Credit to Capabilities

A Sociological Study of Microcredit Groups in India

Credit to Capabilities focuses on the controversial topic of microcredit's impact on women's empowerment and, especially, on the neglected question of how microcredit transforms women's agency. Based on interviews with hundreds of economically and socially vulnerable women from peasant households, this book highlights the role of the associational mechanism – forming women into groups that are embedded in a vast network and providing the opportunity for face-to-face participation in group meetings – in improving women's capabilities. It also reveals the role of microcredit groups in fostering women's social capital, particularly their capacity for organizing collective action for obtaining public goods and for protecting women's welfare. It argues that, in the Indian context, microcredit groups are becoming increasingly important in rural civil societies. Throughout, the book maintains an analytical distinction between married women in male-headed households and women in female-headed households in discussing the potentials and the limitations of microcredit's social and economic impacts.

Paromita Sanyal is an assistant professor of sociology at Cornell University. Her research interests include development, gender, economic sociology, and participatory forms of governance like deliberative democracy (gram sabha in India).

Credit to Capabilities

A Sociological Study of Microcredit Groups in India

PAROMITA SANYAL

Cornell University

CAMBRIDGE
UNIVERSITY PRESS

CAMBRIDGE
UNIVERSITY PRESS

32 Avenue of the Americas, New York, NY 10013-2473, USA

Cambridge University Press is part of the University of Cambridge.

It furthers the University's mission by disseminating knowledge in the pursuit of education, learning, and research at the highest international levels of excellence.

www.cambridge.org
Information on this title: www.cambridge.org/9781107077676

First published 2014

A catalog record for this publication is available from the British Library.

Library of Congress Cataloging in Publication Data
Sanyal, Paromita.
Credit to capabilities : a sociological study of microcredit groups in India / Paromita Sanyal.
pages   cm
Includes bibliographical references and index.
ISBN 978-1-107-07767-6 (alk. paper : hbk)
1. Microfinance – Social aspects – India.   2. Entrepreneurship – India.
3. Poor women – Employment – India.   4. Self-employed women – India.   5. Businesswomen – India.   6. Women – India – Economic conditions.   7. Women – India – Social conditions.   I. Title.
HG178.33.I4S366   2014
332–dc23
2014037191

ISBN 978-1-107-07767-6 Hardback

Contents

Acknowledgments

One summer (now several years back) I arrived in Kolkata (India), with a plan of researching microcredit groups, driven by the desire to bring a sociological perspective to bear on the study of these groups. The people who helped in the initial days by putting me in touch with the key NGOs were Manab Sen and Tarun Debnath. Without their introduction I might not have gained as ready access to the field. The two NGO leaders, who I shall not name (to preserve their organizations' anonymity), graciously allowed me access to the microcredit groups under their implementation and allowed me the use of their organization's residential facilities during the period of my research. The group supervisors took me around to the groups, accommodating this task of showing me around in the initial days within their busy schedules. And, foremost, the women whom I interviewed indulged my many questions, for the most part patiently, taking a break from their hectic daily schedules and juggling their competing demands at home and in their agricultural fields. Without their willingness to talk to me, this project would not have come to fruition. I am full of gratitude toward them, and I hope to return to the NGOs to share this book with the organizations.

In the U.S. the development of this book was aided by comments from and conversations with Marty Whyte, Mary Brinton, Peggy Levitt, Patrick Heller, Raka Ray, and Vijayendra Rao. My colleagues at Cornell University have been great cheerleaders. I would like to particularly thank Richard Swedberg and my ex-colleague Steve Morgan. I have given innumerable talks on this research in the U.S. and all of those opportunities have helped me crystallize my thoughts on this topic and helped me publicize my research. For this I would like to thank all the people who have invited me out to present this research – Lyn Spillman at University of Notre Dame; Monica Prasad at Northwestern University; Patrick Heller at Brown University; Vijayendra Rao at The World Bank; Jeannie Annan at the International Rescue Committee; Elora Chowdhury at UMass., Boston, among others.

My family and friends have sustained me through this long period. My parents Bikash and Jharna Sanyal deserve special mention for their academic encouragement and support. My husband has been a source of constant inspiration and strength. Their love and dedication to my work are pillars on which the book stands. For this I am indebted to them, and some debts can never be repaid.

Introduction

MUMTAZ BEGUM led me to her house through a short, winding path to wait for the other group members to arrive. She appeared to be in her early to mid-thirties and resembled the village women I had glimpsed on my way to this rural hamlet, except for one feature that set her apart. She did not have the end of her saree draped over her head in a *ghomta*,[1] a comportment that is meant to denote the *lajja*, or modesty, that married women are supposed to embody. It was about eleven o'clock during the day, and most of the working-age males were out in their fields or plying their trades elsewhere. I entered her house – a one-room structure made of bamboo, straw, and packed mud with a terracotta-tiled roof – and settled down on a hand-stitched jute mat that she had spread on the floor for me. Noticing that there was no one else in her household, I asked casually where her other family members were. This question, an innocent conversation-starter, made her pause ever so slightly. Then she crouched down beside me and started talking in a hushed tone:

I have a *shotin*.[2] He married again for having children. There's a lot of history. I told him repeatedly when I married him, that I couldn't have children. He said it was not a problem, that it would be OK. I made him promise that he wouldn't take another wife later for having children. He agreed. But such is my fate. See, I was a Hindu girl from Naihati, a proper town not a village like this one here, and

---

[1] Words in *Bangla*, or the Bengali language, which appear in this book have been italicized throughout and explained in the text or in accompanying footnotes.

[2] This term denotes the relationship between the co-wives of a man in a polygamous relationship.

I

I was married once before. But it was against my will. My father was very ill, nearly dying. He was worried that he would leave behind an unmarried daughter. So, after seeing some interested parties, he and my elder brother arranged my marriage. But I was against it. I was only fourteen at the time, studying in class eight. And the man they had chosen was much older than I. He was a widower. I think he paid my father and brother to fix the match. The marriage went through, and I was with him for several years. I even had two sons. But I hated being with him.

Then, one day, as I was passing through the village center, I saw him (the man that would become her next husband). This was a nearby village to which I had moved after my marriage. He was a tailor, and he worked in the ready-made garment shop in this village. We both noticed each other. From then on, we started seeing each other whenever we had a chance. But we were careful not to let anyone know. After some time of this going on, he said he wanted to marry me. He had not been married yet. I told him about my situation. And I told him that I'd had the operation after having two children, and that's why I wouldn't be able to bear children in the future. If he married me, he would have to remain childless. At the time, he said it would be fine. So one day, as we had planned, I left that man and the children and came away with him.

We got married soon after. That's when I got this name and became a Muslim. For quite a few years we were happy; there weren't any problems. Then gradually he became interested in having a child. This was the beginning of tensions. I reminded him of his promise to me. But, finally, he decided to take a second wife. I couldn't do anything to stop him. This time he married into his own community. After the first year or so, they had their first child. And just a few months back she had a second child. That's why she's at her father's house now. At that time, I made a deal with him. I told him that since he had broken his promise, from that time on, I was going to be "free."[3] I wasn't going take on any of the household responsibilities, and I would have the liberty to do as I wished. He agreed.

During these years, I had learnt tailoring from him. It was through my own "idea" though. I used to ask him to teach me how to use the sewing machine. He would tell me to learn handling the machine first. The rest, he said, I would learn on my own with time. I thought that rather than depend on him to teach me, I would try it out on my own. I kept trying and was finally able to do it. Now I can cut and sew ready-made garments on my own. These past eight to ten years I've been doing tailoring jobs. We have cultivation on our land, but most of it is given away on lease. We've retained only a portion of it and employ hired labor for cultivating it, since neither of us knows anything about farming. Both of us work on the sewing machine. The other one (second wife) does all the housework. I don't do any housework. I keep myself busy with my own work and, other than that, I am completely "free." I can go anywhere I want.

---

[3] This word was mentioned in English in the original speech. Throughout the text I have specified similar direct English usage by the women by delineating these words with an additional quotation mark.

Three years ago, when microcredit groups started forming in our village, Firdausi (the leader of her group) told me, "You're 'free'. You should get involved in this work. If you become the leader, then it will be convenient for me, because then both of us will be able to do this work together." I told her that I was too caught up and wouldn't be able to manage it. At that time, I was already working [as an unskilled caregiver] at a nursing home for three or four months. This was a few months after his second marriage. I was desperate to get out of the house. I have a relative who lives in the next village. One day she told me, "You're facing such difficulties in your life. I think, if you involve yourself in some work, you'll be able to live more independently." So she introduced me to the nursing home people. But they had a completely Muslim list.[4] Although they had accepted my employment there, some still had objections. They would make me do all kinds of work, but they wouldn't pay me. And I can't ask anyone for something; this is a problem I have. I wasn't able to say anything. So, I returned home on the day of Eid and never went back. I had worked for them for three to four months, but they didn't pay me a single rupee. They never once thought of the pains I had gone into for doing that work. After some days, I got an offer from them to rejoin. But I declined. After that experience, I had decided not to work for any other establishment ever. I had made up my mind to remain at home and again start doing sewing and tailoring jobs. That would be enough. I finally joined the group during those days, after leaving the other job. I became the co-leader of this group. I am "free." When I'm called for something [group-related work], I'm glad to get away from here. I don't face any restrictions. I've been to many places for attending group meetings and events. My husband never says anything. If I tell him once that's all, I leave. I have no problems going wherever I want to.

Now I sew and supply readymade garments for big orders. Before this I used to make readymade garments regularly, even for small orders. But most of the money I earned would be spent on traveling to and from the shop to get the materials and deliver the finished garments. So now I've stopped that, and I work whenever there are large orders. I pay for the monthly twenty rupees savings deposit from my own earnings. My income is completely separate from his. When I have work, I can earn two hundred or even three hundred rupees in a month. But every month the flow of work is not the same; it's a matter of the number of orders I get. I mostly take orders for blouses. He brings the orders from the shop he works in, and he pays me. He never bothers me about it, that I won't pay you, or why should I pay you. And whatever he earns he keeps with himself. He gives me some of the money for safekeeping and takes it back later. I don't keep track of his earnings. He always lets me know what he does. And whatever I do, I maybe let him know or not. I manage my own affairs.

In group number 144, my *shotin* has an account. From that group (in a hushed voice) we had taken Rs. 5000. I had thought of using the money for a specific purpose, but I couldn't do that. So I gave it to my husband, and he used it and later repaid it. Actually, I had thought of expanding my tailoring business with the loan.

---

[4] A facility restricted to the Muslim community for staff recruitment and patient treatment.

But I had to abandon that plan for various reasons. First of all, whose door-to-door would I go to for getting orders? It's different than receiving bulk orders from a shop. There's another big problem. If I plan to expand my business within the neighborhood, then I have to work on credit [*baki*: i.e., receiving payment after completion of work or delayed payments]. If I have money of my own to take care of my debts (*dena*), then it's not a problem to let customers pay up later. But, if I take a loan and then do work for people on credit, then from where will I repay that loan? On top of these problems, nowadays, our locality is crowded with hawkers, who descend on us regularly. Some of them come with goods loaded on their bicycles. Some walk here carrying their wares on their shoulders and heads. So, it's very difficult to set up a business here. It's possible only if someone has capital of her own.

In group number 116 [the one in which she is a member], we're about to get a loan. I've planned to take a loan from here to buy a cow. I haven't finalized my decision yet. I want to try and build some capital. I have a savings account in the village post office, which has been running for four and a half years now. It's in my name. I started it, and I deposit my hard earned money in it. I don't take a single paisa from him. Everything I have in it [nearly Rs. 4500] is from tailoring. If I buy a cow, then I can take money from the dairy merchant and repay the loan. That's why I've thought of this strategy. I'll continue with tailoring and keep a cow as well, since now I have no plans of going anywhere anymore.

See, what I understand is that the purpose of this [microcredit group] is to make us stand on our own feet, so that we can keep aside some money for ourselves and contribute something (to the household). This is a lot. And also, there's the opportunity to listen to things and to give and take ideas. There's a lot to be had from that, too. Through this and through going here and there, we're now being able to "relax." We now have the independence, the freedom that we didn't have before. This is why I like it. These are the benefits of being in the group. But my situation has improved because of my own efforts. I know a trade. I am independent. I am "free." In that regard, for me this is not a new experience. It's all the same for me. So, what can I say! But I can say this much from my conscience that, since we joined this group, it has triggered a feeling in everybody that we can stand on our own feet. [District: Uttar Chobbish Pargana; West Bengal (India) 2004]

At the end of another day of interviewing, it was time to leave. Mumtaz walked me back through the winding paths to the neighborhood rickshaw stand. It was past six o'clock, and the sun was steadily receding. A sliver of moon and a few stars had already made their appearance, without waiting for darkness to descend. In the fading light, I caught a last glimpse of Mumtaz standing by the roadside, her saree tightly draped across her shoulders, her nose-stud casting a spark of light now and then, like the fireflies darting in and out of the bushes. Her image faded with the telltale sound of cowbells. Somewhere nearby, someone's oxen were returning home after a day of bearing the heavy plough through paddy fields.

Meanwhile, the rickshaw kept carrying me away into the deepening twilight and growing buzz of cicadas.

Microcredit has been hailed in the global media as the savior of economically vulnerable populations, especially populations of poor women. Microcredit has also been widely denounced as the institution through which global financial capitalism has penetrated subsistence economies and rural societies in the Global South for purposes of predatory extraction, profit taking, and market incorporation. In the eye of the storm of propaganda, discourse, and evidence regarding microcredit are women – typically poor women in rural societies in middle- and low-income countries. These women's lives are usually lived out in poverty. Their economic roles are most often confined to the performance of unpaid domestic labor, work on agricultural plots owned or leased by the family, home-based piece-rate work, or, for the most oppressed, casual, day-waged agricultural labor. Their lives are subject to varying levels of patriarchal control that can range from societal and familial prohibitions on their physical movements and social interactions to physical oppression used by their families to discipline their disobedience. The social deprivations that mark their lives severely constrain their civic participation and public presence.

This book offers a close look at women now caught up in the global financial institution of microcredit. It focuses on the institution of microcredit in its social totality within local communities. It examines how women's lives are affected by the financial and associational influences that are unleashed by group-based lending to the poor.

The recent financialization of the lives of the poor in subsistence economies through microcredit has ushered in a new era of female-led financial transactions. Through micro-lending institutions and NGO-initiated micro-lending programs, women are now formally at the forefront of financial transactions. This marks a fundamental shift from an era of largely exclusively male-led financial transactions traditionally made through rural moneylenders and banks. The new wave of financialization through microcredit has produced a new and potentially valuable type of association among women. As they are formed into microcredit groups (also called "self-help" groups) to fulfill the terms of a lending model that uses social capital as collateral, they are put in a position to experience and use their joint liability in potentially empowering ways.

It is crucial to understand the importance of microcredit for the effect it has on women's lives. This effect operates simultaneously through the financialization of those lives and through a new kind of participative associationism it introduces into women's lives. This associationism has profound implications for the expansion of women's roles and voices in civic life in their communities and for deepening democracy at the grass-roots in contemporary times. It is also important to understand the limits of microcredit as an institution through which women's empowerment and the economic wellbeing of the poor in general can be improved.

This study is based on semistructured open-ended interviews conducted with four hundred women in West Bengal during the course of the year in 2004 and analysis conducted thereafter. All were enrolled in microcredit programs that were initiated and administered by nongovernmental organizations (NGOs). The most consequential findings of my study are that, regardless of the economic consequences of loan use and the patterns of loan control, the associational aspects of microcredit promotes women's agency in a large proportion of cases and in significant ways. Microcredit groups also promote social capital among women, evidenced by their increased capacity for collective action for securing public goods and for protecting the welfare of women.

Although there is ambiguity in the findings of economists regarding the long-term economic impacts of microcredit on households, my analysis of the effect of microcredit on women's lives presents incontrovertible evidence in favor of the social impact of participation in microcredit groups by women. Even though all women enrolled in microcredit groups do not consistently experience social gains, the significance of my findings concerning group-based microcredit's capacity for improving of women's agency remains undiminished. Microcredit via the group-based model creates networks of associations with participatory requirements. This firmly establishes women's presence within the public sphere of rural societies and fosters women's direct participation in institutions of local governance and economic development.

The qualitative evidence and explanatory interpretations presented in the chapters of this book provide the dense detail necessary to reveal the social and economic preconditions necessary for women's transformation. My close-grained study allows the reader to see what it takes to turn women into entrepreneurs and independent income-earners – to manage their own livelihoods and convert their membership and participation in microcredit groups into improvements in their capabilities.

In Chapter 1, I outline the institutional history of microcredit and the controversy and contradiction surrounding it in contemporary public media and specify the particular focus of this book. In Chapter 2, I discuss the theoretical debate on conceptualizing and assessing women's agency and outline the approach adopted in this book. In Chapter 3 based on the interviews, I analyze the promise and pitfalls of the loans-to-leverage arguments made by proponents of microcredit. In Chapter 4, I show how and why participation in microcredit groups and the rituals of group meetings hold the key to enhancing women's individual capabilities and their agency within their households. In Chapter 5, I shift focus to collective agency and discuss the remarkable finding of microcredit groups spontaneously organizing joint sanctioning to protect women through collective action. I put forward an argument establishing and explaining the role of microcredit groups in promoting women's social capital and normative influence. In Chapter 6, I analyze the variation in collective action fostered by microcredit groups composed of Hindu and Muslim women respectively. I show how and why the local daily life of socio-religious communities – for Hindus and Muslims alike – is an influential part of the dynamics unleashed by microcredit. I show how daily socio-religious life affects women's participation in microcredit groups and their ability to convert their experience into enhanced agency. In Chapter 7, I focus on the loan-use patterns in egalitarian households and female-headed households, literal and de facto. Exploring how loans are used in households where women already exercise a considerable degree of agency helps us to understand the ways microcredit affects the economic well-being of households in which women are free to exercise their capabilities and to exert significant managerial control. The Conclusion assesses the relation between credit and conjugality. It emphasizes the limits of economistic assumptions regarding the move from "borrowing to bargaining" and the empowerment expected to emerge from it. And, importantly, it highlights the relationship between microcredit and the prospects for deepening democracy. The Epilogue looks at current debates concerning methodological perspectives used to evaluate microcredit programs and their influence on our view of microcredit's effectiveness. I present my views on the role of microcredit in India's poverty amelioration and end with a reflection on the moral choices facing the industry.

Microcredit is the crucible in which the forces of global financial power, multilateral development agencies, and governments and NGOs converge to set in motion an excess of promises: regarding economic and social development, the transformation of poor women's lives, and the uplift of families. These promises are fundamentally based on the projected effects of the democratization of credit ushered in by microcredit. At the same time, analysts and participants both fear the consequences of the realities of capitalist extraction through microcredit in its commercialized form. Intensified immiseration has been reported, and critics worry about the increased presence of debt in the lives of families and households that are the clientele of microcredit programs.

Microcredit reflects all these contradictions. I began my research almost a decade ago. I now offer this interpretive study, convinced more than ever that microcredit holds an essential key to understanding the lives of economically vulnerable and socially disadvantaged women worldwide.

I

The global trajectory of microcredit

Over the past three decades, microcredit programs have become phenomenally attractive as a poverty-alleviation strategy among international aid agencies, global development institutions, and governments.[1] In their original and classic model, these programs provide small collateral-free loans through group-based lending for promoting "entrepreneurship"[2] among the self-employed poor and for supporting their livelihoods. Microcredit interest rates vary by country. They may be the same, or lower, or higher than interest rates in rural banks and credit unions but are usually lower than interests charged by local moneylender.

Microcredit remains a popular source of credit for a large segment of the population because it is easily available, does not require physical collateral, and is largely free of complex bureaucracy. These features explain the appeal of microcredit among its borrowers despite the frequently high interest rates and the prevalence of informal sanctioning (punishment, shaming, asset confiscation) in the event of delays and defaults in repayment. Another appealing feature, especially for its overwhelmingly female enrollees, is compulsory savings. Many microcredit programs require the enrolled members to deposit small fixed amounts, and these savings are secured in bank accounts under the names of each member within her microcredit group. In some microcredit programs

---

[1] Microcredit, nowadays, is often referred to by the more recently minted term "microfinance," which stands for a broader array of financial services including micro-insurance. However, to date, microcredit remains the largest component within microfinance services.

[2] I use this term to reflect its usage in the microcredit discourse. It does not contain any judgment regarding the non-conventional versus conventional nature of livelihood enterprises pursued by borrowers.

(including the ones I studied), a small portion of the interest charged on microcredit loans to borrowers is added back to the corresponding group's savings fund. This fund is then equally divided among all group members. Slight variations in these common features of microcredit programs are not unusual.

Now operating worldwide, microcredit commands vast memberships in South and Southeast Asia, Africa, and Latin America.[3] Microcredit has also been adopted as a means of assisting the less well-to-do in postcommunist nations undergoing economic restructuring. And, most recently, microcredit has spread its reach to low-income communities in the United States. Nothing captures the remarkable pace of its diffusion and burgeoning popularity better than the news reports over the period of its development. In 1986 the *Washington Post* ran a story titled "Third World Bank That Lends a Hand" (Nov. 2 edition):

No other banker in the world is like Muhammad Yunus. He is the founder and director of the Grameen Rural Bank in Bangladesh, the Moslem nation nestled between India and Burma on the Indian Ocean. In 10 years of running the bank, Yunus . . . has loaned $ 40 million, all of it to Bangladesh peasants whose average per-capita income is less than $140 a year . . . [Section: Style, People, Fashion]

Two decades later, in 2006, the *Washington Post* ran a story titled "Micro-Credit Pioneer Wins Peace Prize; Economist, Bank Brought New Opportunity to Poor" (Oct. 14 edition):

The $1.4 million prize will be split between the Grameen Bank and [Muhammad Yunus], the bank's managing director . . . The Grameen Bank model has been duplicated in more than 100 countries, from Uganda to Malaysia to Chicago's South Side. "Yunus's long-term vision is to eliminate poverty in the world," the

---

[3] In some parts of the world microcredit is predated by rotating savings and credit associations (RoSCAs). Although there are similarities between the two financial arrangements, especially in their use of social relations and practice of regular savings, their structures of operation differ greatly. Microcredit programs are funded and implemented by external agencies, which could be global development agencies, for-profit or non-profit microfinance institutions (MFIs), nongovernmental organizations, or government agencies. Microcredit groups are formed through external stimulus from implementing organizations, within the parameters of self-selection of members into groups. Microcredit loans have interests on them that are payable by borrowers. And several members in a single microcredit group can borrow simultaneously. In contrast, RoSCAs are informally organized by friends, relatives, or neighbors and emerge organically. They run the savings and lending operations without any external organizational or financial support. In RoSCAs, loans are generated by members' own savings and are therefore typically interest free, and borrowing from the pooled sum occurs through turn-taking.

Nobel Prize committee said. "Muhammad Yunus and Grameen Bank have shown that, in the continuing efforts to achieve it, micro-credit must play a major part . . . " [Section: A]

These two reports trace the extraordinary trajectory of microcredit from being a risky but innovative experiment involving poor women in the villages of Bangladesh (a place so unknown in the West until then that its demographic composition and geographic location needed to be specified) to becoming a model copied extensively around the world. The shift in reporting on microcredit from the "Style, People, and Fashion" to the "A" Section of a Western newspaper is also noteworthy.

This rapid diffusion of the microcredit model was the result of development institutions adopting the "financial self-sustainability paradigm."[4] Starting in the late 1980s, these institutions, including the World Bank, dramatically shifted their strategy of assisting the poor from providing relief and charitable aid to providing convenient access to credit (Robinson 2001). In theory, such credit was supposed to be affordable and non-extractive. The global Micro-Credit Summit, held in Washington, DC, in 1997, became a turning point for several development NGOs (nongovernmental organizations) around the world that were already implementing donor-funded income-generating programs and experimenting with organizing the poor into groups for participatory financial management. These NGOs adopted this new approach to development and service provision and subscribed to the new plan of forming savings- and credit-oriented "self-help groups," or SHGs. This new microcredit lending model operated via the formation of women's SHGs. The term "self-help group," used in the social banking literature (Thapa 1993) to refer to microcredit groups, emerged from the Western headquarters of the development circuit and has obvious connotations of the concept of self-help (as opposed to dependence).[5] The strategy of basing microcredit SHGs exclusively on female membership was informed by the proclaimed success of the Grameen Bank's women-centric lending model. It is also likely that the concept of forming women's groups enjoyed popular appeal among many American policy-makers because of their historic domestic experience with

---

[4] This paradigm advocates that some of the biggest impediments trapping people in poverty are inadequate capital and the difficulties and high costs of borrowing from banks and local moneylenders. These factors adversely affect the profitability and sustainability of the economic enterprises of poor people.

[5] SHGs may also be formed for purposes other than microcredit. In those cases, SHGs may include or be focused on men. Examples include farmers' groups and water users' associations.

women's consciousness-raising groups, which were a central part of the U.S. feminist movement in the late 1960s. The SHG model of microcredit that emerged was therefore very similar in its financial structure to regular microcredit groups with the vision of "self-help" added in.

In India, microcredit SHGs were targeted at villages because of the concentration of poverty in rural areas and because of the relative geographic stability of rural households and neighborhoods (despite work-related seasonal migration, mostly by men). In India, SHGs have ten to twenty members and are often nested within a federated structure. From an organizational perspective, Indian development planners envision that about fifteen to twenty SHGs will vertically grow into a "cluster association," and that all groups within a village block, often numbering between one to two hundred groups, will form a "federation." The goal is for these bodies to develop links with critical village-level political institutions like the *panchayat* and the *zilla parishad* and the government's rural development departments.[6]

NGOs played, and continue to play, a leading role in forming and managing microcredit SHGs. They are directly involved in implementing and managing microcredit programs. These NGO-managed SHG-based microcredit programs are typically of a non-commercial variety and depend on subsidies and funding from the government and donor agencies to raise the capital required for micro-lending. But operationally these programs can be run on either a non-profit or for-profit basis. The peer-group-based monitoring and evaluation and the sanctioning mechanisms rely on, and make use of, social collateral, although the intensity of the disciplinary practices may vary.

In 2008, an article in the *Financial Times* titled "Microfinance Unlocks Potential of the Poor" (Jun. 2 edition) reported:

Drawn by their corporate responsibility agendas and the promise of profitability, commercial banks have been entering the microfinance market, with Credit Agricole and JPMorgan among recent entrants. In Ghana, for example, Barclays offers deposit accounts to traditional "Susu" collectors. ... Some institutions are starting to expand into insurance and savings, while some banks are delivering services through mobile phones.

---

[6] The *panchayat system* broadly refers to the system of decentralized governance that was federally adopted in India in 1992 through the 73rd Constitutional Amendment. It represents the government's attempt at the devolution of power by delegating some of the budgets and decision-making powers of village-level governance and development to a three-tiered structure of elected political offices: the *gram panchayat* at the village level, the *panchayat samiti* at the "block" level, and the *zilla parishad* at the "district" level.

Microfinance may even become an asset class for investors. In May, the International Finance Corporation, part of the World Bank Group, announced an investment of $45m in credit-linked notes to be issued by a vehicle set up by Standard Chartered to facilitate microfinance lending in sub-Saharan Africa and south Asia. [By Sarah Murray]

The entry of big financial institutions and commercial banks into microfinance and speculation about microcredit becoming investment-worthy reflect the unambiguous transformation of a largely non-commercial, non-profit initiative into a globally expanding for-profit industry. With this wave of expansion and transformation, individually targeted lending started to be offered as an alternative to the traditionally group-based form of micro-lending. Borrowers no longer needed to be part of a group, meet participation requirements, or be held mutually responsible for monitoring and assessment of loan requests, in order to access loans. The purpose for which microcredit loans were theoretically supposed to be given was expanded from the original mandate of productive income-earning investments to include various forms of consumer credit. Lending practices considered by some to be aggressive and risky began to emerge. Many poor households fell prey to the temptation of readily available credit that was procedurally easy to access but financially costly given their low income.

In some places, like the Southern India state of Andhra Pradesh, things came to a head when journalistic reports emerged of some borrowers committing suicide or fleeing after being unable to pay back their loans and being hounded by the agents of commercial lending companies. Politicians and state government officials involved themselves in this matter and declared that borrowers with unpaid loans need not worry about repaying. These announcements threatened to encourage mass defaults. This entire episode received lengthy coverage in the *New York Times* (in the Nov. 17, 2010, issue), making this one of the first widespread negative international exposures of microcredit.

For the first time in its history, the public reputation of microcredit, and microfinance practices as a whole, was tarnished. Coinciding with this debacle in the microfinance sector in India, another fiasco was shaping up across the border in Bangladesh. Muhammad Yunus, the iconic figure most identified with microcredit, was charged in the latter half of 2010, by the prime minister of Bangladesh, Sheikh Hasina, with allegations of corruption and overstaying his position as president of the Grameen Bank. He, Grameen, and other microfinance institutions were accused of "sucking blood from the poor borrowers."[7] Yunus was ousted by the government (a 25 percent shareholder in the Grameen Bank) from his post in March 2011.[8] After a two-month-long legal battle, in the first week of May 2011, Yunus lost his last appeal in the Supreme Court of Bangladesh. This legal defeat made permanent his dismissal from the Grameen Bank, the organization that he had founded in the late 1970s.

These events notwithstanding, microcredit programs and the micro-finance industry are thriving worldwide and in South Asia. Compared to the exponential growth rate of this sector in India during the period 2000–2010, there has been a recent deceleration in the growth rate and even decline reported by some microfinance institutions (MFIs) following the 2010 Andhra Pradesh crisis. Based on self-reported data from ninety MFIs in India, a MIX Market[9] report (Shyamsukha 2011) shows that growth rates of loan portfolios and clients dropped precip-itously from highs of 95 percent and 57 percent, respectively, to 17 percent (for both) during the 2009 to 2010 period. This shows that the growth of the microfinance sector in India has slowed down following a period of exponential growth. The risk level for MFIs shot up from being nearly non-existent to unprecedented highs. According to the same report, the portfolio-at-risk, which stood at below 1 percent in 2009, skyrocketed to an all-time high of over 25 percent in 2010 (with only six months of post-crisis data). The possibility of defaults and loan write-offs also increased (rising from 0.6 percent to 3 percent) as events unfolded through the post-crisis period.[10]

---

[7] See the article titled "Muhammad Yunus loses appeal against Grameen Bank dismissal" in *The Guardian*, March 8, 2011, edition, by Jason Burke and Saad Hammadi.

[8] For an analysis of the events from the perspective of a scholar of microcredit in Bangladesh, see a piece by Lamia Karim titled "The fall of Muhammad Yunus and its consequences for the women of Grameen Bank" (University of Minnesota Press Blog; March 31, 2011). Karim argues that the events are reflective of the "Bengali culture of *irsha* (envy)."

[9] Microfinance Information Exchange, Inc., was established in 2002 with its headquarters in Washington, DC, and regional offices to date in Peru, Morocco, Azerbaijan, and India. On its website it bills itself as "the premier source for objective, qualified and relevant micro-finance performance data and analysis." Its global partners include the following organ-izations and foundations: Bill & Melinda Gates Foundation, CGAP, Omidyar Network, The MasterCard Foundation, IFAD, Michael & Susan Dell Foundation, and Citi Foundation.

[10] Another point stated in the report is that the interest rate at which Indian MFIs have been borrowing is higher than that paid by their counterparts in other South Asian countries. Apparently, in 2009, the weighted average interest rate on outstanding debt of Indian MFIs worth approximately 3.5 billion USD was nearly 12%, with the weighted average term at 42 months (Shyamsukha 2011).

TABLE 1.1: *Summary Statistics on Microfinance Sector in India*

Loans	2.6 billion (USD, 2011)
Active Borrowers	17.5 million (as of 2011)
Deposits	83.3 million (USD, 2011)
Depositors	812,041 (as of 2011)

[These statistics are based on 158 MFIs (including all varieties) that self-reported their data to MIX Market. The reported data in aggregate cover the period spanning from 2000 to June 2012, although all organizations may not have entered data for their entire period of operation.]

TABLE 1.2: *Recent Trends in MFI Statistics*

Fiscal Year	No. of MFIs reporting data	Yield on gross portfolio (nominal)	Return on Equity	Return on Assets
2006	96	16.90%	17.04%	1.45%
2007	78	22.14%	22%	2.50%
2008	99	24.31%	27.52%	4.10%
2009	104	25.13%	25.02%	4.38%
2010	98	25.27%	9.53%	1.86%
2011	44	22.32%	−30.73%	−7.40%

[Note: The percentages presented are weighted averages. There is a precipitous drop in the number of MFIs reporting their data to MIX Market in 2011.]

Beyond these short-run repercussions of the Andhra crisis, only time will tell to what extent the entire microfinance sector in India will be impacted in the long run (for example, through Reserve Bank of India regulations on MFIs, which have begun to be debated and drafted following the crisis). Despite this recent upheaval, the magnitude of the microfinance industry in India remains large and is growing with the gradual spread of microcredit (its various institutional forms included) to states that have not so far been under its coverage. Some recent statistics reported in Tables 1.1 and 1.2 establish the scale of this sector in India, which continues to be significant. The figures (based on self-reported data by MFIs and NGOs) are taken from MIX Market, one of the most credible publicly accessible sources of global microfinance data available.

The numbers of borrowers and depositors and consequently the sums of loans and deposits would all be significantly higher, but the exact data cannot be arrived at in the absence of a complete database on microfinance operations in India. The true scale of this sector in India is significantly larger than reflected here and continues to grow.

THE SAVIOR–SLAYER DICHOTOMY

The development of each human fate can be represented as an uninterrupted alternation between bondage and release, obligation and freedom. ... For what we regard as freedom is often in fact only a change of obligations; as a new obligation replaces one that we have borne hitherto, we sense above all that the old burden has been removed. Because we are free from it, we seem at first to be completely free – until the new duty, which initially we bear, as it were, with hitherto untaxed and therefore particularly strong set of muscles, make its weight felt as these muscles, too, gradually tire. The process of liberation now starts again with this new duty, just as it had ended at this very point. This pattern is not repeated in a quantitatively uniform manner in all forms of bondage. Rather, there are some with which the note of freedom is associated longer, more intensively and more consciously than with others. (Georg Simmel ([1978], 1982), *The Philosophy of Money*, translated by Tom Bottomore and David Frisby, p. 283)

This description by Simmel of the transition from classical modes of labor arrangement under pre-industrial, non-monetized medieval economies to a modern money economy provides a useful framework for understanding the volatility of the assessments of microcredit circulating in the public imagination. Simmel's statement appears uncannily prescient when applied to the public construction of microcredit as it has oscillated wildly during the last three decades between diametrically opposed views: microcredit as the path to freedom (including the liberation for women from patriarchal repressions through enhanced income-earning capacity) and microcredit as neoliberalism incarnate, contributing to the subjection of the poor to ever more intense oppression through debt obligations owed to lending institutions (MFIs[11]), to NGOs, and to the disciplinary regimen of microcredit groups. Microcredit has been portrayed as both the savior of economically vulnerable populations worldwide, especially poor women, and as their destroyer, pushing women from bearable poverty into unbearable destitution. This savior–slayer dichotomy has been endlessly re-circulated among the public through media accounts that alternate dramatic narratives of uplift with traumatic narratives of catastrophic failure.

The story of Saima Muhammad was featured in Nicolas D. Kristof and Sheryl WuDunn's popular book *Half the Sky* (2009, pgs. 185–187) and then retold by Oprah Winfrey on her popular nightly talk show that was broadcast on October 1, 2009.[12] (The excerpt below is an abridged version of the story that appears in the book):

---

[11] Microfinance institutions.

[12] http://www.oprah.com/world/Microcredit-The-Financial-Revolution/1#ixzz1prOPxCcJ

Saima Muhammad would dissolve into tears every evening. She was desperately poor, and her deadbeat husband was unemployed and not particularly employable. He was frustrated and angry, and he coped by beating Saima each afternoon. Their house, in the outskirts of Lahore, Pakistan, was falling apart, but they had no money for repairs. Saima had to send her young daughter to live with an aunt, because there wasn't enough food to go around. . . .

Sometimes Saima would take the bus to the market in Lahore, an hour away, to try to sell things for money to buy food, but that only led her neighbors to scorn her as a loose woman who would travel by herself. Saima's husband accumulated a debt of more than $3,000, and it seemed that this debt would hang over the family for generations. Then, when Saima's second child was born and turned out to be a girl as well, her mother-in-law, a crone named Sharifa Bibi, exacerbated the tensions.

"She's not going to have a son," Sharifa told Saima's husband, in front of her. "So you should marry again. Take a second wife." Saima was shattered and ran off sobbing. Another wife might well devastate the family finances and leave even less money to feed and educate the children. And Saima herself would be marginalized in the household, cast off like an old sock. For days Saima walked around in a daze, her eyes red, and the slightest incident would send her collapsing into hysterical tears. She felt her whole life slipping away.

It was at that point that Saima joined a women's solidarity group affiliated with a Pakistani microfinance organization called Kashf Foundation. Saima took out a $65 loan and used the money to buy beads and cloth, which she transformed into beautiful embroidery to sell in the markets of Lahore. She used the profit to buy more beads and cloth, and soon she had an embroidery business and was earning a solid income – the only one in her household to do so. Saima brought her eldest daughter back from the aunt and began paying off her husband's debt.

When merchants wanted more embroidery than Saima could produce, she paid neighbors to work for her. Eventually thirty families were working for Saima, and she put her husband to work as well – "under my direction," she explained with a twinkle in her eye. Saima became the tycoon of the neighborhood, and she was able to pay off her husband's entire debt, keep her daughters in school, renovate the house, connect running water to the house, and buy a television.

"Now everyone comes to me to borrow money, the same ones who used to criticize me," Saima said, beaming in satisfaction. "And the children of those who used to criticize me now come to my house to watch TV."

A round-faced woman with thick black hair that just barely peeks out from under her red-and-white-checked scarf, Saima is now a bit plump and displays a gold nose ring as well as several other rings and bracelets on each wrist. She dresses well and exudes self-confidence as she offers a grand tour of her home and work area, ostentatiously showing off the television and the new plumbing. She doesn't even pretend to be subordinate to her husband. He spends his days mostly loafing around, occasionally helping with the work but always having to take orders from his wife. He is now more impressed with females in general: Saima had a third child, also a girl, but that's not a problem. "Girls are just as good as boys," he explained.

"We have a good relationship now," said Saima. "We don't fight, and he treats me well." And what about finding another wife who might bear him a son? Saima chuckled at the question: "Now nobody says anything about that." Sharifa Bibi, the mother-in-law, looked shocked when we asked whether she wanted her son to take a second wife to bear a son. "No, no," she said. "Saima is bringing so much to this house.....She's an exemplary daughter-in-law. She put a roof over our heads and food on the table."

Sharifa even allows that Saima is now largely exempt from beatings by her husband. "A woman should know her limits, and if not then it's her husband's right to beat her," Sharifa said. "But if a woman earns more than her husband, it's difficult for him to discipline her." *

Almost exactly a year later, another report on microcredit was featured prominently in the *New York Times*. It told a vastly different story, one of suicides among debt-trapped borrowers (I quote from the *New York Times*, Nov. 17, 2010[13]):

India's rapidly growing private microcredit industry faces imminent collapse as almost all borrowers in one of India's largest states have stopped repaying their loans, egged on by politicians who accuse the industry of earning outsize profits on the backs of the poor. The crisis has been building for weeks, but has now reached a critical stage. Indian banks, which put up about 80 percent of the money that the companies lent to poor consumers, are increasingly worried that after surviving the global financial crisis mostly unscathed, they could now face serious losses. Indian banks have about $4 billion tied up in the industry, banking officials say.

Responding to public anger over abuses in the microcredit industry – and growing reports of suicides among people unable to pay mounting debts – legislators in the state of Andhra Pradesh last month passed a stringent new law restricting how the companies can lend and collect money. ....

Government officials in the state say they had little choice but to act, and point to women like Durgamma Dappu, a widowed laborer from this impoverished village who took a loan from a private microfinance company because she wanted to build a house. She had never had a bank account or earned a regular salary but was given a $200 loan anyway, which she struggled to repay. So she took another from a different company, then another, until she was nearly $2,000 in debt. In September she fled her village, leaving her family little choice but to forfeit her tiny plot of land, and her dreams.

"These institutions are using quite coercive methods to collect," said V. Vasant Kumar, the state's minister for rural development. "They aren't looking at sustainability or ensuring the money is going to income-generating activities. They are just making money." Reddy Subrahmanyam, a senior official who helped write the Andhra Pradesh legislation, accuses microfinance companies of making "hyperprofits off the poor," and said the industry had become no better than the

---

[13] Contributing reporters: Lydia Polgreen, Vikas Bajaj, Hari Kumar.

widely despised village loan sharks it was intended to replace. "The money lender lives in the community," he said. "At least you can burn down his house. With these companies, it is loot and scoot."

Indeed, some of the anger appears to have been fueled by the recent initial public offering of shares by SKS Microfinance, India's largest for-profit microlender, backed by famous investors like George Soros and Vinod Khosla, a co-founder of Sun Microsystems. SKS and its shareholders raised more than $350 million on the stock market in August. Its revenue and profits have grown around 100 percent annually in recent years. This year, Vikram Akula, chairman of SKS Microfinance, privately sold shares worth about $13 million. He defended the industry's record before the India Economic Summit meeting, saying that a few rogue operators may have given improper loans, but that the industry was too important to fail. "Microfinance has made a tremendous contribution to inclusive growth," he said. Destroying microfinance, he said, would result in "nothing less than financial apartheid." Indian microfinance companies have some of the world's lowest interest rates for small loans. Mr. Akula said that his company had reduced its interest rate by six percentage points, to 24 percent, in the past several years as volume had brought down expenses. . . .

The collapse of the industry could have severe consequences for borrowers, who may be forced to resort to moneylenders once again. It is tough to find a household in this village in an impoverished district of Andhra Pradesh that is not deeply in debt to a for-profit microfinance company. K. Shivamma, a 38-year-old farmer, said she took her first loan hoping to reverse several years of crop failure brought on by drought. "When you take the loan they say, 'Don't worry, it is easy to pay back,'" Ms. Shivamma said. The man from Share, the company that made her first loan, did not ask about her income, Ms. Shivamma said. She soon ran into trouble paying back the $400 loan, and took out another loan, and then another. Now she owes nearly $2,000 and has no idea how she will repay it. The television, the mobile phone and the two buffaloes she bought with one loan were sold long ago. "I know it is a vicious circle," she said. "But there is no choice but to go on."

These two cases span the perceptual gap now present in the microfinance industry. Microcredit offered by different institutions differs on four important counts: capital-raising model, cost-recovery model, profit sharing model, and lending model. In the capital-raising model there is a distinction between the non-commercial model – where the capital for lending is raised through financial grants made by governments, international donor agencies, or global development aid institutions – and the commercial model – where the capital for lending is raised directly through the financial market, that is, the stock market, or initially through private equity and subsequently through the stock market by selling company shares to the public. In the cost-recovery model, that is the extent to which the operating cost of microlending is recouped through interest earned on microloans, there is a difference between lending on a not-for-profit basis (referred to as the "subsidized" model) and lending on a for-profit basis. In not-for-profit lending, the interest charged is either at a subsidized rate or just high enough to meet the operating cost of microlending. In for-profit lending, the interest charged is high enough to return a profit after covering operation costs. Non-commercial microcredit includes both kinds of lending practices and is typically run by government agencies or NGOs. Commercial microcredit adopts an exclusively for-profit model of lending that is touted as the financially "self-sustainable" model by its proponents, and is run by corporate MFIs. On the profit-sharing model, the difference between the non-commercial for-profit model and the commercial model is that, in the former, after-cost profits are used for financing other government or NGO sponsored programs, whereas, in the latter, profits are distributed as dividends to private shareholders of the MFIs. Finally, with respect to the lending models, there can be different forms of organizing joint-liability. Borrowers can be required to be part of peer-groups (into which women self-select) and have weekly or bi-weekly group meetings, or, lending can take place directly between MFIs and individual "clients."

Saima and Shivamma represent the Simmelian alternation of human fate in their contrasting experiences of microcredit: as freedom versus exploitation; as a promising path of advancement versus a perilous path of enslavement; as escape from poverty and gender oppressions through entrepreneurship versus erasure through forfeiture of material assets and to loss of social credibility and dignity. For one, microcredit is the ultimate savior, but, for the other, it is the destroyer that annihilates through the violence of dispossession.

Obviously, between these extremes exist myriad experiences, possibilities, and pathways through which microcredit either achieves or betrays its stated goals of economic uplift for poor households and women's empowerment through improved income and agency. This book empirically and intensively investigates the enormous range and complexity of the social and affective experiences that relations of microcredit set in motion. Only in this way can we understand the several pathways and varying outcomes of microcredit for women in their full social complexity. This is essential for adequately assessing the indispensable contribution of group-based microlending programs to women's agency and well-being around the world.

DEPLOYING SOCIAL RELATIONSHIPS FOR FINANCIAL ENDS

Microcredit's "peer-group lending" model combines features that have allowed microcredit to prove almost magically effective in ensuring high repayment rates despite mixed reports on economic gains achieved by borrowers from credit. Some of these features had appeared separately in poverty-alleviation programs attempted in earlier decades. But they had never before been combined into one institution or a single set of mutually re-enforcing social and economic practices. These features are the harnessing of social collateral, the formation of neighbourhood-based peer groups, joint-liability lending, and an overwhelming focus on women.

SOCIAL COLLATERAL: The preexisting structure of social relation-ships is used for dual purposes. It is intended to limit membership among individuals who share mutual trust and feelings of obligation. It is also intended to restrain individual financial behavior such that the temptation to default or delay repayment (arising from opportunism or genuine hardship) is counterbalanced by the fear and shame of being surrounded by socially linked group members whose financial prospects (of receiving future loans) could be hurt by this action. Pleas, threats, and shaming are the main mechanisms for enforcing compliance and loan recovery. Whether microcredit uses social relations effectively or coercively is often a matter of contentious debate and perspective. Economists and anthropologists often differ widely in the positions they take on this question.

NEIGHBORHOOD-BASED PEER-GROUPS: Women are allowed to self-select into groups, which may vary between having five to twenty members. Residential and social proximity play a role in the way women self-select into groups. This usually has the effect of making groups homogeneous on salient social characteristics, like religion, caste, or other dimensions in other countries. Heterogeneous groups exist but are usually outnumbered by homogeneous groups. Each group elects a leader, co-leader, and cashier. The group convenes usually two times a month, but in some cases weekly, in a meeting that is usually held in one of the member's courtyard or in a public place in the village. Here members talk about their loan and investment needs and the state of their livelihood enterprises. Based on this information, and on the informal knowledge of each other's family situation, women assess each other's earning and repayment capacities and make decisions on the appropriate amount of loan for each member.

JOINT-LIABILITY LENDING: An individual's chance of getting a loan depends on the collective financial behavior of all other group members. If one member defaults on a loan repayment, other members will be delayed in receiving their loans until they help recover the due amount through pressure and persuasion.

FOCUS ON WOMEN: The reason why microcredit lending is primarily targeted at women is a topic of some debate. Its proponents profess that this strategy is intended to rectify women's historic exclusion from sources of capital and to promote their self-employment in small-scale enterprises. Some believe that money in the hands of women, rather than men, yields greater benefits for the household. There is also the much-publicized claim that it promotes women's entrepreneurship and empowerment. Critics, however, argue that the focus on women is mainly due to the assumption that women are far more amenable to informal sanctioning and pressure than are men. Their argument is based on the Grameen Bank's initial experiment with male lending groups, which proved to be a failure.

By putting social relations to work, microcredit has successfully overcome the trouble formal sector banks have had in different parts of the world in recovering agricultural and livelihood-related loans from their multitude of rural clients. For example, in the past, many Asian governments had launched subsidized credit programs primarily targeting the rural poor. Often, such priority sector lending programs provided credit as part of a wider set of rural development objectives and administered livelihood schemes through forming women into groups but not allowing women to self-select into groups. Despite very large financial outlays, many of these programs failed. A classic example is India's Integrated Rural Development Program (IRDP), which was plagued by a high rate of defaults, incorrect government identification of the poor, total dependence on government functionaries, poor leadership, and inappropriate choice of economic activities.

CONTRADICTIONS AND CONTROVERSIES

Academic inquiry into microcredit began in the mid-1990s with economists and anthropologists in the lead. Economists were mainly interested in examining the veracity of microcredit's claims regarding poverty-alleviation (Montgomery, Bhattacharya, and Hulme 1996; Morduch 1998, 1999; Menon 2003; Armendariz de Aghion and Morduch 2005; Banerjee, Duflo, Glennerster, and Kinnan 2010; Bateman and Chang 2008). Anthropologists, by contrast, focused on how the system of microcredit worked as a whole, that is, how program staff interacted with the women enrollees, the dynamics within microcredit groups, and the gender dynamics in borrowers' households (Goetz and Sengupta 1996; Rahman 1999, 2001). An economist-anthropologist collaborative team was the first to turn their attention to microcredit's claims regarding empowering women and started exploring this topic through quantitative and qualitative methods and published a spate of studies (Schuler, Hashemi, Riley, and Akhter 1996; Hashemi, Schuler, and Riley 1996; Schuler, Hashemi, and Badal 1998). Soon after, Naila Kabeer (1998), an unorthodox development economist who is well known for her work on gender and livelihoods, conducted a qualitative study on this theme. Finally, a set of development economists in the United States conducted a large-scale quantitative study on microcredit and women's empowerment (Pitt, Khandker, and Cartwright 2006).

Sociologists (in the West) started studying microcredit programs in developing country contexts around the same time as economists and anthropologists (Fernando 1997; Woolcock 1999, 2001). But the interest did not spread among other sociologists perhaps due to the discipline's focus on problems of Western industrialized societies.[14] In 2006 microcredit was at the center of public attention worldwide because the Nobel Peace prize was awarded to the Grameen Bank and Muhammad Yunus. This increased the visibility of microcredit among U.S. economic sociologists, who previously had been focused primarily on markets, firms, and formal organizations. Microcredit found its first mention within economic sociology when Zelizer (2006) cited it as an example of "circuits of commerce" in her programmatic call to study informal relational circuits within which money circulates and economic transactions take place.

Nearly two decades later and despite the multiple studies conducted by economists and anthropologists, the intriguing problem of the contradictory findings concerning microcredit and women's empowerment remains. It was this unresolved question that motivated me to start my own explorations. By the middle of 2004, I was in the field in India, which had until then been bypassed in favour of Bangladesh as a site for examining microcredit. Between then and now, economists have turned their attention to how microcredit groups' social composition affects the dynamics of trust and social capital and in turn affects loan repayment (Karlan 2005; Cassar, Crowley, Wydick 2007; Cassar and Wydick 2010). They have also begun to undertake a new wave of randomized evaluations of microcredit programs, focusing on microcredit's economic impact on household consumption levels and its impact on women's empowerment (Banerjee

---

[14] Much earlier, some sociologists working on immigrant communities in the United States had studied Roscas (Light and Bonacich 1988). In a meta-analysis of Rosca's, Biggart (2001) mentioned microcredit, but only in a peripheral way. After a long hiatus, once microcredit had spread to the United States, American sociologists began turning their attention to it (Anthony and Horne 2003; Anthony 2005).

et al. 2013). Anthropologists have produced further critiques of microcredit (Karim 2011) that are insightful and updated on changing microcredit practices, but are similar in their major themes to critiques published by anthropologists a decade earlier. Sociologists researching microcredit are still very few in numbers (Ahmed 2008a, 2008b).[15] A quick look at the findings of the past studies will help set the stage for the current study and help readers appreciate the significance of this book.

There was one set of studies, by anthropologists, in which the findings ranged from being skeptical to negative. Rahman (2001) found that the Grameen Bank had a "hidden transcript" behind its preferential targeting of women as loan clients. Women were preferred because of their "positional vulnerability" – their limited physical mobility, submissiveness, and the fragility of women's honor in a village culture – which made them easy targets of peer pressure and institutional coercion. These strategies had failed with the men's groups that the Bank had initially formed. Women were given the loans, which they transferred to their husbands or sons for use.[16] In turn, the men ensured that women had the money to make time-bound weekly repayments so as to avoid shaming disciplinary measures. All of these practices, Rahman argued, exploited women's vulnerability and reaffirmed the prevailing male hegemony. He found that often the rising debt liability of the household exposed women to a greater risk of domestic violence, and the much-celebrated system of social collateral also escalated gendered violence by relying on the use of punitive measures.[17] Goetz and Sengupta (1996) confirmed this negative assessment when they found that women borrowers failed to develop meaningful control over investment activities despite their exclusive access to credit. The wholesale transfer of loans to men provided women no particular advantage in terms of increasing their status and power within the household. On the contrary, the instrumental approach to women as "conduits of credit for the family" (p. 55) reinforced traditional notions of womanhood, with women seen as moral guardians of their household and regulators of recalcitrant

---

[15] My own work first appeared in 2009 in the *American Sociological Review* (74:4). This article highlighted only one of the findings from my study that is now presented in Chapter 5 of this book.

[16] Rahman (1999) found that 60 percent of the loan users in his sample were men. Similarly, Goetz and Sengupta (1996) found that 63 percent of women in their study had partial and very limited to no control over loans.

[17] In Rahman's study (1999), 70 percent of all the women interviewed stated that there was an increase in violence and aggressive behavior in the household because of their involvement with the Bank.

men. They, too, found that loan transfer in some cases led to an escalation of household tension, forced women into supplicant relationships with men, and, ultimately, reinforced gendered patterns of dependency (see also Ackerly 1995). Schuler and team (1996, 1998) found that in Bangladeshi villages, credit-group enrollment had mixed effects on male violence on women. The potential of women developing stronger economic roles and leading more public lives opened up the possibility of reducing women's vulnerability to gendered violence. But women's sudden access to financial resources and the implicit challenge to gender norms could also provoke their husbands to use violence to assert their masculinity.

Standing in stark contrast to these largely skeptical conclusions is a range of studies by economists that highlight microcredit's positive impact on women. For instance, Hashemi and others (1996) found that women's participation in microcredit groups of the Grameen Bank and BRAC empowered them by increasing their physical mobility, their ability to make purchases, and their participation in major household decisions. They found that microcredit promoted women's ownership of productive assets, enhanced their legal and political awareness, and increased their participation in campaigns and protests. On a similarly positive note, Kabeer (1998) found that women's access to credit had reduced violence against women and had given women a greater sense of self-worth and had improved their marital relationships. And Pitt and others (2006) found that women's participation in microcredit programs led women to play a greater role in household decision making, have greater access to financial and economic resources, exercise greater bargaining power with their husbands, and enjoy greater freedom of mobility.

The contradiction in the findings has been attributed to differences in the ways different studies make the concept of power operational for observation and measurement (Kabeer 2001). This explanation is valid but not fully satisfying. It should be noted that all the negative evaluations come from anthropologically grounded investigations while the positive evaluations come from studies conducted by economists. What are we to make of the disciplinary divide over how to define, measure, and assess empowerment?

All of the studies that have examined women's control over loans and entrepreneurship are unanimous in finding that women overwhelmingly transfer loans to men and do not gain economic independence in the manner touted by these programs. Does this departure from the stated goal of all microcredit programs invalidate the core assumption that women's direct access to and control over microcredit loans is essential as the catalyst for empowering women? If direct control over loans and the subsequent benefits of entrepreneurship is not the indispensable source of women's empowerment, what is? This question calls for an answer if we are to understand how microcredit can have an empowering effect on women.

This book argues that there could be more than one way through which microcredit fosters women's empowerment and enhances their agency. It demonstrates the advantages of using an expanded analytical frame. In addition to recognizing the role of economic deprivation in women's lives, it seeks to understand the difference group-based microcredit can make in the context of the social deprivations that women face as they negotiate patriarchy and control.

The experience of economic deprivation may be common to all family members in a poor or low-income household. But, because of their gender identity, women are also under the significant weight of social deprivations in many societies both in contexts of poverty and affluence. These social deprivations may vary in form and intensity between societies and may be influenced by poverty differently. It is these social deprivations that make the lives of poor women distinctly different from, and more controlled and limited than, the lives of poor men. In this context of patriarchy and control and the consequent dynamics of gender relations and social deprivations, there are, in fact, two alternative mechanisms, one financial and the other non-financial, through which microcredit influences women's agency. The two mechanisms are described next.

I. Financial mechanisms of agency transformation

The economic mechanism is expected to catalyze women's empowerment from their direct access to capital in the form of loans. It is anticipated that loans will encourage women to start or expand their own small-scale livelihood enterprises and operate them independently of their husband's control. Successful entrepreneurship is supposed to increase women's economic contributions to their household and enhance their command over material resources. It might also indirectly promote women's mobility and interactions, increase women's awareness on various issues, and make them conversant with resources that they and their families might avail themselves of to improve their lives (social benefits but driven by side-effects of entrepreneurship). These economic and social changes, primarily driven by entrepreneurship and command over material resources, are expected to elevate women's position in the household and culminate in enhancing their capabilities. According to the programs' formal claims, this is the mechanism that is expected to increase women's agency, and this is what the rhetoric of entrepreneurship refers to. However, underneath these formal claims are informally held premises. At the operational level, most NGOs running microcredit programs do not make any distinction between women's independent loan-use versus joint loan-use with their husbands and sons or wholesale transfer of loans to men. In their everyday operational view, some NGOs expect that women's very capacity to bring these loans into the household should increase their voice in household decision making, regardless of who uses these loans and how. This logic assumes that if women bring in loans that are profitably used to increase household income, then women will gain agency, even if men are the ones using these loans. NGOs presume this effect on the basis of the general difficulty and the great expense families encounter when obtaining credit from other informal sources. This mechanism is amply illustrated in the narratives and visual representations that are advertised in the websites of various MFIs and NGOs running microcredit programs.

The success of the financial mechanism ought to have the following determinants: *pattern of loan use* – independent use versus channeling to men; *amount of capital contributions* – loans bigger versus smaller in amount; *economic outcome from loan investment* – profits versus losses. These determinants are likely to be influenced most by a woman's marital status, household composition, and the type of economic activity for which the loan was used. All of these features vary on a case-by-case basis. Therefore, the success of the financial mechanism might be expected to vary on an individualized basis.

II. Associational mechanism

This mechanism, in contrast, is spurred by women's regular participation in group meetings, attendance of leadership training sessions, becoming part of an expanded group-based social network, and linkage with NGOs or other alternative types of institutions running microcredit programs. All of these features share the characteristic of being incidental to the program's primary economic goal. Participation in the fortnightly group meetings and in more periodically held events, such as training sessions and annual microcredit conventions, provides women opportunities to cross the familiar boundary of their household and village neighborhood and also the conventional boundaries of their gender roles. Through these experiences women acquire increased social exposure, greater capacity for moving around unaccompanied, increased ability and scope for social interactions across kinship, class, and gender divides, and learn new skills. Increased mobility and interactions have the effect of increasing women's confidence in their own capabilities. Through their contact with NGOs or other types of implementing organizations (like government agencies and staffs), women become exposed to progressive ideas regarding women's rights, the value of women's work, and the importance of civic engagement. These ideas provide alternatives to their conventional modes of thinking and bring substantive changes to women's desires. Women also learn vital information about laws and learn how to access governmental resources and legal institutions. These changes, primarily of a social nature, may in some cases culminate in changes in women's economic roles. These social transformations, driven primarily by the associational mechanism, combine to improve women's agency. The operation of this alternative mechanism has so far been overshadowed by the preponderance of the values and rhetoric of individualist entrepreneurship.

The associational mechanism, because it is premised on women's participation in the microcredit group, is likely to be determined by human and organizational factors, such as the following: *nature of leadership*; *nature of group meetings*; *nature of group participation*; *role of implementing organization*. The associational mechanism can be expected to have a roughly similar effect up to a certain point on all members of a microcredit group. For example, if a group leader is dynamic and effectively enforces attendance in meetings, then all group members can experience a certain level of simultaneous agency improvement from regular group participation.

The role of microcredit in enhancing or diminishing the agency and well-being of the world's poor becomes illuminated in deeply expanded ways when we are attentive to the particular sources and mechanisms of change – flowing from microcredit loans versus from the network-based structure and functioning of microcredit groups. This can profoundly enhance our holistic understanding of the role of microcredit.

Understanding microcredit's implications in a holistic way also requires us to pay attention to some other critical dimensions of its social implications that have thus far been overlooked. It is important to ask if microcredit groups, given that they link women into a sizeable network, make any difference to women's distinctive social capital, particularly their propensity to cooperate for collective action. Asking if microcredit affects social capital is a radical question. This is because our understanding has been dominated by the reverse relationship – how harnessing preexisting social capital (trust and information), that is, embedding groups in a matrix of social relations, enables microcredit to operate with relative success by ensuring loan repayment even in the absence of physical collaterals or formal contracts. The formal sociological concept that comes closest to capturing this understanding is Granovetter's (1985) idea of "embeddedness." Because of the dominance of this perspective many scholars have simply assumed that village societies are tight-knit and high in social capital and that rural women who enroll in microcredit necessarily share a sense of solidarity, have mutually intimate relations, and share information freely. But there is no reason to simplify village societies and assume this without any empirical basis.

Scholarly opinion is split on how social capital may be affected by government aid and development interventions that are externally driven. On the one hand, there is Coleman's (1990) prediction that government aid in times of need, especially the kind that reduces mutual reliance for resources and assistance, could erode social capital. On the other hand, Elinor Ostrom (1994), the Nobel Laureate political scientist, and other scholars (Krishna 1997, 2000; Wijayaratna and Uphoff 1997) have shown that externally initiated development projects may actually end up generating social capital. For example, farmer-managed irrigation facilities (Ostrom 1994), user committees formed for watershed development and public land-use projects (Krishna 1997, 2000), and joint forest management groups (Wijayaratna and Uphoff 1997) have been found to foster social capital by creating networks and inculcating attitudes that promote cooperation and collective action. But whether social capital is enhanced depends on the ways in which development projects are structured. If indeed microcredit connects women into a social network that is unmatched in its size and characteristics by their conventional social ties, then is it possible that microcredit could foster social capital among women? Can microcredit create the potential for women's group-based collective actions? These are extremely important questions.

Additionally, there is the question whether microcredit groups have any effect on prevailing social norms? Sociologists have noted the instrumental role that social networks play in the enforcement of social norms through sanctioning. Social networks facilitate sanctioning through various mechanisms. They reduce the social and psychological costs of sanctioning, which include the risk of retaliation and loss of relationship, while improving the benefits from sanctioning. These benefits include decreased negative externalities, encouragement and support for those who sanction (Axelrod 1986; Horne 2001, 2004), and enhanced reputation (Coleman

1990). Social networks also enhance a group's ability to organize itself to undertake collective actions to respond to deviance from norms (Coleman 1990). The ability to organize is particularly important in cases where the beneficiaries of these collective actions are socially weaker than those at whom the sanctions are targeted (Emerson 1962). This importance is heightened when weaker groups try to stage a challenge to normative practices. The fact that microcredit programs of the joint-liability group-lending variety structure women into networks of groups raises the possibility of increasing women's social capital and their influence on community norms substantially.

EXTRAPOLATING FROM THE EVIDENCE FROM WEST BENGAL

The findings of this study are based on qualitative evidence drawn from intensive fieldwork, primarily on-site interviews conducted during 2004 in West Bengal, India. I interviewed four hundred women belonging to a sample of fifty-nine microcredit groups drawn from two separate but similarly structured microcredit programs implemented by the two NGOs, Sisterhood and Self-Reliance.[18] These programs operated in the districts of Uttar Chobbish Pargana and Nadia.[19] Tables 1.3 and 1.4 outline the scale of the programs and the number of groups selected from each.

The sample includes 286 Hindu and 114 Muslim microcredit members.[20] By including a religiously heterogeneous sample, this study allows for a valuable comparative analysis of the differences, if any, in the manner in which microcredit affects Hindu and Muslim women in rural Bengal.

West Bengal is a politically unique state. From 1977 until 2010, the state had the Left Front coalition, led by the Communist Party of India

---

[18] Although the NGOs did not specifically request it, I have chosen to use pseudonyms to represent them.

[19] Around the time of this research, CARE (Cooperative for Assistance and Relief Everywhere, Inc.), in partnership with some national banks, was one of the largest fund providers for microfinance SHGs through its CASHE project (Credit and Savings for Household Enterprise). Economic activities pursued by members of these groups typically ranged from agriculture and livestock husbandry (63%) to household industry (26%) and petty trade (11%). Average savings of these groups was Rs. 4284. The rate of loan recovery was high, with 70 percent of groups reporting a recovery rate of 81–100 percent. This data is taken from the "Study of Self-Help Groups and Micro Finance in West Bengal," Draft Report, 2000, by the State Institute of Panchayat and Rural Development, Kalyani, Nadia, West Bengal.

[20] Existing research studies on women in microcredit, nearly all of which is based on programs in Bangladesh, do not specify whether they include only Muslim women or also Hindu women.

TABLE 1.3: *Summary Data on Microfinance Programs*[21]

Particulars: 2004–05	Sisterhood	Self-Reliance
Villages covered	502	58
No. of groups	3074 (2247 reporting loan activity)	510
No. of members	36,912	6,162
No. of loans disbursed*	6528	3924
Total number of loans*	Rs 1,328,72,000 ($2.95 million)	Rs 5,14,00,000 ($1.14 million)
Total savings of groups*	Rs 283,41,000 ($0.63 million)	Rs 61,60,000 ($0.14 million)
Repayment rate	98%	93%

[* Denotes cumulative figures from 2002 to 2005.]

TABLE 1.4: *Sample Details*

Ngo	No. of groups	No. of villages	No. of members
Self-Reliance	30	16	221
Sisterhood	29	10	179

(Marxist), in continuous political power through popular election. This communist-led government survived other communist governments in democratic regimes worldwide and other elected opposition governments at the state and national levels in India. This feature often leads external observers to deduce that women in Bengal may be in a more advantageous position than their compatriots in other states and that the general environment in the state must be more conducive to women's emancipation. But sociologists (Basu 1992; Ray 1999) who have studied women's movements and activism in the state have thoroughly debunked this notion.

In terms of economic development, as estimated in 2001, nearly 72 percent of the state's population is rural (this is marginally down from 76 percent in 1951), and 27 percent lives below the poverty line,[22] which is marginally higher than the national average of 26 percent. Subsistence agriculture remains the primary occupation of most rural families, with

[21] The figures in this table have been compiled from the annual reports of these organizations.

[22] This estimate is based on the Planning Commission of India's 2001 criterion of monthly per capita consumption expenditure below Rs 276 in rural areas.

approximately 62 percent of the rural population continuing to rely on agriculture and agricultural labor at the turn of the century. The rural class hierarchy extends from middle-class peasants to poor sharecroppers and agricultural laborers.

The social environment in West Bengal is less influenced by considerations of caste identity than are Southern and Northern India. There are several historical reasons behind this pattern (discussed in Basu 1992). One among these reasons is reform movements within Hinduism, like the Bengal Renaissance, and broader social reform movements, like the Brahmo Samaj, during the nineteenth century. I make specific mention of these reform movements because many of the reforms also had to do with improving the lives of women by freeing them from some of the most oppressive practices of patriarchy. It was during these movements at the height of the British colonial rule that social leaders Rammohan Roy and Vidyasagar launched large-scale campaigns for banishing the practice of *sati* (the burning alive of a Hindu widow on her husband's funeral pyre) and for encouraging female education and widow remarriage.

These initial victories for women did not lead to greater gains in their social and economic status or to a more egalitarian turn in gender relations. Rural Bengali societies are perhaps only slightly less patriarchal than some locales in North India. The foundation of sexual inequality and female seclusion among Hindus and Muslims in rural Bengal lies in the system of *purdah* (curtain or veil), which results in the confinement of women to the inner sanctum of the home, circumscribes their role to the domestic sphere, and denounces their presence in the public sphere.[23] Nevertheless, significant numbers of poor Hindu and Muslim women perform paid and unpaid agricultural labor, cultivating their own family plots or working on the fields of local landowners. But family members and, often, the women themselves do not perceive their work-participation outside the household as desirable. The negative view of such employment comes partly from its low pay, the hard work that is often required, and the

---

[23] There are numerous works that study various aspects of women's status and gender relations within West Bengal and India. I am highlighting here a few of the studies that are most relevant to readers who may be interested in acquiring additional knowledge about these aspects. For a general contemporary account of women's condition in society, see Kishwar's book (1999). For a detailed analysis of the women's movement in West Bengal, see Ray's study (1999). For details on state formation in West Bengal, historical state legacies, and the role of the ruling left party, see Desai's work (2007). For accounts of Hindu women's attempts to use the Hindu Succession Act of 1956 to exercise their claims on family property, see Basu's study (1999). For a discussion of religion and personal law in India, see Larson's edited volume (2001).

TABLE 1.5: *WB's Human and Gender Development Indices (2001)*[24]

	Income Index	Educ. Index	Health Index	Total
HDI	.430	.690	.700	.610
GDI	.270	.681	.697	.549

TABLE 1.6: *WB's Rural Employment Statistics (as percentage of population) (2001)*

	Male	Female
Main workers	46.00	8.87
Marginal workers	8.30	11.83
Non-workers	45.70	79.30

[Note: The Census of India, 2001, defines main and marginal workers as those who were engaged in economically productive work for 183 days or more and less than 183 days, respectively.]

general disdain for work involving physical labor. But part of it also comes from negative attitudes about women entering the sphere of work beyond the home, especially for paid employment. Men and women view such an eventuality as a necessity dictated by circumstances of poverty or because of the male provider's inadequacy in fulfilling his provisioning role. These attitudes impede women's employment and economic independence.

Comparisons of West Bengal's Human and Gender Development Indices (HDI and GDI) and the rural male-female employment statistics illustrate women's relative disadvantage. The "Income Index" is very low. And the female workforce participation rate of only 18.08 percent in 2001 was not only lower than the national average of 25.68 percent, but was, in fact, the lowest in the country, placing West Bengal last among fifteen of the country's major states.[25] Data reported in the National Sample Survey (55th Round, 1999–2000) also show that, in rural areas of West Bengal, women are engaged primarily in agricultural labor and work in small-scale cottage industries, which provide home-based piece-rate work to women.

[24] All the data cited in this segment, including the data in the tables, is taken from two sources: the Census of India, 2001 (conducted every ten years); and the West Bengal Human Development Report (2004), which is also based on the 2001 Census data, and is published by the Development and Planning Department, Government of West Bengal. I have modified the original tables to present only the relevant information.

[25] Himachal Pradesh in the North reported the highest rate (43.69%) in the country.

Women's literacy is another feature in which the state lags behind. Only 53 percent of rural women are literate compared to a 73 percent literacy rate among rural men. According to the 2001 Census, the state ranks nineteenth out of the thirty-five states and union territories in India as far as female literacy is concerned. This lagging behind is ironic, considering that the state was a frontrunner for women's education in colonial India and has had a self-professed politically progressive left-ruled government for more than three decades. Moreover, the state has the lowest proportion of Muslim girls enrolled in middle and matriculate levels of school in both urban and rural areas, has a particularly high middle-school drop-out rate among Muslim girls, and displays the highest intercommunity disparity in the country (Hasan and Menon 2005).[26] The mean age at marriage in West Bengal is lower for Muslim girls (fifteen to sixteen years old) than the already low age for Hindu girls (seventeen to nineteen years old).[27]

Women's political representation and participation have been disappointing and women's movements, which arose in conjunction with similar movements in the global South, are restricted to primarily urban, educated women. Although one of the state government's major planks has been its active role in reforming and reviving the *panchayat* system, women's representation in these village-level political bodies is no better than elsewhere in India (Basu 1992). The state's most dominant women's organization is the one affiliated with the CPI(M).[28] But, according to Basu (1992), these politically affiliated women's groups have become instruments of "sankskritization"[29] and of co-opting women into quiescence

---

[26] Among Muslims in India, the proportion of the community employed in professions and government services was significantly reduced following the Partition of India, when urban and rural elites of this community migrated to East and West Pakistan. A significant proportion of those Muslims who remained had limited education, was economically less well-off, and engaged mainly in skilled manual labor. In general, the Muslim population in the state is highly concentrated in rural areas and is usually landless, agricultural laborers, artisans, or poor craftsmen. In the urban areas, many Muslims are poor laborers or self-employed business owners. Over the past few decades, the Muslim middle-class has grown, but rather slowly (Hasan and Menon 2005).

[27] The legally approved age for marriage for girls is eighteen, and for boys it is twenty-one.

[28] This organization, founded in 1981, is called the Paschim Banga Ganatantrik Mahila Samiti.

[29] This term was coined by the Indian sociologist M. N. Srinivas (1982) and refers to the process by which people belonging to a lower social order begin to emulate the customs and norms of groups higher up in the social hierarchy. In the context of West Bengal, the term indicates that the leftist policies fostered the weakening of class/caste barriers and the poor were encouraged to model their norms after higher classes/castes. And the strict patriarchal norms of the upper classes/castes increasingly guided and constrained gender relations among the poor.

through the party's democratic centralist principles of organization, electoral preoccupations, and class reductionist ideology. Ray (1999), in her work on the same organization, has argued that the problem of unequal division of labor is never brought to the forefront of discussions, largely due to the dominance of men in the party. The problem of domestic violence has been manipulated to serve the interests of the local political culture and the party's own paternalistic ideology.

The larger question of the transferability of the findings of my study to the effects of microcredit on the lives and agency of women in other cultures I leave open for the moment. I do hope, however, that, in the course of reading this book, the reader will come to share my commitment to the integration of the individualist economic and entrepreneurial perspectives associated with global microcredit with the associational side of microcredit groups that emerged as powerfully important for the women I studied. These two perspectives are indispensable to the accurate assessment of the effects of microcredit on the lives of women in all societies and through them its effect on their society as a whole.

2

Agency

Why does women's agency deserve particular attention? Enlightenment-era debates concerning what constitutes "freedom" provide the background to contemporary scholarly debates found in the social sciences and suggest different answers. Sociologists have tried to understand structure and agency and the relationship between the two – to decide, for instance, whether they are fundamentally antagonistic or co-constitutive.[1] Philosophers have tried to determine whether agency and gender are simultaneously sustainable states of being (Butler 2004). And economists have tried to employ concepts of agency and freedom to broaden conventional evaluative frames measuring "human development" and "gender empowerment" (Sen 1993, 1999; Kabeer 1999). The widely differing cross-cultural articulations and lived events of women's lives have given rise to the prickly problem of whether a universally applicable set of freedoms can be identified for evaluating women's agency, or whether a single evaluative measure should be avoided in favor of incommensurable, culturally embedded understandings.

Some scholars feel that it is impossible – indeed, inappropriate – to establish an idealized set of universal criteria for evaluative purposes. These scholars advocate adopting a culturally relativist position. In sharp contrast, advocates of a universal standard criticize the relativist position and argue that lapsing into such a relativist approach courts an intellectual and cultural apologetic that will be used to justify and sustain inequality and injustice.

[1] The most sustained attempt has been made by Giddens (1976, 1979, 1981, 1984) in his proposed "theory of structuration." See also Emirbayer and Mische (1998) on the "chordal triad of agency."

Discussion of women's agency begins with a consideration of the normative limits set on women's individual aspirations and actions in most societies when norms are established and policed by men. Women bear an unequal burden when it comes to explicit and implicit social restrictions. It is also true that not all women experience these restrictions as constraining. They may internalize socially recommended modes of behavior and even internalize restrictive social injunctions, incorporating them into their preferences and desires. Compliance with the normative prescriptions and proscriptions may even come to constitute the core of their self-identity as women. Put differently, for women, social injunctions may become markers of their gender identity, making identity possible through the restriction of possibilities.

Women's contortionist-like pliability under different regimes of control makes it difficult to treat women's agency in one context or at one historical moment as prefigurative or representative of women's agency in a separate context or at another temporal moment. Compared to men's agency, women's agency constitutes a more complex social and intellectual category. Since the mid-1990s, the quality of women's lives has been the object of annual measurement and international ranking efforts following the creation of influential scales by the United Nations Development Programme (UNDP) such as the gender-related development index (GDI) and the gender empowerment measure (GEM). The latter is an assessment of what women are able to do or achieve in the societies in which they live and, to that end, measures women's relative income, access to, and participation in professionally and economically powerful positions, and their political incumbency measured by the holding of parliamentary seats.

These indices and measures are informed by conventionally implicit ideas regarding what constitutes women's agency, ideas that are secondary and subordinated to the priority of meaningful comparable measurability. As a result, these measures are narrowly restricted to easily quantifiable achievements that can be derived from secondary survey data and are biased toward capturing expressions of agency and empowerment among women in urban societies and in economically secure classes.

Without a theory of agency, we run the risk of confusing such measures with the *meaning* of agency. The intellectual usefulness of the theory of agency that scholars adopt should not be limited to academic audiences, however. Its usefulness must extend to policymakers in aid and development institutions that often design interventions based on good intentions, ideas in vogue, or political priorities, but who lack the critical engagement necessary to arrive at an underlying clarity concerning the ideals of agency that they hope to promote.

EXISTING APPROACHES

Sociological theorizing has focused on individual agency, without paying specific attention to women's agency or to the dynamics between gender and agency. In modern sociological theorizing, discussions of what constitutes agency have been a by-product of a commitment to understanding what constitutes social structure. The dialectical relationship between the force of social structure and choice of individual action in practice is where sociologists begin the search for agency. Structure is conceived as being constituted by "rules and resources" that have a purely mental existence as "memory traces" (Giddens 1984: 377). Structure has a "dual" character in that structure shapes and conditions the practices that constitute the social system; it is simultaneously reproduced and sustained by individuals embodying and enacting those practices (Giddens 1981: 27). Social structure has been defined as "schemas and resources" (Sewell 1992: 8, 10), where "schemas" include not only formally stated "rules" of social life but also the "informal and not always conscious schemas, metaphors, or assumptions presupposed by such formal statements" (p. 8) and where "resources" can be conceptualized as "manifestations and consequences of the enactment of cultural schemas" (p. 11). In this conceptualization, social structure is understood as "sets of mutually sustaining schemas and resources that empower and constrain social action and that tend to be reproduced by that social action" (p. 19). This conceptualization acknowledges that the reproduction of social structure through action is never automatic or inevitable. Structures are at risk of being challenged and transformed in each social encounter they make possible. This is because schemas are transposable across different contexts of practices and because resources accumulate unpredictably, meaning different things to different people or groups.

Within this general understanding of social structure, agency is the inherent human capacity present in all individuals "for desiring, for forming intentions, and for acting creatively" (p. 20):

Agency is formed by a specific range of cultural schemas and resources available in a person's particular social milieu. The specific forms that agency will take consequently vary enormously and are culturally and historically determined. But a capacity for agency is as much a given for humans as the capacity for respiration. ... [H]owever, ... the agency exercised by different persons is far from uniform, that agency differs enormously in kind and extent. What kinds of desires people can have, what intentions they can form, and what sorts of creative transpositions they can carry out vary dramatically from one social world to another depending on the nature of the particular structures that inform those social worlds ... Agency also differs in extent, both between and within societies ... Occupancy of different social positions – as defined, for example, by gender, wealth, social prestige, class, ethnicity, occupation, generation ... gives people knowledge of different schemas and access to different kinds and amounts of resources and hence different possibilities for transformative action. And the scope or extent of agency also varies enormously between different social systems, even for occupants of analogous positions. (Sewell 1992: 20)

This conception of agency is useful for acknowledging the possibility that the capacity for agency may be unequally distributed among individuals within a society and across societies and that gender has the power to influence the capacity for agency according to its role within any given society's set of "schemas and resources."[2]

What this sociologically grounded framework takes for granted – that individuals can simultaneously embody gender and possess agency – Judith Butler opens up for questioning in a philosophically grounded framework of agency that emphasizes the "double contingency" of gender in a field of constraints imposed by innumerable and unspecified external actors:

If gender is a kind of doing, an incessant activity performed, in part, without one's knowing and without one's willing, it is not for that reason automatic or mechanical. On the contrary, it is a practice of improvisation within a scene of constraint. Moreover, one does not "do" one's gender alone. One is always "doing" with or for another even if the other is only imaginary ... the terms that make up one's own gender are, from the start, outside oneself, beyond oneself in a sociality that has no single author. (Butler 2004: 1)

This theory of gender performativity emphasizes the Durkheimian "social fact" of gender. A still harsher way of conceptualizing gender is provided by Arjun Appadurai; he argues that gender is a set of "terms of recognition" (Appadurai 2004),[3] that is, a set of conditions and constraints under which the male and female sexes participate in society and negotiate with

---

[2] Sewell's theory of agency, however, may be critiqued for its ideological assertion that everyone possesses an inherent capacity for agency, that is, for forming desires and intentions and acting creatively. We simply do not know how gravely decimated the capacity for agency can become under the weight of "durable inequalities" (Tilly 1998) that some groups face. Another serious lacuna is that it leaves unclear if all desires are indiscriminately indicative of agency, including desires that comply with social conventions that diminish the subject's freedom, or whether desires ought to be judged against an evaluative frame to determine if they are indicative of agency.

[3] Appadurai (2004) coined the phrase "terms of recognition" in reference to the normative terms on which the different caste groups participate in a caste-stratified society.

the social norms that frame their lives. If the "terms that make up one's own gender" and the "terms of recognition" are largely predetermined, and, if individuals become unrecognizable or barred from being recognized without complying with these terms, is it feasible to possess gender and agency simultaneously?

This question has implicitly informed the efforts of development economists to define women's agency as part of their quest to evaluate "development'" and quality of life issues. Amartya Sen and Naila Kabeer are the two most prominent figures in the effort to theorize on women's agency from a "gender and development" perspective.

Sen (1993, 1999) has proposed a "capabilities approach" to agency. In this framework, agency is the freedom to inculcate and achieve "capabilities," which are "functionings" or "beings and doings" that encompass valuable material and nonmaterial goals. These valuable "beings and doings" may range from basic needs, such as nutrition and health, to social needs, such as participation in the life of a community, to the need for self-respect and dignity.

Sen has noted that inequalities and deficiencies in education and other amenities tend to affect women's expectations and desires. Many choices that women make are driven by their conscious or subconscious desire to make their lives more maneuverable within the culturally constructed normative architecture within which they are embedded. At times, their desires are simply reflections of the normative blueprints that are available in the communities to which they belong. Such a notion that women's desires can be coopted by restrictive social norms is also reflected in Sewell's theorizing on agency when he provides the following example: "If they are denied access to the public sphere, women's ambitions will be focused on private life" (1992: 21). This profoundly complicated relationship between gender and desire, that is, between norms and aspirations and their dialectical relationship with autonomous "individual personhood," is powerfully captured by Butler when she writes:

What does gender want? To speak in this way may seem strange, but it becomes less so when we realize that the social norms that constitute our existence carry desires that do not originate with our individual personhood. The matter is made more complex by the fact that the viability of our individual personhood is fundamentally dependent on these social norms. (Butler 2004: 1–2)

It is this vulnerability of desires to gender and social norms that limits the usefulness of a culturally relativist position, or what Sen critically labels a "desire-based approach." Such an approach ultimately results in affirming the status quo and, therefore, remains deficient in understanding and promoting the full possibilities of women's agency. It is this discerning stance on desires that distinguishes Sen's "capabilities" approach to agency from Sewell's "capacity for agency" that may be desire based even as it recognizes the susceptibility of desires to social norms and recognizes the possibility and social value of "transformative action."

In his "capabilities approach" to agency, Sen replaces desire with choice (desire that is pursued through action) and, more importantly, introduces a conception of *value*, or *valuableness*, as a yardstick to evaluate choices for them to be judged as being indicative of agency. In his framework, only those choices (by women) that have an intrinsic relevance for objectively improving the quality of women's lives are to be considered as indicative of agency. "Objective" in this context implies the expansion of possibilities for the expression of personhood and for participation in social, economic, and civic or political spheres of action. This stance reveals an "etic view" of agency, one that stands outside any particular society and that subscribes to using a universal yardstick that incorporates cross-cultural criteria for judging the importance of choices for improving women's quality of life by measurably reliable standards.

This "etic" approach is also adopted in Kabeer's conception of agency that takes into account the substantive content of choices and the psychological and sociocultural motivations underpinning those choices. Kabeer cautions against being misled by women's use of the vocabulary of choice that may falsely assume the availability of alternative options or, at least, imagined alternatives at the discursive level. Such alternatives may be absent in reality, and women's ability to think or act outside of what is prescribed may be compromised.[4]

In Kabeer's framework, to claim that a woman has gained agency entails taking the following analytic steps: stating her goals; discerning her motivations for cherishing and pursuing those goals and the meaning she attaches to the goals; and, finally, evaluating these subjective reasons and objective goals against a universal standard of human welfare and freedom. Kabeer broadens the category of women's agency beyond its sole focus on women's role in decision making (this has been social scientists'

---

[4] Kabeer argues, "The availability of alternatives at the discursive level, of being able to at least imagine the possibility of having chosen differently, is thus crucial to the emergence of a critical consciousness, the process by which people move from a position of unquestioning acceptance of the social order to a critical perspective on it" (1999: 441).

favored indicator) to include a range of previously overlooked behaviors such as cognitive processes of reflection and analysis, bargaining, negotiation, deception, manipulation, subversion, and resistance.

The theoretical perspectives of Sen, Kabeer, and Butler have in common the view that social norms are often constraining and coercive and that the conceptualization of women's agency must engage the critical relationship between the self and constraining norms. Agency is viewed as emerging out of the antagonistic relationship between the individual and norms, that is, from the struggle to establish a transformative relation with the very social norms that define the condition of being. Agency is epitomized as that state of consciousness or arousal that expresses itself primarily through acts that seek to critique, resist, and overcome social norms. Its possibility to materialize lies in the continual enactment of norms, or in Butler's language, in the "iterability of performativity" (Butler 1999: xxiv).

Every performance of a norm opens the possibility of slight deviations from conforming to the norm's socially endorsed meaning and from complying with its precise bodily practice. It is in these interstices between prescriptions and practice that one can find agency. However, there is no progressive ascension to an immaculate state of freedom. Power permeates all states of being, and that means that all agency is riddled with paradox: *"Paradox is the condition of its possibility"* (Butler 2004: 3–4). But the difference agency makes is that it pushes against normative boundaries and strives to achieve greater "livability." Butler asserts that such a critical relationship to norms can be developed collectively even if the collective exists as a minority within a wider society.[5]

---

[5] There is an alternative perspective popular among anthropologists that emphasizes a culturally relativist view of agency and critiques the emphasis on resistance. A recent figure in this critique is Mahmood (2005), who has studied the Islamic revival, or the piety movement, among Egyptian women and who criticizes the previous approaches for conflating agency with antagonism (against social norms). A main criticism of the antagonistic view of agency is the "naturalization of freedom as a social ideal" and the equating of agency with "resistance to relations of domination." Mahmood underscores the possibility that not all women may hold an instinctual hatred for restrictive patriarchal norms or share the desire to be free from relations of subordination and from the structures of male domination. She labels these perceptions as "normative liberal assumptions about human nature" and a "false-consciousness thesis." In the culturally relativist framework, agency is "entailed not only in those acts that resist norms but also in the multiple ways in which one *inhabits* norms" (2005: 15) and in "the variety of ways in which norms are lived and inhabited, aspired to, reached for, and consummated" (2005: 23). I do not subscribe to or adopt this approach to agency in my work.

SOCIAL DEPRIVATION IN A CONTEXT
OF PATRIARCHY AND CONTROL

The social deprivations women face in rural societies in Bengal are rooted in norms, mores, conventions, customs, rules, and practices governing marriage and propriety that determine evaluations of married women's conduct. Class, caste, and religion condition these norms and affect how restrictive they are for any individual woman and on any specific occasion. Practices common to Hindu and Muslim communities alike include: patrilineal descent and inheritance (father-to-son lineage and property transfer); patrilocal residence (married couple residing with or near husband's family and clan); village and clan exogamy with respect to the father's and mother's village and clan (marrying outside the clan and village of parents' birth, which is different in some cases for Muslims); and early marriage for girls.

Girls are typically married away by their parents in their adolescent years. On getting married, they leave their natal village and enter their husband's family and village as complete strangers. They may enter a joint household or form a nuclear household, often only nominally separate as it is often in the neighborhood where the husband's kin reside. Family and community members view these young brides as embodying their family's honor. The ideal is to keep these young women within the household, as opposed to letting them be exposed to the public world of streets and market that are considered perilous and where honor will be put at risk. The result of this restricted physical mobility and confined social engagement is that most of the daily interactions of women occur within a relatively small circle that includes female relatives from the husband's side who live in the same hamlet and non-kin neighbors who also live within shouting distance.

These women usually have daily encounters with each other at the public water tap or at the village pond or well or on their way to and from these shared facilities. These public resources of everyday need usually mark the conventional limits of women's movement. Women's encounters and interactions at these locations do not usually generate a deep level of solidarity. They do not facilitate close social ties that can be relied on when seeking certain crucial types of assistance or that give women the authority to intervene to stop the ill-treatment of women within their circle.

Women's social networks do expand through the life cycle and do contain the power to circulate approval or censure. Nevertheless, the networks remain limited in size and restricted in their capacity to mobilize assistance in solving personal or public problems. The gendered codes of conduct to which all women are subject and their consequent lack of exposure gravely hamper their ability to overcome, individually or collectively, their subordination within the household and in the community.

Structural factors and life-course events are salient in determining the limits of women's domestic power. One of the most important of these factors is the pattern of residence, that is, whether the family is part of a coresiding joint or extended family household or a separate nuclear unit. Women in nuclear households have relatively more opportunity to express their voice in household matters. But, in joint households, it is customary for sons to hand over most if not their entire income to their parents. In such cases, parents-in-law have full authority over income, expenditure and redistribution. The mother-in-law is the only woman in the household who, by virtue of her seniority, enjoys a certain degree of power. Wives, particularly young wives, are lowest in the household's power hierarchy.

Another social factor that influences women's domestic power is childbirth. It is often found that women become more involved in domestic affairs after they have children. Securing the child's future becomes the impetus that drives women to actively participate in household decisions. Tied to this is the theme of women being *notun* (new) versus *purono* (old), terms that reflect the number of years since a woman has been married. It is typical for new wives to have less voice in household affairs compared with women who have been married for longer.

Other factors that have considerable influence on women's domestic power are the husband's migration, age, and health. When husbands migrate for work and there is no other adult male in the household, women become responsible for running the household. Similarly, women whose husbands are old or infirm tend to have more domestic power. The normative inequalities of a patriarchal society also leave women almost defenseless against being deserted by their husbands or being passed over for second wives. Women have few alternatives to accepting men's abandonment and tolerating a second wife's homecoming as men's prerogatives in a patriarchal society.

This depiction is a partial picture of the complex relationship that women have to the patriarchal system of rural society, a relationship that evolves and changes considerably through their life cycle. A young powerless bride who feels alienated within an unfamiliar and hostile environment may, after several decades, when she has become a mother-in-law, become transformed into an agent of rule-enforcement and, occasionally, a source of verbal and physical tyranny to the newly recruited daughters-in-law. This mitigation of subordination and this capacity for exercising dominance are not the results of gaining more meaningful capabilities. Rather, they are the result of gaining proximity to patriarchal power with advancement through the family life cycle.

Some social deprivations, however, are not ameliorated with the progression of age and stage of life and are manifestly an almost universal feature of women's lives in rural societies in Bengal and many other parts of India. These social deficits center on the paucity of women's membership and participation in spheres of sociality outside familial and kinship circles. Even when married women in standard male-headed households engage in income-earning work, it is primarily in daily agricultural wage-work, home-based piece-rate work, or in home-based enterprises. None of these require exposure to the public world outside the household or systematic interactions with women and men outside of the relational circle of the family. Most organic civil society groups and associations in rural communities are composed of male membership and create scope for participation by men only.

AN APPOSITIONAL APPROACH

In light of the various existing approaches to agency, I propose using an *appositional* or *compound vision* approach. This "bee's-eye view" of agency is the best way we can understand agency in all its complexity and fullness.

A bee has "apposition eyes" that are made up of hundreds of single eyes called ommatidium, each with its own lens that looks in a different direction and forms its own partial visual impression. These numerous impressions combine in the brain like fragments of a collage to form a single meaningful representation of an object. Taking any single visual perspective yields an incomplete view.

To evaluate the agency of women within a single culture or society without taking into account the capabilities ("beings and doings") achieved by women in other societies is to mistake a partial impression for a whole picture. To analyze and assess women's agency, we must adopt an appositional, or compound, cross-cultural perspective (not a culturally relativist perspective) and grasp the variety of goals and aspirations, the myriad forms of covert and overt actions, and latent motivations that constitute the reality of women's lives under different regimes of prohibition and possibility. As social scientists, we must become intellectual bricoleurs and assemble a conception of women's agency from a compre-hensive knowledge of a wide assortment of women's lives under different legal and normative regimes. Only then will we be able to create an integrated representation of what women potentially are capable of desir-ing and doing under a progressive relaxation of stultifying norms and laws.

An appositional approach to agency is not an argument for a decon-textualized assessment of agency. Context is crucial. One action in a particular context may represent agency; in another, it may be a coercive routine; in yet another, it may be a deprivation or a forced responsibility rather than a matter of choice. Even within the identical context, an action's significance with respect to agency may vary with changes in the circumstances of women's lives. Uncritically accepting the status quo of any gender regime becomes much less of a risk when combining the perspectives that an appositional approach requires.

A complementary way of thinking about norms is to understand them as social contracts. A contract is a pact between parties that gives each party some rights and simultaneously imposes obligations or restrictions. The degree of power that individuals possess determines the tradeoffs among enjoyed rights, painful sacrifices, and burdensome obligations. Gender norms can be thought of as informal contracts delineating the privilege and differential price of participation in society for men and women. This price can be enforced by the threat of denouncement and violence.[6] Or this price may be extracted with the incentive of entitlements or the promise of privileges. For example, the norm in some societies that married women should focus primarily on their domestic nurturing role is accompanied by women's entitlement to or "privilege" of being provided for by the family's male members or by the state.

When women choose this contract and comply with this norm, to know if it represents agency, we must ask if alternative sets of entitlements are available to them. Do women have the capacity to enforce the entitlements

---

[6] A real-life example of how the price of defying norms – in this case, the norm of intra-community marriage – can be extracted violently is available from an incident that occurred in 2010 in West Bengal. As reported by local newsmedia, a sixteen-year-old girl from the Santhal tribal community in rural Birbhum was made to strip; she was then beaten and forced to walk naked for eight kilometers through three villages by a mob of male members of her own community, who jeered at her and molested her all along the way after it was discovered that she was in a romantic relationship with a boy from a different community. According to local news report, the incident occurred in April but was discovered only in August once videos of the incident recorded on cellular phones by people present during the incident were widely posted and shared on the Internet. The girl, her family, and the village panchayat had all maintained silence until then.

they choose? It is also essential to evaluate whether or not their chosen entitlements increase the opportunities generally available to them to express themselves and participate in all spheres of society. It is usually the case that in strongly patriarchal societies, women do not have the power to enforce their entitlements within the household against other family members. Even if they theoretically possess such a power due to legislative reforms, they may refrain from exercising it in order to retain their promised "privileges." Women often prefer to adopt nonconfrontational strategies of survival. A theoretical choice to uphold a set of norms that can be imposed on women with violence if needed, the entitlements of which cannot be enforced by a woman without negative ramifications, and whose enforcement forecloses opportunities for women cannot accurately be labeled a free exercise of women's agency.

Conceptually, it is important to distinguish between agency and well-being. Both bear importantly on the quality of life, but refer to different aspects of it. Agency, which ought to be viewed from an appositional, capabilities approach, is the capacity for being able to engage in actions that improve the economic, social and cultural, and civic dimensions of one's life. Agency connotes freedom and, therefore, carries underlying connotations of power and relational negotiations that are inevitable in the process of attaining and expressing freedom. Well-being, by contrast, in keeping with its conventional usage, refers exclusively to the material or economic conditions of life.[7] There is no necessary positive correlation between agency and well-being; that is to say, an improvement in individual agency does not necessarily have to be reflected in improvements in individual material or economic well-being.

Historical examples of this decoupling between agency and well-being – instances in which "freedom"/"self-dependence"/"independence"[8] increased together with a simultaneous decline in the material conditions of life – are

---

[7] In contemporary times, the notion of well-being has been occasionally expanded to include a subjective dimension, "happiness," and it has attracted considerable attention from economists concerned with national and international development. These economists have attempted to measure it at the country level and to develop an index and ranking out of these measures. The term "gross national happiness" has been coined (originally in Bhutan) and is now in circulation (see http://www.grossnationalhappiness.com). There has been a recent government sponsored attempt in the United Kingdom to measure the national level of happiness (as an alternative measure to the gross domestic product (GDP)), and the results were published in an article in *The Guardian* dated July 24, 2012 ("Wellbeing index points way to bliss: Live on a remote island and don't work").

[8] These terms come to us via English translation of the authors' original German language usage.

variously cited in the works of Max Weber and Georg Simmel and others. Such transformations were crucial in analyzing social developments in nineteenth-century Germany. Weber wrote of "freedom" in an almost trivializing and disparaging tone, at the same time as he stressed its undeniable pull. Focusing on the changed disposition of workers that made them prefer working as day laborers[9] and, hence, willing to forego the possibility of long-term economic security and the promise of future upward mobility in favor of freedom (from indenture and personal subjection), Weber wrote:

Domestic servants flee the household of the master. Threshers want to sever their close tie-in with the economy of the estate. The laborer on annual contract relinquishes his secure position, in order to make his precarious way as a "free" day laborer. The peasant with very little land would starve than accept a job and work for someone else. Innumerable workers prefer to pay any price to a jobber for a piece of land and to live in abject dependence on creditors who charge usurious interest-rates, all this for the sake of "self-dependence" which they crave, i.e. for the sake of independence from personal subservience to a master ... It is pointless to argue about such elementary movements, which give expression to the tremendous and purely psychological magic of "freedom." In good measure this is a grand illusion, but after all man and so also the farm laborers do not live "by bread alone." The efforts and aspirations of the farm laborers make just this evident to us, that the "bread and butter question" is of secondary importance. (Bendix 1960: 45–6 [Weber 1892: 797–8])[10]

In a similar manner, Simmel made his observations on freedom and well-being in comparing the conditions of the bonded laborer to the industrial worker in the emerging capitalist system. Simmel wrote:

By thus eliminating the pressure of irrevocable dependency on a particular individual master, the worker is already on the way to personal freedom despite his objective bondage. That this emergent freedom has little continuous influence upon the material situation of the worker should not prevent us from appreciating it. For here [sphere of labor and economic relations: insertion mine], as in other spheres, there is no necessary connection between liberty and increased well-being which is usually automatically presupposed by wishes, theories and agitations. (Simmel 1982 (1978): 300)

Agency and well-being also became decoupled in the course of social development during the so-called Golden Age of Victorian England (the

---

[9] Agricultural laborers hired by the day (instead of the whole year/annual contract laborers) on the basis of fixed monetary wage contracts and in exchange of wages alone (no room, meals, or in-kind allowances).

[10] This study was focused on the problem of farm laborers in Germany and was based on a survey of *junkers* (landowners).

quarter-century period from 1850 to 1875) coinciding with the heyday of the Industrial Revolution. Edgar Royston Pike, a British observer, noted the connection between factory employment and liberty and the public's growing preference for independence even as the material standards of life and the prospect of economic security were being compromised:

The liberty which endears factory life to both lads and lasses is in strong contrast with the restraints of domestic service ...[11] The annual or half-yearly festival – the picnic in summer, and the ball in winter – which is a conspicuous event in factory life, excites a vast sensation throughout the neighborhood, and is an occasion of great pride or vanity to the members. Servant-girls and footboys see the vans go by in the summer morning, and hear the fiddles and the dancing in the winter evening, and feel they are "in bondage", and "get no pleasure". They cannot dress as the factory lads and lasses may – buying and wearing whatever they take a fancy to. Worse still, they have not the daily stimulus and amusement of society of their own order. Beyond their kitchen mates, they seldom have any free and prolonged conversation; while the day-workers pass to and from the factory in groups, and can take walks, or spend the evenings together. The maidservant must have "no followers", while the factory-worker can flirt to any extent. Servant-girls rarely marry, while factory-girls probably always may, whether they do or not ...

It may be very true that every freak of idleness in the day-worker entails much loss; it may be true that the liberty of one's own room may be spoiled by the stoppage of the mill and the gnawing care of subsistence; it may be that the gay dresser of the fete-day has her fine shawl in pawn from Monday morning till Saturday night; it may be that modesty and self-respect decay in the publicity of factory life, till the character becomes hard, and the mind coarse, in a large proportion of factory-workers, while the burden of temptation is fearfully heavy to the rest – all these things may be true; but public opinion among the class is in favor of the independence of factory and other day-work ... In one word, it is *independence* against *dependence*. (Pike 1967: 159)[12]

---

[11] This "..." is a punctuation mark used by the author himself. It does not denote the omission of text.

[12] This structural opportunity to pursue freedom and a growing taste for freedom led to significant ramifications in nineteenth-century European societies. It led to a historic and sudden shortage of men and women available to work as domestic servants after a continuous expansion in the demand and supply of servants through the eighteenth and nineteenth centuries in English society (Coser 1973), where being able to afford servant(s) symbolized the achievement of higher social status (Hecht 1956). A similar "acute crisis" in the role of the housemaid was reported in Norway, where the number of housemaids was more than halved in the span of only two decades (falling from 115,000 to 49,000 between 1930 and 1952), their average age increased by about ten years (indicating that fewer girls and younger women were still entering the service and those already past their prime in the service were continuing to be retained), and a significantly large proportion of them held the desire to work in other types of jobs (Aubert 1956: 155). The lack of freedom in the servant-role was attracting women away to industrial jobs. Even though factory jobs

The distinction between agency and well-being is not simply a theoretical one but one that comes vitally into play at specific moments in history.

While the appositional approach recognizes that agency and well-being may not improve simultaneously, it holds onto the perspective that agency must be positively correlated with capabilities (or what Sen (1993) has also termed as "functionings" or "beings and doings") that are achievable by an individual. Capabilities can be categorized into two broad kinds. There are those "beings and doings" that require economic means in order to be pursued and achieved. Hence, they are termed "pricey." There are other "beings and doings" that can be pursued free[13] of an economic cost. Where individual agency increases without a simultaneous increase in economic well-being, we can presume that the enhanced agency is primarily expressed in pursuing a larger array of the "free" rather than the "pricey" "beings and doings." The objective improvement in the social quality of life from being able to pursue a larger array of free "beings and doings" and the consequent sense of liberty that derives from that explains why an individual might prefer freedom even at the cost of sacrificing their present and future material quality of life.[14]

A diagrammatic representation will help clarify which of the two kinds of capabilities are enhanced in different "quality of life scenarios": when agency and well-being are both low (down left-hand corner); when agency is low but well-being is high (down right-hand corner); when agency increases without an accompanying improvement in well-being

were highly regulated and supervised, they were restricted to specified hours. Industrial work did not spill over in the diffused manner of housemaid work to consume their entire time and claim their private lives and personalities. Consequently, new laws were passed at the time in Norway to alter and regulate the working conditions of housemaids in an attempted "occupationalization" (Aubert 1956: 158) of the domestic servant role. The laws introduced specificity along the dimensions of space, time, and work content, so as to make working as a domestic servant attractive enough to retain some women against the pull of industrial jobs. These legislated specificities – like being given her own bed; her own room and one that can be locked; not being ordered to sleep in the children's room; a ten hour limit on working hours so that she is able to spend some of her time awake at her own discretion; free days and limitation on overtime (Aubert 1956) – focused not on increasing the remuneration for the housemaid job but on introducing some degree of freedom and autonomy in the housemaid's life.

[13] I have chosen to use the word "free" instead of "costless" in order to restrict the meaning of "free" to being economically costless and to leave open the possibility that economically "free" actions may prove to be socially costly. Social costs usually take the shape of reproach or more severe sanctions from family members or the community.

[14] Simmel (1982 [1978]), in his chapter titled "individual freedom," recognized this association when he mentioned that freedom is the liberty to engage in the economic exchange of labor (however unfair) with an employer of one's own choosing.

TABLE 2.1: *Capabilities in "Quality of Life Scenarios"*

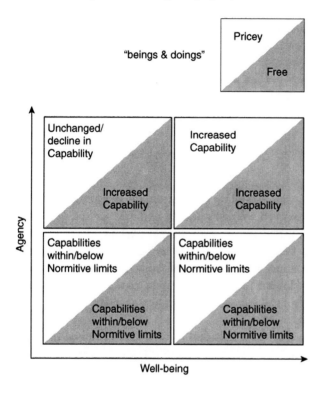

(top left-hand corner); and when agency and well-being both improve (top right-hand corner).

It is important to be aware that a structural opportunity like microcredit may result in any of these four scenarios. One outcome that is particularly observed is an increase in women's agency without a concurrent increase in women's personal income or any dramatic improvement in household economic well-being. In this scenario, agency improves unilaterally because of the greater associational freedom and scope created by microcredit that allows women to engage in a wider set of free "beings and doings."

An important set of such free "beings and doings" is the freedom and capability of *participation* in social and civic life and action. This constitutes an objective improvement in women's quality of life, as having an expanded associational life is intrinsically desirable for individuals and also carries the promising potential for fostering social capital benefits. Agency improvement, even when not accompanied by parallel improvement in material well-being, should not be discounted. Instead, agency improvement should be appreciated for what it achieves – increasing women's capabilities and raising quality of life, and, eventually, deepening democracy by making subaltern publics more capable of engaging in a civic and political life. Agency is a "meta-good," and achieving agency must precede the capability to achieve material well-being through individual efforts.

GENDER "HABITUS"

Incorporating Bourdieu's notion of "habitus" into this discussion can further enhance our understanding of the mutually constraining and enabling relationship between women's agency and microcredit. Formulated in order to capture the dialectical relationship between social structure and individual agency, the concept of "habitus" is particularly useful for understanding the nature and potential of women's agency in a gender-stratified society. "Habitus" can impress upon us the significance of the sometimes seemingly small increments in women's agency within a context of stringent patriarchy.

It should be stated at the outset that in Bourdieu's original theoretical usage, "habitus" was not consciously developed or used with the intention of explaining gendered behavior or in reference to evaluating the differences in men and women's quality of life. But his ethnographic work, centered on Algerian peasant society under French colonialism, brought into focus the bodily and social conduct of men and women within the private space of the household and in public space. It therefore bears directly on notions of feminine propriety and male potency or excellence that structured gender-appropriate conduct and social practices. "Habitus" is easily and usefully shifted from the realm of class stratification into the complementary realm of gender analysis.

"Habitus" is the intermediary individual manifestation, in the form of durable preferences and dispositions, of objective conditions and constraints of life that are experienced and shared by an entire collectivity or group of people and which are determined by the group's structural position in a stratified society. Reframing it, we may say that "habitus" is the individual and subjective manifestation of what Weber called "life chances." "Habitus" represents the subjective and bodily incorporation of the individual through which social structure translates into daily practice and that, in turn, helps sustain the social structure. In Bourdieu's words:

The structures constitutive of a particular type of environment (e.g. the material conditions of existence characteristic of a class condition) produce *habitus*, systems of durable, transposable *dispositions*, structured structures predisposed to function as structuring structures, that is, as principles of the generation and structuring of practices and representations, which can be objectively "regulated" and "regular" without in any way being obedience to rules, objectively adapted to their goals without presupposing a conscious aiming at ends or an express mastery of the operations necessary to attain them and, being all this, collectively orchestrated without being the product of the orchestrating action of the conductor. (Bourdieu 2012 [1977]: 72)

Class and gender are both principles along which society is stratified. Gender also functions as an institution that assigns women and men to female- and male-typed roles in the private sphere of the household. It also influences the extent of men's and women's participation and success in the labor market and in other public spheres of engagement. As a system of stratification, gender is unique for creating and sustaining inequality in the material conditions of life and in life chances, power, and capabilities among two groups that are not only socially proximate but that are also linked through familial and kinship ties and share relational intimacy in the household. The social supremacy and subordination that accompanies occupancy of gender positions orients men's and women's practices in ways that conform to and preserve the gendered social structure. Bourdieu recognizes this in his analysis of the Kabyle in Algerian peasant society when he remarks on the "*centrifugal*, male orientation and the *centripetal*, female orientation" (p. 92). His explanation of the operation of "habitus" is strongly reminiscent of the arguments of Sen, Kabeer, and Butler regarding women's agency and the structured and structuring nature of desire.

Because the dispositions durably inculcated by objective conditions (which science apprehends through statistical regularities as the probabilities objectively attached to a group or class) engender aspirations and practices objectively compatible with those objective requirements, the most improbable practices are excluded, either totally without examination, as *unthinkable*, or at the cost of the *double negation* which inclines agents to make a virtue of necessity, that is, to refuse what is anyway refused and to love the inevitable. The very conditions of production of the ethos, *necessity made into a virtue*, are such that the expectations to which it gives rise tend to ignore the restrictions to which the validity of any calculus of probabilities is subordinated ... (pp. 77–78)

Bourdieu exceeds Sen, Kabeer, and Butler in seeing the comprehensive, totalizing incorporation of the individual's body by social structure, not just the more limited subjective faculties. He talks about "body *hexis*," that is, the embodied form of "habitus":

Bodily *hexis* is political mythology realized, *em-bodied*, turned into a permanent disposition, a durable manner of standing, speaking, and thereby of *feeling* and *thinking* (pp. 63–64) ... a pattern of postures that is both individual and systematic ... and charged with a host of social meaning and values. (p. 87)

In short, the specifically feminine virtue, *lahia*, modesty, restraint, reserve, orients the whole female body downwards, towards the ground, the inside, the house, whereas male excellence, *nif* (twofold meaning of sexual potency inseparable from social potency: insertion mine), is asserted in movement upwards, outwards, towards other men. (p. 94)

Yet, where Sen and Kabeer argue for the need to abandon desire-based approaches to evaluating agency, Bourdieu (owing perhaps to his roots in anthropology) sees the play of agency even within the structured and structuring of "habitus":

Through the habitus, the structure which has produced it governs practice, not by the processes of a mechanical determinism, but through the mediation of the orientations and limits it assigns to the habitus's operations of invention. As an acquired system of generative schemes objectively adjusted to the particular conditions in which it is constituted, the habitus engenders all the thoughts, all the perceptions, and all the actions consistent with those conditions, and no others ... Because the habitus is an endless capacity to engender products – thought, perceptions, expressions, actions – whose limits are set by the historically and socially situated conditions of its production, the conditioned and conditional freedom it secures is as remote from a creation of unpredictable novelty as it is from a simple mechanical reproduction of the initial conditionings. (p. 95)

How are the conditioning influences of structural environments (associated with a particular position in the class or gender hierarchy) and early socialization overcome? If "habitus" cannot be overcome, if it is indeed a permanent disposition, then how can women's desires or practices engender anything else other than that which is thoroughly conditioned by their gender "habitus"? What forms exactly could these conditioned and conditional freedoms take? And do these freedoms pose a challenge to the norms of the group? Do they have a transformative relationship to norms?

Through my research, I show how "habitus" operates in the lives of women who are caught up in the tide of microcredit in rural Bengali society. Even more importantly, my research shows how microcredit groups, because of the new structural opportunities for participation and new practices, have the promising potential of becoming significant sources of secondary socialization that are helping to cultivate women's capabilities. Microcredit enables women to resist and even transcend the conventional gender "habitus" that they are socialized into. Microcredit transforms women's desires and dispositions and demands a new kind of body "*hexis*." Microcredit increases capabilities and enhances women's individual and collective agency. Ultimately, it may promote a level of agency in women that extends beyond conditioned and conditional freedoms.

STRATEGIES OF OBSERVING AGENCY

Translating agency into reliable empirical indicators is difficult, to say the least.[15] I decipher women's capacity to exercise agency by focusing on a range of dimensions.

Three aspects of my approach need to be emphasized. First, I do not simply assume that all women invariably have decision-making powers over aspects that are typically considered to fall within their gender-domain. My interviews with women revealed at an early stage that it was not unlikely that women lacked authority even in aspects of decision making that some scholars consider to fall within the female domain. Interviews also revealed that women in real and de facto female-headed households habitually make decisions that conventionally fall within the male-domain. I use the concept of "domestic power," and the theory of gendered spheres of decision making cautiously and apply these intellectual constructions on a case-by-case basis where and when appropriate.

Second, I avoid a fundamental conceptual error found in many quantitative studies of agency. This is the error of assuming that the various dimensions of agency necessarily change together or change at the same pace. My framework acknowledges the possibility that a woman may have increased agency in a few dimensions and no change in the remaining dimensions or that improvement in some dimensions may far outpace changes in other dimensions. My cases confirmed that these discrepancies across different dimensions of agency are frequently observed. I nevertheless make a unified assessment of agency for each individual case, even though this is a subjective assessment. There is no escape from subjectivity in evaluations of this nature. I have tried to be as explicit as possible in presenting to readers all the data on which my judgments are based.

---

[15] The definitions and indicators of women's "autonomy" used by scholars are multiple. Autonomy has been variously defined as "the degree of access to and control over material and social resources within the family, in the community, and in the society at large" (Dixon-Mueller 1978); "the ability to influence and control one's personal environment" (Safilios-Rothschild 1982); "the capacity to obtain information and make decisions about one's private concerns and those of one's intimates" (Dyson and Moore 1983).

TABLE 2.2: *Themes Covered under Dimensions of Agency*

Social Awareness	Social Interaction	Physical Mobility	Domestic Power	Civic Participation	Collective Action
Knowledge of legal & govt. or political institutions	Ability to interact with people outside the family & kin group	Ability to go to local shops & markets to fulfill needs	Knowledge of domestic income & expenditure patterns	Ability to participate in meetings of the village council	Ability to jointly or individually protest against wrongdoings
Knowledge of financial institutions & options & govt. schemes	Ability to overcome restrictions on appearing in public	Ability to visit the local health facilities	Control over use of money & decisions on financial investments	Ability to contest elections for positions in the village council	Ability to initiate joint actions to address resource & infrastructure shortages
Awareness of & ability to adopt contraceptive measures	Relative freedom in interactions	Ability to go on social visits	Expressing opinions on household management		
Awareness of happenings in the larger community	Changes in the nature & frequency of interactions	Ability to attend non-compulsory group events in other villages (All the above: accompanied vs. independently)	Ability to resist verbal abuse and physical violence		

Third, my approach acknowledges that women may associate different levels of significance to the different abilities listed under each of the six capability dimensions. This might be the case due to differences in individual perceptions regarding the difference these capabilities make to their quotidian lives. For example, some women stated in the interview that keeping track of household income and expenses was not all that important for them because their husbands managed the financial front. Some others stated that the ability to go to markets and shops was not relevant because their husbands purchased everything they needed or they made purchases from the hawkers that came to their doorstep. In order to understand women's subjective valuations of capabilities, I sought out women's narratives of the meanings they assign to the transformations they experience (or their absence) and how they view the difference that any particular capability makes in their lives. Of course, perceptions, like desires, are susceptible to influence by cultural context. I therefore do not take these narratives at face value but subject them to my own analytic and diagnostic sieve. Following this methodological procedure, I am better able to elicit accounts from the women of the desires, meanings, and motivations they assign to their capabilities while maintaining my own independent interpretive stance.

There are two special advantages to a qualitative approach in understanding women's agency. First, the use of qualitative methods allows the adoption of an interpretive approach through which to integrate the wide range of women's responses to capabilities or their lack. The wide range of responses across different dimensions of agency must be made part of any analysis and is central both to the complexity of the issue and to the depth of its social importance. This method gives respondents full latitude in expressing their past and present experiences in their own terms by drawing on their repertoire of colloquial vocabulary and idioms through which they express a very wide range of emotions. In my study, women's verbal recounting was often accompanied by tears of distress, by signs of anger or despondence, by a sense of embarrassment or irony, or by humor and peals of laughter. Taken in their totality, these *vernacular enunciations* plus *gestures* and *emotions* through which women expressed themselves added a great deal to the content of their narratives. These embodied, vernacular elements communicate states of being (with or without agency) that are of indispensable value as sources through which to refine our assessments of women's agency.

Second, qualitative methods are indispensable for deciphering women's own assessment of cause and effect in their lives. What causes individual women assign to their enhanced agency are crucial indicators of their empowerment. Of course, subjective opinions are cross referenced against objective data on such issues as the number of loans they have taken, how the loans have been used and by whom, the degree of participation in group meetings and events, and the intensity of involvement within the social networks associated with microcredit.

PATHWAYS TO AGENCY

Miles and Huberman (1994) have laid out in great detail the specifics of a very powerful methodology of qualitative causal analysis, which has a particular advantage for identifying mechanisms. The fundamental approach of this method is to analyze narratives or interviews with the aim of identifying the underlying variables and processes that are invariably embedded in personal accounts. For this study, their method entails analyzing each individual case or interview with an eye toward identifying the following three factors: the independent variables that have the most influence on agency (loans and income versus associational influence), the mediating variables that affect agency that are present (household composition, etc.), and the effect of these variables on the agency of the subject. All this information is used to draw out detailed causal networks at work in each of the cases in this study. The penultimate step is to differentiate the broad typologies of causal network patterns identified in this manner. These are the pathways to agency. The final step involves counting the number of cases that fall under each of the different causal patterns, or pathways. The numerical prevalence of each pathway helps to identify the dominant and least prevalent strategies and experiences that contribute to improving women's agency.

For each individual case of my study, I took the following analytical steps: (i) I assessed the pattern of agency change – improvement, continued lack, pre-existing agency; (ii) I decided the level of overall improvement – slight, moderate, or substantial; (iii) I determined the predominant mechanism responsible for the changes – the economic, or financial mechanism via access to credit; or the associational mechanism via group participation and social networks; or an unrelated source; and (iv) I identified the social-structural factors operating in each case – household composition, level of education, spousal characteristics, and so on. This analysis produced five distinct trajectories experienced by women with respect to states of agency associated with microcredit. The table below lists the pathways and

TABLE 2.3: *Pathways to Agency*

Pathways	Nos. women
1. Agency improvements flowing predominantly from the *associational mechanism* (occurs regardless of economic outcome from loan-use or loan-transfer)	139 (34.75%)[49%]*
2. Possessing agency prior to enrollment in microcredit due to unrelated factors	116 (29%)
3. Failure to improve agency though reporting household economic gains from loan-use (loan-transfer to men; profitable investment; weak group participation)	76 (19%)[27%]
4. Failure to improve agency & failure to make household economic gains from loans (loan-transfer to men; unprofitable investment; weak group participation)	44 (11%)[15%]
5. Agency improvements flowing predominantly from the *financial mechanism* (loans used independently by women)	25 (6.25%)[9%]

[*Note: The number noted within (%) represents the percentage with regard to the total sample in this study, that is, 400 women. And the number noted within [%] represents the percentage with regard to the total number of women who were found to be lacking agency prior to their group membership, that is, 284 women (400–116).]

presents data on the numbers of cases that shared the same causal pattern. The pathways are presented in descending order of frequency.

The most striking finding of my study is that, of all the women who lacked agency prior to their enrollment in microcredit, nearly 49 percent experienced improvements in their agency due to the associational mechanism. Compared to this pattern, a meager 9 percent of women experienced improvements in their agency due to the financial mechanism (taking into account both its formal and informal definitions). The associational mechanism emerged as the overwhelmingly predominant of the two mechanisms in improving women's agency.

However, the data also reveal that the associational mechanism is not invariably transforming. Its positive effect depends, among other factors, on women's group participation and the quality of group leadership. The requisite level of participation is often lacking and the quality of leadership can vary greatly. Forming individuals into associations and requiring their participation should not be assumed to be the panacea for the problems related to poverty and underdevelopment. Associations do not

automatically or invariably produce positive economic and social outcomes. Nor should the associational mechanism be thought of as a
costless way for catalyzing social change. To be successful, a robust
associational mechanism requires significant investments of time and
energy on the part of both individuals and organizations. Significant
resources from global aid and development institutions are also necessary for women's microcredit groups to have their desired effect and
realize in practice the potential they hold for enhanced agency.

3

Converting loans into leverage

Advocates of microcredit, when they support giving women direct access to credit, often rely rhetorically and ideologically on money's quasi-magical powers to transform women into "entrepreneurs."[1] Such advocates hope that money in the hands of women will become transformed into a tool with which women can counteract the weight of normative restrictions and redress the deficit of their economic constraint in their favor.

Steeped in contemporary, economistic developmental ideologies, NGO leaders and staffs often sincerely believe that microcredit will enable women to launch their own livelihood enterprises, become significant income-earners, contribute financially to their households, and as a result significantly enhance their social agency. Those who are more attuned to the reality of household dynamics and gender relations in rural Bengali societies tend to be somewhat skeptical about the superficially optimistic trope of "female entrepreneurship." In its place, these proponents tend to hope that women's role as the access point for loans will raise women's

---

[1] In the microcredit discourse the word "entrepreneur" is typically used to refer to women who own and run economic enterprises regardless of the nature (conventional or innovative) and scale (small or large) of the enterprise. This is an extremely loose use of entrepreneurship as a concept. The term has a much more specific meaning in the classical works of Schumpeter and others who use it to designate successful and profitable leadership of a capitalist firm (Becker, Knudsen, and Swedberg 2011). During the last few decades, the looser meaning of "entrepreneur" has emerged from organizational studies to mean anyone who starts an organization. A third use of the term has emerged quite recently and applied to the figure of the "social entrepreneur." For further analysis of this term, see Swedberg (2000) and Reuf (2010). I have used the term "livelihood enterprise" to designate the small, self-run businesses of microcredit users.

value in the eyes of their family and alter the social perception of women's worth. In this view, even if men are the loan users, women will be able to use their access to loans strategically to negotiate for rights and freedoms that are conventionally denied them. Both of these hypotheses regarding how loans will transform the lives of women are globally publicized – through formal development discourses and through grassroots perceptions of the social efficacy of microcredit.

In my study I used women in conventionally patriarchal, male-headed households who were economically dependent on their husbands, did not have any livelihood enterprises of their own, and conformed to social expectations about gender roles to examine claims that loans resulted directly in "entrepreneurship" and leverage. Among this category of women in my study comprising 284 women, only 6, a miniscule number, became independent enterprise owners.

An equally small number of women exercised managerial control over loans that were used in economic enterprises that the women had initiated by themselves or in collaboration with their husbands. In these cases the enterprises were run either jointly by the couple or executed by the husbands (three cases). There were sixteen other cases in which the women expressed that they had gained some bargaining capacity by channeling loans to their husbands. Together, these twenty-five cases are the focus of Sections I and II of this chapter. The descriptive Table 3.1 specifies for all these cases the household-type, presence/absence of adult son, and the women's loan-use, income, and repayment characteristics. The narratives that follow my analysis are presented as illustrative of general patterns.

In Section I, I focus on wives who started their own small-scale farm and non-farm enterprises and identify the conditions under which women's "entrepreneurship" is realized. Identifying these factors conditioning women's entrepreneurship reveals the other social and economic dimensions that are crucial to enhancing women's agency under conditions of patriarchy and contradict the validity of simplistic claims of wholesale transformation as a result of direct loans alone. In the second section, I focus on the women who appeared to gain some agency and bargaining capacity through transferring loans. Together, these sets of women compose less than ten percent of the sample of women in conventional male-headed households (9%: 25 out of 284).

In contrast, a strikingly large percentage (42%) of that sample is composed of women who transferred the loans to their husbands yet failed to gain agency (regardless of loans yielding profits or losses). These women are the focus of Section III. These real-life outcomes demonstrating the

TABLE 3.1: *Objective Conditions for Economic Mechanism to Improve Agency*

Loans	Loan-use activity	Respondent	Nuclear household	No adult son*	Initiated loan-use idea	Independent economic enterprise	Income substantial part of livelihood	Independent loan repayment	Effect strong (S) weak (W)
21,500	Farming, Cattle	Niyasha	X	X	X	Partial	X	Partial	W
20,000	Fish trade	Ashima		X	X		X		W
20,000	Business	Lotika	X	X	X		X		W
20,000	Farming	Shabitri	X	X			X		W
19,000	Farming	Lokkhi	X	X			X		W
18,500	Farming, Fish trade	Sandhya	X	X			loss	Partial	W
18,000	Farming	Shoma	X	X			X	Partial	W
17,000	Farming, Nursery, Cattle	Rina	X	X	Joint	Partial	X		S
16,500	Farming	Tarakdashi	X	X	X	X	X	X	S
16,500	Farming	Taslima (M)	X	X	X	X	X	X	S
15,000	Business	Rekha	X	X			X		W
12,100	Farming, vehicle	Bhanu	X	X	X	X	X	X	S
12,000	Business	Sumitra	Mother-in-law	X	X	X	X	X	S
9000	Farming	Arati B	X	X	Joint		X		W
8500+	Farming, Fish trade, Cattle	Shampa	X	X			X		W
8000	Business	Shahida (M)	X	X	Joint		X		S

TABLE 3.1: (cont.)

Loans	Loan-use activity	Respondent	Nuclear household	No adult son*	Initiated loan-use idea	Independent economic enterprise	Income substantial part of livelihood	Independent loan repayment	Effect strong (S) weak (W)
8000	Funeral, Bicycle, Land	Renu	X	X					W
7500	Business	Arati M	X	X	X	X	X	X	S
7500	Business	Probhati	X	X	X	X	X	X	S
5000	Farming	Shobita R	Father-in-law	X			X		W
4000	Farming, Land	Hasina (M)	X	X			X		W
2800	Farming	Shikha	X	X	X		X		S
?	Cattle	Mumtaz (M)	Mother-in-law	X					W
?	Farming	Shobita M	X	X			X		W
?	?	Geeta	X	X					W

inefficacy of the financial mechanism alone in improving women's agency vividly illustrate the obstacles in the way of directly translating loans into successful challenges to patriarchy in the countryside of Bengal. Understanding the limitations and failures of the financial mechanism for married women in conventional patriarchal households re-enforces the importance of microcredit's associational properties for improving women's agency.

WIVES WHO TURNED WORTHY

Married women in conventionally gendered households gain impressive levels of agency from their access to loans when they become independent loan-users – that is, when they control all aspects of the enterprise and repay loans from their own earnings. These women may decide to rope their family members into various enterprises funded by their loans, but this is done by their decision, and they remain in full control of all aspects of the enterprise. In all of these cases, the women are sole loan-users – that is, none of their husbands have parallel access to loans from other sources. The earnings of these women, although not large by any means, are substantial enough to elevate them to being either the principal breadwinner in their family or equal earners alongside their husbands.

These women gain a "prescribing voice," the ability to articulate plans for economically uplifting their households and the ability to influence the decisions and choices of other family members. They gain worth, or value, in the eyes of their husbands, neighbors, and fellow group members, and become praiseworthy within this circle for their pivotal economic role in their households. These changes are tantamount to altering important aspects of conventional gender relations within the household. "Women's entrepreneurship," then, enhances women's agency dramatically, but this is true only in a tiny percentage of cases involving married women with economically productive non-migrant husbands. The vast number of these women simply do not become "entrepreneurs" in the sense implied by the microcredit discourse. Women in this category who do are exceptions and not the rule.

Only in six cases of my study were married women solely responsible for proposing an investment plan and starting and operating their own economic enterprises not related to their husbands' occupations. In only three other cases did women take the leading role in proposing an investment plan or participate actively with their husbands in jointly formulating plans that were then put into practice by their husbands. Having managerial control over loans made their cases different from other cases of loan-transfer. In these nine cases, the financial mechanism facilitated extremely significant gains in women's agency. Analyzing these cases reveals that women's agency achieved through "entrepreneurship" and/ or loan-control was realized only when a combination of social and economic circumstances produced an environment that necessitated, permitted or tolerated women's leadership role in household economics. The enabling circumstances can be summarized in the following terms:

i)   Residence in nuclear household – absence of in-laws in the same unit
ii) Husband's income is extremely paltry – falling below subsistence-level
iii) Husband's attitude is accommodative – not averse to gender-role deviations
iv) No adult son – or, if there is a son, he is too young to manage money

These conditions are revealing in that household material distress or emergency is an important reason for the acceptance of women's leadership.

"I do everything; my husband is nothing!"

We started cultivating crops only after I joined the group. Before that we didn't have any cultivation because we didn't own any land. Now we lease in land or cultivate through sharecropping.[2] Last year I grew paddy, and we have enough rice for this year and enough fodder for the cow. Next year I'll grow paddy again ... I don't take money from anywhere else because now we have a group. If I take anything, I'll take it from the group. We'll take money from the place that helped us open our eyes. (Bhanu Mondol, group: Sharada)

Forty-five-year-old Bhanu (Hindu) looks frail and has an air of being in a rush. Her demeanor is not surprising once she explains that, not long before, she used to work three shifts a day as a farm-laborer in the fields of local landowning families. The family's financial situation, though, has improved dramatically in the last five years since she joined the microcredit group in her neighborhood. These improvements can be solely credited to her.

Five years ago, they were landless and had no money to even rent-in land for sharecropping. The only source of income for the family of seven

---

[2] These are different types of land tenancy systems by which landless farming families rent-in land from land-owning families.

was her husband's paltry daily earnings of Rs 30 from agricultural wage-work that fluctuated seasonally and was vulnerable to the vagaries of nature. Bhanu recalls those days. It is a distressing picture of abject poverty:

> Before I joined the group, I can't tell you how much struggle we had to undergo. For a whole year I couldn't put a grain of rice in my stomach. I'd cook a cupful of rice, and I'd feed my children with it, and I'd have the leftover starch with wild leaves and roots ... At the time my children were very young, and I never used to go anywhere outside the house.

In addition to severe food shortages, Bhanu and her family endured other deprivations of various kinds. Bhanu grabs at the saree she is wearing and talks about how, for years, she was never able to buy a new saree for herself. She always bought her neighbors' worn out sarees for a few rupees, and those were all that she had to wear. Despite near-starvation conditions, she never thought of trying to find work as a farm laborer, although she could have earned at least something if she had done that: "Before I never used to go [outside the house to work in the fields] because I didn't have the habit."

Once she joined the group, she took a very small loan of Rs 600 to pay off the sum they had borrowed at high interest from the moneylender to meet their subsistence needs. Grinding poverty and living in debt to the moneylender had not made her step out of the house in search of paid work. Surprisingly, the urge to repay the group loan and the incentive of taking another loan in the future pushed her against the force of habit into *maathe jon daoa*, "giving labor in the fields." The daily pay for agricultural wage-labor was a meager Rs 20.[3] By the time the loan was repaid, two years had passed. Then she took a loan of Rs 1500 and rented-in some land for cultivating paddy. Later, she stored the rice at home and repaid the loans by continuing to work as a farm laborer. Then, taking a huge leap, she took out a loan of Rs 10,000, a substantial sum considering the family's still fragile economic condition. She used part of that money to buy a "cycle-van," a pedal-driven wooden platform on three wheels, which serves as a mode of transportation in these villages. Her plan was to have the vehicle operated by her eldest son, now in his teens and old enough to start working. The rest she used for cultivation. Then, in order to repay the group's loan, she intensified her efforts to earn more. The

---

[3] The daily wage for agricultural laborers varies by village and region. In the villages I studied, on average in 2004, women were paid Rs 30 per day and men Rs 40. But in this particular village, the rate was Rs 10 lower than the average.

common practice for women who work as agricultural daily wage-laborers is to work one shift a day. But she started working three shifts a day so that she could repay the sizeable loan and maintain her credibility in the group that was essential for receiving future loans.

Throughout the entire day I would work in the fields, sometimes for three shifts: morning, noon, and evening. I'd work, and I'd constantly pray to god. When I gave my son the cycle-van I told him, "Work hard and see that we can repay the loan in time. If we can keep our [financial] behavior all right then, in the future, we can take loans and start cultivating.

It took her an entire year to repay the loan through her own and her son's combined earnings. This is how Bhanu went from being a housebound wife-mother struggling to make ends meet with her husband's abysmally low income to becoming a frenzied worker.

The physical and normative contraints of home and "*gharer bou*"(bride/wife of the household) that kept Bhanu from entering the public world began to lose their hold over her. Once she realized that repaying loans on time meant the possibility of being able to take out more loans and having the chance to put the household on its feet for a lifetime, she shed her inhibitions. Eventually she cultivated land on her own behalf. To supplement her farm-laborer income she started doing various other kinds of work as well. She bought vegetables and flowers in bulk at wholesale rates from the local farmers and then used a combination of cycle-vans, local trains, and her own physical labor to transport the produce to surrounding local markets, and sold them at somewhat higher retail rates. She also hired herself out as a cook at social and religious ceremonies in the village. Bhanu's first micro-credit loan and its repayment started a cycle of performing paid work outside the household that led to a gradual but accelerating dismantling of boundaries and inhibitions.

Since I didn't have the habit before, I was embarrassed to go work on the fields for others. But now, from going and working on my own fields, I've gained the experience, and I'm no longer scared or embarrassed to work for others. Now I earn Rs 600–700 every month on my own. I harvest vegetables for people and earn twenty, twenty-five, thirty, forty, and even sixty rupees some days … When I don't get work in the fields, I buy vegetables and flowers in bulk and go to the markets in and around this area to sell vegetables and flowers and earn something that way.

This is an example of how loans can, under special circumstances, induce a change in "habitus," a gradual shedding of structurally conditioned socialized behaviors and preferences. Only a tiny number of married women in conventional male-headed households experience access to loans as an

economic incentive powerful enough to fundamentally alter the structure
of their desires and behaviors. Loans are experienced as forceful incentives
more usually under the oppressive weight of dire poverty that in extreme
cases pushes the household down below the subsistence level. Whether
voluntary or forced, women's entrepreneurial efforts nevertheless result in
their acquiring agency. Indeed often women's agency improves so much
that, as in the case of Bhanu, a complete shift in the household's balance of
power takes place.

Now we have two bighas of land under cultivation, and I've purchased a plough. I
also bought an ox with the money we made from selling crops. My husband uses
the plough and the ox to plough other people's fields. I still work in the fields . . . I do
everything; my husband is nothing! I take the loans, and I repay them. Even when it
comes to cultivation, I do everything, from planting the seeds to buying and
applying fertilizers and pesticides, harvesting the crop and selling them. I do
everything!

Bhanu's account of the transformations within her household includes
overcoming another gender barrier that would be missed without knowledge of the local context. Among her various agricultural tasks, she
mentions buying and applying fertilizers and pesticides. This is highly
unusual for women unless they are farmers in female-headed households.
Agricultural supply shops are usually owned and operated by men and will
not, as a matter of usual practice, sell these fertilizers and pesticides to
women. They make exceptions only when they are absolutely certain that
their female customer is indeed the person who is in charge of the farm.
This practice is adopted as a precautionary measure, as consuming fertilizers or pesticides is a common way by which village women commit
suicide. The fact that Bhanu makes these purchases herself, despite her
husband being around, is evidence that her lead role in farming is publicly
recognized.

Over the three years since she started farming, the amount of land she has
rented-in for cultivation has steadily grown. Now the earnings from agriculture constitute a substantial part of the household's income. With the newly
acquired plough, her husband's earnings reach about Rs 800 per month
during the paddy-sowing season[4], which lasts for six months a year. For the
other six months, he sits at home idle. Bhanu declares vigorously that she
works all twelve months a year and earns approximately Rs 700 every
month. Her year-round income exceeds her husband's. On the home front,
Bhanu is in charge of making each and every decision, from the allocation of

---

[4] This is about Rs 70 per day and two weeks of hired work per month during high season.

funds for different household needs to the acquisition of agricultural supplies needed for farming and the repayment of debts. Their economic improvement is visible in the land and assets they have acquired, and it is also reflected in her increased creditworthiness among her neighbors:

Now I'm happy. Before, none of these women [pointing to the other group members] would be ready to give me even five hundred grams of rice, leave alone money. But now they'll give me Rs 5000 if I ask for it. Now they'll give because I cultivate and I have an ox, a plough, and a van. So now everyone is willing to give, but before no one used to give me anything. They were scared that I wouldn't be able to return what I borrowed.

Although Bhanu regularly attends the fortnightly group meetings in her neighborhood, she has not attended any group event outside the village because that would mean the loss of a day's work. In her case, all the dimensions of agency have been radically transformed by her active work life that was catalyzed by the availability of loans. Residence in a nuclear household without the coercive presence of in-laws, her family's extreme poverty before joining the group, and the fact that her sons were too young to manage loans or to work were contributing factors. Bhanu's case is especially noteworthy and contrasts with the cases that follow for the fact that she was successful despite her residence in her husband's village and despite his presence in the household throughout the period she gradually displaced him as the family's leading economic actor and manager.

"Things changed because, now, I'm bringing the money."

He would never ever talk about those matters [household matters requiring decision making], but things changed after I joined the group. [Laughs] Well, things changed because, now, I'm bringing the money, so there's no other way but to change! That's why he has changed. And I have to repay this money [loans] myself, so he has to change ... (Taslima Bibi, group: Ujjaini)

Taslima Bibi, a Muslim woman in her mid-thirties with no formal education, bluntly asserts the influence of her newly gained financial power. It is extremely rare for a married Muslim woman in these Bengali villages to have the power to express independent agency through financial power in such emphatic terms.

When Taslima got married, like almost all other women in these villages, she moved to her husband's village. There she entered the joint household, headed by her parents-in-law. Her new home was located, like the home she grew up in in her native hamlet, in a predominantly Muslim community. But here, as the daughter-in-law of a joint household, Taslima was subject to a stringently enforced code of conduct. She was not allowed to set foot out of the house, even to go across the street to a neighboring house. Several years into her marriage, she had three children. With the multiplication of the family's needs, and her husband's single income from carpentry work, she began to feel the pinch. When she got word that a microcredit group was starting in her neighborhood, she joined it. But her membership was short-lived. Her father- and mother-in-law were vigorously opposed to her regular participation in meetings and blocked her from attending them. After only two months of membership, they forced Taslima, against her will, to withdraw from the group. She realized that it would be impossible for her to take advantage of the loans as long as she remained in the joint household. She also knew that it was imperative for her to engage in some kind of economic activity that would bring in income. Her children had started attending school, and the family's need for money had increased greatly. Taslima began persuading her husband to move back to her native village.

After some time, her pleading and reasoning bore results. Her husband agreed with her plan. They moved back and set up an independent household. Now she was free to take out loans and use them for economic activities even when those activities took her outside the house. She was a daughter of this village, not one of its *bou* (brides). She no longer was carrying the weight of the dignity of her husband's family on her shoulders.

The couple worked out an arrangement for sharing the economic responsibilities of their household. He would bear all the household expenses, including their children's education costs, from his carpentry earnings. She would take loans and invest them independently, and she would be solely responsible for repaying all loans from the earnings that she would generate.

Over the past seven years of her group membership, Taslima has taken Rs 16,500 in loans. With the money, she has bought four dairy cows over these years. She buys female calves at around Rs 2000 each, rears them for a couple of years and, eventually, sells them for nearly double the price at around Rs 4000–5000. Every year in this way, she earns a profit of Rs 2000–3000 from selling cows. She has also leased-in land for cultivating vegetables and has started a produce business. In addition to all these works, she works as a farm laborer for a daily wage of Rs 30 in order to pay for the monthly loan installments. All of these loans have been repaid entirely by her from her independent income from these enterprises. She expresses her command over economic activities and emphasizes the opportunity provided by these loans:

The biggest advantage is that now there's a place from where I can get money if I need it. Who'll give me so much money? But from here I can get money for business or agriculture. I've taken money from here, and I've rented-in land and started cultivating vegetables. I've also bought cows.

Her strong affirmation of the benefit of credit and her use of first person are unique. Such sentiments depart from those held by most women in this study, particularly married Muslim women, who say that they have no independent use for money.

She is less positive, compared to many other women, when she discusses the group's associational dimensions. It is difficult for her to miss work in order to attend group events outside her neighborhood, especially since she depends on her own income to repay loans. For the most part, her participation is limited to the neighborhood-based group meeting held every two weeks. Even these meetings have relatively little importance to her for their social value or meaning. She already enjoys relative social freedom by virtue of living in her native village and running the various economic enterprises owned by her, not to mention her escape from the joint-household and the absence of in-laws.

Some normative constraints nevertheless still may apply, evidenced by Taslima's vehement reaction to the question of whether she is able to go to the market: "We [women] don't go to the market. I buy the things I need from the hawkers who come to the house to sell their wares." It is not clear whether this not going to the market is a symptom of social constraints or whether trips to the market have been made unnecessary by the arrival of the market at Taslima's doorstep. (When institutions adjust to compensate for normative restrictions, it sometimes becomes difficult to judge the implications of such accommodations for women's agency.)

With respect to household decision making, the balance of power has changed significantly following Taslima's active economic engagement: "Before, he would do whatever he thought was the best. But now it's better. Now whatever we do, we do it together. We both understand and then act. Both he and I usually go together to check out something before we do it." She ascribes this change to her newly gained financial capacity that now makes her an equal earner in the household.

Despite her increased earnings, Taslima claims that there has not been as great an economic improvement in their household as might have been expected. Medical treatment for her stomach ulcers saps away a portion of her profits at the end of every year. Recently she also spent Rs 5000 on the treatment of one of her cows that had fallen ill, but she was unable to save it. She worries about recovering the losses. Regardless of her financial loss and medical costs, the couple can now afford to hire a private tutor for their children and meet Taslima's medical expenses without taking out high-interest debts. These facts, along with Taslima's emphatic affirmation on the importance of loans, indicate that there have been significant economic improvements.

These two cases show that women can become independent entrepreneurs when they reside in their native village or even in their husband's village so long as they live in households that are fully separate from their in-laws. All the women who became entrepreneurs lived in households that were not surrounded by the households of their husbands' immediate kin. If these women had sons, they were too young to handle money independently or make investment decisions. As the next case shows, a husband's migration also creates an environment conducive to women's independent loan use that in turn contributes to increased agency.

"But now, whether it's a loss or a gain, I have the courage!"

I had the idea that, since we're in this group, I could take money from here and rent- or lease-in land and cultivate it. In that way we could earn more money and keep some of it aside at the year's end. If I did this every year, the money would keep growing ... Before, we didn't have anything, but now we're taking money from here and moving ahead. Now things are beginning to look up! (Tarakdashi Biswas, group: Ujjal)

Tarakdashi is a young Hindu woman in her early thirties with two young sons and no formal education. Her husband, a fisherman, goes away to the nearby delta on fishing trips and returns home briefly twice a month. He is, in a way, a migrant worker. Yet there is a difference between poor migrant workers like him and those workers who migrate to faraway cities and foreign countries to work for lucrative wages. A few men from these villages have migrated to work in the construction industry in Mumbai and in the Gulf countries.

Tarakdashi's husband earns only about Rs 2000–2500 per month, an income that falls far short of fulfilling even the basic needs of their family of four. In fact, before joining the group, Tarakdashi's household was in such dire straits that often she could not feed her children adequately: "The household was in very bad shape, and we simply couldn't go on. I couldn't even buy milk for my children."

She started working as a farm laborer for Rs 30 per day. It was a question of her family's survival. She continued working in the fields of local landowners for two years. Taking up any other economic activity was out of the question. They had no capital and borrowing from the local moneylender was unaffordable given the exorbitantly high interest rate.

Concerned about her family's grim economic situation, Tarakdashi enrolled in the microcredit group that was being formed in her neighborhood. She hoped to use this opportunity to avail herself of some capital, an opportunity she might never have had otherwise. When it was time for the first round of loans to be disbursed, she thought of taking one and starting her own cultivation. Yet both she and her husband lacked experience in farming. Apart from working as a farm laborer, she had no prior experience with cultivation, and her husband was away from home most of the time. When she shared her idea with her husband, he tried to dissuade her, afraid that it was too much of a risk to take a loan given their precarious financial situation. In the face of his fears and disapproval, she assured him that she would manage all the farming activities on her own and promised that she would be able to repay the loan.

Tarakdashi took a loan of Rs 7000 and rented-in some land. Gradually she learned to cultivate by seeking instruction from her neighbors who were experienced farmers. They also helped her by purchasing agricultural supplies and fertilizers for her on their trips into town when buying their own supplies. In this way she managed and continues to manage the cultivation of her rented-in land. When necessary, she even employs farm laborers. So far, she has taken three loans totaling Rs 16,500. With Rs 1500, she purchased a goat and some hens, and, with the rest, she has rented-in more land for cultivation. Her husband continues in his original line of work and still returns home twice a month. She continues to be fully responsible for the daily supervision of the fields and all other aspects of agriculture.

The family's economic situation has improved as a result of her economic initiatives. In addition to the earnings from agriculture, every six months she earns between Rs 3000–5000 from selling goats and hens. Now, whether they make a loss or a profit, she says she has the courage (*shahosh*) to take a loan and to get into the previously dreaded situation of being in debt. Once she started earning money and experiencing financial improvement, it gave her the courage to do the things she had never done on her own behalf before such as purchasing groceries. Although there were grocery stores near their house she never ventured inside before to buy things for herself. She relied on her husband to buy all of the household goods during his visits home. But now she participates fully in all aspects of household decision-making, moves around and interacts with people at her own discretion, and engages in independent market transactions, even when these involve credit:

Before, too, he used to live away from home, but he'd buy everything before he'd leave for work. There are shops nearby, but still I never used to go there. I didn't have the courage to go because I had no money in my hand. How would I repay if I made a purchase? Now, say we need things worth Rs 500, but if we don't have all of the money at one time, maybe we have only Rs 100 or 200, then I go ahead and buy on credit. When he comes home, I repay the debt.

Tarakdashi's transition into a full-fledged farmer shows that a husband's migratory status along with his inability to make enough for the family's basic needs has the unintended effect of encouraging women to become independent, to invest on their own initiative and to repay loans.

"I've built up a small capital."

It was my idea [to start the business]! I thought that if I did it, then I'd be able to make a living. And my husband encouraged me ... This sort of opportunity is good ... In the beginning, when I came here after my marriage, I didn't used to do anything. But, soon, I realized that we needed to bring up our children, and a single person's income wasn't enough for that. (Probhati Mondol, group: Aranghata Gram Sangathan)

Probhati is a thirty-two-year-old Hindu woman with eight years of schooling. It has been four years since she joined a microcredit group. In these few years, she has gone from being the secondary to the primary breadwinner of her family. Her husband's only source of livelihood is selling lottery tickets. His earnings from that are not only very low but also erratic. They fluctuate from a high of Rs 1000 to a low of nothing at all. Probhati admits with a giggle, suppressing her embarrassment, that his abysmal average monthly income of Rs 500 is "just good enough for meeting the minor household expenses." For the initial few years after her marriage, Probhati did not earn any income as is typical for new wives. In the meantime, the couple had two children, and the household slowly ground to a halt because of her husband's failure to meet the family's subsistence needs.

Probhati was forced to take up paid work. She started working in a local toy factory making cheap plastic rattles. From that, she went on to work for a local merchant making paper packets out of recycled newspaper and homemade glue. These packets are widely used in grocery stores to package dry items such as spices and lentils for customers.

Making these was tedious work and the pay was far lower than the already low local rate for *bidi* binding (making hand-rolled unfiltered cigarettes). For every one thousand packets she made, Probhati was paid the standard local rate of Rs 4.[5] Each month she earned a pittance, between Rs 360–480, from making over one hundred thousand paper bags. Their family of four could barely survive on the couple's combined earnings.

When Probhati initially wanted to join the group, her husband had been reluctant to let her enroll in it. He was afraid to take on financial commitments that they might not be able to fulfill given their precarious financial condition. But Probhati convinced her husband of the advantages of joining the group and kept cajoling him until he agreed to it:

> I told him that in this day and age it's impossible to support a household on the earnings of one person. So this could be a way through which I could work as well. He had heard people saying that our money would be lost here. I said to him, "Let people say what they want; let me try it out and see how far it goes." I didn't listen to what the others said; I acted on my own thinking.

After joining the group, she took a very small loan of Rs 500 and made her husband buy old newspapers from the local recycled goods seller. From these she made her own paper packets and told her husband to sell them to the local retail stores. She made a small profit by circumventing her middleman-employer, who pocketed most of the profits. From this experience she realized that, if she could buy more raw materials, she would be able to multiply her profits.

The next time Probhati took a loan of Rs 1000. With the money she purchased twenty kilograms of newsprint. This time the profits were larger, and so she was able to repay the loan entirely from her own earnings. Emboldened by her gradual economic success, Probhati made a big move. She borrowed quite a large sum of Rs 6000 from the group's accumulated savings fund with the intention of making a major investment in her business. With a larger amount of investment, the profits were even larger, and she was able to build up a small amount of capital. Now, every

---

[5] Compared to this rate, *bidi*-making is much more highly paid at Rs 36 for every one thousand. However, in her neighborhood, the only type of home-based piece-rate work available was making these paper bags. Therefore, she did not have a choice in deciding the type of work she would pursue. Not all types of piece-rate work are available in all villages. Availability depends on the merchants and middleman who establish contacts in each neighborhood and village.

day she makes three to four thousand paper bags. Every month she earns Rs 1000–1500, nearly double to triple the amount that she would have earned doing the same amount of work for an employer. She has no immediate plans for taking another loan because the capital she has accumulated is enough to fund her single-person enterprise for a while.

Probhati's husband, although initially opposed to her joining the group, has been supportive throughout. He makes the bulk purchases and sales on her behalf. Reflecting on her role in transforming the economic condition of their household she says, "It was my idea. I thought that if I did this then I'd be able to make a living. And my husband encouraged me. If he sees that I'm doing something good, then he won't say anything; this sort of opportunity is good." She, rather than her husband, keeps track of the financial accounts of the business and the household and allocates money between the different household needs: "I spend some of it on the household and some on my children. I also keep some aside for bad times. My husband gives me money for household expenses, and I also keep some aside from that."

Probhati has derived considerable benefit from the associational aspects of her microcredit group. Attending group meetings and traveling to the organization's office once every month to deposit the group's savings has increased her range of social contacts and personal physical mobility. But the most significant change microcredit has brought to Probhati's life has been enabling her to establish her own business. Her business has made her the primary breadwinner of the household, with a steadier income than her husband's. Her voice in the financial decisions of the house now rings clearly: "After I can take my household to a certain position, only then can I start thinking of opening a savings account [in the bank]. I've started a fixed deposit account in the post office with Rs 1000. I started it after joining the group." The money for this significant step has come solely from the profits generated by her business initiative.

Probhati's case demonstrates that prior work or business experience is important in motivating and enabling women to set up their own small-scale enterprises, especially non-agricultural ones. Some of the women who had started their own non-agricultural enterprises had some prior business-related experience from their girlhood exposure to their fathers' small businesses. Women who had intermittently worked in their fathers' grocery stores as young girls were more likely than others to set up an independent enterprise as adults. Their increased likelihood of business ownership seems to be related to their familiarity with weights and measures and their facility with financial calculations. This knowledge seems to have provided them the necessary confidence to start their own enterprises.

Whether loans will spur women to set up businesses in the line of work in which they are presently engaged appears to depend a lot on the type of home-based industry in which women have expertise. For example, Probhati's case shows that, in some types of work, women are able to circumvent the middleman merchant and start their own businesses with loans. In contrast to this pattern, there is the example of the *bidi* industry that is the largest employer of women in most of these rural villages. In this line of work, where women make *bidi* on a piece-rate basis, it is virtually impossible for these women to individually circumvent the middlemen or to take their place. These subcontracting middlemen are agents of local companies. They supply specialized materials, like tobacco leaf, and provide vital links to markets beyond the limited boundary of the village. They travel frequently to markets in towns and cities maintaining the link between manufacturing bases and retail centers. For women doing *bidi*-binding work there is no scope to utilize microcredit loans to scale up their work or to become middlemen. Women working as bidi binders often remain trapped by the security of a predictable income even though it is extremely low.

It is especially important to analyze microcredit and women's agency in relation to two key features of many women's lives: the abysmal poverty of many male-headed households and their own husband's attitude.

The ways in which poverty and patriarchy interact and the role "impoverished patriarchy" plays in women's lives provide the context for women's direct use of microcredit loans and their transformation into entrepreneurs. None of these women, at the start of their married lives, were engaged in any income-generating work, as is the norm for new brides. But, within some number of years, they were forced to play a direct role in the economic uplift of their households by becoming income-generators, by undertaking paid work, by starting up a business venture, or by taking up farming. Microcredit helped greatly to realize these goals. These women did indeed exhibit "entrepreneurial spirit." But abject poverty and their husbands' failure to provide for the family (a breach of the traditional marital contract between the genders, so to speak) cannot be overlooked. Would these women have overcome the conventional gender barriers and become "entrepreneurs" with their independent businesses and farming practices had their husbands been economically successful providers? If they had economically capable sons, adult enough to profitably invest loan-monies, would these women have taken on the double

burden of running business ventures while fulfilling their domestic reproductive roles? These questions point to the sociological complexity of
microcredit's effect on the lives of real families. "Impoverished patriarchy"
as a context for women's increased agency through economic initiative
must be added to simplistic media reports unreservedly celebrating "wom-
en's entrepreneurship" through microcredit.

These women "entrepreneurs" did not lament the failure of patriarchy
or voice any yearning for a benevolent utopian patriarchy as did the
disadvantaged female Bengali domestic servants studied by Ray and
Qayum (2009). Nevertheless, their ability to take direct advantage of the
financial incentive of microcredit to transform and expand their capabilities was facilitated by the looming insolvency or bankruptcy of household
patriarchy.

To this we must add a discussion of masculinity, without which this
study of women's "entrepreneurship" and agency would be incomplete.
In Ray and Qayum's account, the women servants viewed the men in
their lives, men who were mostly "absent," literally and figuratively,
through the lens of incapacity and failure.[6] In striking contrast, these
women "entrepreneurs" usually highlighted their husband's compliant
and accommodative attitudes even though these men too had failed to
live up to the expectations that accompany masculine gender roles. Their
husbands' flexible and cooperative attitudes enabled these women to fully
pursue their economic roles and yielded room for them to participate in, or
even to lead, household decision making and management. The narratives
these women give of their husbands' accommodation of their increased
agency produce a picture of malleable masculinity and suggest that this
appears to be an essential precondition for women's "entrepreneurship."
Malleable masculinity is a necessary term with which to capture the
parallel transition that men must undergo concurrently with their wives'
growing economic roles. It is also meant to suggest the reality of a less- or
non-malleable masculinity that can obstruct women's access to microcredit and hamper or prevent entirely their increased agency.

Other research on microcredit across the border in Bangladesh has
found the husband's attitude to be an influential factor in determining
women's role in decision-making and dropping out from the group (Pitt
et al. 2006). Typologies of masculine attitudes toward women's agency

---

[6] Ray and Qayum (2009) find that women typically end up as servants in the context of being
orphaned, abandoned by husbands or in-laws, or married to a husband unable to provide
for them.

exist but I find them misleading.[7] I believe it is best to think in terms of *malleable masculinity* because the term accurately suggests the tempering force of circumstances and relational negotiations through which gender attitudes of men are made flexible. Attitudes evolve through the lifetime, and men alter their attitudes regarding the appropriate limits for women's role as they face the vicissitudes of life and realize the limits of their own capacity for meeting their family's needs. This could be the result of the interplay between severe economic constraints and a personality type.

Rigid masculinities, however, as the cases in this chapter demonstrate, also exist and can resist every attempt to challenge or change conventionally patriarchal gender attitudes.

BRIDES[8] WHO BARGAINED

Economic theory holds that one dominant form intra-household dynamics may take is bargaining – that is, a combination of cooperation and conflict. According to this model, members of a household will cooperate to the extent that cooperation makes everyone better off. But within this social dynamic there is a great range of possible cooperative arrangements for sharing resources and performing labor. The deal any particular individual gets within the household can vary enormously, and by no means are all deals equally beneficial for everyone.

Although all members gain relative to non-cooperation, some gain disproportionately. Patterns of asymmetrical gains create scope for conflict. The outcome of conflict (or whose claims to resources prevail) depends on the relative bargaining power of each household member. The bargaining power of each individual depends on his or her individually available fall-back position, or threat points – that is, their options outside of the marital household. This theory assumes that the availability of these options, in turn, is determined by each person's command over material resources. According to this theory, then, women's exclusive access to microcredit – that is, to loans that are less expensive than borrowing from the moneylender and entail virtually no red tape – should augment their bargaining power.

---

[7] Ahmed (2008), in her study of microcredit in Bangladesh, has inductively codified different types of masculinity: "high-minded"; "mixed"; "abusive"; and "lacking in common sense." This typology is conceptually helpful but runs the danger of making masculinity appear too categorical.

[8] I use the word bride to denote the vernacular word "*bou*," which means bride or married woman.

In reality, however, when men are the actual loan users, access to microcredit adds to women's increased agency in an extremely limited way – and not invariably to any increase at all. Certainly, some women claim that they have acquired motivation and social permission to question their husbands on the use of household monies when they are directly responsible for the loans. Because women are now the frontline borrowers and they must answer to their groups for the repayment of loans, they have an interest and feel they have a right in monitoring household finances. This sense of direct responsibility and accountability that women feel for the loan is important. The burden is felt to be more pressing than when husbands borrow from other sources (often without the wife's knowledge). This heightened personal responsibility is mixed with anxiety felt at the consequences of being unable to make a timely repayment – the chronic worry of losing face among fellow group members. Responsibility for loans does sometimes give women a new, even if limited, monitoring authority over their husband's and the household's financial decision making.

There were sixteen women in this study's sample who seemed to gain some degree of increased agency from transferring loans to their husbands (and in one case to an adult son) rather than gaining agency from the microcredit group's associational aspects. Their agency improvements were rather limited. The most these women were able to gain was some degree of monitoring capacity or what I term a "proscribing voice," that is, the ability to ask questions regarding loan-use and investment, to play a supplementary role in the household's financial management, and to sound a cautionary note when the husband's decisions seem of questionable wisdom.

The two strongest gains from household bargaining were among women who were economically active prior to their enrollment in microcredit and who already had significant agency across the range of capabilities considered here. The examples of Kanika Bacchar (Hindu) and Achchia Bibi (Muslim), both of whom transferred loans to their husbands, illustrate this dynamics of cooperative conflict and demonstrate how women's access to microcredit loans affects intra-household dynamics. Even in their cases, however, excessive monitoring led to domestic conflict. Men pushed back, trying to hold on to their traditional privilege of unquestioned authority over household finances. In these two cases it was possible to discern a tempering process take hold, initiated and led by women infused with a new sense of responsibility and accountability and in which rigid masculinities were rendered partially malleable.

Kanika is a sharecropper along with her husband, and they both also work as farm laborers. As a girl, Kanika attended school until the sixth grade and now, as a young woman, looks quite capable of holding her own. When the local panchayat member first approached her about starting a microcredit group in her neighborhood, she dithered. When she proposed the idea to her husband, he rejected it and expressed his strong disapproval. But the party member, who was her well-off neighbor's husband, declared that he would put her name down as the group leader, and assured her that she need not worry about her husband's objections. For the last three years, Kanika has been the leader of her group, and she and her husband have borrowed Rs 20,000 in loans. With the money they have leased-in land for cultivating paddy and vegetables. Before the loan, they had been too poor to cultivate anything beyond their tiny plot of land. Her husband does the bulk of the farm labor while she does all the work for the two cows that they are raising, in addition to working as a farm laborer. Kanika talks about her greater capacity to probe into financial matters compared with before. But she is also quick to point out the precarious balancing act required to question her husband without appearing to be interfering with his prerogatives:

Among ourselves, we discuss how much loans we need to take and what to do with it. From time to time, I try to find out how the money is being spent. If we (women) try to manage everything as we go then we need to ask the men (*purush*) about it. But, it's not really wise to constantly keep probing the *purush* (male). Then that'll cause a *jhamela* (a problem/complication). But depending on the situation, I have to try to know what's happening. For the most part, the money is spent by him, because we use it in cultivation. And he is the one who buys the soil and fertilizers. But within all that, I have to do a bit of *tadanta* (investigation): How much was spent? How was it spent? I used to keep such information before too, but then I never used to give him money myself, like now. But because now the group gives the money to the women and we give it to our husbands, we have to keep ourselves informed, because later we'll be responsible for repaying this money. So women have the right to investigate (*tadanta*).

Women whose husbands adhere to a rigid gender ideology have to exercise caution. Achchia, a Muslim woman in her mid-twenties represents a vivid case of the reality that access to loans does not make bargaining an automatic response. Achchia comes off as very assertive and articulate in her conversation (although illiterate) and is an enthusiastic participant in the interview. It is clear that it is a cathartic experience for her. Achchia grew up as one of seven children in a destitute family, has worked her whole life, and started her own business when she was only sixteen or seventeen. As a young child she worked as a maid instead of going to school until a well-intentioned local man proposed to teach her his trade so that, in the future, she could stand on her own feet. He taught her to weave cotton into the gauze that is used in bandages. Once Achchia had built up enough savings by working for the man who taught her this trade, she bought her own weaving machine. Then she contacted a middleman merchant in a nearby village and convinced him to place orders with her. By the age of sixteen, she had become the main earner of her family, supporting her parents and siblings.

When she turned nineteen, Acchia was married away. Her husband works as a truck and car driver in the city, earning a monthly wage of Rs 4000. Achchia resumed her work very soon after she married, earning about Rs 500 per month. Working had become a habit, and she could not sit around idly. She lives with her brother's family, as she and her husband have not yet saved up enough to set up their own household. The Rs 2000 she had saved up from her work, they recently used to buy a small plot of land.

At her husband's asking, she has taken two loans totaling Rs 4500. He has used them for making some improvements to the automobile he uses for work (or so he claims). Achchia is not entirely sure she says. She provides an example of the tense interplay of leverage and conflict with her husband. Her queries on how exactly he uses the money are met with strong reminders from him that she should stay within the prescribed limits of her gender role:

If I ask him he says, "Why do I have to give you so many explanations? You're a woman, stay like a woman!" But I'm the one who gives him that money, so I need to probe. What are you doing with the money? Then he tells me what he's used it for. I tell him that, if you tell me right away, then there will be no occasion for further tensions. But if you don't tell me then I'll need to probe because I'm answerable to my group. Most of the times he tells me, but every time he'll say, "Why do I have to give you explanations?"

Achchia's husband did not object to her joining the group, but, when it comes to her attending the group meetings, he sounds a note of dissension. This often results in a row:

My husband says, "Why do women of the household need to go anywhere?" I tell him that there are five other women there, and I have to go meet with them. Otherwise, I won't have any dignity or respect (*maan shaman*) left. So then he says, "Do what you think is best!" When he says, "You don't have to go outside," I say that I have [with emphasis] to go outside, because we're human beings too; but staying within the household all the time, we cannot live. We, too, want to live!

Acchia explains why he disapproves:

> He thinks that wives of the house should stay within the house. But women these days don't want that any more. Now they, too, want to work, and they, too, want to enjoy life (*ananda*). But many men don't like that, like my husband.

Strikingly, he never objects to her weekly trips to a nearby village to deliver her finished work and pick up raw supplies. Achchia gets worked up while explaining this discrepancy:

> No, he doesn't object to that because that is a source of income; that is a source of income! But, when I go for group meetings and activities, that is at the expense of my work and household chores. But you see, sometimes for long-term gains, you have to do something at the expense of your work now. For instance, we have to go to group meetings now that, in that sense, are a loss of time and work. But at some point of time it will bring gains. He says that I can't defeat you in words, do what you want.

The role that money generally plays in intra-household dynamics and gender relations is revealed in one of her husband's acute observations that Achchia reports while explaining who pays for the group's mandatory savings deposits:

> I pay for it from my own earnings. That's the reason that husbands today say that you don't give us our due respect; you earn your own money, that's why you don't give us our due value (*daam diye cholo na*). And those that don't earn give their husbands their due respect. I tell him that is a wrong idea. In this day and age, if both [husband and wife] do not work equally, you can't raise a family and run a household.

In contrast to these examples, there are women like Shabitri, who have no income of their own and are vulnerable to losing the modest monitoring authority they have gained from being the bringer of loans. Not having any income of their own, such women are defenseless against their husband's decision to withdraw from the group. Her ability to inquire into financial matters, derived from her direct responsibility for the microcredit loan repayment, will disappear if her husband chooses another source of credit:

> He says, "We won't take any more loans; we're taking money and then we're making losses repeatedly. I can't continue in this group. I'll repay my existing loan, and I'll withdraw." As for me, the money is in his hands. If my husband doesn't give me the money [for mandatory deposits], I can't force him . . . He says he'll keep twenty or fifty rupees, or whatever it is, in the bank. If he really starts transacting with the bank, then I'll still need to probe into what he's doing with the money, but I won't have as much force as I have now in asking him about

things or telling him things. If he does it [switches from the group to the bank] then he'll have more power.

When women lack an independent source of income, however small that income may be, the decision to continue group membership is in the hands of men. Husbands are the ones who pay for the compulsory savings deposits that their wives need to make to retain their group membership. For women like Shabitri there is always the disheartening possibility that the monitoring authority and the "proscribing voice" they have gained from taking microcredit loans will be lost if microcredit loans are replaced with loans from male-dominated financial institutions such as banks and farmers' cooperatives.

MIRED MUTINIES

Given the cultural and practical constraints of the context, very few married women who are not the household heads or are not facing dire economic adversity feel eager or fully competent to take advantage of microcredit loans to start their own enterprises. Men do not usually forcibly wrest control of microcredit loans from women. There are also economically pragmatic reasons that explain why the standard household strategy is to have the man be fully responsible for the loan-use and repayment. In the extant rural eoconomy, households tend to maximize income by principally relying on men to use microcredit loans to expand their existing livelihood enterprise or to start ancillary businesses. This pattern does not disrupt women's existing forms of income where they are engaged in home-based piece-rate work (in bidi binding, for instance). Although extremely low, the income from this type of work is nevertheless predictably secure compared to women taking on the risk of investing in an enterprise whose returns are uncertain.

Loan transfers, by themselves, do not endow women with meaningful agency unless accompanied by dynamics stemming from a strong associational mechanism or undergirded by an independent income earning capacity. There are numerous cases in which women, when they transfer loans (even when these loans facilitate their household's economic improvement), continue to lack agency. These women are unable to fully participate in the group's associational activities and are unable to register their voice in household decision-making even though men's access to microcredit loans depends on their wives' membership in these groups.

"So, now I've stopped wanting!"

I can't ask my husband any questions. He runs everything. There are many women who buy their own saris, or a *shaya* (underskirt), or a blouse, or bangles. But I've never spent even ten paisa wastefully on myself. My husband buys everything for me. If I say, 'Today I need this much money,' then he'll give it to me. But I don't have a single paisa in my own hand! (Marjina Bibi, group: Ananya)

Marjina Bibi's stark depiction of her lack of decision-making power, even within the conventionally categorized female spheres, may lead one to imagine that she is a young, newly wed wife in a traditional extended family household. But she is a thirty-seven-year-old Muslim woman who has been married for nearly two decades and is a mother of four sons and a daughter. Two of her sons are married (although living separately), making her a mother-in-law. Even though her own mother-in-law lives in the same household with them, she is old and has withdrawn from household management. Considering all the facts regarding her position within her family and within the life cycle, Marjina's utter lack of agency appears to depart strikingly from expectations concerning women's power as women advance from being young, defenseless brides to domineering mothers-in-law.

Marjina's husband and youngest son are milkmen by profession and work for a dairy merchant. They milk cows in the surrounding villages and deliver the milk to him for a joint daily income of Rs 80. The family does not own land. Recently, however, they started cultivation through share-cropping with a loan of Rs 5000 from the group, their only loan so far. Marjina tends to the pair of cows and to the goats, hens, and ducks the family owns and earns around Rs 100–200 each month from selling eggs. But Marjina hands over her entire income to her husband, and he pays for her monthly savings deposit.

Marjina has enrolled in two microcredit groups in her village, and she now has a combined savings of Rs 1260.[9] These savings are the family's first and only savings. She hopes to keep this money to ensure her old age care: "I'll try my best to keep the money for myself. But if I see that he (her husband) isn't causing me any inconvenience and he's taking good care of

---

[9] There were very few cases in which I found that women were part of two microcredit groups simultaneously. Technically, one person is allowed to be a member of only one group. But, in such cases, women had joined one group in their own name and another group in the name of their daughter. In most of these cases in my sample, I found that women enrolled in two microcredit groups in order to have more than one avenue for small savings. Saving for a daughter's marriage was a common motive for women with young daughters. There were no cases where women had taken loans simultaneously from both groups.

me, then I'll give it to him." One might expect that her simultaneous membership in two microcredit groups would lead to the burden of double participation, of attending two sets of fortnightly group meetings. But, instead, she expresses frustration about not being able to participate in any of the groups' activities. She does not have her husband's *hukum* (permission) to attend even the mandatory group meetings: "No, my husband doesn't allow me to attend the meetings; he doesn't like it. He says, 'If we have to give money [for the savings deposits] we will, but you can't leave the house to attend the meetings and do all that.' So, without his *hukum*, I can't come." In fact, Marjina's husband does not allow her to go places unaccompanied, even if it is within their own village: "My husband is such a person that he'll come along with me even if I go from here to the next neighborhood to visit the doctor."

According to Marjina, her husband fears that her participation in group activities will compromise her efficiency in performing household chores. In addition, he believes that it is not appropriate for women to participate in meetings. On the day of the group meeting, Marjina usually sends her young daughter, who is not yet a teenager, to deliver her mandatory savings deposit to the leader. Even on the rare occasion that she attends a group meeting, her husband accompanies her. His constant presence prevents her from using this one opportunity to interact with others beyond the surveillance of his gaze: "And if he goes with me, wherever I go then I don't need to speak over him or against him!" Marjina's interactions continue to remain limited within the small family circle. The group has failed to bring even the slightest change in her life:

I haven't gained any experience from this. I'm sitting here [for the interview], but I could be buried alive for this! People talk to other people and through that they overcome their fear of talking to others. But I can't talk to other people. So, if I see someone, I feel scared, thinking that I may say something wrong, which may offend the person ... Even if I feel like coming [to the meetings] at times, there's no way. I don't get to leave the house. So, now I've stopped wanting."

The unremitting surveillance has forced Marjina to curb her desire for the social freedoms she lacks. She confesses that she lives with a real fear of violating her husband's authority:

I don't go out of the house. If there is a very special need only then I go somewhere. I have much to do at home. For instance, now I have to return and cut fodder for the cows and cook. My son and husband work at milking cows all day. My son returns at one o'clock, and my husband might return anytime between two and three, and I have to be home at that time. So, if I'm out I feel scared, thinking that they might return when I'm not there. Everyone is not scared in the same way, no matter how bad a husband may be. But I still have the fear in me; that's the reason I don't go anywhere. Till now I haven't lent anyone even Rs 10 without my husband's permission.

Marjina's freedom is equally limited when it comes to those domestic matters that usually fall within women's traditional domain. She has never made any household purchase independently: "I don't buy anything with my own hands. In a household you see that women buy utensils, plates, bowls, and glasses; but I don't buy anything. If I need anything, I tell my husband." She admits that she has never made a single purchase, even for her young daughter, from the traveling hawkers who come right to the doorstep. Her husband gives their daughter money, and she is allowed to buy things for herself, a freedom of which Marjina herself is deprived. Marina's role as the source of credit counts for nothing.

For women to achieve increased agency, it is essential that there be accompanying changes in men's attitudes and ideas about gender roles. Such changes must include men's increasing tolerance of what they consider to be violations of gender propriety. Without this change in men's attitudes, women's struggle for agency will be in vain. Agency, after all, is always exercised and realized in a context of social relations.

Added to men's rigidly conformist attitudes regarding gender roles, two other significant structural factors obstruct the path women must travel to achieve and express agency. As the next case illustrates, these two factors are: residence in a joint household and a family's relative wealth.

"They tell us, 'You take care of your responsibilities, and we'll take care of ours.'"

No, my father-in-law and husband keep track of all that [household finances]. I don't know anything about it. They tell us, "You take care of your responsibilities, and we'll take care of ours." So I don't try to get involved in it. (Bithika Gayen, group: Iti Mahila Samity)

Bithika is the co-leader of her group, established just over three years ago. She is a thirty-two-year-old Hindu woman, a mother of three sons, and has nine years of school education, which is high by local standards. She comes from a relatively well-off extended family that includes her husband and her parents-in-law. Her retired father-in-law once held a government job, a prized rarity in a village, and her husband owns a furniture-making business. She has taken two loans for his business, one of Rs 20,000 and another of Rs 40,000. At a total of Rs 60,000, she is the highest loan taker in the entire sample of four hundred women. However, being the source of such a sizeable amount of credit has not translated into any additional agency in addition to the basic freedoms she possessed prior to joining the group.

Unlike Marjina, she can go unaccompanied to the nearby health center with her children, and she can even go to the market occasionally to buy clothes for herself and her children during festivals. But her husband is firmly in control of all managerial aspects of the household. He refuses to share with her any financial information about the household or his business. He even disregards her queries about how he uses the loans: "He doesn't want to tell me when I ask him. He says, 'What will you do knowing so much?'" After being repeatedly refused an answer, she has given up her attempts. She laughs a bit embarrassedly and admits, "Since he doesn't want to tell me when I ask him, I've stopped asking. As long as I'm getting what I need, I don't ask."

There are other important aspects of the household of which she is forced to remain ignorant. She and her husband have a joint bank account and life insurance policy. Both were started by him, and he provides the money for them. Although officially she is a joint holder of these accounts, she has no knowledge of the financial details. Her physical mobility, although somewhat less restricted than that of some other women, is sharply watched over by her father-in-law who keeps an eye on her comings and goings. He is somewhat disapproving whenever she leaves the house.

Bithika's case is typical of the behavior of rural Hindu women who are of similarly high social and economic standing. Anjana and Kajal are sisters-in-law in a very conservative and well-off extended family household. Their extended family jointly holds over hundred *bigha* of land, a very significant amount. These women have respectively taken Rs 25,000 (Rs 15,000 used for cultivation and Rs 10,000 to pay for daughter's wedding expenses) and Rs 15,000 (for starting a paddy stocking business) in loans. In both cases the loans were taken at the behest of their husbands and were exclusively used by these men.

These transfers have not resulted in any increase in these women's agency. Both women are completely subject to the authority of their parents-in-law. They rarely attend the mandatory group meetings. When they do attend, it is in response to repeated calls made by their fellow group members. These brief and infrequent appearances serve as their only contact with the world beyond the threshold of their two-story brick and concrete house that marks their family's economic distinction. Even though the loans are for such high amounts and even though they have been successful in generating profits, they have not altered gender boundaries or shifted the dynamics of bargaining.

These women, like most of their peers, lack an alternative to the marital family as a fallback position. This drawback is present regardless of the household's economic condition. Saraswati Sardar, an ex-group leader, now in her forties, reveals this fact in a compelling way. With a stable monthly income of Rs 5000 per month, her family is fairly well-off, a fact which is reflected in their ownership of a one-story concrete house. She has taken three loans totaling Rs 21,000, and all have been used by her husband for paddy cultivation. Asked if she ever calls her husband's attention to her role as the primary channel of credit and if this role has added force to her voice in decision making, she comments:

> No, that would only create tensions! See, I am a kind of person who doesn't like to get into any kind of trouble. I follow whatever someone tells me nicely … Look, I don't have my mother- or father-in-law, my two sons live far away from home, and my daughter will be married soon. So, what is the use of creating such tensions? I don't have my parents either. So, where will I go? You tell me! So, I have to stay with my husband and act accordingly.

Saraswati's condition represents that of a majority of women. In a patriarchal society, most women do not have the option of leaving their marital family, whatever the circumstance. This is not due to women's economic dependence alone. There are equally important issues of honor and cultural injunctions that bind women to their marital families.

Kamala, a middle-aged group member, still vividly remembers her aunt's parting words to her when she was married away at the age of fifteen. She was a frail girl married to a man many times her size and seven years older:

> My aunt who had reared me [after the early loss of her parents] had told me, "You shall not leave and go anywhere else, and you shall not lift your feet and return to me. Now your blood is thin (*patla*), but after you spend years in your husband's house, your blood will thicken (*ghono*). You will have children and your husband will begin to understand you. By then you will have gained much experience."

The experience that awaited her was the discovery that her husband was an ill-tempered man, prone to going into violent rages against her over the slightest deviation from his dictates.

In this rural agrarian social milieu, men are the ones who initiate separations, informally abandoning their wives.[10] Women are not usually

---

[10] In the entire sample of four hundred women, only one (a Muslim) had initiated a separation from her husband following his second marriage.

welcomed back into their natal families. Left without a place to turn, women are unable to use their economic advantage of access to credit as a bargaining tool in navigating unfavorable domestic situations.

Recognizing the salience of these sociological factors should dampen surprise at the finding that loan transfers neither necessarily nor invariably improve women's negotiating power within their households. The absence of even a marginally satisfying fall-back position also explains why often there remains a gap between acquiring agency and being able to exercise it effectively.

Through involvement with their microcredit group, women, who may have been passively acquiescing in their husband's decisions and injunctions, may become aware of the importance of their active involvement in household decision making. They may, additionally, gain a taste for engaging in a broader range of social actions and interactions. Yet, in their everyday transactions, they may not have the capacity to transform this awareness into a capacity for agency when faced with opposition from their husbands. Women's participation in the associational activities of the microcredit group, in cases like these, has a minimal impact on their ability to improve and exercise their agency. They see themselves, and are perceived, merely as conduits for loans whose use is wholly at their husbands' discretion and within their husbands' control.

CONCLUSIONS

This study finds that microcredit promotes married women's agency through independent entrepreneurship or enhanced bargaining leverage only in a minuscule number of cases. The decision by married women in male-headed households to launch independent livelihood-enterprises is usually made under duress and when facing great economic adversity. A very specific constellation of social and structural factors must be present to propel women into the role of successful independent entrepreneurship. These factors include residence in nuclear households, lack of adult sons, and a husband's malleable masculinity that accommodates women's changing economic roles and deviation from gendered conventions regarding their own and their wives' conduct. Merely serving as channels of credit to their husbands does not add to women's bargaining power vis-à-vis other household members. Such an assumption betrays a fundamental lack of sociological understanding regarding the cultural milieus in which microcredit today operates.

These findings notwithstanding, it is crucial to note that when micro-credit is accessed due to hardship and under the structural conditions cited above, it facilitates radically positive transformations in women's agency. The positive correlation of women's entrepreneurship with women's agency under the conditions specified, despite its rarity, has tremendous theoretical and philosophical implications and is not to be underestimated

The pattern of loan use emerges from this study as the more significant predictor of the effectiveness of loans in increasing women's agency than does the amount of the loan. When women are the primary loan users, regardless of the amount of loan, they gain agency from their direct economic contribution to the household. Conversely, when husbands are the primary loan users, regardless of how big the loans and the subsequent profits are, women register no gains or, at best, very weak and precarious gains from their indirect, passive role in the loan transactions.

When men are the primary users and payers of loans, they do not view the loans as women's contributions to the household economy. Often women themselves do not perceive these loans as economic contributions made by them. When the loans do not result in women's running their own economic enterprises (this is true in the majority of cases), access to micro-credit plays a very small part in increasing women's agency.

4

The power of participation

It is late in the afternoon, and the mid-day meal has concluded in most households. The women have a few hours on their hands until evening. The open, unpaved courtyard in front of one thatched house begins to fill up with women streaming in from nearby houses. This is the group leader's house. There is some laughter and banter and a conversation starts up among the gathered women. Some women have brought along their *kulo*, a hand-woven bamboo tray, with little piles of shredded tobacco, *tendu* leaves cut in squares, a reel of white thread, a bowl of ash, and a pair of scissors. Their fingers fly rolling and binding *bidi* as they talk among themselves. When all the fifteen women who make up this microcredit group have arrived, the group leader calls attention to the group's formal business. The meeting begins with the joint ritual recitation of the *"shapathnama,"* a set of oaths handed out to all participants in all the microcredit groups administered by the particular NGO sponsoring this group.[1]

At the conclusion of the ritual, the women sit down in a circle on the straw mat spread on the earthen floor. Some begin to unfold plastic carry-bags. Others unzip small worn out purses or untie the bulging knot at the end of their saree. Little passbooks, rupee notes, and piles of coins begin to accumulate on the mat. The woman who serves as the group's cashier begins to collect the money for the fortnightly savings deposit and loan repayment from each of the women. She updates each passbook with an entry.

---

[1] This model of requiring group members to repeat specific principles (formulated by the NGO running the microcredit program) is similar to Grameen Bank's model of requiring its members to recite the "Sixteen Decisions." However, not all of the microcredit groups in this study were consistent in performing this ceremonial ritual at the start of every meeting.

In the meantime, some of the women have started talking about the business or the crop cultivation into which their family invested their last loan. Some of them lament the loss of their crop due to the unusually heavy monsoon that year. One or two talk of how the plants rotted in the water before they were ready for harvesting. Others talk about the state of the business into which their loan was invested (by their husband or by them or jointly). The focus of the conversation is on the yields from the various livelihood enterprises. Some women talk about the amount of loan they and their husbands are planning to take in the next round. The cashier concludes her accounting work. It turns out that two women have not been able to put together the amount due for this fortnightly period of their loan's installment plan. The leader and group members urge them to try harder, telling them that they are now likely to find it more difficult to put together the payment due for two-installment periods instead of one during the coming two weeks before the next meeting.

The gathering does not break up at the conclusion of the discussion of financial affairs. The women continue talking about the latest events in the neighborhood. They talk about the problems they face in their households, the shortage of this or that public service like drinking water, the declining condition of particular roads, a mishap within a local family – if and how they should help, whether they should pool some money and offer it to the family in need. Some women animatedly talk about their conflict with family members. Listeners share advice and strategies about how to handle a difficult mother-in-law or tame a stubborn husband. If a new government policy or initiative has been launched recently, the group's supervisor, on one of his/ her rotating occasional visits, may announce it at this point in the meeting. After an hour or two passes, the women begin to collect their things and depart. They will be with each other again in two weeks time.

The group's leader and co-leader, meanwhile, will have to attend a monthly cluster meeting with other group leaders.[2] The annual microfinance convention that will be held in the NGO's village headquarters is coming up in a few months. The pair will have to start mobilizing group members to participate. Some groups put on performances of group singing or dramatic skits portraying the social situation of women. The leaders will need to agree about whether they want to organize something along those lines.

The two leaders will also need to decide if they are going to participate on behalf of their group in the next *gram sabha*, the village council meeting

---

[2] A cluster meeting includes the leaders and or co-leaders from about fifteen or twenty groups in adjacent neighborhoods.

organized by the local government. Perhaps they need to discuss what claims they might want to advise the group to make upon the council, including perhaps a demand for an electric power pole or a drinking water tube-well that the neighborhood needs. Amid all this planning, the leaders need to prepare for the next round of loans when the group will need to make some difficult decisions regarding each member's repayment capacity and the amount of the loan to be allotted to each member. Some members will undoubtedly feel hurt or offended. Tensions will have to be resolved or eased using a combination of discretion and persuasion.

This reconstruction of a typical microcredit group meeting highlights the most important aspects of the associational mechanism by which microcredit increases women's agency, individually and collectively. These group meetings, put in place to marshall social collateral in replacement of physical collateral, stimulate the associational mechanism that the preponderance of the evidence from my study shows is the major source of improvement in women's agency. The associational mechanism improves women's agency regardless of any and all financial benefits derived from the loan itself. This is the study's single most dramatic finding.

Almost half the sample of 284 married women in male-headed households emphasized group participation and their membership in the collective network of the group as playing major roles in improving their capabilities. Even if the economic mechanism by which microcredit promises to enhance agency is rendered ineffectual by the persistence of patriarchal domination and control, the associational mechanism by which women's agency can be increased can nevertheless still flourish. Again, it is the associational mechanism that matters most for improving the agency for a significant proportion of women.

The effect microcredit meetings and events have on the lives of the women depends very much on the frequency and intensity with which each woman participates in them. The number of required meetings ranges from mandatory bi-weekly attendance for all group members in neighborhood-based group meetings to occasional attendance at the annually held SHG convention. Some microcredit programs, such as the ones I studied, also require the group leaders to attend monthly cluster meetings in the village and occasionally participate in government sponsored events relating to microcredit groups. These events give women the opportunity to travel beyond the confines of socially restricted local geographical spaces and to interact in public in ways that break with gendered conventions.

The fortnightly group meetings occur in the immediate vicinity of group members' residences, but familiarity of the surroundings belie the far reaching consequences the women's interactions can have. These intense, close-up encounters between women fulfill the requirements of what Erving Goffman characterizes as "focused interactions." The interactions are distinguished in the following strong ways: First, there is a ritual component – the joint recitation of resolutions – that inculcates group identification; there is a direct focus of attention – on the volatile issue of money; there is free-flowing, unsupervised verbal communication; these result in a mutual heightened awareness of each other; and, finally, an emerging feeling of solidarity and mutual identification.

The larger events encompass multiple groups and are significantly different from the fortnightly meetings. The distance that women have to travel to attend these events surpasses any distance most have ever traveled without a family escort. Participation marks a symbolic watershed: Some are invited to address the crowd and talk about the accomplishments of their group. They share the stage with dignitaries.

Usually the women chosen to make public speeches are leaders from microcredit groups that have distinguished themselves either through their financial success or because they have made a significant social intervention by mobilizing group members in some way. The women who do not get the opportunity to make public speeches (these make up the majority) nevertheless have the novel experience of listening to speeches made by women very similar to themselves. Often these moments become the transformative event through which a participant realizes what women are capable of achieving – the event through which women see themselves as being capable, individually and collectively, of imagining and enacting alternative realities. At these larger meetings women also get to listen to bank officials, government bureaucrats, and political leaders exhort them to launch their own livelihood enterprises and to become engines of economic and social change.

Taken together, these associational forms produce a variety of subjective reactions that contribute to changes in conventional thinking, desires, and behaviors. These changes range from small and incremental variations on past patterns to dramatic shifts. Whatever their magnitude, these changes act on the "habitus" to push against the basic conventional structures that shape dispositions and desires.

This discussion of the benefits of association for women's agency will analyze its positive impacts under optimal conditions in order to show both its theoretical and real-life importance for creating positive change.

Women's participation in a microcredit group's associational life has a transformative impact on her life through increasing her agency whether or not the loan actually increases her income-generation capacity or economic contribution to the household. This striking aspect and social dynamic of microcredit has been neglected both by economists and by anthropologists. Economists lack interest in the social sources of women's agency, and anthropologists have so far failed to recognize this as they focus on condemning women's frequent lack of direct loan control, the social harm of the coercive aspects of sanctioning imposed by some microcredit institutions, or the harmful effects on women of the ignominy of being unable to repay loans.

Six capabilities constitute the core dimensions of agency in this study. Five of them will be the focus of the remainder of this chapter. The sixth capability, collective action, will be the subject of the next chapter. My analysis will show how the associational mechanism enhances each of these capabilities through a case-based, life-course perspective. The chosen cases illustrate generally observed patterns. Where appropriate, I have added additional examples from other cases to emphasize some points. In each case, I specify the pattern of loan-usage to show that women can gain agency through the associational mechanism regardless of whether they use the loans themselves or transfer them to their husbands. At the end of this chapter, I discuss the varying significance women attach to the improvements in their capabilities. This allows for a theoretically crucial discussion of how researchers can most productively integrate women's subjective evaluations of changes in their agency with their own analysis.

The most striking finding of this study is that most women attach far greater significance to improvements in their new capacity to be socially aware and analytical, to actively engage in social interactions with a broader spectrum of people than before, to be geographically mobile, to participate in civic institutions more broadly, and to be a part of the group's collective actions, than they attach to perceived increases in their domestic power. This finding appears to contradict – or at least to be in significant tension with – the enormous importance the social science literature assigns to domestic power in determining women's status.

But domestic power is only one dimension – one arena for the exercise of capabilities – when it comes to analyzing women's agency. It does turn out to be the case that the magnitude of gains made by women through microcredit in domestic power is much less than the improvements made in their other capabilities.

This point requires some clarification. Some improvements in capabilities can be considered to be "objectively" large when considered from a universal, appositional standpoint. Others – that by global egalitarian standards of middle-class secular modernity would be considered minor or woefully inadequate – are experienced by women as being of the greatest significance given the extreme social constraints of patriarchy under which they are forced to function.

It is extremely important, this study shows, to recognize the importance of the subjective experience of the enormity of the gains from the women's point of view. For these women, the novelty of being able to do things that they were never allowed previously may carry much more significance than gaining domestic power in small increments. It is important to recognize that domestic power is crucially dependent upon a woman's self-conscious awareness and her freedom to interact with others and upon her ability to move about freely in geographical space.

Effective decision making, including decision making that falls outside of conventionally female domains (a key element in increasing women's domestic power), is only possible when women are informed and aware of opportunities. They also need to be able to convert decisions into actions through gaining physical access to formal and informal institutions and facilities. In other words, increased domestic power is contingent not only on command over material resources, as narrow economic theories tend to imply, but also on command over knowledge and interpretive competence and confidence concerning institutional alternatives and access to the resources to take advantage of them.

Using this analytic perspective, it immediately becomes clear that the women's own evaluations of the magnitude and significance of increased agency they experience in some of their capabilities is not misplaced. The accounts they give of improvements in their capacities for social and physical circulation, civic participation, and collective action understandably take precedence over direct concerns about improving their domestic power. Without the former, there are no meaningful socially realized forms beyond the narrow domestic sphere in which what they have learned and felt in their microcredit groups can find effective collective expression or translation into purposeful action.

SELF-CONSCIOUS SOCIAL AWARENESS

Change occurs from the mind; money can't make the change! If this *saree* of mine gets soiled, I have to clean it, and only then it'll change. In the same way, if my mind is soiled and I have to change it, I've got to mingle with other people. Only then the dirt will be washed away and it'll change. Everything is in the mind. (Saleya Bibi, group: Shanti)

In her final remark to me about the influence of the group, Saleya uses the analogy of cleaning a soiled garment to sum up the role the group's associational life played in transforming her subjectivity. In her first-person testimony, she ascribes her acquisition of agency to the psychological transformation she experienced as a result of her interactions with other members of her microcredit group.

A Muslim woman in her forties, Saleya worked as an agricultural laborer for Rs 35 per day before joining the group. Following her membership in the group, her household experienced a brief spurt of economic improvement. Over the past four years she has taken Rs 9000 in loans and has used the money to rent-in land that she has cultivated on her own through a sharecropping arrangement. She managed all the agricultural tasks single-handedly and, at the end of the first year, produced six sacks of rice for her share.[3] The paddy cultivation improved her household's economic situation enough for her to stop working as an agricultural laborer.

But recently, after four years of group membership, she once again found herself in desperate need of low-paid work. Work in the fields was not available, however, because the fields were still waterlogged from the heavy flooding and no one was hiring farm laborers. She was even willing to work as a maid in the city for a while to tide over the decline in her family's economic fortunes. This recent downturn started with the wedding expenses incurred for the last two of her three daughters who were married in close succession. Saleya had taken an additional loan of Rs 5000 from the group fund for covering these expenses.[4] The family ran into difficulty in repaying the loan because her husband's income dropped following a shortage of work in the *bidi* factory where he works. The economic improvement that Saleya had worked so hard to achieve

---

[3] This was worth six months of consumable rice for their family, which at the time had six-members.

[4] Taking a loan from the group fund is different from taking a regular type of loan from the group. For the former type of loan, usually accessed for emergencies, the money comes from the group's combined savings and not from the external donor or bank fund (administered through NGOs) which finances microcredit. There is a nominal interest of 2 percent, a much lower rate than is charged for regular microcredit loans. The interest money is added back to the group fund when repaid, thus augmenting the collective savings. Finally, there is no fixed date by which a loan taken from the group fund needs to be repaid, so the repayment can be made according to the debtor's convenience. However, further loans cannot be claimed until the outstanding money owed is fully repaid.

remained precarious due to the contingencies of unemployment, under-employment, natural calamities, and large one-time expenditures.

Summing up the overall effect of the group on her life, Saleya says, "My economic condition hasn't improved all that much, but my social experience (*abhigyata*) and capacity (*khomota*) have improved a lot." She gives the example of her raised awareness of family planning and contraception methods that she has gained through her participation in the group: "I didn't understand the consequences before. I had five children. But now I tell my daughters not to have more than one or two." She mentions the group meetings as the source of this changed attitude: "Yes, we talk about it. The fewer children in a household, the more peace there is. The more children there are, the more difficult it is to feed and clothe them well and to educate them properly. This is a point in our *shapatnama*, and we have to recite it at the beginning of every group meeting."

Among the Muslim communities in some of these villages, contraceptive measures are deemed un-Islamic and shunned. Two other middle-aged Muslim women belonging to different groups complained that years back when they had suggested adopting birth control measures, their husbands had threatened them with rejection. One of them had been told that community members would refuse food and water served by her and that none would recite the prayer at her funeral.

In fact, in the initial years, the *mullahs*, Muslim clerics, in Saleya's village were strongly opposed to the women enrolling in these groups. Acting on their accurate intuition that the influence of microcredit groups would destabilize the domestic power equilibrium in their community, the mullahs rallied against them. Their opposition to microcredit was not based on Islamic doctrine concerning the charging and paying of interest on loans. Rather, their fears were direct expressions of acute patriarchal anxiety that hitherto docile women, supposedly steeped in a powerful ethos of subordination and subservience, would now be exposed to, and corrupted by, new ideas concerning independence and its possibilities. Saleya explains:

They [clerics] would say that it's bad to be part of the women's groups. Why should women step out of their houses? Women will gain excessive power ... They said that we'd be corrupted if we stepped outside our homes, that the women wouldn't listen to their men anymore; they would do as they wished; they would become independent and act according to their own wishes.

These clerics' investment in such radically conservative social norms explains why microcredit groups have become a primary source of social awareness for women enrolled in microcredit programs. These groups, originally initiated for economic purposes, have become unintended forums in which women can talk in an unsupervised way about their deepest personal concerns – including their thoughts about such intimate subjects as birth control – and from it gain the confidence to counsel younger women.

Another way in which Saleya's everyday life has changed dramatically as a result of microcredit group membership is the new freedom that she has gained to mingle with people she chooses. Particularly significant is her capacity to interact with men not related to her such as the male NGO staffs and the husbands of fellow group members. Before group participation, such interactions were impossible and considered social and moral transgressions:

Before, I couldn't talk to anyone; I'd feel afraid. But after forming this group, everyone has peace in their minds. Now I can talk to the husbands of all the women in the group . . . Before I'd feel scared while talking to other men, thinking of what my husband would say! But now I know that if he asks me, "Why were you talking to that person?" Then I can say, "He is the husband of so-and-so, who is in our women's group," and then he won't object.

Saleya expresses her previous inhibitions even though, as an agricultural laborer, she was used to working outside the household. She also regularly had gone to the market to do the family's food shopping. This task uncharacteristically fell among her responsibilities because her husband left early in the morning for his work at the *bidi* factory and returned very late every night. Nevertheless, this previous access to the public world of the market had not had any liberating influence on Saleya.

In fact, market participation was not previously experienced as a freedom at all by Saleya because she had to be doubly careful not to be perceived as taking advantage of the opportunity it presented to violate social codes governing traditional male and female conduct. Such constrained gender mobility prevented her from expanding her social network or interacting in any personally fulfilling way beyond her immediate circle of relatives and female neighbors.

In addition to increased social awareness, Saleya has gained a great deal of freedom to interact with a wider range of people since joining the group. These improvements have had a transformative effect on the quality of her life. Her powerful analogy of cleansing the mind through free communicative interaction with peers with the cleaning of a soiled sari implies that microcredit group membership is a way of ridding the self of the destructive and "soiling" aspects of a constraining and unjust "habitus" for women.

Participation in microcredit groups fosters self-conscious social awareness in women across the entire economic spectrum and even in the most adverse domestic circumstances. A compelling example is Shuma, who was living her life in the stranglehold of heightened surveillance of daughters-in-law within an extended family household till she joined the local microcredit group.

Shuma is a lively, vociferous young Hindu woman, a high school graduate, who belongs to a large and well-off extended family household. Her father-in-law owns twenty *bigha* of fertile land and a three-storied concrete house. Because of her family's affluence, her participation in a microcredit group may seem unexpected. But, given their restricted social lives, women like Shuma do join because of the enticing prospect of becoming part of a microcredit group's associational life. The prospect of taking out loans is secondary in most such cases, although when women like Shuma do take loans they can afford to take larger ones because of their family's economic standing.

Tall and thin, her hair tightly pulled back in a bun and the end of her plain cotton sari firmly draped around her shoulders, Shuma radiates enthusiasm. Quickly glancing around her to make sure that no one is within earshot, she explains her predicament. She finds herself trapped by the economic exploitation exercised by her father-in-law. He keeps all the household money firmly within his grasp and provides only for his family members' most basic needs. Her un-enterprising husband is unwell, and neither she nor her husband has money of their own. Shuma therefore came up with a plan to use microcredit to remedy her domestic situation. Since joining the group, Shuma has taken three loans totaling Rs 41,500, a large amount by local standards. Her father-in-law is unaware of this, and her husband, who knows about it,[5] does not know how exactly the loans are spent other than that she transfers the loans to her father, a doctor,[6] to help him run his pharmacy. When her father-in-law asks her to take out loans so that he can use the money for cultivation, she tells him that the group will not give her loans because her father-in-law is rich. Shuma's father repays the money and gives her a proportional share of the profits divided into monthly installments.

---

[5] She could not prevent her husband from knowing about it because all husbands are required to sign along with their wives before loans are disbursed. This regulation was started so that husbands would not back out at the time of repayment, claiming that they had no hand in taking the loans.

[6] Doctor is often used in villages as a generic term to refer to doctors and pharmacists.

Despite profiting from the loans, Shuma has been unable to make much headway in changing her domestic situation. She has been able to secure the basic well-being of her husband, daughter, and herself, but at the cost of taking on the economic responsibilities that she thinks should belong to her husband.

The meager freedoms that she has been able to wrest from within her confinement in her father-in-law's household have been the result of the group's associational mechanism. In fact, these freedoms have given her a new lease of life. Attending the group meetings has become a source of crucial relief from the oppressive household environment. Why did her in-laws allow her to join a microcredit group in the first place and even to become the group leader? According to Shuma, at the time of her joining, they failed to anticipate the impact her joining the group would have. They had imagined that she would merely go to their relative's house next door once a week to deposit some money. They did not foresee that she would seize this opportunity to step beyond the direct control of the household and vigorously embrace a leadership role for the group.

The three things I did three years back were eating, working (inside the house), and sleeping. Since I came here after my marriage, I'd forgotten that an outside world even existed. Sometimes I couldn't even remember what date of the month it was ... They don't allow us to talk to anyone from the outside. Going to watch movies, we can't do that. You want to read a book; no you can't do that. "O she's proud of being educated and she's showing off." This is what their (her parents-in-laws) character is like.

The microcredit group legitimates her escape from her in-laws' domestic tyranny. When another group faces a problem, she is happy to accompany the supervisor to visit the group. She is determined to improve on her leadership skills and gain independence and some measure of autonomy through her connections with the microcredit group.

Yes, I've been through many "struggles," and I know that I'll have to confront many more to get stability in this work (as group leader). But now I think that somehow I will break out of the fence, and by breaking and breaking and breaking, one day I'll gain stability.

Shuma's intensely pursued and cultivated participation in her microcredit group pays off in confrontations with her parents-in-laws. One recent incident included her reading the newspaper, an activity she has started to keep herself abreast of current affairs. She credits her social awakening to being a member of the microcredit group. She is now able to hold her own – and regain self-respect – despite domestic opposition:

Mentally I've been able to change in a big way. The way I'd turned ignorant despite my education is unimaginable to me now ... After coming here I'd forgotten the importance of reading newspapers. Now after joining the group and being able to go out in the neighborhood, I go to the houses of people who subscribe to the newspaper, and I sit there for five minutes and browse through the daily paper. Now I do it for my own sake. I don't listen to what people say behind my back. (In-laws ask) "Why did you go to such and such's place?" I went because I needed to! How will all of you understand the importance of a newspaper? (In-laws say) "Will reading the news earn the rice in your belly?" Perhaps not, but so what! At least I got to know what happened all around the world today.

Participation in a microcredit group changes subjectivity at both ends of the economic and social spectrum. Reflecting on four years of group membership, Shuma says that the biggest benefit has been in being able to connect with the world outside. She relishes "the fact that I've learnt to keep in stride with reality and get to know about the outside world." "I've recovered the real life experience that had been completely 'blocked' from me in the past three years. That is the biggest advantage for me," she says.

Shuma has begun to reach out to her younger sister-in-law after a prolonged period of minimal communication despite their residence in the same household. Shuma is no longer afraid that her parents-in-law will suspect that she is complaining about them behind their backs. Now the two sisters-in-law meet in the group meetings, and Shuma uses this opportunity to train her to speak out against injustices: "I have to prepare her too. I tell her, 'I'm the only one who speaks up; all of you should start speaking up as well! First you speak up and then if they ask you, who taught you all this, then point to me.' But three years back this was unimaginable. I was trapped within the four walls of the house." Shuma is now confident that one day she will be able to fight back with the collective strength she is now determined to build.

The social awareness and courage Shuma has developed gives her the will and the nerve to ask her father-in-law about some of the details of the household's finances, a previously inconceivable act. She is able to do this even as she continues to deny him access to loans. She tells how she asks him about financial details when he seeks her help in writing down the accounts of crop sales. She is the most educated member in the family, but previously, although she aided her father-in-law when he did his accounts, she did not have the courage then to ask him about the details.

Although I helped him with the calculations back then as well and saw how much he made, I would never ask him, father what will you do with the money? I didn't have the courage then. If I asked they might've said, "O my, now she's asking for the accounts (*hisheb*)!" But now I ask him, so you sold the jute and made one lakh, what're you going to do with the money? And he says, "I've seen a piece of land and I'll buy it, this is how much they're asking for it." He tells me and so I listen and get the information, but before I'd be too scared to ask. It's by coming to the group that I've developed this courage in my heart.

Shuma's case illustrates how effectively the associational mechanism increases women's agency even in unfavorable circumstances and also illustrates the cascading effects of the social awakening derived from group membership. This is not to say that gains in agency from participation in microcredit groups do not still leave women's agency incomplete and fragmented. Yet, even if modest in scale, these gains are enormously valuable given the constraints and oppression of the domestic environments in which women are embedded. What money cannot achieve in a rigidly patriarchal context, microcredit's associational mechanism can. The agency gained can, in Butler's terms, greatly increase the "livability" of women's lives.

Microcredit groups have now become participants' primary source of information about various government policies, strategic institutions, and available resources. Access to such information enables women to enroll in economic programs and take advantage of institutional opportunities. Kanika, who belongs to a different group, mentioned enrolling in the government's unemployed laborer benefit program after learning about it from her group's supervisor. She emphasized the critical role of the group in making women like her aware of such facilities: "After joining this group we started getting news about schemes [programs] at the district level; information started circulating. That's how I got to know about it."

Microcredit group participation has led some of these women to become informed about their legal and political entitlements and both to confront and take advantage of law and justice institutions. A dramatic example involved Neoti Basak, an illiterate, sixty-year-old, poor, low-caste widow who speaks out vigorously regarding her increased awareness of the legal system. Referring to the problem of the police frequently arresting young boys in her community on charges of criminal involvement and theft, she describes how their interactions with the police have changed from supplication to confrontation:

[Now] we can get to know about where we should go and what we should do [in case of a problem] ... Have we ever seen a judge with our own eyes or known anything about the law? But today we can get to know something about it ... I can go and confront the policemen alone ... Earlier, when a young boy would disappear from the village, we wouldn't know where to enquire. We'd get hold of a *"dalal"* (a broker or middleman) and go about searching high and low. We'd pay them, and then we'd fall to their feet, begging them to bring our boy back. But now, we call the police station directly and ask if they've taken one of our boys, and we don't have to pay a single paisa. Earlier, we had to bribe the guards at the door and only then they'd allow us to enter the police station and meet with the officer-in-charge. Now we tell them, "We need to see the chief," and they let us enter immediately![7]

Annual microcredit self-help group (SHG) conventions, organized by NGOs or the state, also expose women to new ideas and information. These large-scale public events are used by the NGOs as occasions to increase the awareness of microcredit members regarding such issues as women's rights, the unlawfulness of domestic violence against women, legal recourses available to women, the perils of underage marriage, and other relevant topics. On the day of Self-Reliance's annual microfinance convention, all group members dressed in crimson-bordered white saris and white caps distributed by the organization and marched in procession to the makeshift convention center announcing slogans broadcast through hand-held microphones. The slogans, authored by NGO staffs, included the following: "Women don't fall back, push forward"; and "Women lift up your faces and claim your rights." Dramatic acts of collective participation like these, performed in public, often have cascading effects. They can change how men view women's agency and collective capacities and, even more important, they can gradually change women's own thoughts and perceptions about the reach and effective individual and collective use of their own empowerment.

SOCIAL INTERACTION

We (as Indians) have been free since we gained independence in 1947, yet *we* (as women: emphasized in speech) aren't free. We still have to live under the rule of others, under the dominance of our "guardians."[8] Before marriage we're under

---

[7] One of the reasons the police apprehended young men from this community may be that some of them are involved in the illicit, unlicensed production and sales of country liquor. It may also be that the police use apprehension as an opportunity for extortion.

[8] It is not uncommon to find women (literate or illiterate) in these villages using the English word "guardian." Its most likely source of diffusion among villagers is the government bureaucracy, which has historically required individuals to specify who their "guardian" is for many types of official work. The common understanding is that for men not yet married, their guardian is their father; married men are considered household heads, hence gaining the status of a guardian; women, unmarried and married, are considered to be under the guardianship of their father and later of their husband.

the rule of our parents and after marriage we're under the rule of our husbands and our fathers- and mothers-in-law. (Ishani Mondol, group: "Udayan")

Ishani Mondol, a Hindu woman in her mid-thirties, sums up the condition of women in rural Bengali societies with these stark words and then launches into an incisive critique of patriarchal mechanisms of control. Having graduated from high school, she is the most educated and articulate woman in her group. Her family is also among the better off households in the village. Her husband owns land and is an elected member of the village council (*panchayat*). The couple has a one-story concrete house with two modestly furnished rooms. A small television stands on the bedside table, and her husband's motorbike is parked in the room. In fact, it is their relative affluence that both explains and exacerbates Ishani's feelings of a lack of freedom. Affluence comes with its own "protective" layer of patriarchal control. For her entire life, until she joined the microcredit group, Ishani had never gone anywhere without being accompanied by a senior family member:

When I was young and living with my parents they never let me go anywhere without being accompanied by a "guardian." And after I came here, my mother- and father-in-law became my "guardians." My husband, too, became my "guardian." I never had the opportunity to go anywhere without them, and I didn't have the courage either. That's why, despite the fact that I had desires, I wasn't able to act upon them.

Even routine acts like going to the doctor or taking the children to school have not given her the opportunity to step out of the house independently. She is, in her own words, literally *a housewife*; she spends all of her time indoors. Restrictive norms, even when they are meant to be protective, inhibit the growth of fundamental capabilities in women. They can determine women's self-perceptions and skew them so as to conform, against the women's own gendered interests, to socialized preferences for female subordination. In the language of Bourdieu, what results is a gendered "habitus." Ishani herself is aware of this, and, in so many words, tries to convey the fundamental importance of what Bourdieu has theorized:

The other thing is that we have to hand over the loans to our "guardians"; we don't have the power to control our own money. We just don't have the capacity (*khomota*) to do it. And even if we have the capacity, if we don't have a man beside us, we don't get enough courage (*shahosh*). We have to take them along ... If we have to conduct a business of some kind we've got to travel ... but I've never gone out on my own because I just don't have the training or experience ... Yet, what does Self-Reliance mean?[9] It means standing on your own feet, being self-sufficient.

---

[9] This is a closely approximated pseudonym of the NGO, which implements the microcredit program in which she is enrolled.

If we have to stand on our own feet, we have to start businesses of some sort. But we haven't been able to prepare ourselves to be like that. So, even though we're in Self-Reliance, we're forced to be reliant on others.

Ishani's family has taken out three loans of which the first two were used to start a poultry farm that was eventually abandoned because it was unprofitable. The most recent loan of Rs7000 was used by her husband for cultivation. At Ishani's suggestion, the boundary of their paddy field, land that is usually left fallow, was planted with cauliflowers. Her initiative in proposing this idea was something new. But no other change has occurred in the domestic power dynamics or money distribution in the household.

Ishani's husband is in charge of all financial matters and allocates money among the different household needs. He gives Ishani a small sum for her own spending. Every month she has to ask him for the Rs30 that she needs for the group savings deposit. This is despite that fact that Ishani has been rearing cows for a long time and earning between Rs1000 and Rs 1500 every month from selling milk. That money is not considered her personal income because livestock are considered to be household assets and the cost of their upkeep is met by income from other sources. The labor that women contribute to rearing cattle is socially rendered largely invisible. It is unremunerated.

Ishani had proposed to her group the idea that the only way in which women can retain control over loans is by starting some type of collective enterprise, jointly owned and managed by all group members together. But her suggestion failed to generate any consensus or practical plan because of several obstacles including differences among the women in their skills and ambitions, the pressure of domestic responsibilities, and the lack of the backing of any institutional support.

Despite the failure to gain any economic independence, Ishani still feels strongly that the group has made a substantial contribution to her life by increasing her capacity for social interaction. Now she is able to interact with other women in the group meetings and move around somewhat more freely than before. This exposure, according to her, has given her a sense of courage. She goes out of her way repeatedly to emphasize this:

After joining the group and talking to so many women, I've gained a lot of courage. Now, if there's a need to go somewhere, then I'd tell my husband that we're going with the sisters (supervisors) to a particular place, and he'd let me go. Also, before I didn't know how to speak to people and whom to speak to. But now I know many more people, and I've gained the courage to speak up.

Ishani's life shows how women in relatively affluent households also lack agency. In fact, they are harder hit than poorer women by "Sanskritization," a social and cultural process that limits their economic roles and social circulation.

Courage to socialize independently with a broad spectrum of people and to articulate and assert one's own ideas and arguments comes up repeatedly as a theme in the accounts given by these women. The ritualized participation in a non–kin-based collectivity, and taking part in meetings and events conducted in the public sphere breaks down conventional gender barriers.

Since becoming members of these groups, many women find themselves operating within a greatly expanded social network. Being members of the same group generates a sense of trust and camaraderie that allows women to overcome their wariness and to share private household information and troubles. In the fortnightly group meetings, women can express themselves freely with their peers beyond the disciplining gaze of their husbands and in-laws. The increased freedom and fluency of self-expression is cathartic for many women and contributes greatly to their psychological well-being. Women often express this as "getting peace of mind (*shanti*)" or feeling "free" and "light (*halka*)."

A younger group member considered this aspect to be the most liberating influence of all ten years of her married life:

After my marriage, it wasn't like before when I could go around with a bunch of friends and talk and spend time with them. Only after forming the group I'm now practically "free" again. For me this is the most exciting part, that I can meet and mingle with other people and I can learn about things . . . Whenever there's a group event I come; if there's a meeting I come. I'm a kind of person who never holds on to any resentment . . . I'm always cheerful, but I can't express that in front of my family members, like my father- and mother-in-law. But here when all of us get together and do something, I can express that. (Tuntuni)

Contradicting romantic tropes of traditional village life, women pointed out that, earlier, it was not common practice for them to visit each other without a specific need. Now women have an opportunity to socialize more frequently. One group member points out, "Now we go to each others' houses very often. But, before, we'd go only if we needed something specific, we just didn't go and sit down in other people's houses for a chat" (Bobita).

Group social interaction, whether in the regular group meetings or in the large-scale events, holds special significance for increasing women's agency. Being part of a larger circle of interaction exposes women to a wider range of experiences and safely allows them individually to imagine alternative "beings and doings."

Groups that had undertaken successful collective actions shared their story in the microcredit conventions and inspired other women to imagine that they, too, could one day be like the speakers:

We heard in that meeting that in one village, all the women in the group had got organized and destroyed the illegal [unlicensed] liquor distillery in their village. So imagine the power and force they must've acquired and how much they've improved themselves! In another place, the river's embankment had collapsed, and the women from the group there gathered together with baskets and shovels and rebuilt the levee. It's great to hear such stories and to imagine what if we can be like that some day! We're trying to learn. (Anima)

Whatever the magnitude of actual gains, the greater freedom of expression fosters feelings of interpersonal trust and emotional affinity among group members. These feelings play an important role in strengthening women's loyalty to microcredit groups and ensure their continuing participation even when the economic gains are uncertain.

PHYSICAL MOBILITY

I didn't have the courage to assert myself in this way before. But after joining Self-Reliance and hearing their [supervisors] words in the meetings, we've understood what they say. On the first day of the group meeting itself, they explained to us, "This is what you women have to be like. This is what you've got to learn. And this is what you need to understand!" That is how the change happened, gradually. Now we've been able to break some rules and apply some of these ideas at home! (Rokeya Bibi, group: "Duti Pata")

Draping the end of her sari over her head in a sign of modesty, Rokeya Bibi, a middle-aged Muslim woman, declares that being able to build a toilet adjacent to her house has been the biggest economic benefit of being in the microcredit group. It has saved her from a terrible and shameful inconvenience and has finally restored her dignity.

In the four years of group membership, she has taken four loans totaling Rs 11,000. She has given Rs 4500 to one of her sons for his carpentry business and has used Rs 6500 to build a toilet. But the economic situation of the household is much the same as it was before. In fact, she says they are indebted to the tune of Rs 10,000–11,000 because of her recent surgery. Rokeya's own income-earning potential has remained unaltered by her group membership.

Several years ago she had bought a cow when her father-in-law had separated their family from the joint unit, leaving them only a small plot of land. Since then, she has been rearing cows and poultry, and she has used her income from selling milk to raise and educate her children. She declares proudly that all six of them have seven to eight years of schooling. Rokeya herself has six years of schooling and used to offer private lessons to local children for a nominal fee.

Her husband lost his job in the state-run gun and shell factory some years ago and has begun working on their land and now cultivates it. But their land holding is small and proves sufficient only to meet the needs of their household consumption. He has to supplement his income by hiring himself out as an agricultural laborer. On occasion, Rokeya's husband also brokers the buying and selling of livestock. His income is unstable. There are days when he earns nothing and days when he earns twenty, fifty, or even a hundred rupees. The family has a grove of mango trees that yields a modest seasonal income of Rs 2000–5000 every year. At the end of every year, Rokeya says that they are usually left with a debt of Rs 1000–2000 and, now and then, there are days when "the cooking pot is not put on the fire."

Yet Rokeya gushes about the dramatic changes in her life since joining the group. She claims she has been able to break free from the restrictive environment that for so many years held her captive within the house. Rokeya's first opportunity to leave the house unaccompanied came on the occasion of the annual microcredit convention that was organized by Self-Reliance in its district headquarter.

Rokeya was the most senior and most educated member of her group, and for these reasons she had been chosen to be the first group leader. She also had the advantage of not having dependent children at home. Group members urged her to participate in the convention. Even though her husband was the one who had brought microcredit to their village by requesting the NGO staff to start a group in his neighborhood, he objected vehemently when it came to his wife leaving the household to attend the convention. An intense period followed during which the staff and group members tried to convince him to change his mind. Their persuasion finally made him relent. At the age of forty-three, Rokeya made her first journey outside the house unaccompanied by a family member to attend a non-family event:

We weren't allowed to set foot out of the house . . . The first time in my life I went out was to attend the group convention. My husband simply wouldn't allow me to go. The supervisor explained to him repeatedly, and finally, he gave his consent. A woman from my group explained to him that it was an exclusively women's affair and that we'd have no interaction with men whatsoever. Then finally he allowed me. Yet, on the day of our journey, I was late in meeting up with the rest of the group, so all of them came to my house and helped me pack up and leave. They suspected that my husband might be creating problems at the last minute and trying to restrain me from leaving. That time I went and that was the start. I returned and told him all about it. From then on, he allows me to go whenever there's a program.

Thereafter, when training sessions were held for the leaders of microcredit groups, Rokeya participated. She heard patriarchal gender scripts questioned, challenged, and refuted at these sessions and returned home with a fundamentally transformed perspective on her economic role in the household. Even after four years, she reproduces a dramatic rendition of the program director exhorting the women to think critically:

He asked us, "Say, for instance, the husband earns fifty rupees, and he thinks that his wife doesn't even earn five rupees. But that is not the case. [Voice picks up volume] Women too earn fifty rupees! But, from where? Let me see if any of you can tell me, from where?" Some of the women tried, some were incorrect, some couldn't even think of anything. Then he explained, "Consider this: women tend to their cows, goats, and hens throughout the day. How much do they earn daily doing that? Or, consider how much you'd have to pay if you employed a maid to do the household chores. But husbands never have to pay their wives anything! That money is extra, so that is what women earn!" But we'd never thought in that manner before; we'd never perceived it in that way. Then he said, "OK, let's take independence: men have all the freedoms. But why don't women have any freedom? Because they can't protest!"

The intensity of the effect of this lesson is evident in Rokeya's voice. Its vibrancy communicates the wonder she experienced upon first hearing these ideas.

Gradually Rokeya's expanded forays into the world beyond her household gave rise to changes in her behavior. In the assessment of some of the Hindu women in this group, Muslim women were even more thoroughly entangled than they in webs of patriarchal control. The women found themselves surprised by the reach and subtle, intricate, pervasive depth of that control.

A spontaneous dialogue between Rokeya and a fellow group member, Krishna, her longtime neighbor who is Hindu, reveals their full awareness of the intensity of the patriarchal control that limits them and the changes induced by group participation:

KRISHNA: I think Muslim women have experienced more improvements because, before this, they were completely confined within the house. Compared to them, we'd at least go out a bit in times of need and crisis. But their husbands never allowed them to set foot outside the house. They'd stay inside with their saris drawn over their heads.

ROKEYA: Now we've snatched away some independence from our husbands! What we didn't have the strength to take from them before, now we've taken, whether by explaining to them or whether from their experience of seeing how the group works. Our husbands have now given us a bit of leeway, and we've been able to move forward a bit in these last four years.

KRISHNA: But it wasn't like this before! At least we Hindus eat in front of Muslims; we are less shy in these matters. In our first visit to Bajitpur [regional office for a microcredit-related event], during lunch time there was a long line of women; we were all served rice and all of us sat down to eat. But she (Rokeya) said, "I'm not eating in front of all these other people!" They [Muslim women] don't have the habit of eating in front of others! So, while all of us sat in the verandah and ate, she and another Muslim woman sat inside a room and ate. Imagine that!

ROKEYA: That's how far we had fallen behind! Before, if I had to go somewhere, I would eat at home before leaving and eat again only after returning. Even if I bought some food on the way, I'd carry it all the way back home. But now whenever I go somewhere, if I need to eat, I go into a roadside hotel.

KRISHNA: Now you see how far she's advanced!

ROKEYA: I think for women, especially, their social situation has improved. Even though I had some education, yet, as a woman, I didn't have the language to express the fact that I'm proud of being educated. Only now, as I am approaching fifty, I feel that pride, after earning the wisdom and power of speech from Self-Reliance. But before in our house, the attitude was, it's fine if you're educated, but when you've come to your husband's house, all you do is manage the household and serve the family. This was the problem, but now it's not like that ... Now as my group's cashier, I've counted a lot of money, and I've balanced plenty of accounts ... We had all of this capacity within us, but we didn't have a place where we could express it. Now Self-Reliance has given us that platform through this group.

Issues of comportment, demeanor, and rules and practices surrounding eating have for centuries existed as boundary-markers between groups as they jostled for space within a hierarchically organized social landscape. Women had to remain within the private sphere, the inner sanctum (*andarmahal*) of the household, when it was big enough to allow such demarcations.

Within the constricted spaces of poverty, women were supposed to recede into the household in the presence of male strangers and to send the men of the household to receive strangers. They were supposed to eat last and carry themselves in a way that reflected modesty. Seen in the light of Bourdieu's notion of "habitus," these seemingly minor changes were in fact momentous for the shift they mark in women's achievement of agency.

Physical mobility and exposure to public affairs have set in motion among these women a process of learning from observation and mutual emulation. Women who would not have influenced each other previously, on enrollment in the microcredit group, put themselves in a position to influence each other in profound ways. Here is how a microcredit group transformed the life of Champa Bibi, another Muslim woman from a different group:

In villages, women usually don't go to the market except for specific needs, like say, taking your sick child to the doctor or, perhaps, to buy a saree. But, earlier, I never used to go to the market, not even to buy sarees. But now I go, because now, if my husband buys a saree for me, I don't like the design! So I go myself and choose according to my own liking and buy it. Before, I was afraid that people might comment that, look, what kind of a wife is she? If her husband chooses something for her, she doesn't like it! But now, if I need five things, he buys two and I go to the market and choose three by myself and buy it. I changed after I joined the group, after seeing the ways of the others in the group, and after listening to the things they say. Why should we remain in the darkness any more? ... There are eighteen women in the group, and I can hear eighteen different things from them. I feel good. When I wasn't in the group, I wasn't able to meet others. But now we can all get together and listen to different things. From that we get different ideas, and we feel different from before.

For Rokeya, exposure to the thoughts, ideas, and experiences of the other women in her group allows her to intervene in the day-to-day running of her household in new and empowered ways:

Now, sometimes, I go to the market, but earlier it was out of the question. Before, he'd bring some of the things [items of household need], but the rest he'd forget. If I said anything, he'd say the opposite. Now I explain to him that, see, these are the things you need to bring. It's fine if he understands. Otherwise, I can say, you give me the money, and I'll take care of it myself. We didn't have this opportunity or the intelligence before.

The experience of not having to depend upon her husband because of her new ability to act on her own authority has reduced altercations with him.

DOMESTIC POWER

"Now I've gained some *buddhi* [acumen] of my own from the *charcha* [practice] that I've had"

People would come and ask him [my husband] for money. Back then, I never used to say anything. It's your money; give it to whomever you want! If I expressed my hesitation he'd say, "Why do you have to be bothered about it? I've done what I thought was best!" Now I say, "You do what you think is best, but that isn't right. You're giving him money, and who's to say he won't run away with it? He might not repay you. How well do you know him?" Now he accepts what I say. If I say, "Don't lend him money, he's a shady person," then he says, "Fine, I won't lend to him since you think he might not repay." (Jharna Majumdar, group: "Shantimata")

Jharna has been a group member for four years. Young and vivacious, she talks animatedly and breaks into sudden smiles as she talks. She describes how she and the women in her group started by saving three rupees every week and having weekly meetings. After a year or so, she suggested that the group raise the weekly savings amount from three to five rupees. That way they could save twenty rupees per month instead of twelve, and also claim larger loan amounts. Each group member has saved 920 rupees, and the total group savings amounts to a little over seventeen thousand. She and many other women in the group pay for their own savings deposit. They are able to do this because many of them do bidi-binding work and earn a few hundred rupees each month. Jharna's husband is an agent in this line of work, and he employs the neighborhood women in bidi-binding. This is the first time in her life that she has saved money independently. Asked what she thinks of it, she says:

Maybe my husband will not tell me this, but someone else's husband might tell her, "Will you bring me some money?" In that situation won't he feel a little, sort of, under her (the group members gathered around her laugh). Look, a man saying to his wife, "Bring me some money," isn't it something you feel awkward about? (She gives a look of embarrassment and smiles coyly.) You know, if your husband comes and tells you, "Bring me some money," then it does feel good! (She suppresses her laughter and gives a big grin.) We are the ones always saying, "Give me some money, I need this, I need that." But nowadays, it's the opposite! Now they're telling their wives to bring them some money, "I need it, I'm thinking of starting such and such business, or I am planning to cultivate."

In these few years, Jharna claims to have acquired a greater voice in household decisions. Surprisingly, she has not taken out any loans because they have not needed any. Her income has remained unchanged. Her change from passive acquiescence to active questioning and articulated opposition to her husband's decisions is not due to domestic power derived from a loan transfer or from her increased financial contribution to the household. Explaining her changed attitude, she says, "Now I've gained some *buddhi* [acumen] of my own from the *charcha* that I've had. Now I say what I think is good, like don't do this because it might cause problems."

The concept of *charcha*, used here by Jharna to explain transformation, means a practice, a conscious cultivation through which one can be transformed. It refers to the learning of a skill, gaining competency in something through repeated engagement or performance of actions that are initially new and unfamiliar.

"*Charcha*" needs to be understood in relation to "habitus" to understand its full significance for women's lives. "*Charcha*" is a countervailing energy to be mobilized against the socialized force of "habitus." The thoughts, perceptions, desires, and "body hexis" generated by the constraining structural dynamics of the intersecting gender and class positions occupied by these women in rural society are slowly being unraveled as a result of the women's assertion of their own agency. These women are cultivating skills and performing practices – conventionally associated with men – that are perceived as unconventional, even destabilizing, when performed by women. They are gathering together in meetings, talking about financial matters, deciding on loans and repayment issues, maintaining financial accounts, and deliberating about community affairs in purposive, potentially effective, even activist, ways.

The radical effect of such transformative practice is clearly manifest by the last thing she says as she concludes the interview:

> I studied only till class four, and I had completely forgotten how to read and write. My hand would shake if I signed my name. But after joining the group, I refreshed my memory and practiced on my own. Now I write down all the minutes and transactions in the group's account and resolution book. Now I can also write letters. I developed all of this myself after joining the group.

Practice of this fundamental sort, which entails learning a new set of associational and pragmatic skills through which agency can be actively asserted (rather than constraints accommodated and painfully adapted to) radically transforms and alters the women's experience of the patriarchal gender roles they have internalized. It brings within practical reach their desire to participate in aspects of household affairs that are the traditional preserve of men. The associational mechanism contributes to a subtle, deep, and pervasive improvement in women's domestic power.

With increased agency women are able to abandon the secrecy with which they occasionally or regularly do things that are traditionally disapproved of. With increased agency women are able to act more openly within their households. The transition from secrecy to openness can have immense significance for a woman's exercise of domestic power.

Dulurani Mondol, Dulu for short, is the forty-year-old ex-leader and current co-leader of her microcredit group. A little more than a decade before she joined the group she had taken up tailoring work to supplement her household's income. She tailored garments on subcontract for a merchant and every week she would go by herself to his house in a distant neighborhood to deliver the finished work.

Despite this history of independent movement, Dulu stresses her husband's initial reluctance to let her leave the house to attend group events.

Dulu had to plead with him and explain that, as the group leader, it was her responsibility to attend the training sessions and make sure that the lessons got disseminated to all the group's members. Only after the considerable effort it took to convince him could Dulu attend her first microcredit event outside their neighborhood. This took place in the NGO's local office that was only a few kilometers away. Comparing her life previous to enrollment in her microcredit group, Dulu comments:

Back then we lived within the four walls of our house. We never used to go from this field to that; we [women] didn't even go to each other's houses ... The first time I went out was to Bajitpur for an orientation meeting (of microcredit group leaders) ... Since then I've gone to many places, and I've heard many speeches, and I'm glad I heard them. Before, we didn't know anything! But now, at least, we know something, and we've also gained some experience.

She does not mention here her weekly trips to the garment merchant's neighborhood. She only mentions it when asked if she had any personal savings prior to joining the group to which she answers "yes" and explains how she started it. Some ten years ago, when she used to regularly go to meet with the merchant, she noticed that the neighborhood was economically better off than her own, and many of the residents there had savings accounts into which they made monthly deposits.

Adopting a tone of closely guarded secrecy, she reveals how she started her savings account five years before she joined the microcredit group: "Then I thought, well, I do tailoring work and, at least, I earn something. So I hid it from him (husband) and, behind his back, I opened a savings account in the post office with a recurring monthly deposit of Rs 60. I went to the post office myself; my husband didn't know about it."[10]

For five long years she kept it a secret from her entire family: "I never brought the balance book home; I kept it in the post office. He wouldn't be home all day. In the morning he'd go out to sell fish. So, at that time, I'd leave the house on the pretext of going to the pond to wash up. But, instead, I'd go to the post office nearby and pay for my monthly deposit. So he never got to know about it." But after five years of managing the account on her own, she broke the news to her husband. This was only a few months before the account was due to mature. That year there were

[10] In India, post offices offer a limited range of government-sponsored savings plans and function as rudimentary banks where people may open accounts and deposit money. Post offices are present even in small villages and are therefore used for savings where banks cannot be present.

rumors that the flood that was devastating other parts of the countryside would reach their village. Afraid of what might happen in the aftermath of such a disaster, she let him in on the secret. Her plan had been to start a fixed deposit once she received the lump sum at the end of the term. Now, with her husband's consent, she has enrolled in another savings plan at the bank.

This secretive narrative of a surreptitious savings account discloses the complex nature of the relationship between women's financial capability and domestic power. It points to the importance of understanding the layered meanings and messages contained in covert versus overt actions. When asked why she needed to adopt such secrecy, Dulu responds in an agitated manner: "We're women and we can't work for money!" This even though she was engaged in paid work, not explaining her need for secrecy. A fellow group member, Anima, chimes in: "We have to pinch from our husbands' pockets!" Ichamati, the group leader, fills in the explanation that Dulu's own account lacks: "Actually, all our men are *paragneye lok* [rustic people]; so they don't understand everything, and that's why we always have to do things on the sly." Breaking from this constraining need to employ slyness in marital relations requires more than money.

Dulu's subsequent financial venture clarifies how microcredit's associational mechanism contributes to increasing women's capacity through encouraging transparency with respect to personal financial ambition, desires, and decision making. Six months before the fieldwork for this study, the government had launched a project called the "Swarnajayanti Gram Swarozgar Yojana" (SGSY). Government officials surveyed village households and used a set of indicators to identify the households falling below the poverty line (BPL) and those above it (APL). BPL households were provided the opportunity of forming government-sponsored SGSY microcredit groups that would be provided with subsidized credit and other support measures.

These groups, modeled on microcredit groups, were also exclusively targeted at women and had mandatory savings requirements. Dulu and some others from their group were designated as APL and excluded from the BPL group in their village. According to them, it was an unfair designation based on superficial economic distinctions.[11] Being excluded from the government-run group meant that the women lost an opportunity to

---

[11] The type of dwelling was a selection criterion. Those having brick and concrete houses were designated as APL, and those having clay or bamboo huts were designated as BPL.

save an additional Rs 30 every month. Women value such external opportunities to save because they find it impossible to save informally at home.

Not one to be left behind, Dulu came up with an idea and suggested it to the nine others in the group who had also been excluded. She lowers her voice to a whisper, as if about to reveal another secret enterprise:

> One day I said to her [Ichamati, the group leader, who is also her distantly related sister-in-law], "Can't the rest of us get together and start a two rupee account? ... If they [BPL women] can operate another savings account and deposit Rs 30 a month, can't we start another savings account and deposit two rupees everyday?! In that way, we can save Rs 60 every month and deposit it in the post office!"

Dulu did not suggest this initiative only because her family's finances had improved because of her access to loans. In fact, according to her, their situation had not changed much. She had taken three loans totaling Rs 12,500 over the past four years, and all of it had been invested by her husband in rice cultivation and in his fish retail business. Still, for two consecutive years they have had losses in agriculture. One year there was too little rain and salinity destroyed their crop. The next year there was excessive rain and flooding. Eventually they were forced to take loans at high interest from the moneylender, just like they used to take before. Recently, Dulu had resumed tailoring after a gap of several years. It had become increasingly difficult for them to run their five-member household and repay their debts on the sole income of her husband. She now earns Rs 520 every month. On listening to her suggestion, the non-BPL group members agreed and, together, they decided to let their husbands in on their plan. They felt confident that, since there were nine of them, their husbands would not object and they would be able to overcome any objections. In fact, this financial venture received the full consent of their families, and the women started their personal savings accounts in the local post office.

Saving money in this way means something very different from saving it in the traditional way through traditional channels. When women save money at home in slotted clay urns called "Lakshmi'r *ghat*" (Lakshmi's urn), it is considered conventional behavior and is socially approved. Lakshmi, the Hindu goddess of prosperity, is associated in mythology with all the feminine virtues, especially docility. In popular iconography she is shown holding an urn for saving money. Women who choose to save through modern institutions like banks and post offices rather than

---

Dulu's house is made of brick, plastered together with clay not concrete. So, in her opinion, it is ironic and unfair that her household was labeled as APL.

informally at home are seen as breaking with tradition. Saving in this manner, women cross the gendered boundary of the household, interact autonomously with men, and even save on behalf of themselves alone as individuals.

When women perform such non-traditional, even defiant, acts, strength of numbers creates a tipping point after which secrecy becomes no longer necessary. Participation in microcredit groups gives women this vital strength to declare their individual and collective wills.

In assessing women's domestic power, it is important to pay attention to the distinction between overt actions and covert ones. Although both are capabilities, overt actions represent a greater degree of agency and attest to greater freedom. Covert actions, however subversive, help maintain the status quo of power imbalances between men and women within the household. Overt actions have the capacity to alter the gender dynamics of domestic decision making and modify the balance of power in the household.

While transferring loans lends women monitoring capacities, the associational mechanism of microcredit provides women scope for "*charcha*," the practice that generates self-consciousness about the desire to become active and acknowledged participants in household affairs.

CIVIC PARTICIPATION

"They're going to make plans for the village and we aren't going to be there!"

Yes, we participate in it [*gram sabha*: village forum] every time. The first time I was going to go, he [her husband] said, "What are all of you going there for?" And I said, "They're going to make plans for the village, and we aren't going to be there! Let us go and see what exactly happens there." We're voters and they come to us for votes all right, but when it comes to planning, it's only the men who do that. That's why we want to go. Now he doesn't object to my going anymore. (Urmila Biswas, group: "Ma Sharada")

Twenty-seven-year-old Urmila has been a member of a microcredit group for seven years. She was fifteen at the time of her marriage when she left her parents' home in Bangladesh to start her married life across the border in India. Five years after her arrival, Sisterhood launched its microcredit program and started forming groups. In those days, when people were completely unfamiliar with microcredit, forming a group proved a nearly insurmountable task.

It took Urmila and the few other women who volunteered to join the group nearly three months to recruit twelve other women. It was hard for women to congregate publicly in the village. Urmila faced trouble at home whenever it was time for her to attend the weekly group meetings. To save herself from regular confrontations with her in-laws, every time she had to leave the house for group meetings she had to come up with a pretext such as going to the neighborhood tube-well to wash utensils. Her group would conduct its affairs in a clandestine and hurried manner. Urmila would call group meetings on short notice on days when her husband was away.

Keeping aside money for the monthly savings was difficult because Urmila had no income. She had to fish for change in her husband's pockets, always making sure not to take too much lest she be caught. She stashed each fifty paisa and rupee away in a secret spot.

When the group's loan cycle started, she took a loan of Rs 500 to start a fuel wood retailing business from home. Wood is commonly used as cooking fuel in villages. As a young girl, she had gained some experience in using a hand-held scale to weigh and measure goods and to calculate prices for customers. Her family grew and sold betel leaf, and she made the retail sales during her father's occasional absences. Her husband was a carpenter, and he could help with procuring the stock of wood. Relying on her prior experience and her husband's help, Urmila set up her home-based business.

Her husband bought and stacked the fuel wood outside their hut, and she made the sales from home. The initial investment of Rs 500 resulted in a turnout of Rs 1500. Emboldened by the profits, Urmila and her husband decided to take another loan of Rs 1000 to invest in their business. That, too, turned a significant profit.

Then they took a hefty loan of Rs 5000 for her husband to start his own carpentry business. He made furniture in the evening after completing his day job at an employer's carpentry shop. He purchased an electrical wood-carving tool with the loan and now has a monthly earning of Rs 2500–3000 from his own business. In addition, he still works for his employer.

After repaying the loan, Urmila and her husband were able to accumulate enough savings to consider buying a small plot of land adjoining their house. They took another loan of Rs 10,000 from the group and added their savings to that to purchase the land and register it in their name. Thanks to the loans, they have experienced substantial economic improvement as a family.

After three years, however, Urmila was forced to shut down her fuel wood business. A stiff rise in the price of fuel wood meant that people who could afford to pay were shifting to buying cylinders of cooking gas. The majority who could not afford the cost were shifting to cheaper fuel such as home-made sun-dried pellets of ash and coal dust. A few other families in the village had also taken up selling fuel-wood, cutting into Urmila's customer base.

Once again, Urmila had to rely on her husband's income for paying the group's savings deposit that had gone up from Rs 10 to Rs 20 per month. Now she does not have to scavenge in his pockets for change. Instead, he turns over his income to her, and she has taken on the management of the everyday household expenses. This is a recent development, following years of group participation. It reflects her husband's changed attitude:

Before, my husband would bring everything from the market, and we would eat whatever he brought. He would say, "You're all women and you'll have to eat and wear what we get for you. You'll have to do what we tell you; you can't go out of the house." But now it's not a problem if we go out of the house. That's why now I am the one who goes to the market.

Central to Urmila's transformation is a newly gained capacity for civic participation. Urmila proudly confirms her participation in *gram sabha* or village forums, which are held twice a year. Organized as part of the *panchayat* system of decentralized governance, these meetings are government-instituted public forums in which development plans are ratified, decisions are taken regarding the provision of public resources and infrastructure, and budgetary allocations are discussed and approved through public deliberation.

At these meetings beneficiaries are also selected for government programs of subsidized benefits to below-poverty-line households and to schedule caste families. The meetings are chaired by elected leaders who belong to political parties. Key local-level politicians and government bureaucrats attend these meetings and announce government-funded policies and projects. Villagers are expected to voice their demands and play an active role in determining which public works get implemented in their village and who gets selected to receive various kinds of government-sponsored anti-poverty support.

Women's participation in these civic forums is usually low and has become a government priority. In the popular perception of rural society, these *gram sabha* meetings, held twice every year, were considered arenas for partisan politics in which men battled their political rivals. Ever since joining microcredit groups, however, women have become aware of their equal right with men to participate in these forums and aware of the government-sponsored benefits that can be accessed and fought for at these meetings.

Women in microcredit groups have taken the opportunity to exercise their right to participate in the *gram sabha*. In a few places, the elected members of the village *panchayat* have welcomed women's participation. Some political leaders pay particular attention to informing the leaders of microcredit groups of forthcoming *gram sabha* meetings and invite them to present their demands. Being embedded in a system of electoral politics has forced some political leaders to recognize these women as an important constituency.

In other villages, women's participation in these meetings has met with stiff opposition from men. *Panchayat* council members have persistently ignored women's demands, and men have refused to acknowledge women's right to participate in *gram sabhas*. In these situations, women's participation usually remains marginal. A noteworthy change has occurred, nevertheless. Microcredit groups have provided women a strategic base for exercising their right to participate in village-level public politics as citizens. It is safe to conclude that NGOs would not have had the same positive effects without the empowering collective network of microcredit groups.

Women rarely participated in village council meetings prior to their enrollment in microcredit groups. Among the four hundred women in the study, only six mentioned taking part in such forums prior to joining a group. (Three of these women played a strictly passive role. They simply provided signatures to achieve a quorum and were not even physically present at the gatherings.) Three were members of political parties, and two of them had stood for local elections in constituencies reserved for women. In all three of these cases, there were family ties to political parties. Husbands, parents, or fathers-in-law had been party members. Apart from cases like these, membership in microcredit groups has been the predominant factor influencing women's participation in the *gram sabhas*.

It has become a custom in some microcredit groups for all its members to participate in village council meetings. Women's inhibitions regarding appearing in public and interacting with men has given way to a new assertiveness and a fluency in the vocabulary of civic rights. Urmila and her fellow group members have been participating in village council meetings for the past three years. Aparna, a member of Urmila's group, discusses women's rights as voters:

Before we never used to attend these because everyone would say, "Why should women come here?" But now we've realized that we, too, are voters and as voters we, too, have rights. We've got the right to speak in the village council and to raise our demands. Now, when we're at these meetings, they give us attention.

In Urmila's group, even the women whose husbands are conservative use the language of civic duty to claim their right to participate. Shadhana, a member of the same group, explained to her orthodox husband, "I'm a voter and all the voters need to go." In another village, Alladi Sarkar, an illiterate group member spoke forcefully of her participation in the village forum and pointed to the change that their membership in the microcredit group and their indirect association with the NGO had made in this regard.

Before I didn't used to go, I was a "*bou*" (wife/bride) then. Now, after going to the group, I attend the village forum. Before, women never used to go to those meetings; the men would say, "Since when did women start coming to the *gram sabha*!" Now, after we started going to the *samity* (organization, referring to the NGO) and the *gram sabha*, the men don't say anything. Everyone goes now, all the women and all the "*bou*." Before none of the "*bou*" went, back then men would scold them.

Literate women who had previously provided signatures to fulfill quorums at the *gram sabha* stopped their passive acquiescence once they had joined microcredit groups. Self-aware about their political rights, these women now assume a prominent role in these meetings. One of those women, Sheema, the cashier of her group, explains how they learned to raise their demands:

We just gave our signature at every meeting, and we never protested about it. But after joining the group, gradually we began to ask, Why are we present in the meetings, just to give our signatures? We, too, have some demands! If we wanted to raise our demands, we had to wave our hands to attract their [male political leaders] attention and talk. Whenever we wanted to say something, they wouldn't listen to us ... But this time we were very forceful. We demanded that they build a proper road for us and repair the school building. We voiced our concern about the lack of a playground in the school and raised questions about the problem with the monthly polio vaccination program.

Several women from a diverse range of microcredit groups claim that their engagement with the village forum differs sharply from that of men's. According to them, men are more preoccupied with political issues. By contrast, women claim to be more concerned with raising demands about public infrastructure and resources. The difference is emphatically outlined by Shyamali, Sheema's sister-in-law and the leader of their group:

When we formed the group, we got to know that the village forum meetings were not the sole domain of men. Women, too, had the right to raise their demands there. Some of us didn't have houses and toilets; the river's embankment was collapsing in front of some houses. We could present these complaints to the village council. Men will only think about their party politics, but they'll never let these social issues come to the surface. Even if they bring these up, they're not concerned to check if the demands are being met. They're more concerned with maintaining their party labels. So, in the group, we decided that we would go and collectively raise our demands.

Increased women's agency resulting from participation in microcredit groups can be attributed in part to the collective dimensions of their project. In groups that are cohesive and have strong and active leaders, all group members rally to support each other. In some villages, the supervisors and leaders of different groups have combined efforts to coordinate and inspire their memberships to orchestrate large-scale participation in village forum meetings. The intent is to tip the balance in favor of women so that they can be a voting majority voice that pushes their demands through. Where such mass coordination has occurred, there have been concerted attempts by men to thwart women's participation.

In one village, in the year prior to the study (2003), several group leaders from villages falling under the jurisdiction of the same panchayat successfully mobilized their members to participate in the village forum meeting. On the day of the meeting, one hundred and fifty women from neighboring microcredit groups arrived at the meeting. The women clearly outnumbered the men who represented the different political parties. The women represented a quorum. Their sheer number threatened to eclipse other participants' interests and demands. Faced with this unexpected threat, the men reacted viciously. When the women presented the long list containing their names for inclusion among those present, the council members tore it to shreds and prevented them from joining the meeting. Eventually, the men were successful in illegally ousting the women.

This incident strengthened the resolve of some of the group leaders to continue the struggle. They kept up the pressure on their groups, and, the following year, the women again showed up determined to exercise their civic rights. The political leaders could no longer deny the legitimacy of their presence and were reluctantly forced to relent. Since then, reportedly, on the day of the village forum meeting, two tents are set up to accommodate the public. One is meant for people with political affiliations, and this one is occupied entirely by men. The other is meant for people without political affiliations. This one is occupied entirely by women. Babli, one of the group leaders involved in this civic participation project sums up the men's reaction: "They wonder, what are the group's women doing here! They say we're eating the heads of the women (brainwashing) and bringing them out of their homes."

A handful of Muslim women, usually the leaders of microcredit groups, have also attended the *gram sabha* meetings although it is rare for Muslim women to appear at these events. Firdausi, who is the leader of a micro-credit group composed entirely of Muslim members, describes the way in which she successfully raised her demand in a village forum meeting:

In the past *gram sabha*, I had proposed that a house be sanctioned for a group member who had been recently widowed and left destitute. They had decided to grant the house to a man. But I had argued that, he was a man, and at the end of the day he could earn at least Rs 50, so it wasn't right to give him the house. Rather, here was a woman with two children whose husband had died, and she had no capacity for earning anything. I had created a big fuss in the meeting about this, and in the end she was given the house. This time the member of the village council let me know beforehand that the meeting was coming up. He said that if we had any demands from the women in the group, we should present them in the meeting. I assured him that we'd be there. So now I have all these experiences, but before I never knew or understood any of these things.

Firdausi was the only member in her group who participated in this meeting. Following her successful intervention, she expressed her intention to mobilize other group members to participate in future village forums. Rehana Bibi, another Muslim group leader, speaks animatedly about her increased awareness of the different government departments and facilities. She speaks about her participation in the *gram sabha* meeting forcefully and with enthusiasm:

Before this I didn't know anybody. I never understood what a group was, what a meeting was, and what the five of us were supposed to sit and discuss about! None of us had any experience. Then, when they (group supervisors) said that we should go to the regional (*anchal*) office, we had absolutely no idea of what that was! Now we know that if someone's house is damaged or if there are other property losses, if we go to the (government) office and let them know, then we might be able to get some aid. But before we didn't know about these. We didn't have a tube-well in the village, we didn't have toilets, we didn't have roads, yet we didn't know that we could go to the regional office and let them know about these issues and demand these facilities. Now we can go to the meeting, stand up and speak up for what we need. We need a road; our children can't go to school, and we can't walk. We can't even take a patient to the hospital; the patient is likely to die before we can even get there. The road here was terrible but now the *panchayat* has repaired it.

Although these may be exceptional cases, their rarity does not diminish their significance. The collective power brought to bear by microcredit groups is clear to all their participants. The quality of leadership also makes a big difference. Babli, the young group leader quoted earlier, emphasizes the importance of the quality of leadership:

All group leaders aren't the same. It depends on the leader to make their group members aware and experts in this matter. I want my group to improve. I also want that people should come to my group for exposure visits. But, not all the leaders want that. Some think, there's a group, so there's a group; they've got to save money, so they're saving money. It depends on their whims. But now they show on television how the liquor distillery in one village was destroyed. By whom? By women! In another village gambling was stopped. By whom? By women! Now women can see all this on television.

If the group leader's vision is limited to the financial goals specified by narrowly conceived ideologies of microfinance, there is little chance that the group will attempt to realize its latent capacity for collective civic engagement. By contrast, when a group leader develops a vision for her group that extends beyond the stated financial goals of disbursing and recovering loans and accumulating savings, it becomes likely that she will encourage the group to foray into the civic sphere. Women's capacity for civic participation is contingent upon the quality of their group's leadership but has little directly to do with any individual woman's direct access to loans, income-earning capacity, or household economic condition.

CONCLUSIONS

Participating in microcredit groups affords women precious scope for exposure to the world beyond the confines of their household and culminates in altering women's preferences and dispositions. This study reveals the cumulative change microcredit groups bring to women's lives. Increase in agency begins with changes in less intractable capabilities, like increased self-awareness, and moves in a steady progression to complex and more intractable arenas of struggle and conflict, like domestic power, civic participation, and the ability to take part in collective action and protests.

Of course, fully autonomous agency is never realized in any particular case. Not all women are capable of using their membership in microcredit groups to cultivate the full range of their capacities. Public political agency in particular requires a collectively orchestrated assault on customary practices of female subordination and the dismantling of formidable barriers to full female participation in public life. It is nevertheless true that microcredit groups provide foundational building blocks for women's agency and provide women indispensable experiences central to basic freedoms they would otherwise lack.

5

Microcredit and collective action

The social formation of women into groups capable of effective collective action is an unintended but crucially significant consequence of microcredit as a financial practice. The impetus to foster group-initiated collective action and provide the basis for communal sanctioning on group members' behalf unintentionally leads microcredit to enhance women's agency in ways never anticipated or analyzed within the standard financially focused models of program evaluation.

A third of the microcredit groups in this study used collective action to achieve a public good or apply sanctioning to protect members against customary practices that compromised women's welfare. These actions varied in scope and in the risk they entailed. Some, such as repairing or reclaiming village paths, or confronting the local liquor lobby to stop illicit trade in country liquor were extremely ambitious. Many of these bold undertakings required a sustained struggle against powerful vested interests. Other actions, such as rescuing women from domestic violence and the application of public sanctioning against physically abusive men were also quite daring. These actions broke with the conventions that enforce non-interference in the private affairs of other households and discourage direct confrontation or the disciplining of men.

In fact some of these actions practically redressed the unfair treatment of individual women and sent a powerful signal message to other households. Some mobilizations galvanized the entire community into collective action. The different types of collective action, whatever the scale, were all significant in promoting women's capacity for cooperation and achieving public goods. This is a dramatic finding that existing studies of microcredit have not reported or analyzed.

Increased capacity for cooperation adds to women's "social capital" and the women use this capacity for securing various benefits especially those of a public good character. These may be conventional public goods such as physical infrastructure that is non-rivalrous and non-excludable, including village roads and waterworks. Sanctioning, too, may constitute a public good. According to the group members, sanctioning to protect specific women produces positive externalities that benefit a wider population of women by lessening injustice and inequality.[1] Women's collective agency can produce public goods that otherwise cannot be harnessed by any other means including by state intervention since these public goods can be achieved solely through cooperation or voluntary participation (Fafchamps 2006).

That microcredit allows poor, socially subordinated, rural women to gain the capacity to undertake collective action is an unanticipated finding and even an astonishing one given that these women face an interrelated triad of specific disadvantages and challenging circumstances. First, collective action requires the mobilization of many individuals, and in these rural societies, women have limited social networks. Women are largely confined to their family and kin-group. They are rarely affiliated with village-based producer or recreational societies. The youth clubs, market committees, and grassroots political organizations that exist in these rural societies are monopolized and always dominated by men. Women's employment does not afford them the traditional associational advantages of jobs because women are typically engaged in low-paid agricultural wage labor in the fields or in unorganized home-based piece-rate work. These jobs do not allow women to socialize or regularly interact with co-workers out of sight of their families.

Second, most collective actions by women are directed against men and require extensive interactions with male police personnel and political party members. These men are traditional power holders and all are part of the same patriarchal hierarchy.

Third, and finally, married women, although striving to make economic contributions to their household, are for the most part economically dependent on male figures (husbands, fathers, or fathers-in-laws) and socially dependent on the institution of marriage. Their investments in the institution realistically limit women's capacity to defy household or

---

[1] Some interviewees claimed that punishing wife-beaters had a positive effect for a wider group of women by deterring domestic violence. Because of the degree of cooperation sanctioning requires, I have used the term "collective action" broadly to include it.

spousal restrictions and prohibitions against involvements that reach beyond the domestic sphere.

How microcredit promotes a capacity for cooperation among women in light of some of the critiques that have been directed at it merits our attention. Microcredit has been criticized for being a means by which women are co-opted against their interests into consent to neoliberal capitalist ideological structures that are presumably jointly orchestrated by collusion between government and international aid and development agencies (Schild 2000; John 2005). Related critiques fault microcredit for promulgating a market-based solution to poverty that has supposedly been used by states to evade their welfare commitments and to renege on their responsibility to meet basic needs and provide guaranteed minimal labor rights and protections (Mayoux 1995). These critiques overlook the possibility suggested by Sen's (1999) capabilities approach that, under certain circumstances, market-based ties and interactions clearly can contribute to fostering enabling forms of human freedom for populations that have previously been denied access to market-based institutions.

In fact, there is a fairly rich literature in economic anthropology (Ardener and Burman 1996) and in economic sociology (Light and Bonacich 1988; Biggart 2001) on rotating credit and savings associations (RoSCAs), tontines, and ethnic savings clubs. This work, which predates the microcredit literature, shows how informally arranged credit systems within particular communities were socially constructive and increased the capacity for trust and cooperation in everyday social relations. It was this work that provided much of the empirical data by which the usefulness of the concept of social capital was confirmed (Woolcock 2001; Portes and Sensenbrenner 1993).

Although microcredit groups and RoSCAs are different in important organizational and financial aspects, they are similar in their reliance on social collateral.[2] They are also similar in their reliance on individual household resources as a means of gaining access to the market. It is difficult to see why one system should be viewed as intrinsically repressive while the other is not. Close observational study of microcredit groups allows us to understand aspects of its impact that a solely financially focused analysis blocks out of our field of vision. Seeing how and why microcredit groups undertake collective action and sanctioning provides a new understanding.

---

[2] See note on these differences in Chapter 1.

Analysis of the interviews points to structural features of microcredit groups that contribute to the necessary alteration of the *"habitus"* of poor rural women that permits the achievement of this collective capacity. Group participation itself, with its resulting improvement in collective women's agency overall, is one factor that enables individual women to articulate their demands and voice their opposition. How this gain occurs has already been explained in the previous chapter.

Another feature that plays a crucial role in fostering the capacity for agency-enhancing cooperation is the regular face-to-face economic transactions that promote frequent social interactions among women belonging to a microcredit group. This process builds trust and intimacy among group members. It deepens the ties among group members who may have previously shared kinship and neighborly ties. And it also creates confidence and mutual concern among group members who were not previously related or known to each other.

Finally, the presence of numerous microcredit groups in a village means that women are embedded in a sizeable network and linked to each other within a web of what Mark Granovetter has termed "weak ties." This provides women the structural base required for collective mobilization and also reshapes the costs and benefits of sanctioning in a way favorable to women. These underlying processes combine to promote women's capacity for cooperation leading to the realization of shared, mutually beneficial, and often socially altruistic goals.

COLLECTIVE ACTION AND SANCTIONING

Eighteen out of fifty-nine microcredit groups (approximately thirty percent of sample) undertook collective action and joint sanctioning. This is a significant percentage given the constraints of patriarchy and poverty inhibiting women's agency. Collective action and sanctioning are defined as group-based when any subset of a microcredit group's members joined together to undertake an action proposed by one or more of them, or whenever members joined forces to act under the group leader's initiative. Included in this definition were actions in which members from a number of different microcredit groups joined forces. What stands out is that women drew legitimacy for their actions from their group membership and used that legitimacy to empower themselves, individually and collectively, to launch these interventions.

The group-based actions can be divided roughly according to the character of their intended effects at different levels within their communities.

TABLE 5.1: *Types of Collective Action*

Internal	External	Community-wide
• Domestic violence & conflicts (5)	• Domestic violence & conflicts (4)	• Anti-liquor campaign (3)
• Annulling under-age marriage (1)	• Attempted polygamy by men (3)	• Anti-gambling campaign (1)
• Men having extra-marital affairs (1)	• Men having extra-marital affairs (1)	• Acquiring public goods (4)
		• Organizing community events (2)

[Note: The numbers in parentheses show the numbers of actions reported.]

The actions can be differentiated into *internal interventions*, actions that involve and impact only group members and their households, *external interventions* that involve and impact some non-group member households, and *community-wide interventions* that affect the entire community (Table 5.1). It is noteworthy that most of the collective actions were targeted at non-member households and that some of them had large community-wide impact.

All of these collective mobilizations were successful in achieving their intended goals. Only in two instances, both involving the same group, did the mobilizations fail to produce the desired outcome. This was due to a variety of causes. Descriptions of the most significant incidents of collective action and collective sanctioning organized by microcredit groups follow in the next section of this chapter.

Mobilizing against domestic violence and conflict

Domestic violence against women is a common feature in some villages. Before microcredit groups, female neighbors often played the role of sympathetic but silent spectators. This situation has changed remarkably as will become evident. Several incidents reveal how women intervened to mediate in conjugal conflicts and to stop domestic violence regardless of whether the victims were affiliated with a microcredit group. Women from one microcredit group often intervened to protect a woman who belonged to another.

In the following incident a microcredit group mediated a domestic conflict between a husband and wife who lived in a different village. The wife was not affiliated with any microcredit group. Following an argument, the wife had left her household and, without informing her husband, had returned to her parents' house in another village. A few days later, the husband came in search of her. The two burst into a heated argument. The dispute was overheard by the microcredit group who had gathered together for their monthly meeting. Hearing the frenzied voices from a distance, the group leader rushed to the scene and asked the man about the problem. The leader recalls how he initially reacted at being questioned by a group of women, and how she held her ground with the group's support:

At first, he spoke to me with a hot temper. Then I told him, husbands and wives have problems, but, after some time, they unite. We're outsiders; later when the two of you unite you won't even remember that I tried to calm things down. Then he said, "Who're you?" I said, I'm a person, and I'm telling you what I think is best. But he showed no signs of cooling down or accepting what we were saying. He insisted that he wouldn't take her back. I said to him, "I promise you'll carry her back on your shoulders! You've got to take her back." Then someone from the side said, "These women are from the group." Then he said, "Look, this is what has happened, and I won't take her back." I said, look at it this way, you beat her and she came away without telling you; you've done something wrong and she's done something wrong. Now two people have to live together to make a family, so the two need to cooperate. In this way, after explaining to him, he took her back with him.

Readers may question the wisdom of encouraging and enabling the reunion of this couple and the return of the wife to her marital household from which she had temporarily escaped in response to suffering violence from her husband. The reality is that in many cases, women do not desire to leave their marital household permanently because of the social stigma and the economic hardship such a course entails. The husband, too, perhaps did not desire to abandon this wife despite his threat to do so, given that he had come in search of her.

For all these reasons, the microcredit group considered their intervention a major success. The group had been formed only two years ago, unlike many other surrounding groups that had been in existence for four years or more. That the women had acquired a strong, authoritative voice through the group in such a short period is noteworthy. It is equally important to recognize that the group leader who led them was an unmarried woman (twenty-one years old) in a cultural context in which unmarried women command even less importance than married women.[3]

---

[3] In the social context of this study, being unmarried is usually an indicator of family poverty, that is, the family is so poor they cannot muster the resources required for organizing a

In a more serious case, a number of microcredit groups intervened twice to save the life of a woman who was a member of one of the microcredit groups in this study. The woman, a victim of chronic physical abuse by her husband, was driven to attempt suicide by hanging herself. Her attempt was thwarted as family members broke into the room and saved her. In the process of being rescued, she sustained a severe head injury and was later diagnosed with a cerebral tumor and advised to undergo immediate surgery. Her husband, a poor rickshaw-puller, could not pay for the procedure. When news of this problem reached the adjoining microcredit groups, the group leaders decided to mobilize their members to collect donations for the surgery. Each group from the adjoining neighborhoods contributed Rs 100. The money that was collected was added to contributions from the woman's parents, and this was used to pay for the surgery.

After this initial intervention, the group members retreated until they intervened again following a rather unexpected turn of events. One night the woman's neighbors rushed to their group leader and reported seeing a shaman (*ojha*) perform sorcery in that house. Immediately, the leader gathered some group members and headed for the woman's house. There they interrogated the woman's husband and found out that she had been unconscious for the past seven days. The husband had not only concealed this fact from everyone, but, instead of taking her to the hospital, had hired a shaman (*ojha*) to cure her maladies. By dawn, her condition had worsened. Chanchala, the group leader who had led the action, recalls her reaction on seeing the woman's lifeless form, parts of her face singed from the burning incense used by the shaman in his exorcism rituals:

I shuddered when I saw her! I wanted to give her husband a good thrashing. But if we got started with that, then she would die laying there ... We came straight to Sister [NGO founder-director] and reported everything. She advised us to go to the hospital first. Eleven of us got together and took her to the hospital. We didn't have one man with us, and none of us had any money either. The hospital staff saw her and immediately transferred her to the town hospital. We collected Rs 100 from each of the groups again and ended up raising Rs 1100. Then we went to the nearby army [Border Security Force] camp and requested a ride to the town hospital ... Instead, they gave us Rs 500. We took the money and hired a taxi. First we took her to the hospital, and then we went to the police station [to file a report against the husband] ...

wedding and/or for paying the dowry needed to get a groom. In the case of this woman, her parents were poor and old and did not have a son. So, she was responsible for supporting them, and, for that, she had started working as an immunization agent of the primary health clinic.

The woman stayed in the hospital for fifteen days and accumulated a huge medical bill. For those two weeks, a few women from the adjoining groups went to the local school daily and canvassed students for donations. They contributed these daily collections toward her medical expenses. As she failed to recover, the doctors ordered her transfer to the city hospital. Having exhausted all their resources, the women approached the organization leader for contributions. Meanwhile, back in the village, group members resumed their efforts to raise money for her treatment. After two more weeks, the woman recovered and returned to her house, and the groups' effort in saving this woman was widely recognized throughout the area.

All the groups that initiated action against domestic violence were successful in stopping violence in the targeted households and in rescuing victims. Police complaints and other legal actions undertaken by groups against the perpetrators on behalf of the victims were less successful, however. In one dramatic example, group members rescued a woman from domestic violence and lodged a formal report (FIR) in the local police station in an effort to sanction her husband:

There was a family that lived in this neighborhood. The husband would beat his wife quite often. But we didn't know anything about it because their house was at some distance from here, and she was a member of a different (microcredit) group, and no one had told us about it. Then one night the man's brother came rushing to me and said, "He'll beat her to death; even I can't stop him. Please do something about it. Try to stop him." Once I heard about it, I gathered all the members of my group and some other groups here, and all of us marched to their house. We went and saw that he had beaten her to pulp. She was in such a state that she couldn't even breathe properly, and no one else in the house could approach her. Then four or five of us marched into the room and pulled her out. He didn't try to stop us. We put her on a rickshaw and took her to the hospital. We called the police station to report the incident. When we were returning from the hospital, we saw the police jeep enter the neighborhood. The police came and took away one of the brothers-in-law and his son; they were supporting this man who beat his wife. But, by then, the man had fled. Then we arrived and brought her back to her house. After that he never beat her again, and now they're united. (Tandra)

The disciplinary action initiated by the women did not reach its desired culmination. When the police came a second time to apprehend the husband, his wife begged them to pardon him. Group members admitted that they were disappointed at the way in which the victim thwarted the disciplinary action that was intended to protect her. They had hoped that such a penalty would be a lesson, deterring other husbands from beating their wives.

In another case, a group leader followed through with legal actions against an abusive husband of a group member at great personal cost. Other group members had refused to be drawn into the intervention. Asura Bibi (a Muslim woman), during her tenure as the group leader, single-handedly carried out two significant third-party sanctions, one of which was against a chronic wife-beater. In this case, the accused man, a Muslim, aligned with the lower-caste (Hindu) men in the village who were already pitted against this group leader for leading an anti-liquor campaign in the village.[4] With support from the NGO leader, Asura was steadfast in her support of the victimized woman. She filed a case against the husband and stood witness against him in the local court. At home, she faced her own husband's wrath for involving herself in this matter and, although middle-aged, suffered his beatings and abuses:

I told her (NGO leader) that I'm even ready to give up my life (fighting for this case), but I won't step back if you support me. I returned with her promise, and I stood my ground. No one in the village would stand witness against him (the abusive husband), only I did, and I filed a case against him ... The case went on for two years and, in the end, there was a court order against him. Either he had to take his wife back (and stop his abusive behavior), or else, face prison term. So he took his wife back and now she's going to have a child.

This resolution saved the wife from being abandoned, but it did not put Asura, the group leader, in favor with the victim or her family. Asura's actions had earned her the reputation of a troublemaker among the men of the village. So the victim's husband instructed his wife to shun the group leader's company lest she come under her influence.

In several cases, group members intervened when fellow members of the group were subjected to abuse by their husbands. Rokeya'a husband (see the previous chapter) was quick tempered and frequently flew into a rage. After previous incidents of conflict had escalated into violence, the group leader used her authority and intervened:

We (group members) come and tell them, don't do this. There is no way you can do this, we sit in your house (for the meetings), and we won't allow you to create such a nuisance ... While we're here you can't do anything. Whatever you do (the arguments), do afterwards, not in front of us. (Ekadashi)

In the most recent incident, Rokeya's husband had started arguing with her when she corrected him and showed him the proper way of refurbishing the walls of their thatched hut with clay. He got so angry

---

[4] This will be described in a later section of this chapter.

at being challenged and corrected that he went into a frenzied tirade against her. He was ready to throw her out of the house. Hearing the loud argument, her fellow group members rushed to her residence to protect her:

O he was like Ravana in battle, what a scene it was! Even they know about it; he simply wouldn't keep me at home anymore. He started such a torment. Then all the women from my group came, and even they couldn't work up their courage to interrupt, thinking, god knows what sin she has committed. He was raving and ranting. Then, finally, he left to winnow the paddy, and then they asked me, what did you do? So I told them that he was stacking the hay for the wall, and he wasn't doing it correctly, so I broke it and said I would do it. They said, "Really, he was acting like that and abused you with such insults just for this!" I said well, "If I have *ghee* (clarified butter) in my fate, what can I do but eat it off my plate!" [translated idiom] I have to tolerate this. The group members sympathized with me and said, really, what kind of a person is he, he doesn't understand. I got some peace of mind from being a part of the group. I shared some of my feelings with them and released some of my sorrows; I felt a little lighter.

The group members' presence at the scene prevented her husband's fury from escalating into violence. His departure resulted from the group's presence. Rokeya sums up the change:

Earlier our husbands used to torture us a lot. My husband is very ill-tempered. In the past, I've laid down my back to receive beatings from him, and I've tolerated his insults. But after forming this group, we've [group members] tried to make him understand, and now those bouts have reduced a lot. And now we've learned to protest. So, at times, I protest. This is the main thing I have to say; this is the story of my life!

Microcredit groups that are the most active and attentive to their members' welfare do not allow even minor incidents of violence against their members to pass without notice. In one group, a member who was in a grim economic condition fell behind on her loan repayment. This led to a dispute with her husband that ended with her receiving a beating from him. When this came out in the group meeting, the leader summoned her husband to appear at the next group meeting. There, in the presence of everyone, she reproached him for beating his wife, and he apologized for his actions. In another group, the leader, along with some group members, intervened in the household problems of a member whose husband was well known for his short temper. Although he was much older than most of the group's women, they confronted him and pointed out his bad judgment and ill-considered and false accusations against his wife. Before the formation of microcredit groups, younger women confronting an older man about his conduct within the walls of his private domain simply would have been inconceivable.

All of these actions – sanctioning of husbands of immediate fellow group members, intervening on behalf of women who do not belong to the same microcredit group, and intervening on behalf of women who do not belong to any microcredit group at all – are very significant. It is profoundly awkward socially for women in the same microcredit group to sanction the husband of a fellow group member. Group members often feel close to these men. Disciplining an outsider-man may be less awkward socially but risks subjecting the women to greater opposition and resistance and makes interventions more difficult to execute.

All these actions represent significant gains for women. In fact, microcredit groups have now become an informal source of support to which women can turn in times of personal crisis. Such an institutional source of material, emotional, and moral support did not exist for most women before their enrollment in these groups.

Mobilizing against men's sexual transgressions

Microcredit groups have intervened to help secure the economic and social security of married women when these vital interests have been threatened by husbands' extramarital affairs. Groups have also intervened to defend the rights of unmarried women in cases where men have engaged in sexual relations but have shunned marriage. In such cases, microcredit groups have acted as moral vigilantes, reinforcing the ethical boundaries placed around men's sexual behavior and enforcing the social responsibilities associated with sexual relations.

These interventions provide a window into how these women view the relationships among sexual intimacy, marriage, and economic responsibility. They also reveal how these women define violations of sexual propriety and justice in marital affairs and their practical assessment of what kind of collective action best protects and promotes women's welfare. That these notions may be quite different from contemporary liberal and feminist activist projects concerning women's welfare that have gained ground in urban societies in many parts of the world should not surprise us. Whatever these women's "emic," or localized, contextual understanding of what effective collective action should be in any particular instance, the capacity of these economically and socially disadvantaged rural women to cooperate effectively in defense of women like themselves represents a remarkable change.

Anima, a young Hindu woman, has been a member of a group for the past four years. A few months before the group was formed, she discovered that her husband was having an affair with a local woman who was also married. Anima was infuriated by her discovery. The security of her marriage was shattered. Yet there was nothing she could do about it. She lived in an extended family household with her father- and mother-in-law, her husband's older brothers and their wives. None of them was willing to reprimand her husband for his promiscuous behavior or counsel him to reform. Because she was the youngest member in the age-based hierarchy of the extended household, she was afraid to voice her complaint. Sometimes she would erupt with anger, and this would lead to heated arguments with her husband. Often this would end in violence toward her.

Anima suffered alone. There was no one to whom she could turn. At the same time, a microcredit group was forming in her neighborhood and she, her sisters-in-law, and the woman who was her husband's mistress all ended up joining the same group. Unable to tolerate the domestic turmoil any longer, Anima, as a member of this microcredit group, decided to voice her allegation during a group meeting:

I had to let the group know about this. I would catch him with her here and there, and I would let everyone in the group know about it. That other woman was also in the group, and she didn't dare to say anything. When I brought up the whole thing in front of the group, then the others supported me. They said to her, "She isn't accusing you for nothing if you can't say you really haven't done anything!" My sisters-in-law explained to her that you have children and your daughter is married now. You have to keep your dignity, so you have to stop doing this. She couldn't get the support of the group and after a lot of pressure from the group she straightened out. Slowly both of them were cured. If ever my husband goes out of line again, I can let the group know about it.

Anima reported the incident despite objections from her sisters-in-law who thought it was embarrassing for the family for this to become known. Anima argued vehemently that this role of the group ought to be highlighted in this study because this particular intervention of her group has been far more important than credit in improving her household's well-being. With surprising candor she defended the public divulging of this intimate detail of her conjugal life so as to accurately reveal the extraordinary benefit she has received from being part of this group:

[B]ut if we don't talk about this then how can this side of the group be known ... If my family breaks apart while I'm a member of this group, will the others in the group want that to happen! Then everyone from the group created pressure and the problem gradually straightened out. So joining the group has benefited me. In this

way I've improved the condition of my household ... Now he's completely transformed and the only thought in his mind is of raising his children well.

What is most telling about this incident is the changed capacity for agency
it reveals in an identical cast of characters with and without the presence of
microcredit as a field of social action. Prior to enrolling in the group, her
sisters-in-law seemed indifferent to her problems. Now, as microcredit
group members, they were able to pressure a transgressing woman to
end her illicit affair. What they could not do as relatives living in the
household of their brother-in-law, they could and did achieve as fellow
microcredit group members.

Women from another microcredit group in a different village disciplined a pair of brothers for making clandestine plans for a second marriage. The women discovered that the young men, only eighteen and
nineteen, were already married but had brought home two young girls
aged fourteen and fifteen. It was rumored that both were planning a second
wedding. The collective response of the village was decisive. The people of
the village, mostly men, cornered the boys in a room and beat them up.
Meanwhile microcredit group members confronted the girls for what they
thought of as their loose conduct. Male collective wrath was focused on the
boys and the women called the girls to task. One woman gathered courage
and, with the support of the microcredit group members, slapped the girls
for their misconduct:

Why did they have to follow the boys, just because the boys asked them to? Today
these girls followed these boys. But if tomorrow my son calls them, then they'll follow
after him. So I mustered my courage, and I went forward and gave them a beating.
I had the courage because I'm in the group. That's why I was able to do it.

This cooperative collective action of sanctioning the girls for allowing
themselves to be seduced should not be interpreted solely as being a
conservative measure. Rather, it should also be understood as effective
collective action against men who compromise women's welfare in these
village societies (in this case by possibly luring the minor girls into sexual
relations with the hope of marriage and abandoning them soon after).

Another incident, this time involving premarital sex, dramatically rein-
forces this point. A woman who belonged to a different microcredit group
in another part of the village reported to her fellow group members that her
unwed teenaged daughter was pregnant and only a month away from
giving birth. The mother alleged that the culprit was a young boy from
the village. In a society in which unmarried sexual relations are taboo, this
allegation threatened the honor of both families.

Soon the leader of the microcredit group to which this woman belonged contacted the leaders of the microcredit groups in the part of the village where the boy's family lived. The boy's family, it turned out, was a well-established extended family, and his sister-in-law was a member of the microcredit group in that neighborhood. On a specified day, the girl was brought to the boy's house, and nearly one hundred women from the neighboring microcredit groups gathered at his doorstep. The women tried to convince the family to recognize the girl as their son's bride and accept her into their household.

But the boy denied his responsibility, and the family refused to surrender to the women's demand. Following this stalemate, the women temporarily withdrew from their action. After a few weeks the girl gave birth, and on the very next day, the group's supervisor arrived at the boy's home with the new mother and child. For a second time, all the women gathered at the family's doorstep. They persistently asked that the family acknowledge their responsibility and demanded that they legitimize the relationship by giving the mother and child a place in their household.

But the male heads of the extended family protected the boy from public pressure and refused to let him appear before the gathered women. The acrimonious exchange between the family and the groups' women continued. The women pressed their demand unrelentingly and promised to withdraw only if the boy publicly denied that he was the father of the newborn.

Finally, the family was forced to allow their son to appear in public. On encountering the sight of the girl and the newborn, he broke down and quickly admitted his responsibility. Soon after, the women adorned the young girl with vermillion and shell bangles, the ritual symbols of Hindu marriage, and forced her entry into the household. The couple has since been married and now lives in the same household. Ever since this incident, the groups in this locality have become frontline institutions for solving domestic disputes. Even political leaders and the police refrain from intervening unless approached by these groups.

A second example of forcing a woman's entry into a household is also revealing. Although geographically far apart, these two groups came up with the same strategy in protecting the reputation and future of women whose social standing had been compromised by men's sexual transgressions against them. This microcredit group came to the support of, and socially rescued, a newly married stranger to their village who did not belong to any microcredit group at all.

One afternoon members of a microcredit group gathered together for their fortnightly meeting, but were interrupted by a loud nearby argument. When group members arrived at the site of the dispute, they found one of their local men, a married man with a family, being accosted by an outsider woman who claimed to be his second wife. From the aggrieved woman's account, it appeared that the man had traveled to her village and married her but had abandoned her soon after and returned home to his first wife.

The outsider woman demanded a place in his household, but he rejected her outright. On hearing this allegation, the group members supported this woman and demanded that the man accept her into his household. They argued that, in marrying her and consummating the relationship, he had defiled her, and now it was his duty to accept her into his family. The group leader narrates the incident:

> We decided that he shouldn't get away with this; when he's married her, he's got to take on her responsibility and provide for her. All of us went to him and we told him so. Still he insisted that he wouldn't accept her into his family ... At this, all of us grew agitated ... You will do such fallen deeds and you think the people of this village will simply tolerate it! (Arati)

Although he protested vehemently, he eventually surrendered under the collective pressure exerted by the group.

The matter did not end there, however. After reluctantly accepting the second wife into his home, the husband and his first wife frequently subjected her to physical violence. Once again, the group came to her rescue by going to the police and convincing them to intervene. After the police gave the man a warning, the violence ended. The group members reported that the second woman proceeded to have a child who was now being brought up by the man and his first wife. The woman went to the city to work as a maid.

Although this resolution was not a particularly happy one for the woman, yet the group had done what it could to establish her status as a married person and to protect her from violence. The women themselves recognized that the group's real success in this case was the importance of the symbolic victory they won by forcing the man to accept responsibility for his action:

> We forced him [the accused man] to accept her because he didn't want to. We wanted to teach everyone the lesson that men can't just go around destroying women's lives. And, in the future, no man from this village should dare to repeat this. When we did this, the message went to our own husbands that if they do something like this, then all of us will act together, and we won't spare anyone. (Bharati)

The women intended this action to deter men from having sexual relations outside of marriage and prevent the practice of married men taking another wife, and then eventually abandoning one of the wives. In a more general way, these women's actions were intended to send men the message that their sexual and conjugal misconduct would no longer be without consequences. If men mistreated women or injured their welfare, the price of doing so would be paid.

The agency these women exercised in these matters, it should be said, was not explicitly justified by any appeal to modern activist ideals of feminist liberation. In fact, these actions may appear to some to be conservatively oriented acts of vigilantism. In rural societies such as those in West Bengal, the fact is that a woman's economic security is linked to the fate of her marriage. Normative judgments made by these women are biased toward the preservation of marriage and family even when they also challenge acceptance of men's customary violence against their wives. Women tend to favor reforming men's conduct within these institutions rather than to urge withdrawal from them, given the constraints by which they know full well that women's lives are circumscribed. Nevertheless, their outright protest against the ill treatment of women and their demand for reform even though they do not call for the abandonment of marriage or the family should be seen as representing profound change.

Women understand and appreciate the power to discipline men that the collective agency derived from the group gives them. It is often the subject of joking references and humorously inflected threats. In one group, a middle-aged Hindu member narrated this exchange between a man and his wife to an accompaniment of mirth from her listeners:

After being involved in this group we've gained so much strength that we can even threaten men! I was walking down the street yesterday, and I saw this with my own eyes. There's a woman in this neighborhood who is set on becoming a "vaishnav" of "Nabadwip," so she has stopped touching fish and meat.[5] She's about forty-five or fifty years old. Her husband was a construction worker in Dubai (who has recently returned home for good). Now if she doesn't cook him meat and fish, what is he going to eat? This created a lot of tensions in their household, and he declared that he would marry again. Then she raised her voice and started yelling, "O, you'll marry again! I'm still a member of the (microcredit) group. I'll bring women from

---

[5] "Nabadwip" is a village in the district of Nadia (this group is located in another village of the same district), which is the birthplace of an ancient Hindu ascetic by the name of "Gauranga" who was a worshipper of Lord Vishnu, or Krishna. Hence all followers of this tradition are called "vaishnavs." They practice vegetarianism and other austerities in their daily living.

the group and skin you alive if you marry again." So think of the strength we've gained by joining the group. We can even discipline our husbands because we have money, four hundred and seventy rupees![6] (Shibani)

The power to threaten husbands with reprisals comes not from the paltry savings accumulated over four years or from women's access to loans. Rather, it comes from women's access to an expanded network of women who are now bound to each other with a strong new tie of intimacy and mutual interest. This is captured by Shibani's likening of their microcredit group to a "*harishabhar dawl*," a devotional group in which members are bound by strong affective ties and reach ecstasy by congregating together and singing in unison.

Mobilizing against under-age marriage

In one village, microcredit groups intervened in a case of underage marriage (a conventional social practice in rural India) and forcibly annulled the marriage. One family had colluded with another to surreptitiously marry a fourteen-year-old girl to the other family's son, violating the law that states that girls must be at least eighteen before marrying. It so happened that the girl's mother belonged to a group, even though these groups formally advocate against the practice of underage marriage.

After a time, the local microcredit groups discovered that the clandestine wedding had taken place. A chosen delegation of group leaders and group members, including members of other microcredit groups in the village, paid both families unannounced visits. They could not find the young people who had been secretly sent away to avoid public attention.

The leaders of the delegation threatened to inform the police if the families failed to bring back the young couple within the next few days. When these threats seemed to fail, they cajoled and bribed the families by promising to arrange a proper wedding. Eventually, the young couple was brought back to the village. The group leaders requested a meeting with the families during which they promised to resolve all differences and solemnize the marriage.

A meeting was held to which the families brought political party members for support. The party members suggested that the marriage be socially recognized as it had been ritually solemnized. But the group leaders rejected the suggestion. To them, the solution was simple: the

---

[6] This is the accumulated savings of each member of the group at the rate of Rs 10 every month for four years.

marriage had to be annulled. Any other manner of resolving it would set a bad precedent, they said.

When none of the proposed solutions proved agreeable to the women, one of the group leaders, helped by other members, dragged the girl away from where she was sitting. She was dressed in the attire of a married woman and adorned with all the ritual symbols. They smashed her shell bangles and washed away the vermillion mark on her brow, ridding her of all ritual adornments. Tandra, one of the group leaders involved in this action, declares proudly that the young woman now plays volleyball with the girl's team in the local athletic club, and no one talks of her marriage any more.

This case is important in demonstrating the altruism and action on behalf of the general interest implicit in some of these forms of collective action. This intervention will lead to increased compliance, at a minimum by microcredit group members themselves, with the legally approved age when arranging and contracting the marriage of sons and daughters.

Organizing against local liquor trade

Two microcredit groups in separate districts used two completely different strategies to wage successful anti-liquor campaigns. In one of these villages, alcohol consumption was heaviest among the lower caste "Basak" community, its most populous group. This led to widespread destitution and domestic violence. Women from this community, all members belonging to several different microcredit groups, self-organized under the leadership of Asura, the Muslim group leader profiled earlier in this study.

As a first step, Asura and a handful of members approached the six lower caste families engaged in producing and selling unlicensed "country-liquor" and warned them to close their business. The families, none of whose women belonged to microcredit groups, disregarded the women's warnings and threatened them with retaliation if there was any disruption of their business. Only one elderly woman, a group leader whose son ran a country-liquor business, was able to persuade him to take up another livelihood.

The organized women went to the police and sought legal intervention. The police turned a deaf ear and refused to get involved. Then Asura, disillusioned and angered by the apathy of the authorities, mobilized all the microcredit groups in the village. On a prearranged day about 150 group members marched to the police station and demonstrated, berating the policemen for their passivity. Asura recalls:

We told them [policemen] that they could take off their uniforms, leave their rifles, and vacate their posts. It was our police station, and we could run it better than them. Then they folded their palms and said, "Mothers and sisters please calm down; we'll cooperate with you."

The police intervened and the families were forced to give up their liquor trade. After the success and publicity stemming from the initial intervention had died down, one family tried secretly to resume their business. One day, a group member spotted from a distance a van-driver carting in a barrel of country-liquor. She immediately alerted her fellow members. This group, numbering very few women, seized the barrels. The driver who was carting in the barrel fled the scene. As word spread, women from microcredit groups in the surrounding area started pouring out of their homes. Almost two hundred women eventually congregated at the scene. Bonolata, one of those in the frontlines of the action, describes how they mobilized other microcredit group members to join them:

One person called the other, and that person called another, and in this way two hundred of us got together in a matter of minutes. Many husbands tried to stop their wives from coming, but, despite that, the women came. Some women even fought with their husbands to come and join us. Some husbands beat their wives to stop them from coming.

Once the illicit stock had been seized, a few of the women sought approval by telephone from the NGO leader to carry out their plan to destroy the liquor. Having received it, they proceeded to pour out the liquor and burn the barrels.

This bold action resulted in general threats against the women by the family whose stock had been destroyed and a lawsuit against the individuals leading the action. These conflicts notwithstanding, this action was remarkably successful and benefitted the community as a whole. Since then, their village has been free of liquor shops. The lack of easy availability has reduced alcohol consumption and its associated vices. It should be noted however that microcredit group members did not receive any credit from the villagers for their action. Instead they were targeted with harsh criticism and dragged into embittered disputes and divisive litigation.

In another village, the problem was somewhat different. A family had started conducting an unlicensed country liquor business from their house and it attracted customers from outside the village. These male outsiders roamed the village streets, openly consuming liquor, giving offense, and accosting women. The women of the village felt threatened and feared that these men were subjecting their children to bad influences. At the fortnightly group meetings the women started discussing this problem, and together they made the decision to address it.

The women started by delivering an initial warning to the family and asking them to take their business outside the village. Their warning was ignored. The women got together and raided the family's house. They failed however to find any stock that they could seize. The group members then devised the creative strategy of patrolling the streets to warn off the liquor establishment's clientele. The women agreed that every night by half past eight they would finish all their household chores and by nine o'clock they would step out onto the streets. They would gather at a central meeting place with bamboo batons and spread out through the village streets patrolling them and keeping the intruders at bay. They patrolled the streets for days until the customers were intimidated enough not to enter the precincts of the village. Bharati, a middle-aged Hindu woman, who participated in this action, describes the strategy in detail:

One team would start from that side and patrol the streets for a while. When it was time for them to return, we would come out. And when it was time for us to return, they would come out again ... We used to carry bamboo batons, ready to act if we encountered anything untoward ... There were fifteen of us in each of the two teams. On some nights, both teams stepped out simultaneously, and, suddenly, we would meet at an intersection. Then there'd be thirty of us. Passengers in the busses and cars passing by the main road would be stunned by the sight of so many women on the streets. One day a young man stopped his taxi and asked "Sister, does your husband drink [liquor]?" I said, "Why my husband alone? All men who drink will be taught a lesson." He fled with his taxi ... If it wasn't for the group, we would've never had the courage to do this, and for our whole lives we would've remained like weeds [uncultivated]! But now, at least, we've improved a bit. When our daughters-in-law step in our place they'll improve even further.

The business was eventually forced to shut down for lack of customers. This group's successful collective action won accolades from everyone in the village. The symbolic message sent by the baton-wielding women was a strong and lasting one. This was the same microcredit group that had forced the philandering man to recognize his illegally married second wife and to accept her into his household.

Gambling also afflicts these villages. In one village a microcredit group unintentionally stumbled on a gambling problem while trying to solve a dispute between two warring families. Once it came to their attention, they solved both problems simultaneously by threatening to cast out of the village the family that ran a gambling and liquor establishment.

The group got involved in this problem in a circuitous way. One day, a drunken man slipped and fell in front of a neighbor's house and started shouting expletives at family members. The men of the family rushed out and a fight broke out. A few of the microcredit group's women intervened and separated the disputing parties. A few days later, the family submitted a written complaint to the microcredit group leaders stating that, since the incident, the man had made it a daily practice to pass the house in a drunken state and shout out taunts. The family threatened to take matters into their own hands if the microcredit groups did not intervene.

At first the women approached the accused man and asked him to refrain from his lewd offensiveness. The man ignored the warning and continued his objectionable behavior. One night shortly thereafter, approximately thirty-five women from various microcredit groups gathered at the man's house and confronted him for his actions. When he refused to admit his fault, the women threatened to drag him out by his collar and thrash him.

Eventually, he capitulated and promised to give up his addiction to alcohol and to reform himself. Not content with this, the women resolved that it was not sufficient to correct one fault alone. They decided it was necessary to shut down the gambling establishment where liquor consumption was rampant. One of the leaders explains:

In the house right next to his was the gambling establishment where all the drinking took place. We thought of doing something about it because it wasn't enough to right only one wrong. We went and told the lady of the house to close down the establishment. And we threatened that if they didn't stop within a week, then we'd return and burn down the room where the gambling and drinking took place ... It's for the improvement of society.

The women faced down threats from the family and from some members of the political party who were connected with the family. They refused to be cowed or intimidated. Instead they retaliated using a clever symbolic maneuver.

The leaders of all the microcredit groups in the village met once a month to discuss the affairs of their groups and the village. This "cluster meeting" was held in one of the organization's buildings at the edge of the village in the middle of a compound. The women decided to move the meeting to the heart of the village. To maximize public visibility they chose an open space in which the entire neighborhood could see them assembled. After some time, the family moved their establishment away from that village. The women believe that their successful show of strength and confidence allowed them to prevail.

Organizing for public good

Some microcredit groups have used their collective social strength to demand essential public goods by attending *gram sabha* or village forum meetings together and speaking with one voice. These goods include crucial infrastructure such as safe drinking water, electricity, and roads previously lacking in their villages. Village forums are responsible for applying and disbursing government allocated development funds to plan and undertake construction of local public works. They have sometimes shown willingness to accede to the demands put forward by the women speaking collectively with the authority, and on behalf of, the membership of their microcredit groups.

Occasionally microcredit groups have mobilized themselves to address a specific infrastructure problem whose solution provided no particular benefit to them aside from their general membership in the community. For example, in one village the only road that led into the village from the metaled main road was a narrow strip of clay road that traversed across a pond. This unpaved path had fallen into neglect, and parts of it had collapsed. Bicycle riders and vehicles carrying people had tumbled into the roadside pond as a result. Neither political leaders nor members of the village council (*panchayat*) had done anything to remedy the situation.

The women of a recently formed microcredit group took it upon themselves to get the road repaired. Uma, the group leader, describes how they offered a solution through collective action and how all the villagers joined their efforts enthusiastically:

We [group members] called the men of the village to one of our meetings and said, "Look, the road is falling apart. Is there a way for all of us to get together and repair it?" The men said, "Yes, why not?" Then the men and women joined hands, and we pooled our own money and rebuilt the road with our own hands. Our children dug and brought clay, and with that we rebuilt the road. Some people contributed bamboo and jute sacks; others contributed their labor.

The successful completion of this project inspired the group and gave them confidence. They started attending the village council meetings in their locality. There they raised demands to solicit funds for a house-building grant for a destitute group member and for much-needed public goods such as sanitation facilities, power lines, and a hand-operated groundwater pump for safe drinking water. Except for the last that had been promised previously, the village council supported and then fulfilled all of these demands.

Organizing community events

The microcredit group members who rebuilt their village path had felt bolstered by their success. When the community next found itself facing a crossroads, they again went into action. Every year the community organized two religious festivals to worship the Hindu goddesses "Kali" and "Shitala." The ceremonies had evolved into an important community ritual and took place each year within what had become consecrated space within the neighborhood. Traditionally, such festivals were always organized and overseen by men.

Years ago, the festivals used to be organized on a small scale by consecrating brass pots instead of idols, and the ceremony used to take place in the afternoon. This had all changed when, a few years ago, some enthusiastic men and boys had turned the ceremonies into large-scale events, using life-size idols and holding the festivities in the evenings. But they had not been able to maintain this grander scale for long and had turned back to the small-scale version. In 2002 the men finally declared that the increasing burden of work would force them to discontinue holding the ceremonies altogether unless others could be found who were willing to step in and take charge.

In the past, the women of the community had assisted the men in conducting the ceremonies, but they had never been involved in organizational matters. When the men announced their decision to give the events up, no one volunteered to take over the responsibility. The annual festival was on the verge of being discontinued.

Finally the members of the microcredit group decided to step in and assume the arduous task of organizing the festivals. Krishna explains, "We discussed this in our group. Would the worship really come to an end because none of the men were prepared to carry on the responsibilities?! Then some of us suggested that we should take on the responsibility of organizing it ourselves." Since then, the women have been doing all the work.[7] "We collect money ourselves; we do the marketing ourselves. We hire the priest and the tent-makers and we rent the loudspeakers. We do all of these things and organize the ceremony ourselves," Uma, the group's leader, says beaming with pride.

Another group member, Kamala, enthusiastically describes how they have outdone the men by reinstituting the larger scale version of the ceremonies:

---

[7] At the time of the fieldwork for this study, women had been conducting the ceremonies for two years.

The men would conduct the ceremony during the day by consecrating a brass pot (instead of an idol), but we resolved to make it a big event with a proper idol and a full religious ceremony in the evening ... That night when the lights went on and the sound of drums spread, everyone became curious. They were saying, "What's happening there? O, that ceremony for which they were collecting funds! Well, that's nice! It's not like before when everything would be over by the afternoon."

Women who were not a part of the group were encouraged to participate, making it a neighborhood-wide event led entirely by women. Taking over the ceremonies from the men was not entirely without obstacles. Though they enjoyed the support of some sections of the community, they had to overcome opposition from others, particularly from older men who were quick to ridicule their attempt. Nevertheless, the success of the ceremonies forced the critics to change their minds:

A few had said, "Well, well, now the women's group is collecting contributions for the ceremony! The wives of our houses have come out on the streets to collect contributions! What ceremony will they organize?!" But after we held the ceremony, they realized and said, "Well, the women stepped in and saved the ceremony from being stopped!" (Krishna)

Providing financial help

Microcredit groups have changed the practice and culture of seeking and providing financial help in these villages. Before microcredit, persons seeking financial help, whether for medical or any other purpose, would go from door to door asking for contributions. Villagers who had the means made small financial contributions. Some contributed rice and other agricultural products when members from poor families came asking for financial help for organizing weddings and funerals. As microcredit groups in different villages spontaneously started to mobilize to help each other in times of need, these groups became a new focal point for seeking financial help throughout the community. For group members, the group provides a source of readily available money through the accumulated group savings. This can be given out as interest-free loans to members to tide families over during emergencies.

Most of the financial help provided by groups has been for medical crises. In one group, when a member suddenly fell ill while her husband, a migrant laborer, was away, the members worked through the night to get her transported and admitted to the local hospital. When the local hospital proved unable to give her the care she needed, the group members contacted their group leader and asked for a sum of money for transporting the sick member to the city hospital. This required at least a thousand rupees, not a trivial sum of money.

After consulting the other members, the group leader decided to offer this money as a temporary loan. With this timely financial help, the patient was transported to the city hospital in the care of group members. The capacity of the village women to navigate the hospital bureaucracy by themselves was impressive and testifies to the women's increased agency over a short period of time as a result of their participation in their microcredit group. The woman recovered, and her family paid back the money.

Another member from the same group suddenly took ill and was ordered to undergo surgery. Her husband and mother-in-law approached the group leader and requested the group's help. Once again, the leader of the group took control of the situation. She describes how she went from house to house in the waterlogged village to consult with the group's members:

That time was the peak of monsoon and for a whole month it had rained constantly, and we were practically stuck in our houses. So we had the money from two weeks of collections. Her husband and mother-in-law came to us and told us that she would not survive unless we gave them two to three thousand rupees right away ... I waded through the waist-deep water and went to each of the members' houses and told them about the situation, asking them what was to be done. Everyone said that if money would save her life, then we should give it to her. We gave her Rs3000 and, that too, without a receipt. We had faith that we'd be able to recover the money. (Uma)

The group leader and cashier had to pay from their respective personal households' money reserves to meet the group's monthly deposit and repayment obligations. In the end, the woman recovered, and her family repaid the entire sum.

The women of a microcredit group, all of whom were Muslim, helped their most destitute member, an agricultural daily wage laborer, on two separate occasions. On one occasion, they found her on the verge of being turned out of her home and loaned her Rs 3000 from the group savings to buy up her residential plot of land and home from her estranged husband. Some time later, they again loaned her Rs 1000 from the group fund to pay for the hospital fees for her daughter who had been hospitalized after trying to commit suicide.

In yet another group, the women gave one of their members Rs 500 from the group fund when her daughter had a stillbirth and needed medical attention. These are just a few examples selected at random from a multitude of incidents illustrating the variety of ways in which microcredit groups provide financial assistance. Group members have complete discretion over lending the money in their savings fund and, as in all of the above cases, they consensually decide to allow the needy members to borrow the money interest-free and without a hard and fast timeline for repayment.

Overall, microcredit represents a massive shift in women's ability to provide an infrastructure of informal support for each other. One former group leader remarked directly on the difference between before and after microcredit:

> Before if someone came and asked me for some money, then I wouldn't be able to give any. From where would I get money? But now if someone asks me for money, then I can tell "Bikashda" (the group's supervisor) that a member in the group has a problem, and we need money for that. Then we can withdraw money from the group fund and help the person. We haven't had any incidents like that yet by the grace of god. But if a person did face any trouble, then I think now all of us would come forward to help. But this wouldn't have happened before ... (Saraswati)

The practice and culture of seeking financial assistance in these rural communities has changed accordingly. The locus of trust has shifted. Before microcredit groups existed, financial assistance was an individual matter and depended on individual generosity. Now microcredit groups have become an institutionalized collective framework and socially formalized, participative forum for seeking assistance. If petitioners have not received the approval of the "cluster" (the association of group leaders from fifteen to twenty microcredit groups in adjacent neighborhoods) villagers question the legitimacy of their need and are hesitant to offer assistance.

One group leader, Jayanti, had been part of three cluster-wide efforts to collect money for purchasing copper utensils (a plate and glass and a water pitcher) for three of their village girls whose parents were too poor to afford these traditional wedding gifts. The parents had approached the microcredit cluster for help. The group leaders had readily agreed to lend their assistance, and members of all the groups in that cluster had been asked to donate Rs 10 each.[8] Jayanti contrasts the character and quality of social trust in the available ways of seeking assistance before and after the formation of microcredit groups:

---

[8] I do not consider this assistance as subsidization of the marriage dowry. Instead, I see it as equivalent to the wedding chest and other similar social customs present in many cultures through which the social group helps to provision a new couple's household. In this instance, the donations through the microcredit groups allowed women to coordinate their individual gifts in a way that helped these indigent families preserve their dignity.

They [poor families] would go from door to door asking for help, and we would give two rupees or five at most. This is the way in which people would ask for assistance for their daughter's weddings or for their parents' funeral. Generally, when people ask for money for weddings and funerals, all of us give something, at least . . . But now we don't easily trust anyone who comes asking for money for weddings or funerals because now people have learnt the trick. Yet, we feel sorry when we see people in such a state begging for money, and we contribute two or five rupees. But if someone approaches us through the group, then we contribute ten rupees per head.

EXPLAINING THE CAPACITY FOR COLLECTIVE ACTION

Before we can proceed to understand how women enrolled in microcredit groups acquired the capacity to organize these actions, we must refute and counteract a commonsense notion. We tend to assume that the supposedly overlapping relationships these women share – such as being neighbors or sharing kinship and family ties – contribute to collective agency. But if that were indeed the case, we would expect that similar collectively initiated and executed actions by women would have taken place even prior to the existence of microcredit groups. This is not the case, however.

The women interviewed in this study were virtually unanimous in declaring that before they joined the group no cooperative endeavor for organizing women's collective action, for sanctioning or any other purpose, had taken place. Women who were victims of domestic violence in the past complained that, when their husbands beat them, their neighbors and relatives remained silent spectators. Some even accused intimate bystanders of deriving voyeuristic pleasure from their suffering.

Archana, a pampered daughter from a well-to-do family, laments the passive acquiescence of her neighbors and her hostile in-laws to the harsh and repeated violence to which she was subjected in the early years of her marriage. Her husband once attacked her viciously when he discovered that she had sold off her silver anklet to buy formula for their infant daughter. The formula had previously been paid for by Archana's parents because her husband had refused to do so:

He plucked out a bamboo pole from the fence and beat me over and over again. All the neighbors watched but never uttered a word. They silently enjoyed watching me being beaten (because her parental family was better-off); even my mother-in-law sat there watching.

Neighbors who were sympathetic lacked the power to intervene. This was true in the case of Krishna Ray who recalled her experiences from fifteen years previously when she was repeatedly beaten by her husband, threat-ened with expulsion by her in-laws, and forced to bring more dowry money.

Fifteen years previously, when her son was only a year old, Krishna Ray had been thrown out of the joint household along with her husband and child. Her husband's uncle, a father-in-law by relation, demanded that she bring Rs 300 more from her parents. Only if she brought the money would he allow her back into the ancestral house and to set up a separate room for the family.

During that night her mother-in-law came to where Krishna and her family were sleeping and stole her sleeping child from her. While she lay asleep, her husband too, snuck back to his parent's household. Krishna found herself alone. When she returned, she was severely beaten and ordered to leave unless she brought the money. Her husband stood pas-sively by, a mute spectator, as she was humiliated and expelled from the family. The neighbors watched her plight from a distance and tried to console her after the ordeal:

While I was being beaten the neighbors saw that I was being beaten without any fault of mine. They used to ask him (her husband) why he beat me so without any reason ... When I used to faint from the beatings, then our next door neighbor would come and tend to me with water ... They would console me and say, "Where else will you go? You've got to adjust." No one protested.

Krishna considers how differently things would have gone if their group had existed at the time of her severest trouble. At a minimum, she would have had others with whom to share her travails. Her group might even have disciplined her husband for mistreating her.

Now I have the courage, and I know that I have a place for refuge. I can come and tell the others about my situation and get their suggestions. Now, perhaps, they would've given my husband a talking to. I don't know if they would give him a beating. But, if he went too far, then the women might have given him a few blows. Now women have that capacity! The groups in that neighborhood (across the street) have practically stopped the liquor business.

Some women tried to explain why they were mute bystanders before and never took it upon themselves to intervene. Aparna, a member from a different group who had participated in a collective sanction against domestic violence, admits to having shared in this spectator role and attempts to explain it:

At that time we couldn't come forward. We used to think that if we went forward and intervened then we'd be embroiled in it. So we would stand at a distance and watch, instead of going up to them and stopping them or saying something. We wouldn't be able to do that. If a woman was being beaten by her husband, we'd wait till the husband left the scene, and, only after that, we'd go up to her and help. But now we protest outright. It's illegal for a husband to beat his wife. If she has done something wrong then explain it to her and make her understand. Why beat her!

Preexisting social ties did not mean that women shared feelings of solidarity and empathy or were possessed with the authority or voice to protest against abuse. By themselves, preexisting ties do not foster women's mutual commitment or encourage broader social commitments. Nor do they provide a concrete social network that women can access in times of personal crisis.

As these women tell it, before the formation of the group, the family was the only locus of social and economic interest. Both men and women tended to remain apathetic to happenings elsewhere in the community until the peace of their own home was disturbed. Women in microcredit groups have their own understanding of what has led to a change in this attitude of passive indifference to the sufferings of members of other households. Hearing a pair of group members speak, Lakshmi'di, a local woman who now serves as the group-supervisor, comments:

LAKSHMI'DI: At that time, no one cared to know what was happening in other households. If there was a quarrel between two persons, then they would quarrel. If someone was beating someone else, then let her get beaten. That was the attitude.

ARCHANA: These last two and a half years (since her group membership), I've not been beaten. Now that women are forming groups, they (husbands) know that if they do something like that, then the women will inform the *mahila samity* (women's group). That is why things are much better now.

LAKSHMI'DI: Yes things have subsided a lot. The women here are much better off now, and there is less mutual jealousy.

Other women, too, emphasized the microcredit group as an institution that allows women a forum to voice their concerns and to organize collectively. Saleya Bibi's comment reveals that the group's capacity for collective action and sanctioning had entered the calculus of village men and other stakeholders:

Nowadays the husbands say, "If we say something to our wives then they'll run to the police station and file a case against us. And if we beat them, then they may go to their parents' house, but we still have to work hard and pay them alimony (*khorposh*)." That is why they don't say anything these days ... Now the husbands don't beat their wives anymore because if the woman reports it to one group, then many groups will gather in one place, and they'll demand an explanation. They'll judge whose fault it was, and then they'll pass their judgment ... Also, nowadays, women go out on processions. We have a (microcredit SHG) convention and, for that, hundreds of cars are hired to bring in women from different parts. There are thousands and thousands of women, and men see that happening. And from that they know the strength we now have, so they cannot say much.

The structural and operational features of microcredit enable and promote, to a remarkable degree, the social capacity of women to develop increased individual and collective agency. Social-collateral based models of microcredit rely on the dual pillars of group-based networks and systematic interaction among women enrolled in the group. These features facilitate a set of changes at both the micro and macro levels of social interaction.

At the micro relational level, requiring women enrolled in microcredit groups to conduct economic transactions at regular intervals creates and deepens the ties among them. Systematic communication for shared purposes promotes pro-social behavior. Economic goals (access to loans and opportunity to save) provide a strong justification for women's continued participation in these groups even in the face of family objections on other grounds.

Non-economic purposes may be used as the basis on which to form groups and facilitate frequent interactions. Yet it is impossible to imagine a purpose other than financial interest that would elicit such widespread and sustained membership from poor rural women. Even when enrolling in groups that promise financial benefits, a significant number of women had to overcome household objections. Some women, fearing their husband's opposition, joined these groups secretly and concealed their membership for months. All this attests to the high barriers in place against women's participation in organized and regular activities in the public sphere that is otherwise saturated with the traditional privilege of men.

Added to this is the burden of women's reproductive roles and occupation with piece-rate work. These constraints leave women little time to use at their discretion. Achieving women's large-scale group membership and participation without the motive of a financial incentive is a practical impossibility. Credit does not create the change, but the continuing financial dimensions of its promise are crucial for facilitating women's participation in these groups.

By facilitating frequent interactions, the economic tie transforms the quality of relationship among women belonging to a microcredit group. Continuing economic relations inculcate trust, intimacy, and mutual concern among women belonging to the same group. Prior to joining these groups, women often lacked these feelings even though they resided within close physical proximity. The reaction of Krishna, who belongs to the group that rebuilt the path, organized the community festivals, and helped group members in times of medical crisis, summarizes this transformation:

I've been married for the last twenty-four years. For the first fifteen years, we couldn't step outside the four walls of the house. After that we used to come out a bit. And gradually, in the last three years [since the group was formed], the way we've gotten to know each other, a kind of intimacy has developed among the twenty of us. It's as if we were relatives. Before this we didn't share the same feeling.

On the same point, Ekadashi, a group leader from a different microcredit group, explains how a strong sense of mutual identification fostered by these frequent face-to-face interactions at group meetings now motivates group members to help each other. Domestic conflicts and violence had been a persistent problem faced by Rokeya, who is a member of her group. I asked her what they used to do before. She responded that prior to being part of microcredit groups, women lacked the will and collective authority to intervene. They did not have steady access to news about private matters and domestic conflicts beyond their own. Women were simply not willing to share their problems with each other given this lack of solidarity:

No, we didn't have that before. Back then we never used to get together in one place. But now from the way in which everyone gets together in one place, the mentality has also become one. Mine is yours and yours is mine, that's how we ask about each other. If something happens to one person everyone gets to know about it; something has happened to her, come let's go and see what's the matter. But it wasn't like this before. Back then your affair was your affair.

Ekadashi adds with a note of humor that this has resulted in more burdensome responsibilities compared to earlier times when women did not feel morally responsible for sharing or alleviating each other's troubles.

These days, I say that I was better off when I hadn't joined this group! Joining the group has created a hassle. What hassle, you might ask. If someone falls into trouble, then I can't stay without saying anything nowadays. If there's trouble in their (Rokeya's) family, then I go to their family and say, why will you do this? This isn't right! But, before, I couldn't say this. Now I have more courage. She'll suffer from her own problems! Let the two of us go and say why should he do that? Whose fault is it anyway? I try to mediate and solve the problem.

Another woman, Shefali Mondol, from a different microcredit group in a different district used the analogy of the family to talk about the group, emphasizing the feeling of mutual concern that has now grown between group members:

The way that people helped each other before is different from now. Now, just like you have love and affection in the household, this too is like a household, a "*sansar*." We are getting together when we are called, we can see each other, we didn't have this before. Now we are bound with the tie of affection. So this is like a "*sansar*" now. That is why, if anyone is in a crisis, now we run, first thinking that so and so in our group is in a crisis, come let us all go together. I might call Juthika, she might call someone else, and in this way we can get united and jump into the situation.

Several women mentioned the development of this sense of solidarity.

Frequent face-to-face interactions facilitate discussion on common problems and strategies to redress them. Bharati, a participant in the group that conducted the anti-liquor night patrol and forced acceptance of a second wife, emphasizes this aspect of increased agency. She singles out the microcredit group's role in providing women an institutionalized space for deliberating among themselves to foster their joint welfare:

[Without the group] none of the women would've gained the courage to come out of their homes to do this [anti-liquor campaign]. They would think, let it be the way it is, why should we get involved in it. Who cares what problem is brewing outside as long as everything in my house is fine! Why bother about what's happening outside. Everyone used to think in this way. But now all of us in the group have the opportunity of sitting down together and discussing matters. So together we took the resolution that, no, we cannot allow this to continue in our village.

The group-based lending strategy brings together a substantial number of women regularly and also creates a structure of leadership by designating three women in each group to act as leaders. This creation of a non-kinship-based association expands women's social networks. Aparna, a group member, provides an example of the remarkable difference the microcredit group makes in terms of the size and scope of women's social networks and its impact on their ability to organize:

Before I didn't know anyone; we never used to go to each other's houses. But now, through the group, I can get to know many more people ... I like it that now the twenty of us can get together in one place and discuss different things. If we didn't have this group, then we'd have to spend this time at home ... but here we get to hear about various things, and we get to listen to each other. Through this group, I can get to know people. If we have any problems in the group, then all of us get together and solve it. We repaired the village road. Now all twenty of us go and collect donations from the neighborhood [for the community festival]; before we weren't able to do this. Also, now we attend the village council meetings.

Being part of a group-based network endows women with legitimacy. It lowers their own inhibitions and the reluctance or hostility of their family members in letting them intervene in spheres beyond the household. Saraswati, a group member, pointed out that, before, many husbands would stop their wives from individually intervening in conflicts or problems outside the household. That prohibition has stopped, Saraswati says, because of microcredit groups:

> But this wouldn't have happened before, because back then we didn't know each other well enough. Now the way in which we know people, all of us will jump in to help. But before this the thing was like, if you're in trouble do whatever you can to deal with it. Back then our husbands wouldn't allow us to go out. But now they know that the women are going together and the woman in trouble is also one of our own women. So the husbands won't stop us from going anymore. Before if we wanted to intervene, then they'd stop us and say, why do *you* have to go? Why do *you* have to get involved? But now the husbands know that we've formed a group, and if other women are going ahead then I, too, will join them.

The presence of multiple groups in adjacent neighborhoods connected through a leadership structure means there can be a dramatic expansion in the numbers mobilized when launching large-scale actions. The nesting of these groups into village-based clusters, via microcredit's SHG-based model, further facilitates the ability to organize across neighborhood lines. The social norms literature (Horne 2001, 2004) points out that network size has a significant effect on the propensity for undertaking collective action and on their successful accomplishment by influencing the costs and benefits of sanctioning.

The large networked structure of these groups has two positive effects. It reduces the cost of sanctioning to individual women, and it makes women willing to bear the cost of sanctioning such as facing the risk of being embroiled with the police and with political parties. In addition, the groups gain positive reputation and public recognition of their moral authority and collective power when their interventions are successful. Women deeply value their enhanced reputation and authority. This contributes to a sense of collective effectiveness that inspires these women to undertake further collective actions completely unrelated to microcredit's financial goals.

The importance of reputation to these women is captured in numerous accounts of the public reaction to their group-led interventions. Basanti's gleeful narration of the public reaction following a series of successful collective actions (road repair and organizing festivals) spells this out:

> Now when we go to the market, if we say something, then people make comments like, "Twenty women are together; nowadays you can't even talk to them. If you say anything out of line to one of them, then the twenty will arrive, and they won't let you off easily. We're scared of them!" Now the men are afraid of us. Whenever

we go to the market, they say, "Make way, make way, the women's association is coming," and people make way for us! [Laughs] When I went shopping during the festival season, they were saying, "The association is coming; it's the women's association after all. They have a lot of power; they'll defeat us men!"

From the same group, Kamala reports further on this change in attitude:

When we went to collect donations an elderly gentleman said, "O look at the women's group, now they've come out on the streets to collect donations!" It didn't seem right to him that the women's group should jump into everything. I said to him, "Why not? If I'm happy doing it why shouldn't I be involved! I must go and I will go!" It doesn't matter if it doesn't seem correct to someone. We wouldn't take a step back just because someone chose to pass a comment or lewd remark about us. I told him, say as much as you want to, but we won't let anything affect us. We have a women's group and we won't let the group disintegrate because of what you say. Now he says, "O, the women's group! They have a lot of power!" Now he smiles and talks with me.

A member of the group that forced the wedding of the unwed teen-mother commented on the public reaction in their village:

They [men] said that now we have tremendous capacity. Earlier they'd neglect us, but now they love us. And they're afraid of us too! Now if we see a boy and a girl sitting here and chatting late into the night, we can slap them and call others and discipline them. Word about us has spread everywhere, and there's no one who hasn't heard of what we've done! And it isn't that this has happened only with our group; there was a case in Medinipur [another district] involving another group, and they showed it on television.

Tulsi describes how decision-making power has shifted from local political leaders to these groups, particularly in matters of household disputes:

Now even the police are afraid to approach us! There's a well-known man [the head of the provincial council] here, and even he, when he hears that we're involved in a case, says, "When the group is involved, they'll come to a solution on their own."

Such positive renown is valuable to these women because they function in a social context where women, particularly young women, have been traditionally deprived of social recognition in the household and in the community. For them to receive public, community-wide recognition for their authority and their arbitration and sanctioning capacity takes on tremendous symbolic importance.

Microcredit programs foster women's social capital – trust, network resources, and capacity for collective action – through a complex set of changes centered initially on disciplined techniques of group lending that include structuring women into a network of groups and requiring them to gather for mandatory meetings. No amount of monetization of everyday life through women's incorporation into the world of financial calculation would have facilitated the development of women's social capacity had it not been structured through peer groups and face-to-face interactions. But neither sustained membership in these groups nor compliance with the groups' onerous requirement of participating in fortnightly meetings would have been possible without the financial incentive of receiving loans conveniently and less expensively. This combination of the right incentive and the proper institutional structure has had the consequence of improving women's collective agency and promoting women's capacity for cooperating for collective action and sanctioning, quite unintended to microcredit's original aim.

6

Culture and microcredit: why socio-religious dimensions matter

Microcredit programs are proliferating around the world and operate within an extraordinarily diverse array of cultural and social environments. In South Asian societies particularly community culture appears to have a pronounced influence upon women's participation in microcredit groups. Community culture also influences the collective social behavior of these groups, that is, how they respond to social problems in their immediate surroundings. Factors that constitute and shape community culture in the rural societies of Bengal are many. They include: norms, customs, and social conventions; folk understanding of religious prohibitions and "traditional" prescriptions regarding the conduct of women and wives; and formal legal provisions on matters of civil law that assign rights and obligations to men and women differentially within the institution of marriage. Other shaping factors include the distribution of power within communities mediated by religious institutions such as shariah-based informal arbitrating committees, mullahs and imams, male elders, political leaders, teachers, and other educated and experienced community members. Also included is the extent to which traditional community leaders can wield power to secure or change existing social norms and conventions. Economic and human development issues including poverty, literacy, and education also profoundly shape the life of rural communities. Finally, demographics, in particular whether a community is the numerically dominant one or is the minority in the local context has an important impact on the collective life of rural communities.

All of these factors combine to shape everyday life or the quotidian culture that is a product of the intersectional reality of women's lives (intersecting gender and communal identities). How microcredit groups conduct themselves is very much affected by the culture of everyday life in the particular communities of which they are an increasingly important part. But how the culture of everyday life actually shapes the operation and effectiveness of microcredit groups has not been well studied. How microcredit and the culture of everyday life come together to influence such outcomes as women's agency and women's collective capacity needs scholarly attention. This need is strikingly borne out by an entirely unexpected pattern that emerges from this study's close analysis of the socioreligious composition of microcredit groups in rural Bengal.

Showing how culture influences the social outcomes of microcredit should not lessen my general argument that microcredit, through its associational mechanism, increases women's agency independently of local cultural context and variation. We should never lose sight of the fact that a microcredit program represents a complex and dynamic process whose effects are multi-faceted and sometimes contradictory. I would also emphasize that the very fact of women's membership in these groups, even if it produces minimal participation or little real exercise of female leadership, nevertheless constitutes significant social change in the rural landscape and represents a major social and cultural shift in embryonic form.

Within this broader understanding, we can now study the variation of influence microcredit's associational mechanism can have in different cultural and social contexts. Cultural and social context can amplify the way the associational mechanism within microcredit groups profoundly improves women's agency, and it can also severely circumscribe its beneficial effects.

In some cases, local cultural and social context can prevent microcredit's associational mechanism from improving women's capabilities entirely. In fact, in this study, 42 percent of the women enrolled in microcredit groups appeared not to have been able to enhance their capabilities even after two to four years of membership in microcredit groups.[1] Surprisingly, this category included not only women who claimed not to have experienced any economic improvement in their household (15%), but it also included women who claimed that their household's economic situation had been improved from access to microcredit loans (27%). This fact that financial improvement from loans accessed by the household does not necessarily translate to improvement in women's capabilities is puzzling at first. But it is not puzzling once we consider the sociological factors

---

[1] When considering the total sample of four hundred women interviewed for this study, this is 30 percent.

that prevent loans or group membership from translating into leverage for women.

The effectiveness of the associational mechanism varies greatly from one group to another. There can also be within-group differences as to the benefit members derive from the group's associational mechanism. In some groups, only an inner leadership circle experiences the benefits of enhanced agency.[2] This is largely because of their greater involvement in the activities of the group. They run the meetings, maintain the financial accounts, and participate in a wider network of microcredit training sessions and other events.

In other groups, the gains in agency are diffused throughout the entire group and seem to surpass the sum of individual capabilities. In these groups, collective capacity far exceeds members' assessments of their individual capacities. It is these groups that are the most active in organizing collective actions and that impose sanctions against those whose actions compromise women's welfare. One-third of the groups studied had attained this state of collective agency and group solidarity. But the remaining two-thirds of the groups had not attained this level of collective capacity. This variability in the associational mechanism's impact presents something of a paradox. Through the practice of finance, microcredit injects an autonomous dynamic of social change into whatever context it is introduced while at the same time its ability to affect the agency of women depends greatly upon local socio-cultural conditions.

Another unanticipated finding of this study was that the socio-religious composition of microcredit groups did affect the quality of the group's associational mechanism. In general, microcredit groups composed of Hindu members had a more robust associational mechanism, and were more likely to develop group solidarity and collective capacity, compared to microcredit groups composed of Muslim members. In microcredit groups composed entirely of Muslim women, the study found, the associational mechanism seemed to be compromised because of unfavorable reactions from members' households or from community elders and leaders.

Muslim women, compared to their Hindu counterparts, generally-speaking, faced more stringent prohibitions and stricter patriarchal control. Their interviews contained more personal accounts of rigid and less malleable masculinities than did the interviews of Hindu microcredit

---

[2] Selection into leadership positions is guided by women's literacy levels, because of their need to do basic bookkeeping. Literacy should not be equated with agency. Women who were selected for leadership positions within the group were not necessarily more advanced than other women in their capabilities. Hence, their agency improvements should not be measured by their levels of literacy.

members. Yet, even in the face of opposition, Muslim women formed microcredit groups, and their husbands did make use of microcredit loans even when they forthrightly opposed, or only reluctantly permitted, their wives to participate in these groups. This had a subduing impact on Muslim women's style of group participation.

It was also unanticipated by this study to find that the overwhelming majority of the microcredit groups were either entirely Hindu or Muslim in their composition. This compositional feature can be largely ascribed to the neighborhood-based manner of forming microcredit groups (although one cannot rule out some degree of self-selection based on socio-religious composition). This means that most Hindu women were enrolled in micro-credit groups along with other Hindu women, and these groups were located in Hindu village neighborhoods. Similarly, most Muslim women were in microcredit groups along with other Muslim women, and these groups were located in Muslim neighborhoods.

The individual-level impact of microcredit groups on women's agency and the group-level styles of leadership and members' collective participation must be understood not only as a result of private household and conjugal dynamics then, but also as a result of the norms operating in the different environments of the respective communities. These environments can be discerned from private and public responses ranging from grudging tolerance and tacit approval to subtle censure or aggressive opposition to women's enrollment and participation in microcredit groups.

These differences at the micro group-level cumulatively created larger differences than were at first immediately discernible. The most significant large-scale difference emerged in the distribution of collective action and imposition of sanctions across the fifty-nine microcredit groups. The distribution was unexpectedly skewed once the groups were classified by their socio-religious composition. Microcredit groups composed of Hindu members had the highest rate of collective action, whereas groups with entirely Muslim members did not conduct even a single collective action. Heterogeneous groups that had both Hindu and Muslim women fell in between these two extremes, but their experience of undertaking collective action was very different from that of the microcredit groups composed entirely of Hindu members. Out of the thirty-four microcredit groups composed entirely of Hindu women, fifteen groups undertook collective action and imposed sanctions on men. Some of these groups undertook a single intervention, sometimes collaboratively with other groups, while others undertook multiple interventions. Of the seventeen microcredit groups composed entirely of Muslim women, only one reported a single intervention. This involved the group leader single-handedly imposing a sanction against the in-laws of a woman complaining of ill treatment. This act of sanctioning, albeit bolstered by the group leader's affiliation to the microcredit group, was not a collective action since no other group member joined in the effort.

Finally, out of the eight microcredit groups that had both Hindu and Muslim members, two had been involved in collective action and disciplining men. In one of these groups (*Duti Pata*), the Hindu group leader and some Hindu group members saved a Muslim group member (Rokeya, featured in Chapter 4) from potential violence in a situation of domestic conflict and subtly imposed a sanction on her quick-tempered husband. In the other group (*Baishakhi*), the Muslim group leader, along with Hindu group members, undertook more than one collective action targeted at improving public welfare. She also single-handedly intervened in more than one incident to protect the rights and interests of beleaguered women in her village without the assistance of other group members. Surprisingly, only one collective action (an intense and widespread anti-liquor campaign) was successful. The others got mired in conflict, resulting in the loss of essential public goods such as a public pathway and a tube-well for drawing ground water.

Table 6.1 lists the groups by socio-religious composition and underlines the ones that organized collective actions and imposed sanctions.

To explore the difference of socio-cultural impact on the dynamics within all-Hindu and all-Muslim groups, this chapter will now undertake a closer look at two microcredit groups. So far, we have based our analysis on evidence from the lives of women from all the different microcredit groups. In this section we focus instead on all of the women of two microcredit groups, one entirely Hindu and the other entirely Muslim. This comparison will allow us to illuminate some socio-religious dimensions of microcredit's ability to affect women's agency.

"GROUP STYLES" IN MICROCREDIT

Microcredit groups within a particular microfinance program operate in the same regulatory environment and under identical participation requirements. Yet in reality, there is often a good deal of inconsistency in how closely the different groups follow these requirements.

To understand the differences in the associational styles of Hindu and Muslim microcredit groups, it is useful to employ a pair of concepts that

TABLE 6.1: *Selected Characteristics of Microcredit Groups*

Exclusively Hindu members			Exclusively Muslim members			Mixed Composition		
Group Name	Group Age	Leader Educ.*	Group Name	Group Age	Leader Educ.	Group Name	Group Age	Leader Educ.
Nandita	3.5	0	Nabashakhi	12	0	Tajmahal	4.5	4
Shantima	4	0	Shuhashini	12	0	Ujjaini	7.5	4
Shabitri	5	0	Bipasha	4.5	4	Ashirbad	6	5
Suryamukhi	4.5	4	Nazrul	4	4	Iti	10	5
Shyamama	4	4	Diamond	4	5	Shaheli	7	5
Deepshikha	3	5	Shanti	4	5	Baishakhi	7	5
Sharada	5.5	5	Janakalyan	4	5	Duti Pata	4.5	7
Bonophool	5.5	5	Shalpagram	7	6	Matri	4	8
Mangaldeep	3.5	6	Probhati	2	7			
Pubali	4	6	Shatarupa	4	7			
Shathi	6	7	Ananya	3	8			
MaSharada	7	7	ShonarTori	4	8			
GramSang.	4	8	Janakalyan	4.5	10			
Unnayan	4	8	Shatadal	4	10			
Sanjog	7	8	Nari Mukti	2	10			
Sanhati	3.5	8	Agni Bina	4	10			
Shantimata	4	8	Adhunik	3.5	12			
Barnali	3.5	9						
Beautiful	4	9						
Agni	3.5	9						
Shanchayita	4	9						
Banani	3.5	9						

Sabuj	4	10
Durgapur T	2	10
Rajlakshmi	4	10
Ujjal	4	10
Kamala	5.5	10
Shatadal	4	10
Durgapur G	5	12
Udayan	3.5	12
Radharani	4	12
Debdashi	2	12
Rita	4	12 + 3
Shadhana	3	12 + 3

[Notes: *The group leader's education level is listed in terms of the local grade or class system. For instance, 1 denotes the first year in school at a stipulated ideal age of six and 12 denotes the final year of school completion at an ideal age of eighteen. And 12 + 3 denotes the completion of school and attendance of three-year college.]

are derived from a cultural-interactionist perspective inspired by Erving Goffman and proposed by scholars who study volunteer and community service groups. From this perspective it is helpful to view microcredit and its associated groups as a "scene," that is, as a "strip of action" in which actors have a shared understanding of what is taking place, or "what is going on here" (Lichterman 2012, p. 20). We focus attention on the "group styles" (Lichterman 2012; Eliasoph and Lichterman 2003), that is, on the ongoing pattern of interaction to discover group members' mutually shared assumptions and agreement about what constitutes good or adequate participation in a scene (Lichterman 2012, p. 21).

It has been noted that "scenes" where "participants have been interacting long enough to have routine assumptions about how to coordinate action" (Lichterman 2012, p. 21) appear to give rise to "group styles." In microcredit groups, the shared perception of what actually takes place, or may potentially take place, varies from group to group. It tends to vary between an expansive notion (that lending and savings are associated with collective action such as improving village public goods or imposing sanctions against abusive husbands to protect women) versus a restrictive notion (that lending and saving are self-contained activities and do not extend out into the wider community).

The interactional and participatory dynamics within microcredit groups appear to be influenced by these notions that reflect members' general understanding of what the microcredit group is and can be about. This affects members' implicit practical agreement regarding whether and to what extent they may deviate from the group's mandated financial functions. Culture and context play very important roles in defining what constitutes good or adequate participation and assigning the norms that limit or expand the horizon of what it is feasible for women to do or to imagine empowering themselves and each other to do.

The difference in ideas of good and adequate participation was most apparent in the bi-weekly group meetings. These meetings took place in the neighborhood close to group members' residences and ranged from brief perfunctory gatherings marked by instrumental discussions about loans and repayments and hastily concluded financial transactions to lengthy, involved discussions about group members' household situations and community affairs. In some cases, women spoke of the microcredit group as being an essential part of their lives. They spoke of looking forward with anticipation to group meetings as an opportunity for congregating with their peers. They expressed enthusiasm about participating in microcredit-related events and spoke with great effervescence about the new intimacy and camaraderie that was developing among group members.

In other microcredit groups, women were dismissive about the group's associational aspect and limited their participation to the routine economic activities of taking loans and depositing repayments and savings. They were neglectful about attending group meetings and viewed regular participation in these as an unavoidable inconvenience, a transaction cost they had to incur in order to access microcredit loans. In these cases, the enrolled women did not share deep affective ties with the microcredit group and derived no social gains from their membership in it. Some microcredit groups merely preserved their economic existence and carried out routine financial operations. Other microcredit groups went beyond their narrowly economic mandate to become involved in the community's social life. These tended to evolve to become institutions that served as new sources and centers of legitimacy.

The two groups, *Banani* and *Ananya*, illustrate very well this sharp difference in "group styles." Both groups had existed for three years and belonged under the same NGO-operated microcredit program. In *Banani* a large proportion of the members had gained significant agency, and the group had organized collective actions. In the other group, *Ananya*, except for the leader, the members appeared not to have registered any improvements in their basic capabilities.

As shown in Table 6.2, the women who belonged to the two groups were quite similar in their economic, household, and education profiles.

The only significant difference between these two groups was the religion of group members. In *Banani*, barring one, all the members were Hindu. Originally all the members were Hindu. Later, a few members withdrew from the group, and the leader tried to recruit other women to keep the group at its maximum membership. It was during this period that a very poor Muslim woman joined the group. In fact, however, it was the woman's eighteen-year-old unmarried daughter who attended group meetings. Effectively *Banani* was an all-Hindu group. In *Ananya* all twelve members were Muslim. Both groups reflected the demographic composition of the neighborhoods in which they were situated.

Banani – leadership and group-style

The leader of *Banani* is Uma, a woman in her mid-thirties with nine years of schooling and mother of three teenagers. Throughout the conduct of this study, she exuded enthusiasm in talking about the group. She was

TABLE 6.2: *Comparison of the Two Groups*

Group	Household Type	Monthly Income (Rs): No. of members	Women's Work	Husband's Work	Loans (Rs): No. of members	Educ. (yrs. in school)
BANANI (Hindu) 20 members	Nuclear (1 daughter-in-law in joint HH)	>=3000 +: 3 2500–2000: 7 <2000: 3	Rakhi³-making Bidi-binding Cattle rearing Tailoring	Subsistence agriculture Vegetable/fruit vending Grocery store Bicycle shop Roadside snack vendor Seasonal work in brick kiln	18,000: 1 16,000: 2 10,000–12,000: 4 2000–9000: 6	Leader: 9Y 6 Members: 5–7Y 13 Members: Nil
ANANYA (Muslim) 12 members	Nuclear (2 daughters-in-law in joint HH)	2000–3000: 12	Cattle rearing Poultry rearing Grocery store Tailoring	Subsistence agriculture Vegetable/fruit vending Tailoring Milkman	10,000: 1 6,000: 2 5,000: 1 1500: 1 1000: 1	Leader, co-leader: 8Y 4 Members: 5–6Y 3 Members: 1Y 3 Members: Nil

3 A rakhi is a small decorative disc, traditionally made of combed silk or synthetic thread embellished with other items, which sisters tie around the wrist of their brothers on an auspicious day in the Hindu calendar.

eager to explain her initial interest in forming it. Only fourteen when she was married, she had, in her words, "always wanted to do something." So when a neighbor brought her news of these groups and urged her to come to a meeting to find out more about it, she stepped forward unhesitatingly.

She heard no objection from her husband; he ran the family's grocery store and managed the family plot's cultivation. In the days following the group's formation, Uma proved to be a dynamic leader, holding the group together through the initial months of instability. When some women discontinued their membership soon after they joined, she found other women to fill the vacated spots.

Uma easily could have continued with a smaller group, but she was determined to achieve the maximum allowed – twenty members. When the group stabilized after a few months, some members suggested that the frequency of meetings be reduced from one a week to a biweekly meeting, the stipulated minimum and the schedule chosen by most microcredit groups. Rather than follow her group members' suggestion, Uma convinced them that meeting every other week would increase their financial burden. As long as the group met weekly, she argued, members only had to deposit Rs 5 every week to meet their monthly savings target of Rs 20. (This amount was in addition to any loan repayments that they had to make.) If the group met biweekly, the women would have to deposit Rs 10 every two weeks and she convinced them that it would be much more difficult for them to squirrel away Rs 10 every fourteen days from household expenses than Rs 5 every seven days. Her persuasion proved successful. All members were convinced by this economic argument and gradually accommodated themselves to the discipline of meeting every Wednesday.

Uma reflects on how she has been transformed from being an ordinary housewife inhibited by social customs. Once she used to flee into her house at the sight of an unexpected male stranger at her doorstep and send for her husband to meet him. Now she is someone who interacts with everyone she meets and acts independently to access public institutions and navigate government offices on behalf of herself and the members of her group:

There's always a headman (*morol*) in the village and all the good people, those with all the money. Before I would think, how can I speak to them. And for matters relating to my children, I just didn't have any idea that one had to go to the BDO [Block Development Officer] and the regional office and to offices in Bashirhat. But now I can take my children there and do all the official work myself. But I didn't have this courage before. Or if I went to a hospital before, I'd be afraid. I wouldn't know how to speak to the doctors, but now I'm no longer afraid. And this is what I like best, that I've gained this courage, the courage to speak to other people.

Perhaps I make mistakes, but I believe that a person can make a mistake only once; the second time the person will not make the same mistake ... There is also the money, but what I like best is that I've learnt to speak with other people.

Uma goes so far as to exclaim, "Men are everything and women are nothing! Rather, now I feel that women can do everything, and we need men less and less around us."

This confidence likely comes from the group's experience of unexpectedly having to deal with the illness of one of their group members during her husband's absence. The group's ex-cashier, Basanti, talks about how they got together the money for the member's hospital admission on short notice, and how they accompanied her from the town hospital to the city hospital:

I was the group's cashier at the time Aparna had an asthma attack. First I took her to the nearby hospital and got her admitted; then Uma arrived ... Later the doctor called from the hospital and informed us that she needed to be taken to the big hospital in Kolkata. I had money from that week's collection. Immediately Uma and I took a decision to use that money. We decided to personally repay the shortfall for the time being. We took the money and immediately left for the city with her, and I stayed the night in the hospital.

In the three and a half years that she has been group leader, Uma has shown remarkable zeal in involving her group in social projects. It was her proposal to call the men to their group meeting and suggest repairing the village pathway. She along with other group members together came up with the plan of taking over the organization of the annual religious festivals from the men.[4]

At her encouragement, group members began to attend village council meetings. In these meetings group members voiced their demands for essential public resources such as electricity and safe drinking water. Acting as group leader, it was Uma who had summoned the husband of a member who had beaten his wife over loan repayment problems. It was under her leadership that the group gave money twice from its collections to members in medical crisis. Regular social interaction of group members under her able leadership created a strong sense of group solidarity that was reflected in their new ability to rise above inter-household conflicts. Uma explained this changed attitude:

Look, if people live side-by-side, then conflicts and tensions between households are inevitable. There are disputes related to land and other things. But after forming the (microcredit) group, we've developed a kind of intimacy ("*mon'er meel*"). I

---

[4] These two collective actions are described in detail in Chapter 5.

have problems with you, but when we're in the group, there's no problem between us. I don't think anymore that my family has disputes with her family, so why should I speak with her? This thing is not there anymore. But before, there was this kind of a thing that I won't talk to her; I won't let my children go to her house ... Before, there was a feeling that I don't have any relationship with her, but after forming this group, there's a sense of unity (*"ekata"*) and intimacy among everyone.

The solidarity that has developed allows Uma to invoke a shared commitment to the group's social and civic role that takes it well beyond its initial economic and financial functions.

After considerable success in their early public social endeavors, especially in organizing the annual festival, Uma had the idea of staging a play. It would be performed by the group at the time of the next festival. Once again all the group members welcomed the idea with excitement, and they commissioned a local writer to create a family play that they could perform. Uma showed a remarkable ability to inspire and combine within her group rigorous rule enforcement with a visionary logic of group solidarity. That combination was a central factor in producing the high degree of positive agency transformation that all the members of her microcredit group experienced.

Every Wednesday afternoon, all group members congregate in the earthen courtyard surrounding Uma's house. The meetings begin with a joint recitation of the set of resolutions. Uma recites the set of principles a few lines at a time, and the members repeat them after her. Regular repetition of principles in favor of adopting family planning and advocating against early marriage of girls has had an impact on the attitudes of some of the women. Shikha, a group member, explains how the denouncement of early marriage in the resolution made her change her mind about her daughter's marriage. Before her involvement with the group, Shikha and her husband had planned to marry away their thirteen-year-old daughter soon after she reached puberty. The couple was very poor. After attending group meetings, however, Shikha broke from her accord with her husband, and delayed the marriage. She explains her change of mind:

My eldest daughter is thirteen now, and there've been many proposals for her. But I've said I won't let her marry till she turns eighteen or twenty. If I marry her off at such a young age, then later we'll have to suffer all sorts of tensions. And in the group, too, it's said that we shouldn't marry off our children at such a young age. He [husband] said, "Now all of you are in the group, and you've learnt to think for yourselves! Who can say anything above you'll?"

Regular participation in the group has led to significant improvements in such basic freedoms and capabilities as physical mobility and everyday social interactions. Group members feel much freer to move about and to mingle with others than they did before. Women were full of effervescent enthusiasm as they described how much their social lives have improved. Husbands, forced to confront the changed behavior of their wives, have acceded to the new relations, even if unhappily.

Those particularly conservative husbands unwilling to ease up on the restrictions placed on their wives have succumbed to the urgings and promptings of Uma as group leader. Aparna, a group member, describes how Uma negotiated with her husband and explained to him the need to let Aparna participate in events outside their neighborhood. These group-affiliated movements have afforded Aparna the opportunity to increase her mobility and to gain access to places that were previously out of bounds:

Before, I didn't have the courage to go places on my own. I never used to go to the market. But now, after joining the group, I go wherever I need to ... Once the aunts tell him [husband], he listens to them. Before he would say, "You're the wife of the house, and you want to leave the house and go out on the streets!" He doesn't even listen to his parents, but now he listens to aunt and uncle [the group leader and her husband].[5]

More than half of the members in this group have volunteered more than once to participate in group events held outside their own neighborhood and village.

The active participation of these women in meetings has expanded their social network and increased the range of their social experience and competence. Group members emphasized the learning that took place just from associating with each other in their weekly meetings. Comparing life before and after the group, Parul said:

Twenty people sitting in one place means talking about different things and learning about different things ... Now we can get together as a group and go to other meetings and meet different people. And before this, I'd work all day in the house and in the field, return home, have some rice, roll out the mat, and fall asleep.

Microcredit group members now have each other to draw upon in the event of a problem. Members of *Banani* now collaborate on offering advice and coming up with solutions when one of them confronts a problem. Such close

---

[5] "Aunt," in this usage, is a form of addressing group members that are senior to the speaker. It does not indicate any kin-relationship.

and intense communication has proved cathartic for the women and has deepened social ties of mutuality and solidarity.

Such trust and intimacy produce an appreciation among members of the strength of numbers. Basanti explains, "When the twenty of us sit and discuss things, we get more courage because we get to know the troubles that all of the twenty women are facing." Deepened social ties ease and aid the diffusion of the changes that group members experience in their attitudes and that they express in their actions. Close ties aid in the mobilization of group members to accomplish a common purpose when the need arises.

Women are no longer confined within the narrow limits imposed by their family's restrictions when participating in the associational activities of the group. Their domestic obligations no longer pose obstacles to wider social and civic engagements. The day of the group meeting, traditional wifely and motherly roles are temporarily suspended. Meeting day is special and has its own rituals. Krishna, a group member, describes the change in her household:

On that day, I serve my son's lunch on a plate, cover it, and leave. I tell my father-in-law to ask my son to have his meal when he returns from school. He returns in the afternoon and eats on his own. But on other days, he won't eat like that. He'll say, "Ma, give me rice." . . . But now we don't have these problems anymore. We're free! At the beginning [of group membership], my youngest son would say, "Now you go everywhere, you and that aunt [Uma]. Don't you have anything else to do?" And I would say, "Why do you say that? Look, when we go to those places, we get to know and understand about different things; we can return and explain the same things to the other group members." Nowadays, at times he says, "Ma, you're late today; why haven't you left yet?"

The brief yet regular suspension of women's traditional duties that microcredit meetings create marks a significant change in an environment in which domestic duties are rigidly gendered. Uma and other members described similar changes in their households.

Household decision making showed variation among the women in this group. Before they joined the group, some women did not involve themselves in household decision making at all. A few gave their husbands suggestions, especially about saving money. These were usually ignored.

Things have changed since then. The most vivid examples of change appear in women's reports of their new capacity to answer back in domestic dispute with their husbands. This capacity testifies to the gains these women have made through group participation in acquiring negotiating power within their households. Aparna comments on her new reaction to domestic disputes:

I was like a village wife before. I never involved myself in taking notice of household income and expenses ... Before, people would say things like, "Women are like shoes [fit to be under men's feet]," and they never gave women any value. Now we've learnt to answer back. Nowadays if there's a tiff between us [her husband and herself], then I answer back. If he says, "I'll leave you and go," then these days I say, "If you go away, then the group will come, tie you up, and present you in front of everyone!" But before, I'd never be able to speak like this; I'd be scared.

Parul cites a similar instance of domestic negotiation:

Now even if he [husband] gets to know that I'm here [in a meeting], he won't tell me anything. "It's for my work that she's gone," that's what he'll think ... If he says anything, then I'll stop coming to the group, and I won't take any more loans [other group members laugh]! I'll tell him that I'll cancel my name from the group, and I'll see from where he can get Rs 5000 without paying Rs 250 in interest every month!

The new capacity to trade threats and engage in aggressive repartee is not simply a result of their access to loans. Rather, their increased range of social circulation and their increased agency through group participation, together with the confidence that comes from group solidarity, imbue them with the courage to speak in ways that violate conventional norms of feminine and wifely propriety.

Increased domestic power for these women included the ability to reform uncooperative husbands and to overcome many normative restrictions traditionally placed on women. Going to the market and making purchases without the knowledge of their husband is one such expression of power. Shikha notes this change and underscores the expanded freedom of action it entails:

Before, since I wasn't allowed to go to the market, I'd tell him what I needed and he'd bring what he could. Often he wouldn't get what I wanted or less of it. And sometimes he simply wouldn't bring some of the things at all. He'd say, "I don't have the money" and leave. Now I go to the market on my own and buy what I want depending on what I want to feed my children. One day he came home [saw all the groceries] and asked, "Who brought all this?" I said, "I brought it! Will I wait around all day for you? And you won't bring half the things, so does that mean my children and I won't eat? You're thinking that I must be sitting at home, but now I don't sit around anymore. I'm in the group now, and I've learnt to move around as I wish and to talk to other people." He said, "Well, all of you are in the group, but does that mean you're [group members] not going to obey us [husbands] anymore?" I said, "Of course, we'll listen to you, but we'll pay heed only to those things which can be followed, and we'll answer back for those that can't!"

Some women exercised increased domestic power by voicing the rare demand for equal division of household chores between husband and wife. Dipali, a member of *Banani*, provides a striking example of this increased agency:

Before, I'd never speak defiantly over my husband, but now sometimes I do, and he says, "Now all of you have the group; we can't deal with you anymore!" Once he said, "You better do this today," and I answered, "I can't do it; do it yourself!" He said, "Well your group has gained a lot of muscle it seems!" My point is that, whatever work it might be, why should I do it alone? Let us do it together. If I do your work, then why shouldn't you do some of mine? He said, "You weren't like this before." I said, "I'm becoming like this now [laughs]." He said, "You never used to answer back to my face!" And I said, "Well, I'm becoming like this, can't you see, and you know how our group is!" He went away laughing and said, "Well I've got to put up with it; now all of you are heavier in numbers than us!"

Just how authoritative the group has become is illustrated by the group's intervention in the household of their most senior member. The group undertook to counsel both her and her much older husband and to mediate their conflicts. Uma describes how she, along with other group members, challenged and reasoned with Kamala's husband. Note how he is forced to listen to the women:

Now dada[6] listens to us, knowing that we're united and good. If we go as a group and tell him, "Dada, what you're doing is wrong," he'll listen to us. When he creates a row in the house and scolds her [Kamala], then we go and tell him, "Look, dada, this is not didi's wrong doing, so why are you accusing her?" He listens to us. And if it is something that didi has done wrong, then we tell her that too.

Only where a vibrant associational life makes a group this cohesive is it possible for women to assert their negotiating power in such bold and effective ways. These challenges to male authority do not mean that conventional gender roles have been completely transformed or overcome, of course. These challenges do nevertheless indicate significant changes in gender dynamics among married couples. They also show how masculinities can be made malleable in ways that may have appeared impossible before. Basanti captures this dynamic in her graphic description of the change in public opinion concerning the group:

When we started the group, people [local men] would tease us, "O, the women have formed a group! What do they think of themselves? Women are like *ol* (taro, an edible tuber that grows underground): they should remain under the stem." But now everyone says, "No they can; they've got courage and power (*khomota*)!"

---

[6] "Dada" means older brother and "didi" means older sister. These are commonly used forms of address for people older than oneself.

Now no one says a thing. So from there, we've come this far. Let's try and see if the *ol* can climb on top of the stem. We're trying. Let's see if we can do it!

Ananya – leadership and group-style

The leader of *Ananya* is Firdausi Bibi, a thirty-year-old Muslim woman with eight years of schooling. Married at the age of fifteen, she is the mother of four school-age children. She explains how she started the microcredit group of which she is now the leader:

First of all we are the "*bari'r bou*" (bride/wife of the house), and we don't have the good fortune to go out of our houses. We listen to the radio at home once in a while and, in that, I first heard about forming (microcredit) groups. Then I started to enquire around and found out that there was such a group in the next village. Then I gathered other women in the neighborhood and told them about forming a group. I said, let's see what the benefits are. When we started to form the group, we faced a lot of obstacles; our husbands wouldn't let us attend any meetings. But we overcame all the barriers and proceeded in our work. After the first six months of forming the group, one of the women needed some money for her child's (medical) treatment. So we withdrew money from our group savings and lent it to her. Then we understood that if we had the group, then we might be benefited in this way … So we carried on with it. After some time, we got loans and we handed them to our husbands. Gradually, sometimes, we even kept some of it (loans) for buying hens, ducks, goats, and cows.

Firdausi is quite similar to Uma in the enthusiasm she expresses for the difference the group has made in her life. She, personally, in fact, has made enormous strides. She has emerged from being a village wife, confined to traditional household duties, to become a leading woman in the community with membership in several village-level committees. She talks of her personal transformation with great passion:

Before, I was a "*bou*" (wife) of the Sardar household and would never step foot outside the house. It was only after forming this (microcredit) group that I gained so much experience. Now I can go everywhere. Of course, I am present anywhere there is a meeting of the (microcredit) groups. I have also become a member of the ICDS committee (government-sponsored Integrated Child Development Scheme), and I take part in their meetings held in the primary school here. I am also part of the group that has been formed to deal with the arsenic contamination problem in the village, and I try to be present in those meetings. I am also in touch with the dairy-association, and I am trying to be part of that too. Then in the last *gram sabha* (village forum), I had proposed that one destitute member of the (microcredit) group be given a house (under the government-sponsored housing scheme for below-poverty-line households). The council members had suggested that they would give it to a man. But I had argued that, at least, he was a man and at the end of the day he could earn fifty rupees, so it was not fair to give him the house. Rather, here was a woman with two children whose husband had died and she had no capacity for earning anything, so she should be allotted the housing benefit. I had created a big fuss in the meeting about this. In the end the house was allotted to her. This time the *panchayat* member let me know from beforehand that the *gram sabha* was forthcoming and said, if we had any demands from the women in the (microcredit) group, that we should place them in front of them at the meeting. I reassured him that we would be there. So I have all these experiences. Really, I never used to know or understand anything before.

Despite her personal transformation, however, Firdausi has not been successful in imparting or spreading her positive influence to other group members.

Unlike the collective changes experienced by Uma's microcredit group, members of *Ananya*, experienced little to no improvement in their capabilities after three years. The pattern of group participation in *Ananya* explains this disappointing outcome.

Group meetings were held twice a month in *Ananya* and even these were unevenly attended. A number of members were regularly absent or attended only briefly each time in order to complete the necessary financial transactions. Some members continued to face fierce household opposition to their participation in the microcredit group and its meetings.

Some members themselves felt apathetic toward the group. None of the members in *Ananya* mentioned being influenced by any of the resolution-principles, and none of them mentioned learning anything new from group meetings or collaborating to help one another with domestic problems. None of the women claimed increased social contacts or increased freedom of mobility or social interaction. A few of the members had accompanied their leader to meetings outside the village, but they had not converted that experience into wider physical mobility. Even after three years, the women faced the same burden of normative restrictions that they faced before. Unlike members of *Banani*, they refrained from challenging those restrictions.

Forty-two-year-old Salema Bibi had two accounts in violation of the one-member-per-household rule. In addition to these two accounts in *Ananya*, she had two additional accounts in a second microcredit group in the same neighborhood. In total she had four accounts, one in her name and three in the names of her three daughters, all of whom were minors. Her main intention was to save money for her daughters' weddings. Because she had these several memberships, Salema felt morally compelled to attend some of the group meetings and events to prevent other members from complaining about her non-participation. Even so, Firdausi, as group leader, had to plead with Salema's husband for his permission. Firdausi had to assure him that the events Salema would attend were women-only events, and that Firdausi would be accompanying Salema at all times during her absence from his household. Salema explains:

> I have to coax him to allow me to go outside; otherwise, he doesn't allow me to go anywhere. The leader comes and persuades him. He is a father to her [through extended kinship ties]. She comes and says that mother has to attend this event, and there are only going to be women there and no men. He says, "She'll go only if you're going." So that's how I can go.

Asked how she had benefited from her group membership, Salema responded curtly and with surprise: "How will *I* (emphasized in speech) be benefited?!" Then, urged to explain further, she says, "My son has profited in his business with the loan, and we've done well." Probed further about the nature of group meetings, she says, "We talk about money matters; there's no time for household gossip." Not unexpectedly then, Salema viewed the group only as a means of access to financial opportunities and resources. She did not share any affective bond with it despite her multiple memberships.

Marjina, another group member, rarely attended group meetings because of her husband's objection. (See Chapter 3.) Even on the rare occasions when she did attend, her husband unfailingly accompanied her. He kept a watchful gaze over the proceedings and spoke on her behalf. Marjina remained a passive spectator. Usually she sent the savings deposits through her young daughter. Marjina did not have the freedom to leave the house without her husband's permission and was rarely out of his sight. Within the household, she had no decision-making power even over those aspects of family life conventionally managed by women.

Another member, Firoza, was among those who rarely attended group meetings and who had never attended a group event outside the village. She ran the family's grocery store from home and claimed it was impossible to leave the store no matter what the rules of the microcredit group required. Firoza argued that her absence from the mandatory group meetings was not a problem because the group leader, Firdausi, was her sister-in-law. Firdausi's participation in all group events, she said, more than adequately represented the entire family's participation even though she and Firdausi resided in separate households.

Only one member of the *Ananya* microcredit group mentioned the presence of in-laws in the household as hindering her attendance at group meetings. She claimed that she could not find the time between caring for her elderly father-in-law and looking after the family's cattle and poultry. Another woman said that caring for her four young children prevented her from fully participating in the group events. She briefly attended the biweekly group meetings and then stopped. She left her home only once to attend a group event at the NGO headquarters. Only two group members, besides the leader and co-leader, mentioned attending group events outside their neighborhood.

These reports of passivity and lack of participation stand in marked contrast to the pattern observed in the other groups in which more than half the members volunteered to attend group events outside their village. Another member, Lalbanu, rejoined the group after discontinuing her membership for six months following a fight with her unsympathetic, uncooperative husband. Lalbanu was a mother-in-law herself in her joint-family household, and, although middle-aged, still had no control over household finances. At times, in order to pay for her savings deposits, she had to rely on financial help from her mother and brother.

Mumtaz, with whose experience this study opens, was the group member who enjoyed the greatest freedom to participate in the associational activities of this group (Ananya). The circumstances that allowed her that freedom were nevertheless far from favorable. She was free to do what she pleased because she had withdrawn herself from the day-to-day running of the household following her husband's second marriage. Her liberty came from having been superseded in the household and her consequent desire to find social and economic engagement outside the home.

Given that the overall rate of participation in *Ananya* was so poor and fluctuating, it is not surprising that not one of its members, apart from the leadership, experienced a meaningful gain in agency. Almost all of the women still played a very limited role in household management and not one of them challenged the conventional boundaries of their assigned customary gender roles. Men's attitudes toward women remained unaltered.

Lalbanu encountered fierce opposition from her conservatively minded husband when she attempted to inquire about household income and expenses. Mimicking his anger, she says:

Why will he give me the accounts (*hisheb*)? He won't give me the accounts. Men will never reveal the accounts to women, but they'll demand the accounts from women. At times I probe him, but then we have problems. He says, "Why do I have to give you the accounts? You're the one who's supposed to be answerable to me!"

Only Firdausi spoke of household members taking any actions or making any accommodations so that she could attend and actively participate in microcredit meetings.

In the absence of collective actions or any imposing of sanctions by this group, it is difficult to know whether domestic violence or other social problems existed in this neighborhood. One comment from Firdausi does reveal the possible existence of domestic violence:

(In a serious tone) If there's a woman whose mother-in-law is giving her a hard time and she mentions it, we discuss it. We talk about why women are subjected to such torture. (Transitions to tone of humor) Sometimes we say in jest, "Listen, from now on if anyone's husband beats them, then all of us will go as a group (and intervene)."

It is important to note how Firdausi has to use the subterfuge of humor to broach the possibility of the group imposing sanctions on wife-beaters in the community in the future. The suggestion has to be made tentatively, half in jest. There were no incidents of the group intervening to mediate in domestic disputes in the households of group members or in the neighborhood at large. Even when one member (Lalbanu) withdrew from the group following a fight with her unsupportive, uncooperative husband, the group remained passive.

Similarly, Firdausi's plan to mobilize several groups to attend a village forum meeting came to naught. Talking about this, Mumtaz uses vague and cryptic phrasing:

We had thought of attending it. There are many resources and benefits that can be demanded in those meetings. We also wanted to know about the many things that are discussed there and move ahead. But it didn't work out. I can't answer the question right now. I don't know why it didn't materialize. There are differences between the group members that need to be resolved.

The likelihood of any such mobilization taking place in the near future seems very slim.

How do we explain this difference in participation and commitment between microcredit groups composed of Hindu and Muslim women? To fully understand this we must consider the normative differences. But we must also go beyond these to seek a way to understand how culture, preferences, choices, and temperaments are produced socially – how they are embedded in the economic, religious, and demographic conditions of the respective communities.

IN SEARCH OF EXPLANATIONS

The historical origins of the Muslim population in Bengal derive from the invasion and conquest of Islamic rulers – Afghan, Pathan, and later Mughal – from the northwestern frontiers of the subcontinent beginning in the fourteenth century and continuing intermittently until the beginning of Mughal rule in the sixteenth century. For the next two hundred years (1576–1757), the Mughals reigned over Bengal, promoting infrastructural developments and introducing bureaucratic systems that were largely successful in managing the predominantly agrarian economy. It was during this time that Islam spread among the local Bengali population through conversion from Hinduism. For higher-caste Hindus, the conversion process tended to be motivated by the desire to be closer to power. For lower caste Hindus, conversions were spurred by Islam's promise of a formally egalitarian casteless community in which converts could expect to be free of the oppressions and exclusions of the Hindu *samaj*, or caste community. The Mughal regime was succeeded over the next two hundred years by first British East India Company rule (1757–1857)[7] and then British parliamentary rule (1858–1947). The colonial period ended with the partition of the country along lines of religion. Partition was marked by forced and voluntary migration of Muslims from the newly redrawn lines of the Indian nation to the newly created nation of West and East Pakistan that were carved out of the areas of Muslim concentration in Punjab and Bengal and the migration of Hindus from these newly redrawn areas of Muslim concentration across the new borders into India.[8]

Sixty years after emerging from the tumultuous history and population shifts of partition, West Bengal, at the present time, has the third largest population of Muslims among all the Indian states and union territories (following right after Jammu and Kashmir and Assam). As of 2001, 25.2 percent of its 80.2 million citizens identified themselves as Muslim.[9]

---

[7] In 1757 the Company defeated Nawab Shiraj Ud Daula in the Battle of Plassey in Bengal. In 1857 there was the uprising of Indian soldiers in the employ of the Company, termed in history as the Sepoy Revolt or Mutiny.

[8] The Indian Boundary Commission under the chairmanship of Cyril Radcliffe was responsible for drawing the new boundaries that partitioned undivided India into India and Pakistan.

[9] This percentage is far above the overall proportion of Muslims in India, which is reported to be 13.4 percent in the 2001 Census of India. A more recent estimate is available from the 2010 Pew Research Center report *The Future of the Global Muslim Population*, which pegs the proportion of Muslims in India to be 14.6 percent.

An overwhelmingly large percentage of Muslims in West Bengal (varying reports range between 85 to a full 100%) has been classified by the state government as being "other backward classes" following the reclassification effort undertaken on the recommendation of the National Commission for Religious and Linguistic Minorities, popularly known as the Misra Commission (established in 2004 with its report submitted in 2007).[10] This caste-classification of Muslims was based on education and occupational surveys of current population. The educational and occupational similarity between Hindu OBCs and Muslim OBCs brought out by the survey indicate that both groups face a comparable degree of social and economic disadvantage.

Data presented in the report issued by the Sachar Committee (a committee set up by Prime Minister Manmohan Singh four years after the 2001 national census to investigate the social, economic, and educational status of the Muslim community in India) show that the self-employment categories of "'own account worker' / 'employer' / 'unpaid family worker'" cover 61 percent of the total Muslim workforce compared to approximately 55 percent of total Hindu workforce. Although percentages for both are high, in general, Muslims are even more reliant than Hindus on self-employment.

Disaggregating Hindus into the constitutionally codified caste-groups reveals a more nuanced picture. The Sachar Committee data on the overall Indian rural sector reveals that Hindu "scheduled castes" (SCs) and "scheduled tribes" (STs) are the most reliant of all groups on casual work. Their reliance on casual work severely limits their ability to engage in self-employment. These two groups are followed by Muslim and Hindu OBCs (Other Backward Classes). These populations seem to be roughly

---

[10] Classification of local castes and sub-castes among Hindus into SC (Scheduled Castes) and OBC (Other Backward Classes) is undertaken for the purpose of determining which caste-groups to include in affirmative action policy affecting education and employment. The idea that Muslims, who are the largest minority, are being left out by not being able to access the benefit of affirmative action because of the official absence of caste-like hierarchies in Islam prompted the Commission to undertake occupational surveys of Muslims. Based on educational and occupational data, Muslims were identified by this Commission as falling into various caste-categories. And a large percentage of these caste-categories were included in the OBC list. None of these categories, however, could be declared as "scheduled caste" or "schedule tribe" (considered to be worse off in terms of disadvantage) because the Indian Constitution recognizes SCs and STs to be strictly limited to Hindu lower castes, neo-Buddhists, Sikhs, Christians, and other population groups with animist traditions.

equal in their reliance on self-employment and casual work.[11] Households depending on the earnings from casual daily labor are worse off than households of the self-employed. This is because of the greater precariousness of obtaining waged agricultural labor and other kinds of paid casual work in villages. (Seasonal work in brick kilns is one example of non-agricultural casual labor to be found in villages.) Members of SCs and STs are likely to be the economically worst off populations followed by Muslims and Hindus who are classified as members of OBCs.

Gender norms and social expectations

Based on this data, one would suppose that rural households relying on self-employment and casual work would be enthusiastic about enrolling in microcredit because of the prospect of receiving loans that are free of collateral obligations and bureaucratic red tape. Although there is active willingness and enthusiasm in some quarters, there is considerable apprehension and resistance in others.

The biggest stumbling block against the uptake of microcredit might seem to be the interest rate charged on microcredit loans. This rate at the time of the study was 12 percent at a flat rate that was usually charged as 2 percent monthly interest on six-month loans.

From the perspective of economic rationality, it is perhaps astonishing to find that very few Muslim women reported that their husbands' main objection to their joining microcredit groups was reservations regarding their loan-repayment capacity. Rather, Muslim women spoke of facing opposition based on men's fears that enrollment in microcredit groups would open the door to women violating the norms of gender propriety and would incite women to become insubordinate. In rural Bengali societies, it was the patriarchal Muslim households that most intensely felt the cultural and social threat posed by microcredit. Muslim households were not the only ones feeling anxieties from this quarter, but they felt them the most acutely.

The nature, scale, and sources of these apprehensions are revealing. Saleya's experience (see Chapter 4) of encountering opposition from the mullahs (Muslim clerics) in her village was not unique. A few other Muslim

---

[11] Rural Hindu upper castes show the lowest reliance on casual work (although close to 20% of them are in casual work) and have the highest levels of self-employment and salaried jobs, the former being much higher than the latter.

women also reported facing similar coordinated opposition from the local clergy or from the men and elders in their community. Rehana Bibi, a lively young woman, spoke agitatedly of the fierce opposition members of her group faced in their Muslim community in a village quite distant from Saleya's:

At first, five of us poor women[12] had come together to form the group. But we faced a huge amount of problems. Different people would say different things. Some women came to my house saying that they wanted to form groups, but they had to leave the group after only a few days because their husbands would say all kinds of things, "No you can't be part of this group. The Americans will come, lift up your sarees, stamp your legs (presumably with a seal of Christianity) and take you away. We don't need that kind of money; we won't be part of such groups ... "; "We won't allow our women to form groups and go from the house to the streets to speak to unknown men. We don't want that." In this way many women were forced out of the group by their husbands ... People used to say that I'm pulling away all their women and other bad things ... I struggled for one whole year to get everybody in line.

Rehana's widowed mother, Sophura Bibi, who was one of the early initiators, corroborated this account separately complaining that the men and clergy would say, "We shouldn't take this money because the American government is giving this money."

In another village, Shahida Bibi, a similarly vocal young Muslim woman and member of another Muslim microcredit group (whose name, "*Adhunik mahila samity*," means Modern Women's Association) had a similar story:

There was a huge storm over our going to meetings. Our mothers-in-law scolded us about what kind of women ever join such groups and hold meetings, what kind of things are meetings! My father-in-law said that the book[13] that the daughters-in-law have started, this is like the way our countrymen surrendered to the British; it is like that! We said, do you know how much the country has progressed! These days the government has many schemes [policy initiatives] and opportunities for women. Forget what happened before and look at what's happening now. After I said this, he didn't say anything.

The women in this group faced intense criticism for attending the biweekly meetings. So intense was the opposition that when the time came for them to attend the annual convention of microcredit groups sponsored

---

[12] This initial five included her mother who had long been abandoned by her husband and who supported herself by running her own small paddy-processing business.

[13] Here reference is being made to the individual passbook in which each member's loans and savings accounts are maintained.

by their supporting NGO in its headquarters nearby, they decided not to attend. Instead they hatched a plot to send their mothers-in-law in their place. Mariam Bibi shares what happened next, recounting an incident that dramatically testifies to the severity and collective social reach of the opposition that individual Muslim women enrolled in microcredit groups frequently have to confront:

We would only go to the group member's house where we had the (biweekly) meeting, and people would pass comments like, "All the wives and daughters are leaving their housework behind and going to hold meetings! What the heck are "meetings"? We haven't seen any meetings or anything in our generation, and now the daughters-in-law are holding meetings! They don't regard their husbands and in-laws; we ask them not do it, but yet they don't obey us." So the time came when we had to go to Kolsur for the big meeting. Then all of us decided that we would not go to the meeting. We thought that if we were alive then we would attend the next event. For this one, we decided we would send all the elderly (women) who objected to our activities. We sent them thinking that with their continuing objections we would not be able to have a solid footing in this. If we wanted to start another book, they wouldn't allow us. So thinking of all this, we sent them. They all went and saw that there were only women and women in that event, and there was a play about mothers- and daughters-in-law and how the mothers-in-laws were punishing the daughters-in-laws! They returned and talked about it at home, and we heard about it from them. From that time on, they started objecting less to what we did. And that's how we were able to come this far. That's why we've not been anywhere, since there were no events after that. We just attend our twice a month meetings, and they don't object to that anymore. (Mariam Bibi)

Muslim men seemed to be generally more apprehensive about their wives' involvement in microcredit groups than their Hindu counterparts. They particularly resisted women's participation in meetings and other deliberations. They also were more resistant to changes in conventional gender roles than Hindu men. The possibility of women mingling and interacting with men outside the relational circuit of kinship ties posed the inherent risk of these women losing their feminine modesty. This anxiety was acutely felt in the Muslim community. Twice Muslim men and elders were reported (by the women) to have expressed an association of women's agency with apprehension regarding foreign influence (of American money and equating enrollment in microcredit with surrendering to British colonial powers) and with the fear of forcible conversion.

In entirely Muslim microcredit groups, the generally passive and acquiescing nature of group leadership can be viewed as an adaptive strategy of the women for coping with cultural pressures from the community.

The apathetic attitude among these women and their lack of interest in expanding out from the strict economic functions of borrowing and saving can be interpreted as reflections of Muslim women's reluctance to engage in activities that could have a very high social cost. In the non-experimental settings of real life, it is nearly impossible to separate out how much of this dampening effect comes from internalized gender norms and how much of it is the result of external social coercion regarding feminine propriety. If women truly believe that they ought to remain within the private sphere, their interest in organizing collective action and imposing sanctions will be minimal. But it is equally possible that women's realistic assessment of the hostility collective action or imposing sanctions on their part will generate may lead them to balk at undertaking them through the microcredit groups for the fear of being disciplined.

In fact, gender norm socialization usually takes into account the high cost of gender norm transgressions. There are examples that both low interest (conditioned by costs) and high social cost act as deterring influences. For instance, the leader of an entirely Muslim microcredit group expressed reluctance in her response to my question concerning why they had not acted to stop the prolonged persecution of a group member by her mother-in-law even though the group members were well aware of the situation. According to Aklima Bibi, the group members were unwilling to undertake sanctions against the abusive mother-in-law because they did not want to flout the authority of the woman's husband, that is, transgress the normative boundaries of traditional marital relations: "If her husband protested and said [to his mother], why do you scold and beat her, then it would be something. But we're '*bou-manush*' [married women], can we go and say such things!"

By contrast, even when women may want to go against the prescribed codes of conduct, social expectations may restrain the women from intervening in affairs considered to be the exclusive preserve of families. The restraining effect of social expectations was revealed in another Muslim group when the cashier, Madina Begum, explained why they had not acted against similar problems in their neighborhood: "We haven't had the courage to do anything like that yet, because it's within the village and we're women. If we mobilize for something like that, then the men-folk might say things!"

Expressed in these examples is the fear that going beyond the narrow financial aims and engaging in collective action might jeopardize or even reverse their community's and household members' acceptance of microcredit. Group members may not want to risk an overturning of the hard-won permission that they as Muslim women have wrested from their communities to participate in microcredit groups.

Hindu microcredit group members also sometimes faced criticism from elderly conservative men in their community. It appears that in those cases, however, that the criticisms waned after awhile and that, despite the criticism, the women proceeded with the planning and execution of their public interventions. In some cases they had even won the support of a coterie of men in their community and were able to change the minds of their critics. I would note that in the Hindu groups that did not conduct social interventions, I did not hear any women speaking of any pressing situation in need of urgent intervention or any comments that led me to think that they were being coerced or oppressed by men's stringent enforcement of norms or social expectations regarding feminine propriety.

Religious institutions and the clergy

At first glance, microcredit groups immediately raise the moral issue of women's membership in circuits outside of kinship ties and their increased contact with non-kin men (male NGO staffs, for instance) outside of family oversight and control. These moral issues opened up the scope in some of the Muslim communities for the local religious institutions to intervene. Added to this, the Islamic injunction against taking or paying interest served as a readily available moral avenue for the Muslim clergy to protest women's enrollment in microcredit.

In one village neighborhood, the role of the *"haji shaheb"* (person who has undertaken haj in Mecca) was mentioned in explaining the uphill struggle of the early microcredit adopters in enrolling other women into their group. Firoza Bibi, who took the lead in forming a microcredit group in her Muslim neighborhood, reported on this issue. She clarified that both she and her late husband used to do the *namaz kalaam* but that her husband did not object to her enrolling in the group.[14] Here her emphasis is on the economic behavior of people as a guide to religious morality as opposed to the authority of a cleric's hypocritical and authoritarian religious prescription:

All those who tried to obstruct us, stole away at night (under the cover of darkness) to borrow money from the village moneylender. There are many who think,

---

[14] Her school-going son played a crucial role in the initial stage in convincing his father that the NGO that he had visited to attend a youth program was a reputable one.

I'll go in the daylight and people will say that so and so takes money on interest. In our (Muslim) community it is said that it is '*haram*' (sin) to pay or charge interest. There is a person here who is the head of the community; he is a '*haji shaheb*' (undertaken haj in mecca) and reads the namaz. If he goes upfront and borrows money from someone, then the villagers who've made him the head will say, 'O, you're the head, and you are borrowing money; so if *you* pay interest on the money, it is not a sin and if *we* pay interest, then it is a sin'! So, that is why they have to steal out at night and borrow money (from the moneylender) on the sly. But many are realizing now that, when we're bringing money on the sly and paying more interest, then why not let the women of the house do this by sitting in the house and having meetings. They can save Rs 20 per month and get more money at low interest. This is an advantage.

Anthropologists have done groundbreaking work on the confrontation between the Muslim clergy in Bangladesh and NGOs operating microcredit programs. Lamia Karim (2011) in her recent study conducted across the border from West Bengal in Bangladesh notes that the Muslim clergy frequently bring up the allegation of forced conversion to Christianity. Karim gives an account of a clergyman, who is also an important madrassah leader associated with a famous mosque, claiming that NGOs have started converting women from Islam to Christianity by offering them loans. The clergyman claimed that he knew of a young woman who had been offered a loan of twelve thousand rupees by a prominent NGO and was told that she would not have to repay it if she allowed them to put a Christian seal on her lower abdomen. The cross-border circulation in West Bengal of an identical anxiety of women being converted from their faith (complete with the detail of a seal being imprinted on an intimate part of the female body, violating her modesty) is noteworthy.

It is also interesting to note that this common anxiety exists despite the contrasting demographics of India and Bangladesh. In India Muslims are a significant minority of the population, and in Bangladesh Muslims are a dominant majority. This story may be evidence of some degree of coordination among the Muslim clergy in this part of the subcontinent. There may be a collaborative effort to try to stem the tide of women's enrollment in microcredit programs.

Village-level clergy in the Hindu and Muslim communities are vastly different and create very different religious contexts for the operation of microcredit groups in rural West Bengal. Men of religion within Hinduism who function as priests (*purohits*) in these village societies are limited in their role. They conduct religious worship and preside over social ceremonies, mainly marriages and funerals. Beyond this ceremonial function the Hindu priestly class no longer has power or much influence over social and cultural practices. They do not have a direct governing role in their communities. Such powers and roles belonged to the pre-colonial and colonial periods of Indian history.

The colonial period marked a watershed by introducing a formal legislative process led and imposed by the British colonialists but frequently motivated and aided by indigenous Hindu social reformists. This legislative process initiated the long transformative replacement of the interpretive and governing powers of Hindu clergy on social and cultural matters with formalized secular law. This transformation continued under the newly independent national government that took upon itself the task of "modernizing" or reforming Hindu traditional regulations pertaining to marriage, divorce, and property inheritance.

Neither the colonial and nor the post-colonial nationalist administrations made any attempt to modify Muslim personal laws or to bring them under its legislative jurisdiction. Since these laws were based on the Shariah, a body of Islamic moral codes drawing on the prophetic tradition within Islam (divided into multiple schools of thought and liturgical interpretation), local-level Muslim clerics have continued to remain influential in social and cultural matters.[15] It is a reflection of this pattern that the Muslim cleric, *imam* or *mullah*, in these same villages had a say in the social and cultural matters of the Muslim community.

Marriage laws and informal arbitration

Marriage laws and customs may also help us to understand why Muslim women are reluctant to translate the increased agency microcredit potentially affords them into legitimate and legitimizing interventions into the domestic affairs and power relations of members' households. Most grouped interventions by Hindu microcredit groups were against domestic violence and men's sexual conduct. In comparing the two communities, it is important to recognize that the existential situation of Muslim women in rural Bengal is somewhat more precarious than that of Hindu women, despite numerous similarities.

The main difference concerns the customary practice of men committing polygamous marriages. This practice was prevalent among both Hindus and Muslims in pre-independence India. The Hindu Marriage

[15] These religious leaders are also in charge of the madrasah educational system, schools for Muslim children with an emphasis on Quranic religious education and learning Arabic.

Act (passed in 1955),[16] however, has ruled polygamy to be illegal for Hindus. But, because Muslims abide by Sharia law on personal matters, Muslim men may legally marry up to four wives. Even more importantly, Muslim men enjoy the unilateral and discretionary right to divorce their wives by simply uttering the word "talaq" three times.

Irrespective of differences in law, the practice of a man informally abandoning his first wife to marry another is common practice among poor Hindu and Muslim men in rural Bengal. Without systematic study, it is difficult to say among which community the practice is more prevalent. But the legal provisions allowing Muslim men to have simultaneous multiple marriages, and giving them more grounds than wives to dissolve their marriages, makes the marital status of Muslim women more insecure than that of Hindu women. That insecurity may work to rob Muslim women of the effective moral authority to protest domestic violence or impose sanctions on men who engage in more than one marital relationship or who abandon their wives.

Others have commented on the impact made by the differences in laws and community norms that exist among Muslims and Hindus (SMS 2003). Both the Hindu and Muslim communities rely on the age-old *shalishi* mechanism. This traditional institution reflects the community norms and the distribution of power in these communities. It is an informal, community-based arbitration procedure that has existed since Mughal times beginning in the sixteenth century. It was adapted and modified in succeeding centuries, and operates in parallel with the formal legal system. It is often the first resort for villagers embroiled in a conjugal, family, or property dispute.

For poor villagers and women, arbitration under the *shalishi* system is often their only recourse to justice. Typically, the aggrieved and accused parties or their spokespersons present their opposing cases to a supposedly impartial male community elder or group of elders. The verdict may include admonishment and shaming punishment, fines, or agreeing upon a settlement. Those who mete out justice within this system (a system that has become increasingly politicized in recent times) are governed by community norms that have the preservation of the family as their primary, even overriding goal. They certainly are not in favor of forwarding feminist-inflected ideas of women's rights.

A recent study (SMS 2003) found that when an NGO initiated an NGO-led dispute resolution (after getting domestic violence complaints), and invited all the stakeholders and community leaders to participate but also

[16] The Hindu Code Bills were meant to revamp the traditional personal laws.

allowed the aggrieved woman to speak for herself, Muslim women benefitted greatly. This procedure stands in sharp contrast to the usual practice
in Muslim communities in most Bengali villages. Women are not usually
allowed to be present during the deliberations that determine the judgments of culpability.

One strong-willed and independent Muslim woman, an ex-group leader
named Asura, condemned the gender-bias in the conventional arbitration
mechanism and claimed that it was the inequality and injustice she witnessed
in it that provided the incentive for her to join the microcredit group:

> We have meetings in our village where ten or twelve men-folk get together and do
> *bichar* [pass judgments in informal arbitration]. I would sneak out and listen to
> them. Among us Muslims, women aren't allowed to attend or participate in these.
> Most of the times, I didn't agree with the judgments. They were always one-sided,
> and there were never any protests against faulty judgments and wrongdoing [of
> men against women]. Like my husband would beat me a lot, and everyone would
> say, it was my fault. But I have a conscience, and I believed I wasn't in the wrong.
> From that time on, I had a kind of sadness within me and would keep thinking
> that only if I could organize people, then I could confront and challenge them. So
> when I got the opportunity to join the *samity* (association or NGO accessed
> through enrolling in the microcredit group), I did.

The conventionally male-led dispute resolution process combined with
Shariah-based personal law (interpreted by the local patriarchy to its
own advantage) further compromise the security of Muslim women. The
sometimes overwhelming force of these institutions works to reduce wom-
en's interest or ability to expand the potential agency microcredit gives
them directly into social domains beyond the strictly financial.

Position in the social hierarchy

Another factor contributing to the reduced social agency of women in
entirely Muslim microcredit groups is the minority position of the
Muslim community in India. An experimental study on the influence of
caste on sanctioning found that low-caste individuals exhibited a much
lower willingness than high-caste individuals to punish norm violations
that hurt members of their own caste.[17] This study also found that a

---

[17] Hoff, Kshetramade, and Fehr (2009) studied sanctioning behavior among *dalit* (low-caste)
versus upper-caste individuals in rural Uttar Pradesh, in North India, where caste is
extremely salient and repressive. These authors found that low-caste individuals exhibited
a much lower willingness than high-caste individuals to punish norm violations that hurt
members of their own caste.

strong sense of in-group affiliation (with the caste-group) was crucial for cultivating the willingness to sanction norm-infringement against in-group members by out-group members, and, compared to upper-caste individuals, low-caste individuals displayed a less strong sense of in-group affiliation. The study interpreted this finding to suggest that there is a cultural difference across caste status in the concern for members of one's own caste-community – upper caste individuals share greater mutual concern for co-caste members than do low-caste individuals. The authors explain this discrepancy by suggesting that "life-long position at the ... bottom of an extreme social hierarchy" prevents individuals in subordinated groups from developing a strong sense of in-group affiliation.

Applied to microcredit groups composed entirely of Muslim women, this finding suggests that members of these groups will be more reluctant than Hindu women to undertake sanctions and collective action to protect their interests. Supporting this suggestive hypothesis, Muslim women interviewed in this study were typically reticent when probed on domestic violence problems in the community. Even though they did not directly report a lack of mutual concern, their inaction in various situations can be interpreted in that light. It was rare to hear Muslim women expressing the desire to stop such incidents or to punish perpetrators. Firdausi Bibi from group *Ananya* could only talk of initiating protest half in jest.

By contrast, Hindu women sometimes voluntarily reported such a lack of concern prior to their enrollment in microcredit. They, too, were at the bottom of the gender hierarchy after all. Previous victims of domestic violence complained with anguish how their sisters-in-law and neighbors stood watching. Some, they even suspected, took secret voyeuristic pleasure in watching the victim being abused. Some Hindu women who had previously found themselves in the role of passive observers in such situations admitted that they did not want to take on any trouble as long as they themselves were not directly affected by it.

Following their membership and participation in the microcredit group, these women described a dramatic change in their attitude toward such ill treatment. Evidence of this is available in the several incidents in which Hindu groups intervened on behalf of women – group members and non-members – to rescue them from domestic violence. Collectively the group found that they could successfully punish the perpetrators, put a stop to men's extra-marital affairs and informal polygamy, and annul illegal under-age marriage. The Hindu group members who initiated and took part in these collective actions and imposition of sanctions were from various "Other Backward Classes" and "Scheduled Castes" categories. There were negligibly few upper caste women in the study's sample.

Based on this difference it is plausible that, Muslim women, being a double minority – in the gender hierarchy and in the demographic hierarchy – are hindered in the development of a strong sense of mutual concern for each other's well-being. This lack of solidarity works to inhibit the development of women's autonomy and agency.

This argument implies the corollary possibility that in regions where Muslims are the majority, like neighboring Bangladesh, the double minority factor does not inhibit Muslim women's agency. Therefore, in such areas Muslim women in microcredit groups may be relatively more empowered by their participation than Muslim women in rural villages in West Bengal. In such Muslim-majority areas we may also find that minority Hindu women have weaker in-group affiliation and lack mutual concern for the well-being of co-religion members. They consequently may have less ability to expand the agency microcredit gives them into wider social spheres within their communities. These speculations call for further regionally comparative empirical studies.

CONCLUSIONS

Microcredit groups seem to offer intriguing interpretive paradoxes. On the one hand, the ties among group members can be interpreted to act as channels for disciplinary surveillance instrumentalized to ensure against financial delinquency. Some scholars have argued this to be one of the most coercive elements of microcredit, resulting in shame and indignity. Yet, on the other hand, these ties within the microcredit group – along with the vast web of weak ties among clusters of several microcredit groups – also operate as the arterial system through which feelings of solidarity flow and as informal channels through which help arrives in times of crisis. That help, as we have seen, is not only financial in nature but social and even proto-political.

In this fluid and dynamic process, the socio-religious composition of microcredit groups matters. It influences the group's capacity to cooperate outside and beyond the mandated economic goals and the extent to which effective social networks become established among group members. These are commonly recognized elements of social capital.

This raises a second, seemingly paradoxical aspect of microcredit. As a financial institution it seeks to bring change while embedding itself deeply in the conventional fabric of neighborhoods and local rural households. On the one hand, microcredit seeks to be an agent of financial transformation for the poor. Its goal is to support poor people's livelihood enterprises and, in doing so, inject an ethos and discourse of "entrepreneurship" that the classic sociological literature asserts marks a fundamental break from traditional patterns of economic and social relations and fundamentally restructures the existing patterns of alliances (Ruef 2010; Becker et al. 2011).

Being constructed on a foundation of neighborhood-based peer-groups, microcredit overlays conventional patterns of residential concentration organized by religion and caste. This leads to a preponderance of groups that are homogeneous in their socio-religious and caste composition. This allows the existing cultural environment of a community (dynamically produced and conditioned as it is) to influence the nature and intensity of women's participation in microcredit groups via the *"habitus"* of women and via the outlook produced by traditionally conservative rural community and family norms.

The pattern of difference between Hindu and Muslim microcredit members may be particular to Bengal and may not hold for other parts of the world. Alternatively there is a possibility that a similar pattern is to be found across other states in India where microcredit groups have been operating, in some cases for a longer and in some for a shorter period of time than in West Bengal. The issue of how microcredit functions in relation to women's agency in different socio-religious communities across India warrants further exploration.

This issue is particularly important because microcredit is viewed in some quarters as the intervention that will solve the problem of the gap in the "financial inclusion" of the Muslim community in India's current economic development. The Sachar Committee report ends with these words of promise regarding microcredit: "The SHG-bank linked Microfinance programme of NABARD (National Bank for Agriculture and Rural Development) is one of the largest in the world, and has tremendous potential to improve the economic conditions of rural Muslims[18] ... One of the important ways to help communities living in

---

[18] The report notes that, out of 16.18 lakh SHGs assisted by NABARD up to March 31, 2005, only 1.36 lakh SHGs (approximately only 8%) are found in forty-four minority (Muslim) concentration districts.

poorer areas, both urban and rural, is to provide microcredit, especially to women. A policy to enhance the participation of Muslims in micro-credit schemes of SIDBI (Small Industries Development Bank of India) and NABARD should be laid down" (GOI 2006: pp. 136–137).[19]

---

[19] The Sachar committee looked into the access Muslims across the country have to banking systems and credit in the 2000–2005 period, especially in light of the "Prime Minister's 15-Point Programme" that was launched beginning in 2001 in forty-four minority concentration districts across the country. The report states, "While the share of Muslims as account holders is satisfactory at the all-India level, there is a 12% deficit (compared to the population share of Muslims) in the 44 minority concentration districts. If the quantum of priority sector advances is considered, one finds a deficit of about 9 percentage points at the all India aggregate level and an even higher deficit of 25 percentage points in the 44 minority concentration districts" (GOI 2006, p. 125). This pattern was not true for those populations categorized as "other minorities," which included Christians, neo Buddhists (most of them former *dalits*), Sikhs, and Zoroastrians. For these groups, their condition was found to be "relatively better, particularly in the 44 minority concentration districts, where their share in accounts and amount outstanding is twice that of their population" (p. 125). In West Bengal, where 25 percent of the population is Muslim, "just above 29% of accounts are held by Muslims, 4% more than their share in population; but the share of amount outstanding is an abysmal 9.2%" (p. 127). This pattern matches that of other states with a significant Muslim population, "a depressing scenario" (p. 127), in the words of the report.

Another interesting all-India pattern is the difference between public sector banks versus private sector banks in terms of servicing Muslims. The report states that in terms of the total number of accounts held by Muslims, the public sector banks seem to outperform private sector banks. However, the private sector banks seem to be performing better in extending advances (i.e., credit) to Muslims relative to other communities. Although the absolute magnitude of advances made to Muslims by public sector banks is higher than that made by their private sector peers, "The share of Muslims in amount outstanding is 7.9% in public sector banks as compared to 9.9% in private sector banks" (p. 129). Dividing the forty-four minority concentration districts into four groups by their proportion of Muslim population [above 40% (11 districts); 26–40% (12 districts); >22–<26% (10 districts); 22% and less (11 districts)] also reveals discouraging patterns. "In all four groups, the availment of credit by Muslims is poor with respect to their population share" (p. 129). Along with that, the worst patterns, according to the report, seem to be emerging out of districts where Muslims are above 40 percent and where they are less than 26 percent. The report concludes from this pattern that "as the share of Muslims in populations increases, their share in amount outstanding tends to decrease" (p. 129). However, the districts of Nadia (one of the two districts in my study) and Maldah in West Bengal along with ten other districts in other states are outliers in that the amount outstanding per account of Muslims is higher than that for Other Minorities. Therefore, in light of the Reserve Bank of India's directive to focus on giving minorities access to credit in these minority concentration districts, the Sachar Committee report concludes that it appears that all minority groups but Muslims have benefitted out of it.

Apart from the commercial banking structure, India has two specialized lending institutions – Small Industries Development Bank of India (SIDBI) and National Bank for Agricultural and Rural Development (NABARD) – that focus on providing credit to the small-scale sector and to rural economic enterprises. With regard to SIDBI, the Sachar

In light of recommendations like these, it is clear that microcredit can become yet another institution and policy initiative across which unequal outcomes may emerge among the different socio-religious communities in India. This time inequalities may repeat themselves and persist across the social, cultural, and political domains of women's agency, increased empowerment, and access to social capital.

Inequality in social capital can theoretically be of two kinds, "capital deficit" and "return deficit" (Lin 2000, p. 790). "Capital deficits" have been defined as unequal quantity and quality of network-connections possessed and acquired by groups in society and have been theorized as being the consequence of "differential opportunities" available to and "differential investments" made by various demographic groups (Lin 2000, p. 791). In the context of this study, "capital deficits" refer to the inequality existing in the capacity to cooperate that women develop through their membership and participation in microcredit groups. Microcredit may be an institution in which this structural opportunity has not been equalized across communities. The "return deficits" are apparent in the achievement of public goods, including protecting and promoting women's welfare.

This inequality in social capital – in the effectiveness of social networks and the capacity to cooperate for public goods and to protect women – has the following characteristics. It is intangible compared to other forms of inequality that can be quantitatively measured (income, education, employment, and promotions). It is not amenable to direct observation and harder still to address with targeted measures.

Perhaps its only positive feature is that, considered from an equity-perspective, it is a form of inequality that does not have discriminatory

Committee report found that a paltry 1.5 percent of accounts within it were held by Muslims; the amount of credit authorized [sanctioned? What does this mean? Yes, it means sanctioned] toward these accounts was 0.6 percent; and the actual amount disbursed was 0.5 percent. In terms of actual numbers, the total amount of credit authorized to Muslims (including direct and indirect loans) in the last six years (2000–2006) was Rs 180 crores from a total authrorized credit amount of Rs 31,806 crores. With regard to NABARD policies that focus on small and marginal borrowers for farm- and non-farm livelihoods in the rural sector, the report reveals that only 3.2 percent of production credit (i.e., Rs 291 crores: Short Term Refinance for seasonal Agricultural Operations) and 3.9 percent of investment credit (i.e., Rs 333 crores: Refinance in farm and non-farm sector and rural housing, etc.) have been provided to the Muslim community on an average annually during 2004–2006. In West Bengal, the percentage of production credit and investment credit to its 25 percent Muslim population was each only 6.5 percent. This percentage was better than other states where the proportion of Muslims was far lower. However, it was far worse compared to Kerala (24.7% is Muslim; 11.7% share each of production credit and investment credit to Muslims) and Uttar Pradesh (18.2% is Muslim; 6.9% share each of production credit and investment credit to Muslims).

effects. The distribution of this type of social capital and the welfare that results from it is not a zero-sum game between the communities. Group members from a particular socio-religious community being able to accrue higher levels of social capital and more public goods from it does not mean that group members belonging to other communities are forced to endure lower levels of social capital and get fewer benefits. Physical public infrastructure for the neighborhood or village is non-excludible and non-rival. Opportunities for collectively imposing sanctions are not limited or competitive. The capacity to cooperate for public goods is not of a limited nature.

Finally, it is important to note that the women who belong in the microcredit groups that are not as effective in inculcating social capital are not worse off than they were before as a result of other groups developing more social capital. Despite these non-detrimental features, the inequality in social capital can be extremely consequential for creating or accentuating gaps between contextually proximate communities in the welfare and freedom of women. Ultimately this will be consequential for "development" in its most human and expansive form, namely, "development as freedom" (Sen 1999).

7

Loans and well-being

What effect do microcredit groups have on women who already possess considerable agency? A significant proportion of the study's sample (116 out of 400 or 29%) exercised impressive social capabilities before enrolling in their microcredit group. The keys to their empowerment lay in education, the liberal outlook of a husband, confidence gained from previous successful personal initiatives, or the wisdom won from hard lives.

No existing study of microcredit has studied at any significant depth this question of the relation between microcredit and already empowered women. A few first-wave studies noted the existence of female-headed households and found that women who were widowed or separated had greater control over microcredit loans than did any other group. They used the loans, these studies showed, directly in the economic enterprises they themselves operated. But, beyond this, almost nothing is known about the influence of microcredit on such women, especially whether it improves their overall well-being.

This category (empowered women) included women living in a complex variety of household types. A very small proportion of these women were married and lived with economically productive husbands who showed accommodating and liberal attitudes regarding their wife's agency. These women had nine to twelve years of schooling and two of them had college degrees. Some of these women exhibited enterprising, entrepreneurial spirit independent of any pressures exerted by adversity or immediate economic threat.

Another group of empowered married women living with husbands exhibited a very different economic profile. These women were unencumbered by traditional restrictions precisely because of the relative poverty of their households. Poverty created the need for these women to participate equally in income-generation and household management prior to their involvement in microcredit. Their husbands, too, tended to be liberally minded regarding their wives' initiatives. It is difficult to tell whether this was because of personal character or because of the force of circumstances. Most of these women had no education at all or just a few years of primary or secondary schooling.

Still another group of empowered women were husbandless. These were widows or wives who had separated or had been deserted and presided over genuinely female-headed households. A fourth sizeable group was comprised of women who were de facto household heads because their husbands were economically unproductive or generally inept or disinterested in managing household affairs. Finally, there were women whose husbands did not live continuously in the household because they had become migrant laborers and had moved to either other parts of the state or to other states for work.

The women in all but the first two of the groups described above were involuntarily pushed to take on the mantle of the primary household manager. Most of them therefore developed agency under duress – as the byproduct, as it were, of some intense adversity (widowhood, separation, husband's ineptitude), real loss (the death of a husband), or the effective absence of a male household head (economically unproductive or migrant).[1] Many of these women therefore experienced the need to exercise agency as a responsibility born from adversity. These women came to exercise unrestrained freedom of interaction, physical mobility, and decision-making in both traditional and non-traditional matters and across the entire gamut of market-transactions. But for many of these women, the freedom to exercise agency was experienced as indistinguishable from the constraints and unfreedom of poverty. The enormous diversity in marital status, spousal characteristics, and household economic circumstances among these women immediately stands out.

It is instructive to trace the loan use patterns in three distinct household types of these already empowered women: egalitarian households, de facto female-headed hosueholds, and truly female headed-households. This will allow us to understand the ways and extent to which microcredit affects the economic well-being of households in which women are already free to

---

[1] Male labor migration, regardless of how low paid or economically lucrative the work is, poses constraints and compulsions for those left behind to manage the household. It puts those left behind under duress.

exercise their capabilities and possess significant if not complete managerial control. The analysis focuses first on Muslim households and then on Hindu households. Apart from a single pattern of difference that emerged in the loan use of Muslim and Hindu women in de facto female-headed households that had husbands and sons present, there were great similarities in how Hindu and Muslim women with agency made use of microcredit loans and were able to accomplish higher levels of household well-being.

EGALITARIAN MUSLIM HOUSEHOLDS

In egalitarian Muslim households, the range of loans taken by the women varied from sums as high as Rs 32,000 and 20,000 to lows of one and two thousand. Ajima Bibi and Anjuara Bibi (who belonged to different groups) each took Rs 32,000 in loans. Ajima Bibi was in her mid-forties and attended grade school only up to class four (i.e., until about age nine or ten). She had a husband and four sons. Two sons were studying for their master's degrees at the university and two were enrolled in college. She also had a daughter-in-law, a sixteen-year-old studying in class ten (the equivalent of the 10th grade) in the village school.

Ajima explained that her husband's family had a real knack for education because her father-in-law was educated. In addition, her sons worked hard to earn money to pay for the expenses for their education. There were days when her youngest son worked as a paid farm-laborer on other people's fields early in the morning and went to college later in the day with the money he earned. The family is not poor by any means, and the sons have helped out a great deal by setting up different livelihood enterprises such as a poultry farm and a village medical store. Ajima has taken out loans to finance these businesses:

First I took Rs 2000 and started a poultry farm with it. Within fifteen days of taking the loan my son had jaundice. I was in deep trouble then, and I came and told the other group members, and with their consent I took another Rs 2000 from the group fund. I repaid the Rs 4000 gradually. After that I took another loan of Rs 3000 for the poultry farm. After that I took Rs 5000 and I used it for cultivation and our mango business, we buy mango trees. Then we took Rs 10,000 and used it again for the poultry farm and for buying mango trees. We repaid that, and this time I have taken Rs 10,000 rupees. I have used some of it for the medicine store that my son has just opened, and some of it I have kept for another son who is planning to open a grocery store.

Ajima's husband cultivates a bit of land that they own and runs the seasonal mango business. The poultry farm is managed by him and one of the sons.

Ajima finds it difficult to comment on the household earnings because "it is spread out all over the household" she says. The loans are repaid from the businesses they have been taken out to fund. The Rs 20 monthly savings deposit, however, comes from money Ajima herself has found a way of earning in various ways:

> I have a cow and a goat, and I stitch coverlets, make fuel sticks with cow dung and sell them, sell wood and do this and that because I have to get the money for the group deposit. I can't always ask my sons for the money and expect that they'll give it to me. I know that this is *my* responsibility, so *I* have to get the money.

The family is in the process of constructing a house for which they have already spent one and a half lakhs, out of which Rs 9000 is her own money, from two savings accounts she opened in the local post office and in the Bank long before she had joined the microcredit group. Even though Ajima Bibi does not have an independent business, she has been the main financer behind all the economic activities of the household. Because the household members are all cooperative, she has no reluctance and shows no hesitation in transferring the loans to her husband or sons.

Anjuara Bibi is in her thirties and has a class eight education (i.e., eighth grade). She has a family of four that includes her husband and a school-age daughter and son. Talking about how she joined the group, she says:

> My husband was the one who encouraged me to join the group and start saving. They (NGO staff) had come to tell me about the group, but I had gone to the pond to wash something so they ended up talking to my husband. When I returned he said, "See, these people have come all this way for your earning!" He was joking. I asked what they were saying, and he said, "They are asking you to keep money, so that all of you can stand on your own feet." He was laughing, because we were joking. Then he said "You should join; let's see what they can do for you." He was the one who gave me money.

The family owns a tractor that her husband operates, hiring out his services to other farmers. They acquired this tractor for Rs 95,000 a few months before joining the group by selling off some land they owned and borrowing from moneylenders. Then they spent twenty to thirty thousand rupees to repair it to make it operational. Now every year it yields an annual income of about Rs 50,000, a little over Rs 4000 per month on average. Anjuara does embroidery work on the side and rears ducks. All in all, every month she earns Rs 100. Besides these activities, she has the important responsibility of taking down the bookings for their tractor from villagers who come to reserve it for transporting sand and bricks and for other jobs. "I am the one who takes down all the deals. I can't negotiate the price, but he tells me what to ask for and then I ask them to call later when my husband is there."

Sometimes, the clients bring the payments to the house, and Anjuara has to make a note of the payment and keep track of the money. The family also hires another driver and she has to pay him and keep track of the payments he brings in. In the three and a half years that she has been a member of this group, she has taken Rs 32,000 in loans, most of which has been spent on the existing tractor and to acquire an additional one:

I took Rs 2000 once to pay off certain external debts we had. Then I took Rs 10,000 to buy a new engine for the old tractor. Again, this time I have taken a loan of Rs 20,000 to buy another tractor. We still don't have all the parts to start running it. We need another Rs 20,000 to 30,000 to bring it up to working condition.

The family has significantly improved their economic condition compared to when they relied solely on cultivating their land. But this has also meant taking loans from the group and from external sources to finance their business. For the last three years, the family has been contributing to a life insurance policy through which they save Rs 2200 every six months and into which, so far, they have contributed Rs 13,200.

Mumtaz Bibi and Samsunnahar Bibi are both in their thirties and have a class eight (eighth grade) education. They have taken Rs 20,000 and 21,000, respectively, for their family's building materials and construction supplies businesses. Mumtaz passed on the loans to her husband who ran the business from his building materials shop in the local market. Samsunnahar runs her building materials retail business from home.

Samsunnahar's husband has a truck transportation business for a long time, and he, along with hired drivers, transports goods over long distances in their trucks. Samsunnahar asked her husband to start a construction supplies business for her to run from home. This arrangement would give them a double income. Her idea and her husband's help yielded Samsunnahar a business one year before the group started.

Because many people in the village made purchases on credit and failed to pay on time, a crisis arose. Meanwhile a year had gone by and the microcredit group had started and Samsunnahar had enrolled in it. In the first round she took a loan of Rs 6000 to tide her business over during its initial troubles. After repaying that loan from the business's earnings, she took out a hefty loan of Rs 15,000 for re-investing in it:

I manage everything. We have a phone at home, and we have fixed dealers. I call them and let them know that my truck is going on such and such time and ask them to load the cement and rods on it. We send our trucks to get the sand and stones etc.

and we store them at home. Then when people come to buy those materials I have to deal with them and calculate the cost and take the money from them.

I didn't have any experience (of how to run a business) before. But now, in the process of running this, I've learnt the ropes. I have to keep track of things like, I have bought sand for so much and stones for so much, and how much did I sell them for. And 15,000 is not enough, even to bring a truck-full of cement. I need much more than that. I have two cows at home (bought a year and a half ago with money from elsewhere) and they give milk and calves. This time I needed money, so I was able to take Rs 5000 from Ghosh (dairy merchant) on the promise of milk from the cows.

Every month, her business yields a profit between Rs 15,000–20,000. She explains that the profits are more because they own their trucks and therefore do not have to pay for transporting the materials from the dealers to their home. But the trucks have been purchased on installment, for which her husband has to make an installment payment of Rs 22,000 every so often. Overall, combining their incomes and after meeting all their expenses, their household has a Rs 30,000–35,000 surplus every month. This makes them one of the better-off families in the neighborhood.

Some families invested loan-monies in jointly managed agricultural projects and in creating joint family assets like building a house for the extended household. Forty-year-old Marjina Bibi, a mother of five children, is very articulate and outspoken. She has only three years of schooling (i.e., until third grade). Renu, her adolescent school-aged daughter, explains that her mother is so smart because she is a *"road'er side'er meye,"* "a roadside girl." What she means is that her mother was born and grew up in a village that is close to Machlandapur, on the main highway, that has the nearest railway line connecting surrounding villages to the city Kolkata. Growing up near this transportation hub, Marjina, her daughter argues, enjoyed the benefit of restriction-free movement and a wide range of interactions.[2] Marjina talks about her decision to join the group:

---

[2] This is the full extent of what Renu volunteers by way of an explanation and comparison between her mother's native environment and upbringing and her own very different one. This excerpt highlights important factors that are conducive to fostering women's agency: "My mother is a 'girl of the roadside' (*roader sider meye*). We are village girls, we are studying, and I have taken my class ten exam. If we are, at least, able to go out of the village twice a week then we can gain some experience. But first of all we are not allowed to go absolutely anywhere on our own. And if we do go somewhere then we have a 'passenger' along with us, so imagine that. That's what I mean when I say that my mother is smart and articulate and clever. If one is not conversant with the outside world then one cannot gain experience, and it is not enough to just use the innate intelligence that one has. One has to get to know about the outside world. Without it, one cannot be developed in every respect … In case of my mother, she is 'smart' in every respect; she has the experience of

First I did not join because I wasn't sure that my money would be safe here. But after the others had saved up to Rs 150, I paid the full amount and joined. My "guardian" (husband) did not know about it; I hid it from him and joined the group. There is a cooperative bank here called Ramchandrapur Bank, but that belonged to men. It didn't belong to us. There they would have to write off their land titles, and here we (women) have united and formed a group. Now at least we (their family) don't have any more transactions with the cooperative bank.

Her husband came to know of her group membership six months later when the group gave out its first loan and she took a loan. Then, seeing the financial benefit of being in the group, he did not object. They have ten *kathas* of land and five cows, hens and ducks, assets that they had before joining the group. Every year she earns about five to six thousand rupees from selling milk from the cows, and if everything goes well with their crops, the family has a surplus of Rs 8000–10,000 by the end of the year. The loans Marjina has taken in the three and a half years of group membership have been used in cultivation. But the most recent loan, the most significant sum that they have borrowed up to now, is being used to build a brick house. Having taken out more than Rs 18,000 in loans, Marjina comments on how they manage the repayments:

First I took Rs 2000 for buying rice for the family (for its consumption purposes); that year we didn't grow paddy. Then I took Rs 3000 to take some land on "bondok" (taking possession of pawned away land). After that I took Rs 3500 for taking more land as well. This time I have taken Rs 10,000 for building a house. Our mud house fell in the last flood. We will repay it from cultivation. Say, for instance, right now I have a kind of bean in the field, and at the end of every month this season I am selling it and repaying the loan. In the meantime I have also planted *potol* another summer vegetable that will be ready for harvest during summer. Then there is another kind of bean that will be ready in the meantime. Then we also have date palm trees, and we make molasses out of it and sell it in the market. These are the various ways that we manage the repayment. If there is an income then it is not a problem. Repayment depends on income.

going places, talking to people, mixing with Hindus and Muslims equally, knowing how to talk to different sorts of people so that they will be pleased, how to behave with others. When she was in her native village near Machlandapur, she did not face any restrictions in her movement. But you know how it's like for us – even if we go from here to the market in Masia then someone will go with us. Even if I ride my bicycle, someone will have to go with me in my passenger seat. We do not have the '*hukum*' (permission) of going anywhere on our own. When we went to school, even then a bunch of us girls would go together. If there is a good cinema playing, and you think let us friends go watch it, but we don't have the '*hukum*' to go watch a cinema. And it is not only a question of our parents but the whole village environment where there is a lot of social pressure. Say if I do something wrong, it will be all right with my parents because a child never becomes bad in his or her parents' eyes, but the surrounding environment will talk and create pressure. And the biggest thing is honor, everyone has to look out for their honor. Otherwise one's honor will be tarnished."

Marjina is an equal manager in the household finances. She explains her active role as a necessity for keeping the household strong and healthy:

The household belongs to both husband and wife. So, if both don't put their heads together for everything, then how can the household be run? One has to keep track of everything; it is necessary for both the man and the woman to do it. It is necessary because what if my husband earns twenty rupees and spends thirty rupees, then where will the money come from? That is why it is important to keep track of the expenses. Those who don't keep track are in a bad situation. And those who do keep track have a healthy household.

These examples show a variety of loan use patterns. In all of these cases, including those of partial or full loan transfer, the women were aware of all the financial transactions of the household and the expenditure and use of loans. Overall, there was no case where women were put in a suppliant position in relation to their husbands or sons because of the loan transfer or because of the need to make timely loan repayments to the group. The cooperative nature of the husbands of these women (a very small minority proportionally) meant that the distinction between loan transfer, joint use, and direct loan use was not significant in the lives of these women. Loan transfers did not reflect an unequal distribution of power between the spouses in the household. An egalitarian balance of authority prevailed in which both spouses exercised their prescriptive and proscriptive voices as they conducted the pragmatic affairs of the household for their mutual benefit.

DE FACTO FEMALE-HEADED MUSLIM HOUSEHOLDS

Only six Muslim women said that their husbands were inept and incapable of running the household. There were no cases of husbands working away from home as migrant laborers. Generally, women who were de facto household heads because their husbands were either inept or disinterested in managing household affairs handed over loans to their adult sons. Mothers and sons usually collaborated on the plans for investing the loans, and the actual work was then usually carried out by the sons.

"And then you have to take on your actual form"

Saleya Bibi and her husband have some cultivable land of their own. They lease additional land, and they have three cows and some goats and hens. They have two sons. One is currently in college and the other has completed college and is about to commence his studies for a master's degree.

Saleya says that the decision for her children to pursue education had not come easily, and they have all had to overcome enormous adversity to make that possible. Talking about her life prior to joining the microcredit group, Saleya shares the story of her family's hardships and how she came to take the decision to step out of the house to start laboring by her husband's side in a floor tile factory:

> He (her husband) couldn't control the household being the only earner. Now with this money (loans from the group), we have been able to cultivate and have improved our situation a bit. I have to help out with the agricultural work. My son is still studying and there are several expenses. If one has to bring up their children in a situation of hardship, one always needs to be on the lookout and see from where they can earn a bit of money. And then you have to take on (or reveal) your actual form. . . .I left with my husband to work in the tile factory (six months of work and residence on the factory site). I would go and cook for him and work as his assistant. He would do all the heavy work of making the tiles. I didn't go to steal there but to work; we all have to work to feed ourselves. In this way we were able to improve our situation with the blessings of the one above us.

In the meantime, Seleya learned that a microcredit group had started in her neighborhood. She decided to join on the condition that she would not have to attend the bi-monthly group meetings for the six months that she was away working alongside her husband. It has been four years since she joined the microcredit group. In this time, she has taken five loans, starting with Rs 2000, then Rs 2500, then Rs 3000, then Rs 6000, and, most recently, Rs 9000. All of this money has been used for cultivating paddy. Saleya keeps track of all the loan investments and repayments. She also keeps track of all the household income and expenses. Explaining her leadership in deciding how much loan money to take out, in what amounts, and how best to use it productively, Saleya says:

> His father isn't that clever. He was never into taking any household responsibility. He never thought that he had to keep aside a few bucks for the household, or buy a bit of land and bring up the children. Otherwise, he is good when it comes to working and all that, but if he gets angry, he loses his temper and then he cannot control himself. I have to step in and manage everything . . . It is for bringing them up that we have struggled so much. Today we are working as laborers with the hope that when their time comes, they don't have to feed themselves through their physical labor.

Saleya's eldest son has now started earning by giving private tutorial lessons to village children. This has eased the burden of loan repayment, since he can now manage his own expenses and contribute to household expenses. Overall Saleya claims to have benefited greatly from the loans that now total a little over Rs 22,000.

Rashida Bibi is thirty-nine and has a class eight education. She is another example of a woman who has a husband who is not quite reliable when it comes to practical household matters. All she says of him is that he gets angry frequently. Rashida has been the person in their household who plans what loans to take out and how to use them. First she took a loan of Rs 5000 and bought a cow. Then she took a hefty loan of Rs 15, 000 and made some honeybee boxes with it, so her son could expand his small honey-making enterprise. The initial idea came from her brother who gave his nephew seven boxes of bees and told Rashida that if she could give him some more, then they would not have to worry about supporting him. Now he has a total of thirty bee-boxes with the loans Rashida has taken out. She says that being in the group has made it possible for her to realize her plans:

I think that joining the group has been good. If I had this opportunity, I would have done it five years back. I have benefited from it in every respect. All the things I wasn't able to do because of the lack of money, I've been able to do. I can proceed gradually now with the help of the loans. In the future, I have hopes of doing more. Before I would feel helpless and would think that hoping was useless, but now I don't think that anymore. Now I think that, even if it is delayed by two years, my hopes will be fulfilled. I will be able to establish my sons.

That task has become easier for her with the cooperation of her husband and sons who all now voluntarily report back to her with the details of their financial transactions since she has taken the lead in taking out and repaying the family's loans. Rashida reports:

Yes I would (keep track of transactions) because what would we do if we spent more than we earned? So with that thought I would keep track of transactions. Now, even without my asking for it, they come and tell me about the transactions and tell me about the income and expenses. This is a big benefit because a lot of things become easy. Now that I have to repay the monthly installments, I don't have to worry about the repayments if I am fully informed about the transactions and know from where and when to expect the money to come. And I have told my son so he too sends the money on time. I have not missed even one installment. I am the first one among all to repay the loans.

Anjuara Bibi is now in her mid-fifties and has a class six education. She has adult sons on whom she depends for her basic sustenance. Anjuara has been a member of a microcredit group for the past seven years, having joined one of the very early groups in the region. Recalling her initial experience she says:

Objections! I was beaten so many times for it (attending group meetings). I used to steal my way here. When he (husband, now deceased) would go to the fields, I would come here behind his back. He would come and ask, "Where have you been?" and I had to make up excuses. My husband had a bad temper. He would scold me a lot saying, "Don't go there, people will talk badly about you if you go to meetings." Now everything is open access (*khola bajaar*[3]).

Anjuara has four sons. All of them used to work as farm laborers for Rs 30 per day. The first loan she took from the groups was for Rs 3000. With that money the family took some land for cultivation on a sharecropping arrangement. Her sons grew paddy, and, with the money they made from selling it, they took up more land for cultivation. Then her sons suggested the idea of buying some agricultural land and asked their mother to get a loan for them. Anjuara took out a loan of Rs 4000 from her group and one of her sons borrowed Rs 4000. With this money, they purchased eight *kathas* of land that they now cultivate. It has been two years since they bought the land, the family's first experience of land ownership.

All these households show improvements in their economic well-being. Improvements range from significant markers like purchase of land and expansion of the acreage taken up for cultivation to being able to establish sons in businesses that provide a secure livelihood. These women's heavy reliance on adult sons for initiating and running income-earning enterprises is particularly striking. In return, the sons not only contributed to the general household finances, but sometimes took on the responsibility of assuming the position of primary breadwinner for the family. Strictly independent loan use by Muslim women was not found in this small category of female-led households with active husbands and sons present.

TRUE FEMALE-HEADED MUSLIM HOUSEHOLDS

"I've got to scale up the tree step by step"

Sophura Bibi belongs to a predominantly Muslim group that she helped to establish seven years ago. Now in her fifties, tall and lean, she wears a discolored white saree draped across her bare torso and leaves her head uncovered like many elderly women in these villages. What makes her unlike the others is her outspoken manner and her air of assertive self-sufficiency. She has been running her own small-scale home-based paddy-milling enterprise (manually processing paddy into parboiled rice) for nearly two decades.

---

[3] "Bajaar" means market and "khola bajaar" means open market. What she means here by using the analogy of the open market is that now everything is out in the open.

Like all women from these rural parts, Sophura married at a young age. But the marriage lasted a very short time. Soon after her marriage, she gave birth to her first child, a daughter. Unhappy at this outcome, her husband left her in her father's house where she had come to give birth. Her husband married again. The baby was only two months old at the time.

Sophura could have recovered and returned to her marital home with her husband and claimed her place as the first wife. But she decided to remain in her father's house that was also home to her married brothers. Sophura continued living with her aged father and her brothers' families.

Self-conscious of her economic dependence on her married brothers, Sophura started a small paddy-milling business to support herself and her daughter financially. She bought harvested paddy in bulk from the local rice-farmers, frequently traveling to wholesale grain markets in the surrounding villages. She then had to hire local "van" drivers to transport the sacks of grain to her house. All of these transactions entailed haggling and required the ability to make speedy calculations. Once home, Sophura manually husked the paddy to separate the rice from the chaff and then parboiled and dried the grain at home. The final step was selling this stock of semi-processed grain to the local rice-mill where the rice-grains are further milled and polished and then sold at wholesale prices to rural and urban retail establishments. Sophura recounts:

You can't do this business without money. So, I had to take money from the moneylenders at an interest of ten percent (monthly). If I take Rs 5000, then I have to pay Rs 500 at the end of the month as interest. If I didn't borrow, then I wouldn't be able to run my business. And Rs 5000 was nothing (compared to what was needed).

Sophura continued in this way for some years until her sister, who had been married into a wealthy family, decided that Sophura should get her share of their father's land. This would prevent the possibility that she would be "beaten and kicked out" empty-handed by her brothers after their father's demise. Their father owned twelve *katha* of cultivable land that was to be eventually divided among his two sons and two daughters. Sophura's sister insisted that he divide the land equally between the four siblings while still alive and relinquished her share to Sophura. This entitled Sophura to six *kathas* of land.[4]

---

[4] According to Shariah law (applicable for Muslims), for parents with sons and daughters, a son gets twice the share of a daughter. Following this principle, Sophura should have received 2.4 kathas from her own and her sister's share (1.2 each). But the equal division

Their father, afraid that his sons might disapprove, asked Sophura for payment in exchange for the land, forcing her to buy what should have been hers by right of inheritance. He decided to sell it to her a little below the market value, but her brothers insisted on the full market value. Sophura was forced to borrow Rs 6000 from her business contacts in order to buy the land. Her next step was to build a house and set up independent residence. The land she had acquired had a pond, so she borrowed an additional Rs 13,000 and had the pond filled and built a thatched clay hut on it. To acquire these assets and keep her business running simultaneously, she regularly borrowed from the local moneylenders at high interest.

Pointing to herself, Sophura emphatically proclaims, "Everything that I've done is with this body of mine." Subsequently, while still in her child-bearing years, Sophura had another daughter and, following that, a son by the same man from whom she had separated. However, he did not make any financial contribution toward the children's upbringing. She bore all the expenses single-handedly, and, when the time came, she arranged for her daughters' marriages. For these marriages, too, she had to borrow money from the local "*mahajan*" or moneylenders. Through the years, Sophura had become a familiar face to them. Women like her could ill-afford to borrow at high interest but were nevertheless reliant upon it for their survival.

In 1997, almost a decade after she had started her business, Sophura heard about a local NGO that was forming groups through which women like her would have access to low-interest loans. With her external high-interest debts piled high, Sophura enthusiastically volunteered to form a group in her neighborhood and worked hard at gathering other women. The initial months of the group were difficult. Men taunted them whenever they walked to their group meeting carrying their balance books.[5] Yet, as the group leader, Sophura remained firm: "We didn't pay any heed; we'd take our notebooks and go to the 'club.' Why would we listen to what they said?! We would act according to our own will!"

---

of land among the four siblings was done on the insistence of the oldest daughter. Among Hindus, equal property apportionment among sons and daughters was legally established only in 2005 with the Hindu Succession (Amendment) Act. This was an amendment of the original Hindu Succession Act of 1956 that was formulated by the Indian parliament in order to provide a cohesive set of laws to bridge the differences between the Dayabhaga and Mitaksara schools of Hindu personal laws that had differing guidelines on inheritance.

[5] It was in this village that there were rumors that the NGO staff would make the women bare their legs and stamp them with a seal. And it was here that some men argued that the loans were being provided by the American government and should be shunned.

Once the loan cycle started, Sophura entered into a series of transactions. She took low-interest loans from the group and repaid her high-
interest debts with the moneylenders. She then used her income from the
business to gradually repay the group loans. In her seven years of group
membership, she has taken seven loans totaling Rs 20,000. This was the
highest sum of loans taken by a Muslim woman who was a true household
head and who was unsupported by any income other than her own. With
these loans, she has repaid all her external debts. Explaining her financial
strategy, she says, "I've got to scale up the tree step by step. If I try to jump
and get on top of it at one shot, then I'll fall and break my leg!" With her
latest loan, she has bought a stretch of cultivable land adjacent to her
house. She says with indignant pride, "I have debts from buying the land,
not from eating!"

Sophura now has a savings of Rs 1075 in the group. Three years back,
she opened a savings account in the post office, and in that she has an
additional savings of Rs 1540. She has also started a life insurance policy in
the name of her teenaged son, and for that she pays an annual premium of
Rs 2480. Even though she knew of these opportunities long before joining
the group, she was able to enroll in them only later. She thoroughly
appreciates the financial relief that the group has brought to her life:

What I like most is that now, even if there's a shortage or crisis, I don't have to
spread my palms in front of others and beg for a bit of rice and worry about who'll
give me a little bit of money ... There've been times when I've paid more interest
than capital. But in the group the interest is low. So we can take loans, repay the
interest and capital, take another loan, and plan for investing it in business. I can
buy ten, fifteen sacks of paddy with these loans. When I need money, I take it from
the group and work with it. I don't have problems any more.

Socially being a part of the group has made little difference for Sophura.
Although she now gets an opportunity to congregate with other neighborhood women at the bi-weekly group meetings, even before these group
meetings she had full freedom of movement and interaction. She sums up
the influence of the group on her life, once again repeating the benefit of
the loan:

I didn't have a "guardian"; I was my own boss. So I had to take the initiative and
introduce myself to others. I had to do everything from buying to selling on my
own ... To buy paddy, I would go to the weekly markets in Keosha, Chandipur,
and Sarapur, which are all very far. Everyone loves me; I can get help from
whomever I ask. Taking money from the moneylender was the biggest blight. We
would be paying interest forever, and the capital would still remain unpaid. But
the situation improved gradually after joining the group. Now we're operating in a

healthy way. At least I don't have to beg my neighbors for help: "Lend me Rs 2000 now, and I'll give you an extra Rs 200 when I repay you."

Sophura and women like her who have been single-handedly managing on their own for decades had an intense awareness of the cost of borrowing from moneylenders. They were emphatic about the relief microcredit had brought to their lives.

"In times of crisis and need, in good times and in bad"

For some women, especially those undergoing the shock of recent widow-hood, a microcredit group can be a lifeline preventing descent into destitution. Firoza Bibi is in her mid-forties and had eight years of schooling. Firoza took a loan of Rs 1500 planning to use it for cultivation. Her husband was a farm laborer and they were used to cultivating land together on sharecropping arrangement. Just a week after taking out the loan, Firoza's husband fell ill. The entire sum was spent for doctors and on his treatment. She had to sell her cow to repay the loan from the group.

Since Firoza's husband failed to recover, she had to borrow money privately from the woman who was the group supervisor. The illness continued, and after some months he died. At the time of the study, Firoza was completing her second year in the microcredit group, and it was a year since she had been widowed. During this year, her teenage son, who was in the tenth grade in school, had to abandon his studies and start working as a mason to earn a livelihood for the family.

Firoza's daughter has continued with her studies and attends the ninth grade. Firoza took a second loan of Rs 2500 for buying a dairy cow and books for her daughter. She raised the cow for a while and earned money from selling milk. She repaid the loan by selling off the cow and took another loan of Rs 4000 and, with it, bought two calves and some paddy. She talks about her future plans for loans:

What I will do is, next time I take a loan, I will use some of that money to buy paddy during the harvest season. I will boil the paddy and make rice out of it, and then I will sell off my cows to repay the loan. Later I will buy a cow with the money I make selling the rice.

Firoza earns about five to six hundred rupees every month and her son, who now works as a mason, earns one thousand to twelve hundred a month. Firoza hires herself out for any task that a family in the village needs done, from cooking for large gatherings to cutting grass for fodder. If her family is invited to eat where she has been hired to cook, she ends up saving a kilo of rice from that day's quota of consumption. This is how her family survives. On the difference the group has made to her, Firoza says:

After joining the group, I see that in times of crisis and need – in good times and in bad – I am helpless now because I am a poor; I am helpless. If I come to you and tell you, I am in great need, please give me five rupees, no one will give it to me. They know that if they give me five rupees, then I won't be able to return it. But now, after joining the group, I can see that in times of need I can tell Shahanara (the group supervisor). I haven't taken anything yet, but still if I tell her that I need ten or twenty rupees right now, or even two hundred, then she will say that if you really need the money, then we can withdraw the money out of the group savings deposit … So now I know that I can get a hundred, two hundred, or even two thousand if I need it.

Firoza anticipates that she will need money from the group and, presumably, from outside sources as well at the time of her daughter's wedding. For her son, she hopes that she will be able to take out a loan in the future and help him set up in a business. And for herself, she hopes that the money she is saving in the group will provide her a safety net in her old age:

And in my old age, when I have this money (savings in the group), then my daughter-in-law will know not to ill-treat me because if she does, she will know that I will give the money to my daughter. Am I saying anything wrong? When I don't have a 'guardian' (husband), I have to think about my own future. I have provided for my sisters-in-law, but with the current generation it is doubtful whether the new woman (daughter-in-law) will feed us.

Firoza ends with these emphatic words, "Till the day I can walk about, I will continue with the group. I will never leave it, ever."

Firoza's steadfast conviction that the group could always be relied upon in times of crisis was based on the group's coming to the rescue of Muslima, another group member. A thin, even emaciated woman, Muslima was deserted by a husband and left alone to provide for her four children. Her husband worked seasonally in a brick kiln factory. (Laborers usually stay at the work site in temporary homes for this work.) During his seasonal absences from home, he developed a relationship with a woman that worked in the kiln and married her.

Muslima and he started having problems, and, as a result, he stopped giving her money for food. Left with no other recourse, Muslima started working as a casual maid in the better-off houses in the village. In the meantime the microcredit group in her neighborhood started and Firoza and a few others insisted that she join, since she received no financial support from her husband. Muslima joined, she says, with the prospect of being able to save Rs 10 every fifteen days. That was three years ago.

Since then, she has started working as a daily-waged farm laborer on the land of the group leader's family (they cultivate seven to eight bighas of land). From the Rs 35 daily wages, she has to meet the basic expenses for a family of five.

She took out an initial loan of Rs 1000, a low sum reflecting the poverty of her household, to buy her son a bicycle. He had been insisting on one for some time. He was still young but grown up enough to start working around the village. In the meantime, her husband married a third wife. The group leader confirms that he doesn't do anything for Muslima. The only thing that he continued to do for her was to allow her to stay in the thatched house on the plot of land he owned.

Eventually, Muslima's husband made the decision to sell the house off. This news came as a shock to Muslima who was already virtually destitute and responsible for caring for four young children, both sons and daughters. If her husband sold this plot, she would be left destitute and homeless.

When she broke the news to the group, the group leader called a meeting and, together, the group members decided to withdraw Rs 3000 from the accumulated group savings and lend it to her. This way Muslima could have immediate access to the money she needed (instead of waiting for the next loan cycle). Loans from group savings are virtually interest-free and come with a flexible repayment schedule that depends on the repayment ability of the borrower.

With this money, Muslima was able to buy the land and house from her husband and have it registered under her own name. This averted an enormous crisis in her life. She is repaying the loan now with her farm-laborer earnings.

While still repaying her two loans, another crisis hit. Her daughter, who had been married away just a few years before and who had left her abusive husband and returned home, secretly consumed some poisonous fertilizer in a bid to kill herself. (She took the fertilizer from the house of the group leader for whom her mother worked as a farm laborer.) Muslima's daughter was admitted to the local hospital with the help of some villagers. She recovered, but the doctor refused to discharge her until the hospital charges were met.

Muslima again turned to her only lifeline, the microcredit group. When she notified the group of what had happened, the group came to her rescue. They lent her Rs 1000 from the group savings fund. Muslima is now paying off all of these loans from her own earnings. Her son, who has now started working, has taken charge of the expenses of the household. The group leader comments on the difference the group has made:

If we didn't have the group, maybe she (Muslima) would have to borrow from somebody. And you can't get money for free. Now since we had a group, all of us were able to help her out. If we didn't have the group, we wouldn't be able to help her out in this way. We have Rs 18,200 as group savings, so when she had trouble, we took some money out of that and helped her.

Muslima agrees that without the group she would in all likelihood have had to borrow at high interest in these times of crisis. Reflecting on the savings she is accumulating in the group (Rs 930), she says, "If my son doesn't give me enough to eat in my old age I can feed myself."

Some women then make completely independent use of microcredit loans to run their own small businesses or support their own livelihoods enterprises. Even when they have sons who are old enough to work, only a few seem to work in the mother's enterprises. Mostly, the sons' lines of work are separate from their mothers'. The loans are used by the women exclusively to support their own income-earning enterprises. These women deserve our attention.

As we have seen, there is wide diversity in the economic vulnerability exhibited by these women's households. Importantly for these women, especially for the many who live on single incomes, microcredit groups provide a source of certain and low-interest credit (compared to other informal sources). This, as we have seen, had enabled women to expand existing enterprises, to purchase land, to buy homes to prevent eviction, and to start new savings plans and life insurance policies. Microcredit has also become an extremely valuable source of financial assistance in times of crisis. No longer do the ordinary shocks and blows of rural life necessarily expose these women to sudden impoverishment, begging from neighbors and relatives, or permanent indebtedness to village moneylenders at ruinous rates of interest.

EGALITARIAN HINDU HOUSEHOLDS

Saraswati Mondol is in her late twenties and has a class six education. Very soon after joining her microcredit group, she took out a relatively large loan. Her husband had decided to buy a power tiller that he would use to plough the fields of other farmers on hire. He had inherited only a small portion of land after his father's land had been divided among all his sons.

In the beginning, when Saraswati was newly married, the family made do with whatever they earned from cultivating the land. Their economic prospects were extremely limited. Her husband decided not to rely on cultivation alone for the family's livelihood and proposed the idea of buying a power tiller:

First time I took Rs 1000 for cultivating summer paddy. The second time I took Rs 10,000 with the thought of buying a power tiller, but due to the fault of my fate I couldn't buy it that year. I had kept the money only for three to four months and had returned the money because if I kept the money, I would have to keep on paying the interests. Next time I took 15,000 and with that I bought the power tiller. I needed a lot of money to buy it; the loan was a part of it. We had some money at home, and we had to borrow some from outside. I repaid the 15,000 by doing "*halkhatha*" at the beginning of the cultivation season (debtors pay up at the beginning of the Bengali new year or at the start of the cultivation season). After that I again took 15,000 and paid off all the outside debts at high interests. I also bought oil (diesel) with the money, because we have to buy a lot of oil for tilling almost four to five hundred *bighas* of land (other people's fields).

Now the family earns Rs 60,000–70,000 in a period of two months every year during the plowing season. They have sold their existing power tiller because of the wear and tear from three years of use, and they are arranging to buy a newer one. Saraswati continues to rear livestock. For the last two years she has been growing and selling mushrooms in the winter, a skill she learned from the organic agriculture department of the same NGO that operates the microcredit program in which she is enrolled.

Kalyani Bayen's life has given her a remarkable story to tell. On the verge of becoming a college graduate, she withdrew before taking the final examinations. From a poor family, her father had contracted tuberculosis and could not cultivate the family land. The land had to be given up for sharecropping and the cows had to be sold off. Kalyani, the eldest child, had to take on the responsibility of earning a livelihood for the family.

She enrolled in the livelihoods training program offered by the NGO that now operates the microcredit program and learned to operate a knitting machine. For the next three years she remained affiliated with the NGO program and produced machine-knitted woolen garments. Gradually she saved up enough to buy herself her own machine.

After a few years, she got married and moved to her husband's house with her knitting machine. Her in-laws are better off economically. They own a concrete house and four bighas of cultivable land. Cultivation is managed by her husband, a college graduate. Failing to find paid employment, he now employs and oversees the work of the hired farm laborers who do the actual work.

Kayani's now-deceased father-in-law had accumulated a bank balance and the monthly interest they earn from that covers their monthly household expenses. Right after her marriage, Kalyani started knitting and selling the manufactured items to a trader. Seeing her at work, after a few years her husband learned from her how to operate the knitting machine. Both of them started producing knitted garments that they sold in bulk to the trader.

When microcredit loans started to be given out, Kalyani took a loan of Rs 7000 and with a part it she bought more supplies, hired ten women whom she taught to operate the machine, and set them to work for her. The rest of the money was spent on cultivation. Kalyani and her husband continued to work for the trader and on the side set up their own business.

In the next round, they took a loan of Rs 8000 and expanded their business further. In the meantime, she started teaching and recruited more workers and placed them in her employment. The most recent loan they have taken out is for Rs 10,000, and that, too, has been spent on the business. Now Kalyani has fifty people working for her, and, as of last year, she and her husband have stopped working. The entire business is run on hired labor. Having taken out loans worth nearly Rs 25,000 from the group in the three years since her group membership, twenty-eight-year-old Kalyani has gone from being a hired piece-rate worker to an entrepreneur in the truest sense. She explains:

This is a seasonal business and for instance in the last season we gained Rs 30,000. This time we have two to three lakhs worth of products, so this time the gains are likely to be more. But this time the price of wool has gone up and the number of people selling knitted garments has gone up too, so the prices of the products have fallen. The selling season lasts for three months; the rest of the year we make the garments.

Both of us keep track of the loan money. When we get the raw material, I have to show the employees what kind of things we want made. As for the accounts, my husband keeps track of most of it, but I do know the basics of what we earn and spend. When he is not there, I have to take care of things. If someone comes to buy the things in bulk, then I have to negotiate with them and make the final sales. Then every Friday both of us go to the market to recover the money the retailers owe us.

Egalitarian households included women from poor sharecropping families including forty-year-old Kalyani Majumdar. Her family of three (including a husband and a son/ daughter) does not own any land. They do own some livestock, two cows and a few goats, hens, and ducks. She rears the livestock and her husband works as a farm laborer earning Rs 30–40 every day that he gets work. In the five years that she has been part of the group she has taken Rs 20,000 in loans for expanding their sharecropping operations:

I took Rs 5000 a long while back for cultivating on sharecropping. We have to give half of the crops to the landowner, and we get to keep half of the crops. It requires money to be able to cultivate, say paddy for instance. What he earns through his work as a farm laborer is not even adequate for running the household. If we take the money from here (group) and cultivate paddy then at least we have some paddy at home for our own consumption and the hay can be kept for the cow. Then a second time I took Rs 5000 again for paddy cultivation. This time I took Rs 10,000, all for sharecropping.

The family is no longer in the precarious financial situation it was when they had to borrow even tiny sums like one hundred and two hundred rupees at 10 percent interest. They had found it difficult to repay even these small amounts and debt had held them back from cultivating. The family had had to depend on their paltry incomes to buy staple food grains at market prices. Kalyani explains the difference microcredit has made: "Now at least we can cultivate paddy and have just enough for our home consumption through the year. We have to sell a bit of it to pay off the loans." The family's general economic improvement is reflected in a change in the shopping practices of the household:

I used to go to the market. We had hardships in our household, so I did the marketing, because I could keep things within a tight budget and save a few rupees. A man can never do the marketing within a tight budget. Now my husband does the marketing. Now we don't have to calculate that with this money we have to buy rice and with this money the rest, we have rice at home (from the paddy they grow). The last five years or so I stopped going to the market.

There is now the added responsibility of repaying the loans for which she has to remain concerned:

After joining the group, I have the worry that every month at the end I have to keep aside twenty rupees. Yesterday I sold ten rupees worth of eggs, and I put the money aside knowing that by the end of the month I would have to deposit twenty rupees ... If I don't keep track of it, how can I repay? I have to pay the installments at the end of the month, so whenever I get some money I put it aside. If he gets forty rupees from working as a farm laborer, I keep aside twenty. I might even sell five hens and put aside the money. If we are in a situation where we can't repay, then we might have to sell a sack of paddy and repay the loans. If I take a credit, I have to pay off the credit. No one is going to let me off if I don't clear my credit. Before, I didn't have these worries, compared to now when I have to worry that I must pay such an amount by the end of the month.

Among other gradual economic improvements, after two years of being in the group, Kalyani has started a life insurance policy in her name. She reveals this with slightly embarrassed laughter. "I started it by getting in touch with the agent. I discussed it with my husband and told him that it was high time to think about my future." It has now been running for three years and she needs to deposit Rs 500 in it every year. If she doesn't have the money at the time when it is due, she borrows it from the group savings to make the installment payment.

DE FACTO FEMALE-HEADED HINDU HOUSEHOLDS

A sizeable group of twenty-seven Hindu women were *de facto* household heads either because their husbands had migrated for work (about ten women) or because their husbands were generally inept in managing household affairs. The highest loan taker in this group was Swapna Biswas. She is thirty-two years of age with a class eight education and has taken Rs 52,000 in loans. The money was used by her husband, a puppeteer with his own puppeteering troupe of seventeen men who travelled to different parts of the state putting on puppet shows six months of the year. Swapna explains:

He is the owner of this puppet company. He earns six months of the year and the other six months he is at home without work. At the end of every season he earns about 2 to 2.5 lakhs. There is one season a year. If he earns 2.5 laks then there is some extra but if he earns 2 lakhs he breaks even, because it is very expensive to maintain such a large team. Their monthly expenses along with show expenses are Rs 25,000 to 30,000.

Before the microcredit group started, they would have to regularly borrow lump sum amounts as large as thirty, forty, fifty thousand from the moneylenders at a 10 percent monthly interest rate. Swapna recalls that once they borrowed Rs 12,000 and had to repay Rs 24,000:

We went on like this and, in the end of every year, we would have no money left over, and the situation would be difficult every time. In the middle of all of this I fell ill and had two operations. Then in the year of the floods we lost almost one lakh. Then after we joined the group and took loans at 2 percent (monthly) interest, we gradually improved our situation. Usually it works this way. We take a lump sum of money as a group loan, then within the group the money is divided among everyone according to their needs. I take whatever is left over and put it into my business. First I took Rs 12,000 for the puppet business, then I took Rs 5000, then this time I took Rs 35,000, all for the business. Now we've built a brick house.

Swapna reports that now they do not have to borrow even a rupee from outside. She herself earns Rs 300–350 from bidi-binding work, which is common in the village.

Six women in this egalitarian household group had husbands who were migrant construction workers who worked in the city. In one case the husband worked in another state and returned home only periodically. All of these women took out loans of varying sums (Rs 16,000 in one case,

Rs 13,000 in two cases, and Rs 7000 in two cases). Most of them had used it for acquiring livestock and for cultivation that was then managed by these women in all cases.

Tulsi Ray is thirty-five years old with no formal education. Her husband is a construction worker and has migrated to the western state of Gujarat to work on contract. His earnings range between two and three thousand rupees per month, and he remits back what he has left over after meeting his own living expenses. Tulsi has been managing the household ever since her marriage. Her husband has always been a migrant worker.

When the group started in her neighborhood, she played an instrumental role, along with a few other early enthusiasts, in convincing other women to join. In the beginning she was shooed away from many households.

When the loan cycles started, Tusli took a loan of Rs 7,500 and bought a jersey cow. A considerably more expensive breed than the local breeds, jersey cows have a higher yield of milk. A jersey cow gives twelve kilograms of milk per day. Tulsi says, "I know that even if I have to work all day after it, at the end of the day, it will give me at least thirty or forty rupees. I have been able to stand on my feet by selling the milk."

But Tulsi's next loan of Rs 8000 was used to buy another cow that she hoped would consolidate her financial success. But it failed to deliver the same results due to an unpredictable turn of events:

It was my idea (to buy the cow); I told him (her husband) about it. I have been able to repay the loan by selling milk even before it was due. I thought of buying another cow, and both of us would work on the cows. If he is there, it is convenient because tending to a cow is a lot of work since I am on my own. This time I took a loan of Rs 8000 and bought another cow. The cow delivered the calf and, right after, it was infected with tetanus. Now, the cow has just a few bones left, and I have to spend a lot for its treatment. Just the other day, I paid the doctor Rs 500 to treat the cow. Now the situation is such that I don't have any money and whatever I had made through the past year I have to spend on the cow, but we still cannot say if it will live or die. So with this right now our situation has fallen a bit. If the condition of the cow was not like this, then I could have bought another one. But now it is such a disaster that I have to think of how to make ends meet. I still have to repay the loan. Now they (group members) are saying that take your time and see if the cow recovers and then sell it and buy another one. If this hadn't happened, then my situation would be very good and it's all because I joined the group. He (husband) had returned home prepared to give up his construction job (and participate with her in livestock rearing), but now he has had to leave again. He suffers from high blood pressure, and it is difficult for him to work from a height, which they have to in that line of work, but he was forced to leave again because we have to repay this loan at the end of the year.

Despite this crisis, there has been one other positive change in the last two years. The change concerns savings rather than loans. Tulsi has started a life insurance policy for which she has to pay Rs 514 every three months. She had wanted to enroll in such a plan for some time, but it became possible only after she joined the group:

No, he (husband) wouldn't listen to what I would say. If I said I wanted to start a savings account, he would say, "Forget it, I am earning. You just eat. What is the use of saving money and all that. After I'm dead will you feed the money to the flames?" But now he can understand the mistake we have made. Now I have started an LIC (life insurance corporation) savings policy. I don't even ask him for his opinion, I don't ask should I do this, what do you think, I don't ask him. But he never returns and tells me, why didn't you tell me you've done this? I did this (signing up for the policy) on my own. There is a boy in this neighborhood who is an agent and I went to him and I said I wanted to start one. I have to pay Rs 514 every three months toward this. It has been two years since I started this. He had been telling me from before to start this, but I hadn't because I wasn't sure from where I would get the money. But then two years back I thought that if ever I get stuck for money, then I would be able to take money from the group and pay for the deposit for this. So after that thought, I started the scheme. But before, I would wonder, from where will I get the money, perhaps I might have to borrow the money at 10 percent interest to pay for this. Then the situation was difficult. But now I am no longer afraid. I am no longer afraid of doing anything; I know that we have our group.

Jayanti Biswas is thirty-six years old and has had four years of schooling. She joined the group four years ago at a time when her husband worked as a farm laborer and earned daily wages of only Rs 30–40. In the last three years he has started working as a construction worker and now earns Rs 3000 per month. They had four bighas of land and they had to borrow at a 5 percent monthly interest from the moneylender to cultivate it. Before her husband migrated, he would manage the farming activities. She would watch and learn and occasionally help him with some of the agricultural tasks.

Now Jayanti borrows from the group for her farming needs and is solely responsible for managing the farming activities. First she borrowed Rs 3000; then she borrowed a hefty Rs 10,000. "I have to go to the field. I have to decide what to put in the field and when (referring to fertilizers and pesticides). I have to decide on how much labor to employ and when." She is the co-leader of the group, and talking about attending the group meetings and looking after the affairs of the group, she says:

Before there was no time for me to do all this (group related responsibilities), because there was so much to be done in the house: cooking, giving my children food on time for school. Now, too, it is hard for me to find the time, but I try and make time.

When she was probed further on how she finds the time now that her responsibilities have multiplied, Jayanti breaks out into a laugh and says, "That is the thing, and now I also have to do what my husband used to do before!"

There were some women belonging to the group of *de facto* independent household heads whose husbands were non-migrants. In these cases, the husband's infirmity or general ineptitude and lack of skill in household matters had thrust these women into taking on managerial control.

Angurbala and Kanan were two such women. Each had taken out large Rs 19, 000 loans. Angurbala is forty-five years old with no education and has taken out at least two loans in the three years that she has been a group member. She notes the improvements that she has been able to make because of the loans although she finds it hard to state the gains in terms of income. Her husband has cancer, and for many years she has had to take over the reigns of the household. She has had to become the principal earner in the household that includes their three children, two daughters, and a son:

I don't remember how many times we have taken loans but I remember that last year I had taken Rs 8,000 and this year we have taken Rs 11,000. We use the money for cultivation. We used to have to take money from the moneylender before, but now we take money from here and do the cultivation. We don't have to get into debts elsewhere. We can also cultivate more land than before.

Comparing her situation to conditions before she joined the group, she concludes that she has benefitted overall from escaping the moneylender with a 5 percent monthly interest rate:

Before we had barely enough to eat, so I had to work as a farm laborer, cultivate our own lands, take loans and get into debts and, in this way, I've brought things so far. And then we had this opportunity (loans from the group), everyone said this would make things more convenient for us, so I did it. From this I have received benefits ... I was paying 5 percent (monthly) interest before but now I have to pay less interest.

In addition to the financial support provided by the group, Angurbala comments on the help she has received socially. Her fellow group members, who are now aware of her husband's illness, provide her with the indirect support system that she needs. Angurbala has now also accumulated a savings of Rs 1600 in the group. This is her first savings.

Thirty-seven-year-old Kanan Biswas has no education and has a husband, a son who is studying in school, and an eighteen-year-old daughter who was married at the age of fifteen but was brought home to save her from an abusive husband. The family has no land of their own, so they have taken possession of pawned away land in order to cultivate paddy. Her husband works as a farm laborer and earns daily wages of Rs 35 for the days that he finds work.

In talking about her husband, Kanan says that he is lacking in wits, that he is less clever than the average person. For that reason she has had to manage everything. He is very good-natured, never demands any explanations, and is also a hard worker, but lacks any practical sense. Kanan singlehandedly manages the finances and makes all decisions concerning crop cultivation and the running of the household. This includes managing all the arrangements for her daughter's marriage.

In her four years in the group, Kanan has taken Rs 19,000 in loans for cultivation:

I do the work of cultivating the land we take. My husband understands less, so I have to budget and manage the cultivation and do the entire farming work. I ask others how much fertilizer and pesticide we need for a piece of land, and I go to the shop and buy the things as per their suggestions. And then my husband puts it in the field. All the shopkeepers sell me the pesticides and fertilizers. My husband doesn't quite understand these things, and everyone knows that it is not a problem to sell me these . . . First I took Rs 8000 to take possession of a piece of land (pawned away). Then I took Rs 10,000 for cultivation. I have twice taken Rs 500 from the group fund for cultivation.

In addition to farming, Kanan rears four cows and a goat. Having this livestock provides the security of being able to pay back loans by selling them if the need arises. So far, this has not been necessary. Instead she has been able to take up more land than before and expand her cultivation. Before she joined the group, the family refrained from borrowing from the moneylender fearing the high interest rate. But with the relatively lower interest microcredit loans she says she gained the courage to borrow and expand the scale of her farming on credit:

Before, the way we always had shortages and complaints, we don't have that any more. Before we didn't have the courage to take money from anywhere and do something with it, but now we have the courage. I have saved some money. I have the courage in my mind that after some days I will get the money and do a particular work. We have courage in our hearts now.

Kanan now has a life insurance policy through which she saves one hundred rupees every month.

A smaller group of women who were *de facto* heads of their households took out loans of Rs 5000 or less. The husbands of these women were unfit to work, and in many cases these families did not own any land. These households were economically extremely vulnerable.

There was forty-five-year-old Shobita Shaha, who was the sole provider for her family of five that included her husband and three children. Her husband, having suffered psychiatric problems, was unfit to work and could no longer continue with his work as a vegetable vendor. When the household economy ground to a stop, Shobita had to come up with a way to earn a livelihood. She went to a toy factory in the neighborhood and learned how to make plastic rattles. Then she took a microcredit loan of Rs 3000, bought the raw materials with it, and she and her son started making the plastic rattles at home. Her twenty-eight-year-old son sells them to retail stores in the local market. She earns approximately Rs 1500 per month, half of the average monthly earnings of households with working husbands. She was one of the poorest members of her group. Her family did not have a residence of their own and lived in another person's house for free. Nevertheless, even in her present dire condition, she is better off than before she joined the group:

Things are better now than before. Back then things were barely running. Some days he would give me twenty rupees and on others he would give me ten. We used to earn less than Rs 1500 a month then, and we had to struggle hard to make ends meet.

Fifty-five-year-old Monica Biswas has a husband who is now eighty years old and too aged to work or earn a livelihood. They have no land of their own. They cultivate on sharecropping arrangement and own a cow. Whatever they earn is just enough to support the family of three. The loans totaling Rs 5000 that they have taken so far have all been used for cultivation.

Forty-year-old Bimala Ray has a husband who is "lacking in wits" as it is commonly put in these parts. Though he is a construction worker, he is usually without work, sporadically earning Rs 50 per day. Bimala has had to take up working in the house of her better-off neighbor and earns Rs 500 per month. The family has some livestock, and she says, "I sell my hens and raise goats and then I sell my goats and raise cows." She has taken two loans for cultivating, but has not yet been able to get ahead:

I have taken Rs 3000 for cultivating sugarcanes. I did more work for it, but in the end it turned out to be a loss. I had to work and pay off the loan. This time I have taken Rs 2000 from the group savings and have cultivated peas.

Forty-five-year-old Hemlata Sarkar has a family of five that includes a non-working husband who was paralyzed from a fall four years ago and a son who attends college and works as a farm laborer on his free days and earns Rs 35 a day. The family has two bighas of land that they cultivate with loans taken from the group and that provide their subsistence. The loans she has taken out have been for very small sums:

Last year I took Rs 1000 for cultivation and then I paid it off. Then, at times, I take money from the group savings, 200, 300, 500, all for cultivation. My earnings are less. If I take more than this, then I will be in difficulty to repay. That is why I take money in small amounts.

As the circumstances of these women's lives demonstrate, the improvements in well-being from microcredit in *de facto* female-headed Hindu households varied enormously. At one end of the spectrum were households that had been able to use microcredit to build sizeable successful businesses and practice agriculture and to achieve significantly improved income levels. At the opposite end of the spectrum were women who had taken out very small loans because of their severely limited economic capacity. With these loans, they were just barely able to ensure the survival of their family, prevent descent into complete penury, and marginally improve their household's economic well-being in the face of extreme economic vulerability.[6]

What made the biggest difference, predictably, was whether the husband was also an income-earner or, at least, able to work on the household enterprise led by the wife or earn a small secondary income. Despite the wide variance in the loan sums and gains from loan use, the most remarkable fact is that a substantial portion of the women became independent cultivators and expanded the land under their cultivation by using microcredit loans.

TRUE FEMALE-HEADED HINDU HOUSEHOLDS

Ilarani Mondol has no education and is now in her early forties. She was widowed two decades ago. At the time, she moved back to her parents' house with her young son. While her father was alive, he provided for them

---

[6] Comparing Hindu and Muslim *de facto* female-headed households we find an unanticipated difference in the pattern of son-reliance. In Hindu households of this description, we do not find the kind of reliance on adult sons for using loan monies that we do in comparable Muslim households.

and Ilarani would do little jobs around the neighborhood and village earning three to four hundred rupees a month. Ten years ago her father passed away, leaving the household composed of herself, her son, and her mother without a principal breadwinner.

Having no other option, Ilarani went to the city to work as a cook and caregiver for another household. She has been doing this work for the past ten years, supporting her family with her income. In the meantime, she has arranged for her son's marriage. She always had the desire to build a house of her own, and with savings from her income she was able to buy a plot of land. But for building of the house itself she needed more money than she had saved. She took her first microcredit loan of Rs 10,000 for building the roof of the house. After repaying that loan by herself, she took out another loan of Rs 15,000 for completing the plastering of the house and to put in the flooring and window grills. She is going to repay this loan from her income and from contributions from her son who now works as a laborer.

Jayanti Biswas has no education and is thirty-five now. She has been widowed since she was twenty when her son was only three years old. Her husband had two bighas of land, and his family had received some more land through land redistribution. The family has also owned a shallow-machine (groundwater irrigation pump) from his time.

After her husband passed away, Jayanti's younger brother-in-law took charge of the family cultivation for a while and bore the responsibility of providing for everyone. After some years, he married and established his own household. Since then, Jayanti has had to take charge of the cultivation. Her teenage son is still completing his education. Jayanti single-handedly manages the entire cultivation:

I have to manage everything, from putting fertilizer in the fields to operating the shallow machine (for irrigation). In the beginning, I would ask people how to do things and, in that way, I learnt. It's been nine years since I've been cultivating on my own.

For five of these nine years Jayanti has been a member of the microcredit group, and she has taken out several loans that she has used for cultivation. She does not remember all the loans she has taken, but she recalls that at first she took the small sum of Rs 1000, then she took Rs 2000, and gradually, as she gained confidence in using and repaying loans on her own, she started taking larger sums. Most recently she has taken Rs 10,000, a substantial sum, for using in cultivation. Now three times a year she produces nuts, paddy, and mustard. At the end of the year, after she has met all the household and agricultural expenses and paid for the hired farm laborers, she reports she has between Rs 2000–4000 left. She claims proudly that this is more than what they used to make when her brother-in-law managed the cultivation.

When asked about her experience of being in the microcredit group, she responds by comparing it with her previous experience of borrowing from moneylenders:

What experience will I have! I am saving some money. If I were to take money from outside, then I would have to pay more interest, or say that the moneylender I usually go to refuses to give me the Rs 2000 I need, then I might fall into difficulty with my cultivation. If I need money to buy fertilizer now, it doesn't help if he gives me the money ten days later. I don't have these problems with the group.

Mangali is desperately poor and in a very different economic situation from that of Ilarani and Jayanti. Mangali's husband abandoned her and married a second time. She is a mother of four young children and has been supporting her family by making packets out of recycled newspaper for the past twelve years. Earlier, she would receive some financial help from her unmarried brothers. But that stopped after the young men got married.

Mangali and her four children live in one room adjoining her husband's ancestral house, a room that she arranged to have built and for which she bought some of the materials on credit. It has been three years since she joined the group. At first she took a loan to have a toilet built for the family because they did not have a facility that they could use. After she was able to repay these loans, she became emboldened and took a loan to start her own packet making enterprise. She began selling the paper packets directly to grocery retailers and in this way got rid of her middleman employer. This increased her earnings from a miserable wage of six rupees for every one thousand packets cut and glued together to a profit of two rupees for every kilo of packets she sold.[7] She reports making and selling several kilos on her own in addition to continuing the work for her former employer:

First I took only Rs 1000 because I was too afraid that I wouldn't be able to repay it. I didn't have a toilet that we could use, so with that money I got a well dug out. Then I took Rs 2000 and with it I bought bricks and lined the well and got the toilet built. I repaid it, and then again I took Rs 2000 and started my own business ... Now I have my own business and I am better off.

---

[7] The most likely explanation for the abysmal wages for making "*thonga*," or packets (the lowest wage that I encountered in my sample) is that these packets are free goods for the customers. Grocery retailers who pay for it do not recover the cost they incur by having to buy this packaging material.

Still, her income is extremely meager for supporting a five-member family. She described how she manages the household on her paltry income:

We can just about survive after meeting all our expenses. There's no saying what we eat, just boiled vegetables and rice. And maybe once a year we eat fish or meat. We survive on my earnings, and we don't have to ask others for help, like, "Give me Rs 10 for buying rice." I can't say exactly how much I earn because I never see the whole sum. Whenever I get some money, I use it for household expenses or pay off my debts ... I don't calculate at the end of the month how much I earned; I just know that the room I built is still standing. It's built of bamboo taken on credit, and I still need to pay for them ... The day I arrange for my daughter's wedding, I'll have to beg from everyone, or else I won't be able to manage. It's an enormous struggle for me. I don't eat or live too well.

Mangali has no other savings apart from the meager amount she has accumulated in the group as part of the mandatory savings deposit:

Rs 500, this is my only fall back. If I were not a part of the group I wouldn't have been able to save this either. All of it would have gone inside our stomachs. Now at least, I have saved Rs 500. However much I might have to struggle to bring up my sons, when they grow up they might not provide for me, then if I have this Rs 500 then, at least, I'll have some courage in my heart that I have Rs 500.

Widowed women who had adult sons showed some advantage over widows without grown sons in consolidating greater levels of household gains from the loans.

Bimala's young sons started working as farm laborers, but work wasn't plentiful, and they were paid the wages of a single worker because they were new and inexperienced in this line of work. When things became too difficult to manage, the family (living in Bangladesh at the time) wrote to their son-in-law in India (one of her three daughters had been married off to a family in West Bengal). Following their son-in-law's advice, the family decided to sell off their property, two bighas of land and a house, to the neighboring "miah" and migrate to India:

I can't tell you the truth because it brings tears to the eyes ... The day before we left, the "miah" gave us only 1500 taka for all the property. We lost everything we had and started on the road with 1500 taka, which we spent in five days in the journey across the border. Wherever we stayed, we had to eat something, and for that we had to pay the middleman. We couldn't bring back anything with us, not even a paisa. We put up in my daughter's house for a year, and my son-in-law took my sons to work as farm laborers in other people's fields. My sons worked for several years and were able to acquire a bit of land on "bondok" (taking temporary possession of pawned away land for cultivation). My youngest son used to work on a man's sapling nursery, and he realized there were gains in it. Slowly he started getting into that work. Now we have taken five bighas of land on lease and have planted our own mango sapling nursery. First I took Rs 3000 for making the saplings, then Rs 5000, then again Rs 2500, all for the same thing.

In the four years that she has been a group member, Bimala has taken four loans totaling over Rs 10,000, all used to expand the plant nursery business that her son had started in a small way with his savings a year before she joined the group. The business has grown substantially because of the loans taken out from the microcredit group. There was no question of borrowing from moneylenders, Bimala says, because no one would lend them money, as they were new migrants and supported only by daily wages from farm labor. They did not have the long-term ties or recognition in the village necessary for traditional rural credit worthiness:

My five bighas of land can be sold for three or four lakhs right now. So I am gaining. My sons are benefiting. I am bringing in money for them, and they are making improvements with it. My sons love me. I have to supervise the work of the laborers who work in the nursery. I have to pass on the instructions from my son. My sons leave for ten to twelve days at a time with all their saplings. Now they have gone to Dinajpur to sell saplings. Before, my two sons used to work as daily-wage farm laborers, and I would make do by stitching coverlets for others. What else could I do before? Who would give us money?!

The transformation in Bimala's life is quite remarkable. The transition from a family surviving on the income of agricultural day wage labor to the status of employers of farm laborers who own a nursery business and who continue to acquire land is no small accomplishment.

The well-being improvements for these Hindu households were similar to their Muslim counterparts. Improvements varied from substantial economic improvements to small, less secure, yet vital survival gains. There was a complex set of factors involved in each case that explained why some women in these female-headed households were able to make larger economic improvements than others. These factors included: the individual woman's business or work-related prowess; the income-earning potential of the woman and her sons (if she had any); the preexisting asset situation of the household (whether the women had inherited land from their husband or father, for example); and the profitability of the chosen line of business for which loans were used. The lines of business that the women chose usually depended on the kinds of work with which they were familiar, the work typically available in the village, and the businesses that their relatives may have suggested or helped them establish or work that their sons picked up through employment by others. No single overriding factor leading to increased well-being holds true across all of these cases.

CONCLUSIONS

What is most remarkable and deserves emphasis is the substantial proportion of women who successfully make independent use of microcredit loans. They do so across a wide range of circumstances and often single-handedly. The narrative of loan transfer in conventional male-headed households has been so dominant in the microcredit literature that scholars have neglected to focus on this crucial category of women. By focusing on women who are not among those struggling to gain basic capabilities, we can find much to learn and to celebrate regarding the economic impact of microcredit on improving household well-being.

For the most economically vulnerable households, the improvements these women experienced in their earnings, on which the welfare of their entire family depends, are very small and incremental in absolute economic terms. These families' lives are far from being lifted out of poverty. Microcredit loans, however, remove entire families from the terror of imminent catastrophe and the immediate risk of food scarcity and other critical basic needs failures. This is a crucially important impact.

For other households, as we have seen, the well-being improvements ranged from women starting or expanding independently run businesses to relief from dependence upon borrowing at high interest from village moneylenders. The degree to which all these well-being gains can be sustained over longer periods is an important question, but one that only time can answer. Households engaged in agriculture or keeping livestock were prone to suffering economic losses in times of natural calamities such as monsoon floods.

All of the examples in this study suggest that for the economic element of microcredit to be successful, and for women to play a major part in it, women must secure basic levels of empowerment and freedom. It is the way that women's agency interacts with particular family and economic conditions that determines outcomes of increased well-being for entire households.

8

Interpreting microcredit

LOOKING BEYOND THE SALVATION–EXPLOITATION DICHOTOMY

This study finds that microcredit generates multiple pathways that significantly affect women's agency in addition to affecting household income. And microcredit improves women's agency through two distinctly separate mechanisms.

Married women in conventional male-headed households experience improved agency as a result of the *associational mechanism* inherent in the membership structure and participatory requirements of microcredit groups. This improvement in agency appears to be available regardless of the economic outcome from the loan's investment and whether the borrower uses the loan for herself or transfers it to her husband or adult son.

Sometimes, women possess significant agency within the constraints of their poverty prior to their involvement in microcredit owing to prevailing household conditions. This agency can be the effect of a wide diversity of circumstances and can have complex social and personal sources. A large proportion of the women who exhibit prior agency are the owners and operators of farm and non-farm enterprises through which they support themselves and their families. Microcredit releases these women from their sole dependency for credit on monopolistic village moneylenders who charge higher interest rates and often make more onerous demands on women who do not have the back-up support of male earners.

For the women in truly female-headed households and *de facto* female-headed households microcredit can be crucial for keeping their households afloat financially. It can even sometimes raise families above the grinding struggles of chronic destitution. There is, nevertheless, no observable improvement with respect to agency in these women's lives unless their microcredit group made the leap into understanding themselves as exercising a social, political, and moral power over their own and others' lives above and beyond the simultaneous performance of any narrowly economic function.

Women in microcredit groups who are subjected to harsh constraints of patriarchy experience no improvement in their agency despite reporting overall economic improvement in their households through the use of microcredit loans. (The loans, in these cases as we have seen, are taken out by women but invested and managed by the male members of their households.)

A few women in the study neither experienced improvements in their agency nor saw their households benefit financially from the use of microcredit loans. However, no women in this study were worse-off in matters of agency as a result of their involvement in microcredit. (A few studies of microcredit programs elsewhere in India (Garikipati 2008) and in Bangladesh (Karim 2011) have found such negative outcomes.)

Some married women in households with continuously co-residing husbands with access to microcredit loans have become independent entrepreneurs and have achieved impressive levels of agency. The *economic mechanism* in such cases turns out to play a major role in significantly increasing the agency of these women. But this leap into entrepreneurship occurs so rarely that it tends to underscore the nearly insurmountable roadblocks most women face when they try to translate access to credit into entrepreneurship. These roadblocks are both social and economic in nature and would seem to require both pragmatic and normative change if they are to be overcome.

Overall, microcredit's associational mechanism appears to provide the crucial resource that allows women to undertake actions that extend their reach beyond their own homes and go against the grain of traditional gender restrictions.

These findings point to the limitations of the "Does it work?" question that is frequently asked in policy and project impact-assessment reviews. The question risks premature position taking strongly in favor or strongly against microcredit. The reality is that microcredit, like many other development and anti-poverty interventions, has a complex combination of impacts.

Microcredit works, and works well, for some women in certain types of households. There are also situations in which it does not work well and may make bad situations worse. A wide divergence of outcome may be observed even within the same microcredit program implemented with relative uniformity by a single organization.

The gains themselves may be of two broad kinds – those pertaining to economic well-being (income and standard of living) and those pertaining to agency (enhancing capabilities). The economic gains may accrue to women in two ways: directly in the form of increased income-earning capacity from investing loans in self-owned and self-managed businesses; or indirectly in the form of increased household income and an improved standard of living from transferring loans to husbands who invest the monies to augment or diversify their families' sources of support. Even in these cases of an overall positive economic outcome, married women in households with productive husbands do not benefit independently or autonomously from benefits gained through microcredit nor does an increased standard of living derived through microcredit translate into equal authority over household income. This is an important finding, but to make it a reason for condemning microcredit outright would be misguided and shortsighted. I give my arguments for this view below.

As we have seen, in real life, women's entrepreneurship is most often experienced as the measure of last resort for struggling households. This reality obviously contradicts the idealized model propagated in the official discourse of microcredit. That model always suggests that targeting credit at economically vulnerable women will act as a universal solution incentivizing all vulnerable women to start their own livelihood enterprises regardless of their household composition, spousal characteristics, or level of deprivation.

There are several factors that work against married women becoming owner-operators of independent livelihood enterprises. These factors include a woman's often limited range of skills, her lack of access to markets, and often her own sense of unpreparedness to invest sums of money on her own. In addition the gendered division of household labor leaves women exclusively responsible for major household tasks like preparing meals, caring for children and elderly fathers- and mothers in-law, and other mundane chores. These domestic reproductive duties are time-consuming and constrain women's mobility outside of their homes.

These conditions explain the prevalence of home-based piece-rate work on which women rely for income such as *bidi*-binding, packet making, garment embroidery, and tailoring. In piece-rate work, a middleman supplies the raw materials and buys the finished products at a pre-decided rate. This precludes piece-rate waged businesses as enterprises women can benefit from by investing their loans in. In addition to this, there are factors like distance to wholesale and retail markets and the possibility of market crowding that rule out the scope for women becoming middlemen entrepreneurs by investing microcredit loans to start businesses on a subcontracting basis.

In rural Bengal, it is usual to find the husbands and adult sons of female enrollees in microcredit groups using the loans the women take out in livelihood enterprises operated by them. The men then repay these loans from their earnings. From a household economy perspective, this arrangement optimizes the economic opportunities available for a married couple in a conventional household structure under existing market constraints. Women can continue to engage in home-based piece-rate work, at which they are adept, and earn independent incomes (albeit paltry but predictable incomes), while their husbands invest the loans in already existing agriculture or trade or in new businesses.

These microcredit loans are therefore not construed as economic contributions made by the women. The infusion of money into the family's productive activity by women taking out microcredit loans does not by itself make any significant difference to the existing structure of female subordination within her particular family or the community at large.

Even when women take charge of parts of the microcredit loans, they use the money in traditionally female economic activities such as rearing dairy cows and goats. Incomes from such activities are normally much lower than husbands' earnings. The earnings from this kind of activity are not regular but are intermittent and in lump sum amounts. The cost for rearing livestock is borne from the regular income of the husband. Money for repaying the loan is drawn from the household budget where usually the lines between individual incomes become most blurred.

Even though women perform the primary physical labor in rearing livestock, the income from these activities is not viewed by men or even by the women themselves as properly belonging to them. This kind of income does not have the kind of transformative effect on domestic gender relations that is claimed by some proponents of microfinance. Nor will this kind of loan use, by itself, do anything to change gender relations at the societal level.

Overall, then, in the socio-economic context of rural South Asia, *access to loans by itself makes no notable difference with respect to agency for a vast majority of women.* The money is incorporated into the male domain and is robbed of its supposed real and symbolic power to challenge traditional structures of female seclusion and subordination.

The associational aspects of women meeting among themselves does make a positive difference with respect to agency for an overwhelming majority of women enrolled in microcredit groups. At the core of the associational mechanism's success in increasing women's agency are microcredit's networked structure and the face-to-face interactions within group meetings. Women's participation in regular group meetings, held in public places, defies conventional codes of conduct that drastically restrict women's basic freedoms.

The network structure of the groups expands the social networks of these women, simultaneously creating strong and weak ties. Regular attendance at group meetings increases women's physical mobility and encourages them to seek access to public places that before were out of bounds. Group participation increases the range and intensity of women's social interactions and increases women's social exposure to the world beyond their households. Belonging to a group often initiates a process of empathetic learning whereby women belonging to a group observe the changes taking place in each other and proceed to emulate one another. This promotes the diffusion of changing tastes, preferences, ideas, and dispositions among the participants of a microcredit group.

The associational mechanism imbues women in microcredit groups with collective agency through an *associational assertiveness*. This confident collective spirit opens up a social space for negotiations concerning the immediate coercions of patriarchy in the household and in the community at large. I use the term *associational assertiveness* to emphasize that the capacity of women to be assertive individually and collectively derives from being connected through a capacious web of group-anchored networks. This is similar to the "associational power" that industrial labor is able to gain from workers' membership in unions and parties (Wright 2000).

"Assertiveness" needs to be conceptualized somewhat differently from associational "power." Power connotes control, authority, and influence. Assertiveness emphasizes the boldness, brazenness, even insolence that women need to stand against the tide of normative coercions to challenge cultural practices that perpetuate and exacerbate gender inequities.

Associational assertiveness emboldened women enrolled in microcredit to create well-functioning groups that have shifted members' fundamental mode of demeanor and address from the traditionally approved feminine *habitus*[1] of *lajja* or modesty (humility, shyness, restraint) to

---

[1] Bourdieu (1977)

becoming imbued with a centered confidence about their rightful place at the center of their households, communities, and villages and about the validity and cogency of their opinions.

Changes of this nature that affect and permanently alter the interior structures of subjectivity take time. They are not easy to capture in crude, standard survey. Agency is a subtle dimension of the self and it may take a while before its transformation shows up in survey data as changes in "women's decision-making role," a variable that social scientists commonly rely on for their diagnosis of women's empowerment.

The legitimacy and credibility that women enrolled in microcredit have now gained in many villages coincides with their growing social capital. In some respects rural women enrolled in microcredit may have gained an advantage over their urban working-class and even middle-class counterparts who lack access to any such broadly based and immediately available non-kin network of women or to a forum where they can regularly engage in "focused interactions" with other women.

We do not know how long the positive impacts of microcredit's associational mechanism will last. How will the second generation in these villages, the children and adolescent sons and daughters of villagers, be affected by watching their own mothers, female relatives, and neighbors participating in fortnightly group meetings, saving money for themselves, and being at the frontline of loan transactions? Is it possible that these young girls and boys will grow up to hold different ideas than the previous generation regarding what it is appropriate for men and women to do? Will they have liberal ideas about gender roles, and especially the role and place of women?

Will the daughters of participating women, when they marry and migrate to other villages, look for microcredit groups to join, and will they be able to improve on the gains made by their mothers? Will the sons of participating women grow up to be young men who become liberal-minded husbands who embody a kind of masculinity that is accommodative and encourages their wives' engagements beyond the domestic sphere?

In the very distant future, will these young girls and boys grow up to be mothers- and fathers-in-law that do not restrict their daughters-in-law with the fetters of convention and propriety? These questions on the intergenerational impact of microcredit require that the time horizon of the *longue durée* be adopted as the proper frame for measuring, valuing, and understanding the full sociological impact of microfinance programs.

Credit and conjugality: microcredit and marital bargaining

In societies where being married is a crucial determinant of women's social standing, it is rare for money to directly translate into bargaining power within a marriage. This pattern holds in both poor and wealthy households. A strong fallback position is an essential precondition needed for bargaining (a combination of cooperation and conflict) between spouses to be effective. In the bargaining model of the household, a person's fallback position is comprised of the options outside of the marital household available to either partner if she or he decides to walk out of the marriage. Also termed the "threat-point" in the household economics literature, the fallback position is assumed to be directly and strongly correlated with access to income and wealth.

The feminist critique of the bargaining model of the household (Agarwal 1997) has argued effectively against the narrow assumption that income, wealth, and economic assets, by themselves, can bolster women's bargaining power. The very category of women's "self-interest" has been interrogated to reveal its complex constitution. In fact, there are determinants of bargaining power that themselves need to be bargained for – social norms is a classic example. What aspects of freedom and division of labor can be bargained over between husbands and wives at a particular point of time are governed by normative boundaries.

Mere access to loans does little to bring about a significant increase in women's bargaining power vis-à-vis their husbands for the majority of married women who do not transform themselves into entrepreneurs. These women gain some interrogative power over their husbands. For the tiny minority of women who become entrepreneurs, bargaining with their husbands was unnecessary. This was primarily because these men already embodied a malleable masculinity (likely because of the grim hardship of poverty) that did not resist a recalibration of gender roles in the direction of egalitarian relations.

The other major obstacle to microcredit translating into bargaining power is the centrality of marriage and the marital family in Indian society. The social acceptability and generalized protection (from other men) that being within the institution of marriage provides to women in Indian society is often preferred over any non-marital alternative. Returning to one's parents' home or going to live in the brother's household as a dependent or living alone on one's own are often experienced as simply unacceptable alternatives. The normative centrality of marriage is not a pattern unique to Indian society. The pattern is broadly prevalent in other

South Asian countries and was a historical pattern that prevailed in many pre-industrial Western nations until the early twentieth century.

Given money's lack of bargaining leverage within marriage, the most surprising finding in this study is the truly remarkable associational assertiveness that a significant proportion of women in microcredit groups have been able to gain. This assertiveness, instead of enhancing women's bargaining power in the classic way portrayed in the cooperation-conflict theory of the household, is found to enhance women's *normative influence* within their households and beyond it. Defiance and disciplining of husbands, using the solidarity of the microcredit group as their source of psychological and moral authority, is what these women achieve rather than competitive bargaining. The fact that improvement in agency occurs in the absence of any objective improvement in women's fallback position is remarkable.

But perhaps defiance of patriarchy and disciplining of husbands are finally of greater practical importance than cultivating a strong fallback position for women within marital bargaining. This may be especially true in a social and economic environment in which exiting a marriage is a desperate measure to be undertaken only as a last resort. It is noteworthy that microcredit groups' ability to discipline and to impose effective sanctions upon men constitutes a kind of agency that takes women far beyond the sphere and patriarchal control of familial circuits. This demonstrates the broad scope of associational assertiveness and its potential to carry a woman past the threshold of her own home. The public-good oriented collective actions conducted by microcredit groups carry radical and radicalizing implications for the potential scope of women's agency that microcredit unintentionally may have brought to the surface and given institutional means of expression and enactment.

Microcredit's inability to substantially increase married women's control over loans and household resources has been criticized by many observers as proof of microcredit's ineffectiveness in promoting women's agency. Without dismissing this shortcoming, I propose an alternative view.

Given the existing structure of rural Indian societies, it is economically and socially more beneficial for both women and men to reside within marital households. Rather than debate the merits of economic independence outside of marriage, I argue that what we should focus on is the quality of the conjugal relationship and whether or not microcredit is able to produce a shift within it.

This study found the following three types of conjugal relation shaping the lives of women who participated in microcredit groups: cooperativecompanionate; cooperation-conflict; and hostile-subordination or authoritarian-non-companionate. These three types of conjugal relations ranged from being *compassionate* (mutually caring and considerate) to being *compliant* (husband demanding obedience and submission from wife). At its most extreme, authoritarian-non-companionate marital relations were *coercive* due to the presence of a bullying husband.

It is an extremely important question as to whether microcredit can affect change across the entire gamut of conjugal relations away from a coercive model to a compassionate model. The qualitative data gathered in the course of this study indicate that microcredit does have such a potential by making women's lives much more visible and public than they were previously. The weekly or bi-weekly group meetings make women's lives publicly visible and make their enhanced capabilities visible and tangible to each other in ways that were not available before.

It turns out that this structural feature of peer-group-based microcredit increases the accountability of men in the private sphere of their marital relationships with their wives. It is not simply men's fear of undesired publicity from the imposition of sanctions from group members that produces change. Women's participation in microcredit groups encourages wives and husbands to reform and expand their normatively informed notions regarding what constitutes proper and just marital relations. For women, the reappraisal of conventional boundaries of gender propriety comes from direct exposure to changes in each other's attitudes and actions.

As the range of acceptable behavior for women expands, husbands' demands for compliance gradually begin to give way to accommodation. This process of change has the long-term potential to bring a positive shift in the very nature of conjugal relations, and this has a direct impact on women's agency and well-being. It would be foolishly shortsighted to allow the poor rates of women's entrepreneurship and the weak statistics on women's control over income to mislead us into underestimating the social potential that microcredit actually holds for an overwhelming proportion of female microcredit members.

Microcredit and civil society

Taking a historical view can be a sobering exercise. Some critics of microcredit emphasize the vast indebtedness being created by microcredit institutions and warn that microcredit is being used as an instrument of incorporating the poor into the global neoliberal economic order. Such dire warnings contain within them a romantic illusion concerning the past prior to the availability of microcredit.

The reality is that the poor have always needed to borrow money – to go into debt to fund their livelihood enterprises. Marginal landholders need capital to cultivate their lands. Poor sharecroppers need lump sum amounts of money to lease-in land to practice agriculture, to buy agricultural inputs, and to pay to have their fields irrigated. For small and marginal landholders and landless peasants, borrowing from the village moneylender was never a matter of choice but one of compulsion.

But surveying the rural scene in any region in India will quickly reveal other reasons why poor villagers have always needed to go into debt. There is always the need for all sorts of ritual expenses, including expenses incurred for marriages (especially for the parents of daughters who must fund their wedding feasts and dowry payments), celebrating the birth of grandchildren with normatively prescribed gifts, and for funerals' necessary rituals and feasts.

Occasional but predictable social commitments mandating expensive ceremonies and celebrations have always made getting into – and remaining perpetually in – debt a historical pattern for the poor. Borrowing large sums of money for customary ceremonial costs that far exceed the financial means of the poor predates microcredit by thousands of years.[2]

---

[2] Traditional figures who could fulfill these credit needs included economically better-off relatives, employers (*malik*), and moneylenders (*mahajan*). Indian vernacular literature and cinema abounds in fictional portrayals of the miserable consequences confronting villagers fallen on hard times with no recourse beyond the mercy of the usurious moneylender. In Mehboob Khan's classic 1957 epic film *Mother India* the evil moneylender, Sukhilala, gains power over the mother-in-law of Radha, the female protagonist, who has taken out a loan of five hundred rupees from him to fund Radha's wedding with her son, Shamu. The newly wed couple, Radha and Shamu, begin their conjugal life under the heavy yoke of debt. The repayment terms of the loan are ambiguous, but the village elders decide in favor of the moneylender. The subtext is that these men, too, have to rely on the moneylender for credit in their times of need. Following this decision the couple are forced to surrender a third of their crops from every harvest as interest payment on the loan, with no hope of repaying the principal sum. Thus begins an unrelenting cycle of impoverishment. The couple gives birth to two sons. Hoping to increase their household income, Shamu works hard to bring more of their land under cultivation. An accident (his arm is crushed by a boulder) leaves Shamu permanently injured and unable to work. Ashamed at his inability to work and provide for his family, Shamu leaves the house never to return. Within a few months Radha's mother-in-law dies and Radha gives birth to a third child. Sukhilala, the moneylender, approaches the young and struggling Radha, and confronts here with a tempting proposition. He offers to pardon her debt if she will agree to marry him. Radha refuses, viewing this as an immoral selling of herself. She continues her labor to make the repayments and provide for her three young sons. A family tragedy unfolds from here: Radha's youngest son perishes in a storm while still a toddler; one son, Ramu, grows up, gets married, and subjects his wife to the

Given this long history, microcredit (in its group-based lending model) represents a radical move in a positive direction. This is especially true when we emphasize the formation of peer groups of women with participatory requirements. The significance of groups of women exercising agency in the public sphere of village life cannot be overstated. The rush to assess the economic impact of microcredit must never diminish the importance of recognizing women's empowered agency as an important *and independent feature* of microcredit.

Microcredit groups have a public life in both the literal and figurative senses. These groups literally have a visible physical presence because they hold their meetings in village public spaces or in the open courtyards adjoining the homes of group members where they are noticed by the village men, their in-laws and extended kin, by children and adolescent boys and girls, by village elders, and by the formal and informal power-holders of the village.

Figuratively, microcredit groups are public institutions in that, although formally they make private decisions about the amounts of loans to make and to whom, these groups also involve themselves in decisions of a public nature. As we have seen, microcredit group members collectively intervene to reform conventional practices that undermine women's health and welfare; they work to enforce marital security when necessary; and they redress public goods deficits in the village. In effect, microcredit groups are becoming important components of rural civil society.

To argue that institutions that increase debt (through giving credit) could be fostering civil society may appear controversial, even perverse to many. But the signs that this is already happening are widespread in India, especially in those states in which microcredit groups have existed for several years.

Microcredit, by providing the occasion for women to form groups and take advantage of its associational features, carries the potential of

vicious cycle of unrelenting poverty in which his own family is enmeshed; the other son, Birju, grows up to be a bandit who returns to take revenge on the moneylender years later on the day of his daughter's wedding but is shot and killed by Radha (his mother) to fulfill her promises to abide by the terms of law and the loan. The message of the film is Radha's ability to preserve her moral integrity and dignity even in the face of persistent poverty and the incapacitating burden of debt. Credit in the film is depicted as inherently uncivil by nature – barbarous even. Creditors are always discourteous and rude, usurious in their will and intentions. Creditors lend at extortionist interest rates, seize mortgaged land without hesitation, force debt-trapped individuals to perform unpaid labor (*begar khata*), and capitalize on distress. These depictions accurately reflect a reality in rural India that long predates the introduction of microcredit programs.

promoting women's civic participation in institutions of local governance. For instance, it is noteworthy that women attend *gram sabhas* in the South Indian states of Kerala and Tamil Nadu in large numbers and often present themselves in the meetings as members of their *kudumbashree* and *mahalir sangam*, the vernacular names for state funded microcredit programs.[3] *Gram sabhas* in these states provide forums for discussions on loan opportunities for women and small-business ideas. From this present set of observations, we can confidently conclude that in many village societies microcredit groups are becoming important constituents of local civil society. These groups have begun to play important roles in informal civil arbitration and imposition of sanctions, in regulation and reform activities, and in organizing collective actions for promoting public goods and protecting women.

Microcredit groups so far have not become a political force in Bengal in the way that traditional factory-workers unions, farmers' unions, or, more recently, the Autorickshaw Operator's Union have. However, in some Indian states where the microcredit model has been incorporated by the state into its toolkit of development strategies (usually in the form of the SHG model)[4] there are some interesting signs of microcredit groups beginning to turn into political constituencies.[5] It is interesting to observe how,

---

[3] These observations are based on *gram sabha* data collected by Vijayendra Rao and me. For an article based on this data set that discusses how gender, among other characteristics, conditions deliberative strategies used in the gram sabha, see Rao and Sanyal (2010).

[4] For more on SHGs, see Chapter 1. SHGs (Self-help Groups) are microcredit organizations using group-based, federated models of operation.

[5] One example is microcredit SHGs in Tamil Nadu (TN) established under the *Mahalir Thittam* program by the TN Corporation for Development of Women Ltd. These microcredit SHGs were first launched in 1989 (under the male Chief Minister at the time, M. K. Karunanidhi of the DMK party) in a single district. Funding came from the International Fund for Agricultural Development (IFAD), a U.N. agency for promoting the economic empowerment and food security of agrarian populations around the world. By the years 1992–1993, four additional districts were added to this program's coverage (under the next Chief Minister Jayalalitha (female) of the AIADMK party). In the following years, the state's positive view on the performance of these first- and second-wave SHGs led it to adopt SHGs as a major state-led and funded initiative. The *Mahalir Thittam* project was launched statewide in 1997–1998 (under the Chief Minister M. K. Karunanidhi, who had returned to power). This program has been in place for more than a decade. In the 2011 election, campaign promises made by the two top contenders demonstrate the way these SHGs (and women in general) have become a field and arena of political competition. When DMK's Karunanidhi, the then incumbent chief minister, promised women various kinds of food processors, his challenger, AIADMK's Jayalalitha, outbid him by promising women a longer list of benefits. Included among these benefits were ten lac rupees (Rs 10,000,000) as loans to microcredit SHGs with a 25 percent waiver of interest. The promise of increased

in the course of the past decade, microcredit SHGs and more broadly women have risen in public awareness and have been placed much higher on the agendas of political parties and their leaders (regardless of leaders' own gender).[6] Women participants in microcredit groups are becoming a political constituency. With what political ideologies microcredit will become associated and affiliated in various contexts within state-level politics in India is an open question.[7]

loan amounts and waivers, designed to benefit women enrolled in microcredit SHGs (over and above government sponsored policy measures targeted to benefit below-poverty-line families) is a clear signal that politicians are now beginning to view the membership of microcredit programs as a crucial constituency to be wooed for its political support.

In Andhra Pradesh, the encouragement state governments gave borrowers to rescind their loan repayments during the 2011 controversy concerning practices of commercial MFIs (Microfinance Institutions) that had led to suicides was interpreted by some as an attempt by politicians to gain the support of a new electoral base.

[6] Most recently, Rahul Gandhi, vice president of the Congress Party, selected Koppula Raju, an IAS (Indian Administrative Service) officer from Andhra Pradesh, to be part of his personal team in the AICC (All India Congress Committee). Raju distinguished himself with his work on issues related to rural development and women's empowerment, particularly with his implementation of women's SHGs in AP. Rahul Gandhi has reportedly involved Raju in implementing his pet project Umeed (translates to Hope), which is a Rs 750 crore centrally funded project to empower women in strife-torn Jammu and Kashmir through an SHG model. According to news reports, the UMEED program (launched in 2013) intends to establish ninety thousand self-help groups linking nine lakh women in 143 blocks covering 4,098 panchayats of Jammu and Kashmir in the next five years.

[7] Microcredit groups are becoming a recognizable force in civil society. This is a positive development for its clientele of mostly poor and economically vulnerable women. It is important to recognize that civil society itself can become an important resource for political reform. Civic associationism, according to the neo-Tocquevillian perspective, can protect against hegemonic political takeovers by bringing together individuals who are otherwise socially dispersed and by facilitating the growth of a center of autonomous power distinct from the power wielded by the state. It is also important to note, however, the Gramscian perspective that alerts us to the reality that civic associations can also promote or be recruited to serve authoritarian regimes. Strong civic associations can encourage the formation of authoritarian parties and help these parties to extend their reach more easily throughout society.

In his study of Italy during the interwar years, Dylan Riley (2005) has argued that the strength of the associational sphere in north-central Italy provided organizational resources to the fascist movement and party that helped them become more authoritarian than they would have been had associationism been weaker. Riley shows how Mussolini's fascist party grafted itself onto, and expanded its base of popular support, by tapping into preexisting patriotic veterans' associations and agrarian associations. These associations helped with recruitment and expansion for the fascist party and provided it with a blueprint of organizational techniques that included revenue generation, cultural activities, and family social assistance. And in her study of Germany, Sheri Berman (1997a, b) has shown how the Nazis infiltrated preexisting choral societies and bird-watching clubs to win over popular support in the course of coming to power. Therefore, civic associations historically have allied with democratic forces, but have also aided authoritarian ones.

Microcredit and the prospect of democratic deepening

Microcredit groups, when democratically articulated with institutions of local self-governance, have the potential of enhancing the political capabilities of subordinate groups, despite deep and persistent inequalities. This is a crucially important finding for how we understand the prospects for democratic deepening in India and elsewhere.

In promoting a path of democratizing credit, relying on individual household initiative, and preferentially targeting women as the frontline clientele, group-based microfinance programs have inaugurated an associational space in which women have to participate in order to receive financial benefit. These are not "invited spaces" (Cornwall 2004) because they are not mechanisms originally created for enabling public engagement in governance and they do not bring together a heterogeneous assembly of people who vary by status and power. Rather, microcredit groups are relatively homogeneous in the status and power of members. They privilege exclusive participation by women in a social context of patriarchy, allow voluntary membership, facilitate interaction without intermediaries, and do not privilege already established wealth or credit.

The associational and participatory space of microcredit is carved out by women through their recruitment of other women. That space is constituted by physically congregating in a location in the village neighborhood in which it is possible to express openly and legitimately defiance and deviance. It is a social space in which women are able to step beyond the private sphere of the household.

The financial incentive of collateral-free credit initially provides the raison d'être of microcredit and there is NGO facilitation in the initial stages of group formation. But the actual task of constructing this space relies on women's participation in the group meetings and in the other associational activities of the group. Once created, the microcredit group becomes a space in which women are initiated into the practice of democratic participation. It habituates them to articulating their opinions and arguments and gives them valuable opportunity to hone their skills of persuasion and coordination.

The associational and participatory dimensions of microcredit groups hold the powerful potential of becoming a springboard for women's participation in local governance and in "invited spaces" such as the *gram sabha*. Through microcredit, women can reconstitute themselves as members of publics brought face to face with elected leaders, representatives of the state, and government bureaucrats.

Microcredit groups can be seen to function as "subaltern counterpublics" (Fraser 1990), alternative publics and parallel discursive arenas where women, who are gender-subordinated in a patriarchal system, gather together and engage in their own discursive exchanges. Parts of these exchanges are indeed about mundane financial matters relating to loans and repayments. These mundane matters, we can now see, have a radical transformative potential through *"charcha,"* the vernacular term for the cultivation of a skill through persistent practice.

Other parts of the microcredit group exchange, as we have also seen, animate a counter-discourse of women's place in the household and in the community. These counter-discourses are reflected in groups' challenges to age-old notions and practices of women's subordination. Counter-discourses are implicit in microcredit group participants' challenges to women's exclusion from the public sphere and from governance institutions.

Tentative, emergent conversations about rights as citizens and the right to participate in grassroots institutions of democracy have led in some cases to these "subaltern counter-publics" invading the male bastion of the *gram sabhas* and the discursive contestation inherent in the selection of beneficiaries of government subsidies and the collective determination of the allocation of resources for public goods.

From an exclusively economic perspective, the multiplication of micro-credit groups can be interpreted as the democratization of credit that has ushered in new sets of economic freedoms. It can also be interpreted as subjecting rural societies to increased liabilities of debt.

From the social perspective, this study concludes that the exponential growth of microcredit groups can be viewed positively as a proliferation of "subaltern counter-publics" that entails "a widening of discursive contestation" (Fraser 1990, p. 67). This ought to be considered a positive development in stratified societies. Microcredit, this study concludes, can be seen as an important move in the direction of achieving "participatory parity" (Fraser 1990, p. 68), again, a good thing in stratified societies.

Microcredit does not depoliticize social participation as some critics have charged; rather, it builds political capacities among socially and economically disadvantaged rural women.[8] This takes us directly to the

---

[8] A recent impressive example is the week-long "day and night agitation" (*rapakal samara*) mobilized by Kudumbashree (microcredit SHGs) women in the southern state of Kerala in October 2012. Kudumbashree SHGs (officially known as the State Poverty Eradication Mission) were launched in 1998 by the State Government of Kerala and the National Bank of Agriculture and Rural Development (NABARD). This was at a time when the incumbent Chief Minister belonged to the leftist CPI(M) party. These microcredit groups have the conventional goals of reducing poverty, promoting entrepreneurship, and empowering women. But, in addition, this state-led and managed microcredit program has the goal of working in tandem with local self-governance (*panchayat*) institutions. The total strength of the Kudumbashree SHG network is about thirty-seven to forty lakhs.

In the first week of October 2012, women enrolled in the Kudumbashree SHGs organized a demonstration and assembled in large numbers in front of the state secretariat in

heart of the issue of democratic deepening and decentralization. When a non-commercialized model of microfinance is wedded to goals of local self-governance, participatory democracy sustained by a vibrant civil society becomes possible.[9]

Thiruvananthapuram, the capital city of Kerala, to protest a set of measures by the state government perceived to undermine the strength and vitality of the Kudumbashree SHG network. Led by the All-India Democratic Women's Association (AIDWA) and supported by the CPI(M), the protest was launched against the United Democratic Front (UDF: the current ruling coalition led by the Congress Party) government's decision to reverse the process of decentralization, implement a substantial cutback in the budget set aside for the Kudumbashree poverty eradication mission, and block resource devolution. As Biju and Kumar (2013) have noted, the UDF government raised the interest rate on government loans from 4 percent to 12 percent; indefinitely postponed the promise of a "Gender Budget"; relocated its expert administrative staff; and, most importantly, issued an order permitting Kudumbashree members to become members of the newly created NGO, Janasree, that had launched its own microfinance program. The UDF thereby encouraged women to hold dual memberships in both microfinance programs. It is alleged in some quarters that this was an effort by the Janasree Mission to compete with and undermine the Kudumbashree program. The Janasree Mission includes several development and livelihoods programs including microfinance targeted at women. The Kudumbashree program is seen as having a deep association with the CPI(M)-led LDF government, as it was launched by them and has succeeded because of the party's commitment to decentralization and people's mobilization.

The Kudumbashree SHGs put forward their own set of demands including that the Kudumbashree be made the coordinating agency for the centrally-launched National Rural Livelihoods Mission (NRLM), another new microcredit plus program being rolled out in several states across India. (The latter program was funded by soft loans from the World Bank to the Government of India and by the government itself.) Other demands of the protest included: reduction of interest on loans to four percent; dues write offs on housing loans from another government program; increased budget outlays for Kudumbashree lending programs; and cancellation of budget allotments to the Janasree microcredit program floated by the UDF government. According to commentators (Biju and Kumar 2013), there were twenty-five hundred permanent volunteers from different Kudumbashree SHGs permanently stationed in front of the state secretariat on indefinite strike. "They sat in groups representing different districts. Crowds of women from SHGs from different districts came to the city and participated in demonstrations on a daily basis and their numbers swelled day by day" (p. 25). When the state government refused to yield, the Kudumbashree Samrakshana Vedi (protection committee) threatened to spread their protest across town and to district headquarters. Finally, the government was drawn to the negotiating table and conceded to several of the demands. This included a promise to make Kudumbashrees the coordinating agency for the centrally managed NRLM program; subsidizing the interest on loans to bring the interest rates down to 5–7 percent (reduced from the proposed hike to 12%), and writing off Kudumbashree loan dues of Rs 25 crores under the housing scheme.

According to news reports, the women sang and danced in front of the secretariat after their week-long demonstration ended with the government acceding to so many of their demands. This is one of the most impressive examples of the success that comes when the political power inherent in microcredit SHGs is linked to the state through properly articulated local governance institutions.

[9] Baiocchi, Heller, and Silva (2011) argue in their book *Bootstrapping Democracy* that "civil society is critical to the quality of democracy because it supports collective action" (p. 142).

Microcredit contributes significantly to the emergence of new associational spaces and new collective actors. By so doing it promotes a strengthened civil society and facilitates the mobilization of groups of people who are underrepresented and who cannot otherwise access other institutionalized channels of democracy.

This book strongly highlights the importance of the associational spaces opened up by microcredit groups. It emphasizes the role of these spaces in making rural civil society more inclusive by incorporating large numbers of women into group-based structures with important financial functions. It is crucial that these spaces are largely self-governed by women who are otherwise enmeshed in governing structures dominated by men.

Microcredit promotes discursive democratization by creating associational spaces in which women belonging to "backward castes" and "scheduled castes" and minority Muslim communities can discuss family and conjugal concerns and community matters in ways that transcend personal concerns. Microcredit groups also provide women who lack social or political identity beyond their family, kinship, and caste/religious affiliations, with an institutional identity and effective social network permitting entrance into male-dominated spaces.

If democracy is conceived as "a set of practices that links civil society to public authority" (Baiocchi et al. 2011, p. 142), then microcredit should be celebrated for multiplying those links. Democratization of credit and democratization of development both have risks. They also carry enormous potential for improving the lives of socially marginalized and economically vulnerable people, never more so than when they positively transform women's capacity and instill in them empowered agency.

9

Epilogue: the future of microcredit

The future of microcredit depends in part on the way its social and economic impacts are measured. There is a growing movement that advocates measuring economic and social interventions through randomized experiments (i.e., implementing an intervention in locations selected through a process of rigorous random sampling and having a matched control sample that does not receive the intervention). This methodology has been increasingly employed since the mid-2000s. Although seemingly strictly a technical academic matter, it has widespread ramifications for the future of microcredit because it shapes the kinds of research and the research findings that scholars, policymakers, and funding agencies around the world take seriously.

Until now methodological debates have focused on measuring microcredit's economic impact with the understanding that microcredit's goal is to ameliorate poverty by delivering financial credit to the doorsteps of the poor. Microcredit's economic impact has not been a major focus of this book. I nevertheless want to comment on this methodological issue because of its relationship to what I believe is emerging as the dominant reality concerning microcredit's impact on household economics and role in poverty alleviation.

How microcredit is evaluated in India is crucial because India is one of the largest markets in the world for microcredit and related financial services for economically vulnerable families who are not yet within the ambit of formal banking systems. The financial choices the global microfinance industry makes in India will have a wide impact on the rest of the world. How much interest will it charge? How will it package interest rates for clients? How will it decide to recover the cost of lending? Will it pursue for-profit, "self-sustainable" lending as a goal, or will it pursue a model of subsidized loans supported by philanthropy, international donor agencies, and state subsidies? Each of these choices will ultimately lead to very different futures for the industry as a whole and for the lives of the vast numbers of economically vulnerable families microcredit will eventually affect.

METHODOLOGICAL DEBATES AND DIRECTIONS

There is now a large and contentious literature concerning microcredit's impact on household economy. The debate has recently become tied to a methodological disagreement among economists about accurate methods of impact assessment. This debate is not centered on techniques or tools of quantitative analysis but, rather, one focused on fundamental issues of research design.

Among economists who have long studied microcredit's economic impact, there are those who rely on quasi-experimental designs, sometimes referred to as "natural experiments." This method entails studying differences in outcomes between a randomly selected subset of households participating in a microcredit program that is already running and a randomly selected subset of households, similar to the former set, but not participating in a microcredit program. Most studies evaluating microcredit's economic impact undertaken during the decades between 1990 and 2010 have followed this approach.

These quantitatively based studies claimed methodological superiority over ethnographic and qualitative studies of microcredit because they were able to correct for selection-bias and other issues arising out of what, in the language of economics, is called "endogeneity," or the nonrandom placement of microcredit programs. This methodology, its advocates claimed, corrected for the unmeasured attributes of villages in which microcredit programs operate, and the unobservable household characteristics of those participating in microcredit, all of which could interfere with isolating the effect of microcredit.

A notable study following this approach is that of Pitt and Khandker (1998). Their study reported a positive economic outcome from microcredit for participating households in Bangladesh, especially for women. It found an 18 taka increase in annual household consumption expenditure for every 100 taka borrowed by women compared to an 11 taka increase experienced from loans in the hands of male borrowers. Pitt and Khandker's study is distinctive for finding a positive effect on consumption expenditure that is uniformly observed across all participating households surveyed.[1]

In the last few years, there has been a dramatic change of opinion among economists studying the impact of development interventions regarding the methodological accuracy of studies with a quasi-experimental design. The change has come from a small but influential group of economists affiliated with the Abdul Latif Jameel Poverty Action Lab (J-PAL), based at MIT.[2] The group developed an analytic protocol that randomized experiments in ways that emulate the testing procedures pioneered in the field of clinical medical trials and the agricultural sciences. The goal is to develop a rigorous and scientifically unassailable method of impact assessment. It can also be seen as an attempt to replace one kind of methodological orthodoxy with another.

The major difference between the quasi-experimental approach and randomized experiments is that, in the former, the researcher is forced to select the research sample from populations within preexisting program and non-program locations. This may introduce unobserved biases as a result of organizations purposefully choosing some locations over others as sites for implementing an intervention based on the locations' specific advantages. Randomized experiments, by contrast, are those in which microcredit programs, or any intervention, are randomly assigned to locations (termed "treatments"). Microcredit is introduced to a sample of sites randomly selected from a larger cluster of matched sites. Sites that do not receive the intervention are termed "controls."[3]

Randomized clinical trials were pioneered in 1747 by a Scottish physician named James Lind. Lind was employed as a doctor in the British Royal Navy. His task was to find a cure for scurvy among sailors. He used

---

[1] The findings of this original study were severely contradicted in a recent replication study conducted by Roodman and Morduch (2009) who concluded thus: "As for PK's headline results, we obtain opposite signs. But we do not conclude that lending to women does harm. Rather, all three studies [Pitt and Khandker 1998; Morduch 1999; Khandker 2005; insertion mine] appear to fail in expunging endogeneity. We conclude that for non-experimental methods to retain a place in the program evaluator's portfolio, the quality of the claimed natural experiments must be high and demonstrated."

[2] The group was started in 2003 by Abhijit Banerjee, Esther Duflo, and Sendhil Mullainathan and later joined by Dean Karlan and Jonathan Morduch. The J-PAL website as of May 2012 reported having sixty-six academic economists affiliated with it (http://www.povertyactionlab.org/about-j-pal).

[3] Another level of randomization can be achieved by randomly assigning individuals to microcredit programs. Instead of individuals self-selecting to participate in a program, the opportunity to participate in microcredit is distributed among a randomly selected group of individuals.

six different interventions (a quart of cider, a dose of elixir vitriol (sulfuric acid), vinegar, sea water, oranges and lemons, and electuary of garlic) on six pairs of scurvy-ridden crewmembers aboard *The Salisbury* (Bartholomew 2002). The method was refined in the field of agricultural experimentation with the introduction of matched treatments and controls. This methodology diffused back into medical research and clinical trials.[4] It also attracted the attention of social scientists and policy makers engaged in devising tests to measure the effectiveness of social and economic interventions for human subjects. Few social science research studies have the capacity, however, for adopting this method.

Randomized experiments on the impacts of microcredit are only just beginning. Banerjee, Duflo, and others (2010, 2013) have done the first such study on "first-generation" borrowers in a microcredit program (very small, joint-liability, female-directed loans) operating among the urban working poor in Hyderabad city in the southern Indian state of Andhra Pradesh where microcredit has expanded at a rapid pace.[5]

Their study is a useful complement to mine in that it confirms that microcredit has a heterogeneous set of economic impacts. Researchers found that microcredit differs in how it affects a dependent set of outcomes – creation and profitability of small businesses, investments, and consumption – depending on a household's business potential (that is, whether the household already operated a business, had a high propensity to start a business, or had a low propensity to start one).

After fifteen to eighteen months of having access to microcredit loans (at an interest rate of 12% on non-declining balance; equivalent to 24% APR), expenditure on durable goods (especially business durables) rose and the number of new businesses grew by a third. The authors correctly interpreted these results to be "significant and not insubstantial impacts" (Banerjee et al. 2010, p. 3). "Treatment-area households who had an existing business before the program invest more in durable goods, while their non-durable consumption does not change. Households with high

---

[4] The most infamous of these is the Tuskegee syphilis experiment (1932–1972), conducted by the U.S. Public Health Service among six hundred poor African American male sharecroppers in Macon County, Alabama.

[5] The microcredit program was part of Spandana Sphoorty Financial Limited (one of the largest MFIs (Microcredit Financial Institution) in the region). The study was done by opening branches of microfinance institutions in fifty-two slums (permanent settlements of the urban poor) that were randomly selected out of the 104 slums in Hyderabad city. The authors surveyed 6,850 households after a fifteen- to eighteen-month period initiation of lending.

propensity to become new business owners increase their durable goods spending and see a decrease in non-durable consumption,[6] consistent with the need to pay a fixed cost to enter entrepreneurship. Households with low propensity to become business owners increase their non-durable spending. Their non-durable consumption increase is too large to be due to the income effect of paying off higher-interest debt, suggesting that these households are instead borrowing against future income" (Banerjee et al. 2010, p. 4).

This pair of economists investigated but found no impact of microcredit on women's decision making[7] or other human development indicators such as health and education. It is important to note that the study provides no information on loan-use. The study tells us nothing concerning whether men or women used these loans or whether they were used for common household purposes, saying only that the organization gave these "general loans" solely to women. The particular MFI under study recognized loans to be fungible among different needs, and it did not insist on "transformation in the household" (Banerjee et al. 2010, p. 5).

The evidence from econometric data then also appears to confirm that the effects of microcredit are heterogeneous differing by household type (in this case households distinguished by the presence or absence of business initiative or the stage of business initiative's development). The availability of microcredit does have an effect on household level investments in durable goods (helping to expand or start small businesses in entrepreneurial households) and on non-durable consumption (decreasing, increasing, or leaving it unaffected, depending on the business initiative of household).

A noteworthy impact is the decrease in spending on "temptation goods" (tobacco, alcohol, betel leaves, gambling, and food consumed outside the house) among households starting new businesses. The authors argue that this "fits with the claim often made regarding microcredit, that microcredit changes lives" (Banerjee et al. 2010, p. 20). But the long-run effects of these patterns on household economic status are not known and are difficult to predict. As the authors argue, these patterns could, on the one hand, increase the future consumption levels of entrepreneurial

---

[6] This reduction in non-durable spending includes a cutback on what the authors call "temptation goods," that is, alcohol, tobacco, lottery tickets, and food eaten outside the home.

[7] The dimensions included in the study were: food; clothing; health; home purchase; home repair; education; durable goods; gold investment; silver investment; levels of spending on school tuition; school fees; other education expenses; medical expenditure; teenage girl's school enrollment; teenage boy's school enrollment; count of female children under one year and one to two years old.

households (when the businesses turn profitable) and of non-entrepreneurial households (when microcredit loans are used to pay off debts with even higher interests and that results in greater amount of the income becoming available for consumption). Such an impact would add up to a positive impact on alleviating poverty by reducing its harshness or pulling families out of it.

Conversely, the same short-run patterns could also lead to a decrease in future consumption levels. For entrepreneurial households, their "existing businesses may or may not become more profitable when they scale up; new businesses may or may not generate future profits that compensate their owners for the drop in consumption that partially financed their creation" (Banerjee et al. 2010, p. 4). Non-entrepreneurial households "may be borrowing unsustainably, leading to eventual lower consumption" (Banerjee et al. 2010, p. 4), or they may be pushed off the precipice into poverty when anticipated incomes against which families borrow are interrupted due to various contingencies like illness, for example.

Therefore, these mixed future possibilities along with the finding that microcredit has no effect on average monthly per capita expenditure (i.e., no uniform effect on consumption) or on education, health, and "women's empowerment" in the short-run, all lead the authors to conclude that "for all these groups, the welfare impact is ambiguous ..." (Banerjee et al. 2010, p. 4). They end their paper with the following interpretation of their findings: "Microcredit therefore may not be the 'miracle' that is sometimes claimed on its behalf, but it does allow households to borrow, invest, and create and expand businesses" (Banerjee et al. 2010, p. 31).

The appropriateness of using a fifteen- to eighteen-month time frame to form any judgment at all on a complex outcome like women's decision making is never questioned. Also "decision making" (albeit on several dimensions) is the only variable used to reach the dimension of "women's empowerment" (Banerjee et al. 2010, pp. 3, 20, 31). My own study has shown that "decision making" is quite tardy in changing within conventional households with economically active and co-residing husbands. This is so for complex sociological reasons, including: the primary importance of the marital household for women; the complexity surrounding bargaining; and the inadequacy of money alone (especially in the case of loan transfer to husbands) in redressing the balance of power in favor of wives. But other important dimensions of agency are far quicker to change.

This study was followed closely by another study conducted by an international group of J-PAL affiliated economists (Crepon et al. 2011), which focused on the microcredit program of Al Amana (the largest MFI in rural Morocco). The study concerned joint-liability loans to groups of three or four members that were open to including women and men. Seventy-four percent of the existing self-employment activities at the time of microcredit's launch was declared to be managed by men.

As with the previous study, these authors, too, found that the impact of microcredit was heterogeneous, differing across households with or without self-employment activity at the time at which the microcredit program was launched in these villages. "Households with an existing activity had large increases in their activities through increases in sales, expenditure, and savings associated with reduction in consumption, especially in social consumption. Households without an activity at baseline, although they had an increase in the amount of microcredit, had no significant increase in their activities and had an increase in their consumption (in food and durable expenses)" (Crepon et al. 2011). More specifically, these authors found that in the rural Moroccan context, the main effect of microcredit was to expand the scale of existing agriculture-based and livestock-based self-employment activities.

For existing agriculture-based livelihoods, there were significant impacts on sales (26% increase compared to control villages) and profits. For livestock-based activities, there was an increase in the stock of animals held, an increase in sales (11%) and self-consumption (11%), a diversification in the type of animal held and animal product sold, but no significant impact on profits (Crepon et al. 2011). Microcredit was found to have no effect whatsoever (with respect to creation, expansion, or profit) on small businesses that were distinct from agriculture/livestock enterprises, such as handicrafts-based petty production and sale.

For agricultural and livestock-based households experiencing increased profit, a part of it was saved, often in the form of livestock. On average, households in treatment villages (which include data for participating and non-participating households) had 6.3 percent more in assets than similar households in control villages, and they also had to sell off fewer assets in the previous year (Banerjee et al. 2010, p. 4). But a portion of the profit was spent in compensating for an average 6.8 percent drop in the wage earnings of households in treatment villages (this would be a 44 percent drop in wage earnings if this effect could be exclusively attributed to households receiving credit). This wage-earnings data is reflective of the related finding that households in treatment villages reduced their labor supply outside the village. The decline was sufficient to offset much of the income gains from self employment. This data combined with the other finding that members of microcredit-receiving households did not increase their labor supply on their own enterprises led the authors to conclude that "treated households may be consuming more leisure" (Crepon et al. 2011; Banerjee et al. 2010, p. 13).

Because of this way in which household members adjust their labor downward with increasing incomes (from their own agriculture and live-stock based enterprises), the authors find no net effect on average consumption, which is one of two commonly used proxies for measuring poverty. Among households that had an existing "self employment activity" at the time of microcredit's launch (two-thirds of the sample), the study found a significant decrease in consumption within the two-year period it covered. For households that did not have such an activity at baseline, there was a significant increase in their food expenditure and purchase of durable goods. Their overall consumption was positively affected (but not statistically significant) (Crepon et al. 2011).

Therefore, these authors, too, found no effect on poverty (as measured by changes in average per capita consumption expenditure) in the short two-year period. However, they argue that the possibility that households may be enjoying more leisure should be factored into the total increase in welfare.

These authors also find interesting, albeit "limited changes (p.14)," in the ways that the allocation of money to different consumption goods (among food, schooling, health, temptation goods, social events, non-durable, and durable goods) shifts in households getting into debt with microcredit loans. Compared to control households, treatment households are more likely to spend on health and less likely to spend on social events such as marriages and religious celebrations (Crepon et al. 2011).[8]

Interpretation of findings is important. Randomization of experiments does not make interpretation of findings any less important. And experimental findings on their own may not automatically lead researchers to appropriate conclusions or recommendations. For instance, Michael Bartholomew (2002), adding to the sizeable scholarship on James Lind's work on scurvy,[9] which inspired randomized experiments, writes:

---

[8] With regard to "women's empowerment," these authors admit that the expected probability of change would be minimal given that a majority of direct microcredit borrowers in rural Morocco are men. Few women in remote villages take loans (p. 14). Expectedly, the authors find no effect on their considered quantitative and qualitative indicators that include: "women index (indicators not specified in the working paper), % household self-activities managed by women, number of women activities, women work total hours, women work hours in business."

[9] Published in 1753 in a 358-page book titled *A treatise on the scurvy in three parts*.

Lind's Treatise on the Scurvy did not inaugurate a new epoch in the understanding on scurvy ... Only with twentieth century hindsight can the brief passage recording the Salisbury experiments be made to stand out as being of especial significance ... There was no swift emergence, during the second half of the eighteenth century of a universal conviction concerning the sovereign curative properties of oranges and lemons, and of the uselessness of most other treatments. Rather, the debate about scurvy, as a number of historians have shown, was wide open. The Treatise did not narrow the debate and channel it inexorably toward the Admiralty's eventual decision to issue seamen with lemon juice (Bartholomew 2002). This eventual decision, pushed forward by a physician named Gilbert Blane, came in 1795, forty years after the *Salisbury* experiments.

Bartholomew is not unique in making this argument. He points out that other historians such as Kenneth Carpenter have noted that the experiments seemed "to have made very little impression (1966 [1988])" on researchers investigating the cures of scurvy during the next half of the eighteenth century and is largely an artifact of modern twentieth-century readings. The main explanation lies in Lind's own neglect of his experimental results due to their failure to fit with his theory regarding the disease.[10] Bartholomew (2002) writes, "his theory, and maybe his preconceptions about what keeps seamen generally healthy, direct his attention away from diet" (p. 5). This is just as the theory that credit should empower women (which experimental results disprove) has for so long directed attention away from microcredit's associational mechanism that actually improves women's agency. And in a similar fashion, the evidence supplied by randomized experiments concerning the impact of microcredit programs, while rigorous and useful, may not lead inexorably to correct conclusions about microcredit's effect on women's empowerment.

Combining my findings on the question of how microcredit influences women's agency and the findings from these recent studies on microcredit's economic impact, I want to emphasize the reality that microcredit has heterogeneous results. Microcredit's impact differs by type of household and by the regional context. And this is true for its economic and social impacts.

Emphasizing that microcredit has heterogeneous impacts is a less sensational finding than that microcredit lacks uniform or average effects either

---

[10] His general belief about the disease was that it represented the putrefaction of the body and was caused by a multiplicity of factors, chief among them the environmental conditions of life on board a ship.

on women's agency or on poverty. These statements perform very different interpretive work. The first approximates the messy but nevertheless potentially generative possibilities of lived reality. The second works to discredit microcredit as a means and channel for women's increased empowerment because of its lack of standardized and average effects.

The second statement, moreover, implicitly imposes the assumption that interventions ought to have uniform effects on communities, households, and individuals, despite the reality of diversity that everyone elsewhere acknowledges exists. Economic and social interventions are not medications that can be reasonably expected to have standardized effects on different populations. In fact, research emerging from the field of pharmaco-genomics (Burroughs et al. 2002) has begun to show that even the effects of standardized drugs that were previously believed to have uniform effects actually vary by patient's genetic variation.[11] It seems regressive then that social scientist, policy makers, donors, and the general public should expect a particular economic or social intervention to have standardized effects on the poor, whether considered across different countries or across different regional and household contexts within the same country or even community.

MICROCREDIT'S PLACE IN POLICY

Some social scientists (Krishna and Shariff 2011) have begun to find and emphasize regional heterogeneity in movements into and out of poverty across different Indian states. These findings can help policy-makers understand how microcredit can best be used as a tool for addressing poverty. Examining panel data from over thirteen thousand randomly selected rural households across sixteen states covering a twenty-year period, from 1993–1994 to 2004–2005 (a period during which India experienced high growth rates), Krishna and Shariff have shown the following: Large numbers [22%] have fallen into poverty, even as many

---

[11] Differences in the polymorphisms in genes, that is, the structures of genes and the products they encode, like drug metabolism enzymes, receptor proteins, and other proteins involved in drug response and disease progression, have been found to influence the effectiveness of drugs. These genetic variations lead to significant variations in the metabolism, clinical effectiveness, and side-effect profiles of therapeutically important drugs for populations with different genetic polymorphisms (Burroughs et al. 2002, pp. 3–4). According to Burroughs et al. (2002), there is hope in the medical researcher community that technological advances and the availability of data from the Human Genome Project will enable doctors in the future to provide "individualized pharmaceutical therapy" (p. 3).

others [18%] have moved out of poverty (p. 535). This movement in and out of poverty is observed among all castes. Among Scheduled Castes and Scheduled Tribes, 23.7 percent fell into poverty, while 20.6 percent escaped poverty. Among higher-caste Hindus, 17.5 percent fell into poverty, while 14.7 percent escaped poverty (p. 537). With respect to occupations and livelihoods, the patterns were dramatic: Cultivators (who accounted for 38% of their sample) experienced the largest increase in poverty, with the ranks of poor farmers multiplying by 11.5 percent in the twelve-year period (13.8% escaped while 25.3% fell into poverty); agricultural laborers also experienced a 5.7 percent net increase in poverty; escapes from poverty outnumbered descents into it only among non-farm manual workers, non-farm self-employed, and especially among the regular salaried groups (p. 536).

According to their study:

"Overall, the stock of rural poverty has increased, but there is considerable variation across states and among regions within states ... Rural poverty has fallen in states (such as Himachal Pradesh, Kerala, Rajasthan, and West Bengal) where more people moved out of poverty than fell into poverty ... Over the same period rural poverty increased in a second group of states – including Andhra Pradesh, Bihar, Gujarat, Haryana, Maharashtra, Madhya Pradesh, Orissa, Tamil Nadu, and Uttar Pradesh – where more people fell into poverty than moved out of poverty. (p. 534)

Krishna and Shariff show data for the apparent lack of a relationship between the level of economic growth experienced by a state and its poverty dynamics. For example, Andhra Pradesh (AP) and West Bengal (WB) had similar rates of economic growth, but their poverty dynamics were radically different (AP experienced increased poverty, while WB experienced reduced poverty). Punjab and Rajasthan had low overall economic growth but they did better than average in reducing their rate of rural poverty. Gujarat and Tamil Nadu (TN) had relatively higher rates of economic growth but experienced a net rise in the number of rural poor (p. 537). The four states in which poverty has decreased have a far less and more recent presence of microcredit than Andhra Pradesh and Tamil Nadu that have the largest presence of microcredit of all the states. AP has had private microfinance institutions (MFIs) such as SKS Microfinance operating since 1998. TN has had donor-funded and state-subsidized microcredit (following the SHG model) operating statewide since 1997–1998. Rural households are being pushed into poverty despite the widespread presence of microcredit in some states. This raises the question of what the factors pushing rural people into poverty might be, and how microcredit interacts with these factors.

Krishna and Shariff (2011) shed light on this question. Analyzing the data for all sixteen states, they found that, in aggregate, the factors that were associated exclusively and significantly with escape from poverty were "location within 5 km of a town" and the "presence of an adult son." Both these factors are outside microcredit's influence. Factors that were significantly associated with both escape and (reducing likelihood of) descent were "women's media exposure," "remittances," and "prevalence of telephones." Another set of factors that were associated with lowered risk of descent into poverty (although not significantly associated with escapes) were "education of the household head to secondary level or higher"; "ownership of land and other rural assets"; and "engagement in rural social networks, participation in civil society, and trust in village panchayat [local government]" (p. 4).

Krishna and Shariff write, "Reasons for escape and descent vary considerably across state boundaries. The factors that made a significant difference for escape (or descent) within one Indian state mattered little or not at all within other states and regions" (p. 534). Take for instance their variable "women's media exposure." This refers to women's access to and awareness of information. In aggregate this is strongly related to escape and (lowered risk of) descent. In rural societies, "Having better informed women in one's household resulted in raising the odds of escaping poverty and lowering the risk of falling into poverty" (p. 539). However, using a state-focused analysis, the authors show that the strong association between women's media exposure and escaping poverty is driven by data from Bihar, Madhya Pradesh, Punjab, and Rajasthan. In eleven out of fifteen states there is no such association. What association there is is limited to women's media exposure lowering the risk of descent into poverty (p. 541).

Based on their fine-grained analysis, Krishna and Shariff advocate the following guidelines for policy intervention:

A *preventive policy* – intended to thwart descents into poverty – would, among other things, aim to strengthen local social networks, raise civil society participation, bolster village *panchayats*, and give larger numbers of women access to information and education. Simultaneously, a *supportive policy* – aimed at raising the number of escapes from poverty – would seek to improve road and rail networks between villages and cities, spread further the network of mobile telephones and landlines, and enable more village residents to gain access to non-farm sources of income while also targeting other factors identified by aggregate analysis of the past. (p. 541)

Using this perspective, microcredit contributes greatly to, and fits right into a preventive policy designed to avoid descent into poverty. Microcredit groups strengthen women's social networks, promote their participation in civil society and in local government institutions, and facilitate women's access to information. For all these reasons, the group-based lending model of microcredit has the potential to reduce the risk of decent into poverty.

Microcredit's fit with supportive policies, however, is tenuous. The nature of livelihoods enterprises that microcredit catalyzes differs between the rural and the urban sector. The market constraints of the rural sector are not something that the availability of microcredit, by itself, can correct.[12] The multiplication of non-farm sources of livelihoods for rural women and men is dependent on macro-structural factors (such as the availability of salaried jobs) and on their skill and familiarity with non-agriculture and non-farm-based occupations and other types of petty trades and businesses.

Clearly, given this crucial macroeconomic dimension and its implications for Indian society as a whole, we must analyze and assess the fact that a significant portion of rural microcredit loans are invested in agriculture and in farm and livestock based enterprises. In this regard, it is important to stress that how foreign direct investment (FDI) in retail (including the retail of agricultural produce) will affect the earnings of farmers is, in the long run, a crucial question that warrants deep and careful examination. Much depends on what India decides about allowing FDI in multi-brand retail.

To rectify these constraints – of market size, of limited availability of viable livelihoods if all else remains the same, of the depressing effects of market crowding – what is needed is purposive action to strengthen and enlarge the markets for the goods produced through microcredit loans. In addition, product innovation, better connectivity between rural production zones and urban markets, and vocational training in non-farm livelihoods will all be important.

Special economic zones (SEZs) come to mind when contemplating the need for creating non-farm based salaried work on a large scale that opens up opportunities for waged employment for significant numbers of rural men and women with limited education. Some far-reaching policy initiatives will be necessary if the goal is rural industrialization. Rural industrialization employing women as waged factory workers is widespread in

---

[12] Refer to the comments made by Mumtaz Begum in the Introduction to this book about the constraints facing her when she took out a loan and thought of starting her own tailoring shop in the village.

several Latin American countries, China, Indonesia, Bangladesh, and Sri Lanka. Rural shop-floor jobs in the garment, electronics, and other light manufacturing industries have proliferated around the world.

The often less than fair wage structure of these jobs, the poor labor safety standards, and, particularly, the coercive labor practices prevalent in this sector have long been matters of serious concern.[13] Sociologists who have studied women's factory employment in foreign multinational companies hold diverse opinions regarding how it affects women's economic independence, social empowerment, and gender relations within the household and in the factory setting. Sweatshop-like conditions and the use of gender as an organizing principle of global capitalist manufacturing are important issues that have to be addressed even as we recognize such employment as a potential non-farm source of income for rural women and men.

PHILANTHROPY, FREE MARKET, AND CHOICES FACING MICROCREDIT

Microcredit is one of the very few economic policy innovations originating in the Global South (in the early 1970s) that then diffused into the economically developed North. Nearly three decades after its appearance in Latin America and Bangladesh, it sprouted up in the United States and more recently has appeared in Eastern Europe and the Balkans. The South still remains its largest field of operations.

Over the past four decades, microcredit has become a key tool for American capitalist-entrepreneurs who are making it into a centerpiece of their philanthropic ventures and their ideologies of global finance. Some of them see microfinance as containing within itself an irrefutable financial logic and dynamic through which both global economic development and the fulfillment of human freedom will be realized.

Microcredit has been seized on by the private foundations run and financed by capitalist-entrepreneurs who see it as an effective instrument for achieving a triad of mutually re-enforcing goals simultaneously: giving the poor access to the tools of finance, alleviating global poverty, and promoting women's individual empowerment through entrepreneurship.

---

[13] In this context we should remember the recent (April 24, 2013) garment factory disaster in Bangladesh in which more than one thousand people (mostly female garment workers) were killed by the collapse of a commercial building, Rana Plaza, that housed many garment manufacturing units and that violated safety standards.

The influence on microcredit by philanthropy is profound. The choices major foundations make as to what type of microcredit they support have been – and, more importantly, for the future – will be decisive regarding microcredit's economic effects and particularly its social effects influencing the agency and empowerment of women. Will the future of microcredit be primarily commercial in nature? That is, will the lending capital for microcredit be raised in private equity markets? Or will lending capital be created based primarily on non-commercialized sources such as financial allocations from the government, soft loans from international aid agencies, and philanthropic grants from private donors? The question of commercialized versus non-commercialized and subsidized versus for-profit structuring of microfinance ultimately has enormous implications for interest rates on loans and therefore on the very nature of microcredit itself as a social institution and as a policy tool. How the choices are made between these two alternatives will determine the future of microcredit and therefore its effect on women's lives.

The massive scale and enormously consequential global social thrust of philanthropic-inflected microfinance is brought home by a brilliant piece by Connie Bruck in *The New Yorker* titled "Millions for Millions."[14] The piece provides a vivid account of a private meeting that took place in November 2004 between Mohammad Yunus and a group of young and wealthy Silicon Valley entrepreneurs in the home of venture capitalist John Doerr.

The meeting included leading figures from the world's most powerful corporations including Pierre Omidyar, the founder of the Internet-based auction site eBay, and Sergey Brin and Larry Page, the co-founders of Google. The meeting, billed as a "learning session," was organized on the initiative of Omidyar and some of his peer entrepreneur-capitalists. They comprised a group of businessmen-entrepreneurs whose technological innovations in the computer industry had led to enormous personal fortunes and the direct control of immense corporate wealth. All of them had become interested in making philanthropic donations so that they could "give something back" to the world that had enriched them so handsomely. Microfinance loans were one of the contributions they could make that interested them the most.

Omidyar emerged as an ardent advocate for bringing free-market principles to microcredit. He saw his engagement with microcredit as identical to the mission he brought to his eBay venture: the realization

---

[14] See the October 30, 2006, issue of the magazine.

through technology and management of perfect capitalist free market conditions.

The discussion during the meeting became centered on the prospects for converting microcredit from a philanthropically based enterprise to a market-based one. The trouble with philanthropy, of course, was that it meant that financial endeavors were perpetually reliant on external funding and subsidies from governments, development agencies, and private philanthropic organizations. Only a commercialized venture could sustain itself in any permanent or economically sustainable way by generating its own profits and raising loan capital in global capital markets.

Under the commercial model, raising capital through philanthropic donations and aid grants would be limited to the start of any microcredit program. When a microcredit program reached its full-scale development by providing credit coverage to all poor households, the goal was for it to go commercial and become self-sustaining. The interest charged on micro-loans would then be required to cover the entire cost of bringing credit to the doorstep of the poor and to leave a profit margin attractive enough to lure investors to invest their personal money in microfinance institutions (MFIs).

Not all attendees were convinced or enthusiastic about the prospect of commercializing microcredit. According to the article, Yunus told Bruck (the author):

I had a long debate with Pierre ... He says people should make money. I said, let them make money – but why do you want to make money off the poor people? You make money somewhere else. Here, you come to help them. When they have enough flesh and blood in their bodies, go and suck them, no problem. But, until then, don't do that. Whatever money you are taking away, keep it with them instead (i.e., use the money earned as interest or profit to fund other programs to benefit the same vulnerable populations instead of distributing the profits as dividends to private shareholders as might be the case in commercialized MFIs: insertion mine), so they can come out more quickly.

Later in the meeting, the Grameen Foundation President and CEO, Alex Counts, introduced the idea of a "guarantee fund," an idea that originated at Grameen. A guarantee fund would consist of pledged capital from individual donor-guarantors that could be used by Grameen to underwrite financial instruments backed by national and private banks worldwide to encourage them to provide loan-capital to MFIs for direct micro-lending. The Grameen Foundation hoped that such a guarantee might convince banks to lend MFIs greater amounts of capital at lower interests. The donor pledges were to be called on by the banks only when MFIs defaulted on their repayments.

On the spur of the moment, at the end of that November day, the learning session turned into an impromptu fund-raiser to raise capital for such a guarantee fund. The host, John Doerr, announced that attendees should consider pledging no less than 0.1 percent of their net worth for such a fund. By the end of that day nine people (Omidyar not among them) had pledged a total sum of $31 million. The goal of the group became to raise $50 million.

Omidyar, Bruck relates, left the meeting that night with his interest in microcredit kindled. Almost exactly a year later, in November 2005, he donated $100 million to start the Omidyar-Tufts Microfinance Fund, a fund targeted to promote microcredit in its commercialized profit-making form. In 2010 Omidyar joined the ranks of Microsoft's Bill Gates, investor Warren Buffet, and forty other billionaires who have pledged to donate half of their wealth to charity. In fact, Omidyar has promised to give away to philanthropy over the next two decades all but 1 percent of his wealth. (*Forbes* magazine estimates his net worth to be $3.6 billion.)[15]

The Omidyar Network, set up in 2004, describes its philanthropic mission on its website this way: "ON is a philanthropic investment firm. We create opportunity for people to improve their lives by investing in market-based efforts that catalyze economic, social, and political change." The network does support non-profit ventures, a vast number of them in fact, in their "Government Transparency" portfolio.[16] So what is at issue here is not Omidyar's lack of support for non-profit ventures or his belief that all ventures should be aimed at profit-making, but his conviction that microcredit should be pursued in a fully commercialized way – that it should be able to return a profit to people and institutions who contribute their money to it. This in effect turns micro-lending to the poor into an

---

[15] http://www.achievement.org/autodoc/page/omio bio-1.

[16] For instance, it supports *Ushahidi* (Swahili for testimony), a computer-based technological application developed by a pair of U.S. trained Kenyan software programmers, which enables users to crowd-source information and create real-time visual maps of events as they develop from data submitted by dispersed individuals via mobile phones, instant messaging, Twitter, and so on. This platform facilitates emergency communication during times of crisis and promotes transparency in reporting and democratizes reporting on important political and natural events. Created at the beginning of 2008, during violent riots that followed the 2007 presidential election in Kenya, since then, Ushahidi has been used to track oil spill damage in the Gulf of Mexico and to locate trapped persons following the 2010 Haiti earthquake. Ushahidi is hosted by its eponymous non-profit technology organization and the software itself is free and open source. Recently, the organization made available Crowdmap, a free user-friendly web-based version of the application. Both Ushahidi and Crowdmap have received extensive philanthropic financial support from the Omidyar Network.

investment opportunity for the non-poor, and thereby supposedly ensures microcredit's ability to sustain itself without philanthropic subsidies.

For Omidyar, microcredit represents seamless congruities with eBay. "Both eBay and microfinance allow people to discover that they can be entrepreneurs. Both are based on trust. Both can be viewed as demonstrations of free-market principles. Both can be seen as businesses whose profitability is linked to their social impact. Bruck writes, "Omidyar stopped talking about microfinance as a way to end world poverty, and instead described its mission in a way congruent with the eBay experience," that of enlivening free-market principles in ways that change the world.

Still, the Omidyar Network uses the conventional tropes of poverty alleviation and women's empowerment in its website to explain the purpose of microcredit and downplays the use of free-market principles to "strategy" directed at achieving the more publicly virtuous goal:

Goal: We aspire to make high-quality, affordable financial services widely available to the poor so that they may gain financial security and escape poverty. Women, who are especially vulnerable, can use microfinance services to start a business and earn status in the family and community. When people have access to financial services, they can stabilize their sources of income, build up assets, and plan for the future. We hope these activities will set off greater economic growth in emerging markets and contribute to the revitalization of poor communities.[17]

Strategy: We further strive to demonstrate that these ventures can be self-sustaining and profitable, and thus more attractive to traditional investors. We believe this will foster greater competition in the market and create economies of scale that both drive down costs and improve financial services for the poor. The aim: better service for microfinance clients.[18]

The Network's microfinance portfolio includes a list of twenty-four organizations, a mix of non-profits and for-profits, spread across the Balkans, Asia, Africa, and Latin America, some operating regionally others globally. Among these organizations are known names like the internationally based BRAC and Kiva. There are also new and innovative mobile banking organizations like Mango Financial, Inc. (based in Austin, Texas) that is aimed at providing a variety of financial services, such as prepaid debit cards that include direct deposit, savings, renter's insurance, bill pay, and remittance, to the working poor and other "unbanked" adults in the United States.

Most of the non-profits listed under their "Financial Inclusion" portfolio are not themselves MFIs; rather, they are organizations geared to

[17] http://www.omidyar.com/investment_areas/access-capital/microfinance.
[18] http://www.omidyar.com/investment_areas/access-capital/microfinance.

providing various types of support for MFIs and for further developing and expanding the market for microfinance products. These non-profits include research and development (R&D) organizations that provide research support for developing new financial products for the microfinance sector. An example is "MicroSave" (launched in Uganda in 1998, now operating in India and Africa), that "works to build the infrastructure of the microfinance industry by offering comprehensive, strategic advice and training to MFIs and organizations that support their work."[19] Its services include not savings facilities, as its name might suggest, but research on the "financial needs and preferences of the poor,"[20] field research on MFIs, toolkit development, technical assistance and training, and information sharing with microfinance practitioners. ON's support to MicroSave is geared toward the organization's expansion in India, where it is working to develop and test financial products, conduct research, and "build a community of informed consultants in the microfinance industry."[21] Other microfinance related non-profits getting ON's support are network associations, like Sa-Dhan in India, which provide capacity-building services (financial and policy tools) to affiliated MFIs.[22] ON's non-profit support to BRAC and Kiva are not directed to the micro-lending services of these organizations but to furthering other sectors of their work.[23] The actual MFIs and "Equity funds" the foundation supports – that are involved in providing micro-credit and other financial services to individual clients and in providing finance capital to MFIs – are for-profit organizations that the foundation invests in on a for-profit basis.[24]

---

[19] http://www.omidyar.com/portfolio/microsave.

[20] http://www.omidyar.com/portfolio/microsave.

[21] http://www.omidyar.com/portfolio/microsave.

[22] The complete list of microfinance-oriented non-profit organizations that the ON supports on a non-profit basis include the following: Boulder Institute of Microfinance; BRAC; Consultative Group to Assist the Poor (CGAP); International Association for Microfinance Investors; Kiva; Microfinance Center; Microfinance Information Exchange; MicroSave; Opportunity International; Sa-Dhan; SEEP Network.

[23] In the case of BRAC, ON's support goes to expanding their Human Rights and Legal Aid Services (HRLS) program to address property rights of the poor (http://www.omidyar.com/portfolio/brac). For Kiva, ON supports the development of their technology platform, the expansion of their network of field partners, and promotes efforts to invest in its due diligence and monitoring capabilities across its financial portfolio (http://www.omidyar.com/portfolio/kiva).

[24] The complete list of ON's "investees" under their "financial inclusion" portfolio include the following for-profit organizations: Balkan Financial Sector Equity Fund; BlueOrchard; Catalyst Microfinance Investors; Elevar Equity; Finestrella; Global Commercial Microfinance Consortium; LeapFrog Investments; Mango; MFX Solutions; MicroVest; Mobile Transactions; Prosper; Rev; SOLIDUS Investment Fund.

Google's Brin and Page, who were also participants in the conversation with Yunus in October 2005, established Google.org, the philanthropic arm of Google. Since then, it has been allocating seed money of $1 billion to various causes. Bruck's report, written in 2006, mentions that microcredit is expected to be an important part of their philanthropic portfolio. But microfinance has not yet made it onto Google's list of philanthropic initiatives. In a 2008 interview to *The Economist*,[25] Larry Brilliant, who led Google.org from 2006 to 2009,[26] announced the organization's decision not to engage in microfinance was due to the fact that, in their view, this sector is now "awash with money."

Two other leading executives in the computer industry, Michael Dell of Dell Inc., and Bill Gates of Microsoft, have made significant contributions to the spread and diversification of microfinance services through their respective family foundations. India has been a special focus for the philanthropic work of both men.

The Michael and Susan Dell Foundation (MSDF) is focused on working in the United States, India, and South Africa, and has been making substantial financial grants to MFIs in India. The Foundation's top commitment is to education, followed by childhood health, community, and finally, "family economic stability" under which microfinance falls. From 1999 until the end of the first quarter of 2012, grants committed to each of these causes total respectively $460.7 million, $149.2 million, $88.6 million, and $27.5 million. India is the only country in which the organization supports microfinance (along with other interventions) starting in 2006. Between 2006 and 2013, this foundation has contributed $27.5 million in grants and equity investments to "early-stage, high-potential, socially motivated"[27] urban MFIs in India working to increase the coverage of microfinance services (loans, savings, insurance, and pensions) to include the urban poor residing in slums in and around the major Indian cities. The foundation's website states its view of microfinance "as a tool that can help give underprivileged Indian children a chance at stable, productive adulthoods"[28] by promoting family economic stability. It emphasizes the intergenerational nature of poverty, especially the way in which poverty impacts children's prospects and adulthood trajectories and their later visions for

---

[25] "Face value: Google's guru of giving," *The Economist*, January 17, 2008.
[26] Brilliant moved on to become the director of the "Skoll Global Threat Fund" set up by Jeff Skoll, the first full-time employee and president of eBay. Jeff Skoll also established the Skoll Foundation, which concentrates its focus on social entrepreneurship.
[27] http://www.msdf.org/programs/family-economic-stability/in-india/urban-microfinance.
[28] http://www.msdf.org/programs/family-economic-stability.

their own children. The urban focus is explained by the desire to build a "strong urban microfinance industry"[29] to rectify the avoidance and neglect of the urban slum-dwelling poor by most first-generation MFIs.

The three criteria that guide the foundation's selection of MFI "investees" are described as follows: "The MFIs client or customer-centric approach; The ability of the MFI to cost-effectively reach an increasing number of clients; The intended impact on the quality of life of their clients."[30] The foundation claims that by now the urban "microfinance market" in India has an estimated seven million clients. It has provided grants and equity investments to *Ujjivan Financial Services Private Limited* (launched at the very end of 2004), operating in and around Bangalore, *Arohan Financial Services Limited* (launched in 2006) in Kolkata (serving urban clients in West Bengal, Assam, and Bihar), and to *Swadhaar FinServe Pvt. Ltd.* in Mumbai (launched in 2008 with the formerly existing Swadhaar FinAccess, a non-profit MFI started in 2005, transferring its lending portfolio to the for-profit division), and other urban MFIs.

The launch dates of these urban MFIs coincide with or follow the two-year period of 2004–2006, during which the ON and MSDF made available their grants and equity funds for promoting for-profit and urban microfinance respectively. The MSDF website, unlike ON, does not disclose the foundation's financial approach or philosophy behind urban microcredit – whether they subscribe to lending on a non-commercialized and non-profit basis or on a commercialized, for-profit basis. However, the "private limited" nomenclature of the three urban MFIs receiving the foundation's capital infusion gives away the commercialized character of credit in these cases.

This pattern highlights how newly available streams of private philanthropic finance can spawn new financial organizations that have widespread reach into economically vulnerable populations; be a force in the process of constructing "markets" and creating "clients" (the deserving yet neglected urban working poor); and catalyze the creation of new financial products, unleashing hitherto unavailable opportunities that simultaneously entail unfamiliar risks and burdens.

A look at *Ujjivan's* loan offerings will illustrate all three points. *Ujjivan* (meaning "regenerate"), within only seven full years of its operation (2005–11), claims to have nearly three hundred branches across twenty

---

[29] http://www.msdf.org/programs/family-economic-stability/in-india/urban-microfinance.
[30] http://www.msdf.org/programs/family-economic-stability/in-india/urban-microfinance.

states in India and nearly 1.5 million customers to whom they have disbursed Rs 31,558 million in loans with a 98.32 percent repayment rate.[31] *Ujjivan* has a bifurcated lending model offering group-based loans and individual loans and sees its organizational objectives as "forming well-entrenched relationships with our clients while remaining innovative and maintaining our position as a market leader."[32] As is evident from this organizational self-presentation, poverty alleviation is not among the stated objectives of this organization. The loans given through the group-based lending model, with Grameen-style five-member joint liability groups, can be of two types: *Business Loans* for households engaged in petty trade and commerce and *Family Loans* for meeting family needs, such as education expenses, expenses for social and religious ceremonies and celebrations, buying consumer durables, and paying off high-interest debts.

Both types of loans have a lower and upper limit of Rs 6000–25,000 and have an interest rate of 26 percent per annum at reducing balance, that is, the annual percentage rate, or APR. These loans are payable within a year for loans under Rs 15,000 and in two years for loans above that sum. For its "Graduate Clients" – clients who have completed at least one loan cycle under group lending – *Ujjivan* offers individual lending, allowing individuals to borrow directly from the MFI on a individual basis. Under this individual lending model five types of loans are offered: *Individual Business Loans* between Rs 10,000–100,000 for meeting the working capital and fixed assets needs of individual micro-entrepreneurs who have a running business (at an interest rate of 30% per annum at reducing balance; payable within six months to two years); *Short Term Business Loan* for meeting the working capital needs of individuals running seasonal businesses; *Livestock Loans* between Rs 15,000–35,000 for financing the purchase and upkeep of cattle for households earning incomes from dairy and animal husbandry (at an interest rate of 26 percent per annum at reducing balance; 1 percent of loan amount withheld and charged as processing fee; payable within a year); *Housing Loans* between Rs 10,000–50,000 to help finance housing needs such as rentals, leases and house improvements for clients (at an interest rate of 24 percent per annum at reducing balance; 10 percent of loan amount is withheld as a security deposit and is refunded on loan repayment; payable within six month to two years); *Bazaar Loans* between Rs 10,000–30,000 for meeting the working capital needs of small-scale business owners who operate their

[31] http://www.ujjivan.com/index.htm.   [32] http://www.ujjivan.com/lending_model.htm.

businesses in local markets (at an interest rate of 30% per annum at reducing balance; payable within six months to a year). House loans and bazaar loans fall under the 15 percent non-priority sector lending permitted to MFIs by the Reserve Bank of India.

It appears all these five types of individual loans are charged a "processing fee" of 2.24 percent of the loan amount. This "Individual Lending business model" has been developed under assistance from Women's World Banking (WWB) with whom *Ujjivan* has been collaborating since 2008. WWB is a network of thirty-nine MFIs operating across twenty-seven countries. Headquartered in New York, it helps its affiliate MFIs to develop innovative financial products.

Ujjivan is one among several examples of MFIs that have since 2004–2005 cropped up in the urban and peri-urban landscape of India and represents the new corporate face of microfinance. The mission and rhetoric of this type of corporate microfinance are dramatically different from its original NGO predecessor. This is evident from their terms of choice: "financial inclusion" instead of poverty-eradication/alleviation; "clients" and "customers" instead of enrollees or poor households; and "market-leader" and "business model" instead of development or empowerment. Also, the lower and upper limits of the credit allowed, both of which are high by average rural loan amounts, belie a shift away from the poorest urban population segment. In addition, the fact that loan offerings made through individual lending are kept at a higher sum than the offerings made for group-based lending reveals the organization's desire to move individual borrowers, other than the least well off among them, out of the group-based lending model that requires fortnightly or weekly meetings. This measure limits the reach of a stable associational mechanism from which women might otherwise benefit. It divides women into separate categories by their loan-bearing capacity and puts the burden of participation on less well-off women.

The difference in interest rates charged by corporate microfinance and microcredit's other institutional variants may not be dramatic. The rates vary a great deal by country. As previously mentioned, nonprofit NGOs and governments may operate their microfinance program on a non-profit basis or on a for-profit basis. Interest rates for rural microcredit in India dominated by government, donor institutions, and NGOs mostly range between 12 and 14 percent at a flat rate. This flat rate typically amounts to an annual percentage rate, or APR, of 24–28 percent. By contrast, the trend among urban MFIs is to charge interest on a declining balance basis (usually between 24 and 30%), which adopts the APR method.

Interest rates charged by MFIs in India are actually on the lower end of the industry spectrum. A CGAP study (Rosenberg, Gonzalez, and Narain 2009) found that the median interest rate for profitable MFIs worldwide that self-reported their data to the MIX database was approximately 26 percent in 2006 and the median return on MFI equity in the same year was 12.3 percent. There are outliers to these general patterns. Take the example of Compartamos[33] in Mexico that, as of rates calculated and published in April 2012, charges APR of 78.56 percent on their "Credito Mujer" (credit for women), 77.91 percent on "Additional Credit," 74.94 percent on "Grow your Business Credit," 84.24 percent on "Merchant Credit," and 69.23 percent on "Home Improvement Credit."

These rates are lower, having fallen from the even higher rates of 85 percent (plus a 15 percent tax paid by clients) prior to 2006, which produced an annual return of 55 percent on shareholder's equity (Rosenberg 2007). It is little wonder then that the most profitable 10 percent of the worldwide microcredit portfolio (not MFIs), according to the CGAP report, produced returns on equity in 2006 at above 35 percent. The real surprises, however, are that almost two-thirds of the 555 profitable MFIs (on whose self-reported data the CGAP study is based) are NGOs, cooperatives, public banks, or other nonprofit organizations. A large-scale government funded and operated MFI is one of the highest profit makers. An example of such a large-scale government operated MFI is Bank Rakayat, Indonesia, that has its roots in the late-nineteenth- and twentieth-century people's credit bank initiatives initiated by the Dutch colonialists.

The move to commercialize microcredit was spearheaded by local Latin American non-profit NGOs that, in order to expand the scale and coverage of their micro-lending services, converted themselves into for-profit MFIs. Some eventually transformed themselves into microfinance-oriented commercial banks. Accion,[34] a non-profit organization initially providing

---

[33] Compartamos (meaning "let's share") started as an NGO in Mexico City in 1990. With the expansion of its microcredit services, the non-profit organization changed itself to a for-profit in 2000. Eventually, in 2006, its scaled-up commercialized micro-lending services led it to become a registered private commercial bank, Banco Campartamos.

[34] Accion was founded in 1961 as a non-profit grassroots community development initiative in several shantytowns in Venezuela. It began its microlending activities in the 1970s and expanded across several Latin American countries through the 1980s–1990s. In the course of its expansion, Accion came to the decision that microcredit, in order to be pursued self-sustainably in a scaled-up manner, needed to be commercialized. Eventually, Accion became Accion International, a network of Latin American institutions, and retained its non-profit character by becoming a capacity-building organization. Now, instead of directly engaging in microfinance, Accion helps build MFIs. In the last three decades, Accion has focused on

microcredit on a non-profit basis, was the first to recommend the commercialization of microcredit. BancoSol in Bolivia, an affiliate of Accion, converted itself from a nonprofit organization to become in 1992 the globally first-ever private commercial bank focused on microfinance.

Defending the interest rates charged by the microfinance industry, Elisabeth Rhyne of Accion,[35] who is a frequent contributor on her microfinance-related blog hosted by the Huffington Post, writes that the interest rates of international microfinance often give Americans "sticker shock":[36]

Interest rates face an uncompromising arithmetic of three main cost elements, all context-specific. How big are the loans? What is the maximum loan officer caseload? How much are loan officers paid? A lender making $1,000 loans in a dense city market with a labor market that allows modest loan officer salaries can charge a much lower interest rate (think Bolivia, with rates in the 20s) than a lender making $100 loans in the rural parts of a middle income country where loan officers earn a lot (think Mexico with rates in the 60s) …. Microfinance grew to reach 150 million clients worldwide by pursuing financial sustainability – and profitability – as the ticket to reaching more people permanently without heavy donor dependence. Most of today's international microfinance providers believe the poor should be treated as clients, not recipients of charity. This point does involve moral judgment. Is it more moral to help (a few of) the poor through subsidies or to provide (many of) them with services on a business basis?[37]

This is an accurate summary of the way the industry perceives the moral quandary facing it. For some industry leaders, however, there is no moral quandary. A co-CEO of Compartamos is quoted in a Bloomberg Businessweek piece on the organization saying:

"A lot of people have suggested that financial inclusion can be a poverty alleviation tool," he says. "We're not out to prove that. We're out to provide financial services as opportunities to these clients, realizing that some people might make better use of them than others."[38]

helping establish partner MFIs in Latin America and the Caribbean, the United States, Africa (Cameroon and others), and Asia (India, China, and Inner Mongolia).

[35] Rhyne is the current managing director of the Center for Financial Inclusion at Accion International. Formerly, she was the senior vice president of Accion, and before that the director of the Office of Microenterprise Development at USAID.

[36] Huffington Post, business section, blog post, May 28, 2010. http://www.huffingtonpost.com/elisabeth-rhyne/why-are-microfinance-inte_b_593359.html.

[37] "Why are microfinance interest rates so high?" Huffington Post, The Blog, posted May 28, 2010. http://www.huffingtonpost.com/elisabeth-rhyne/why-are-microfinance-inte_b_593 359.html.

[38] "Compartamos: From Nonprofit to Profit," *Bloomberg Businessweek*, Dec. 13, 2007. http://www.businessweek.com/stories/2007-12-12/compartamos-from-nonprofit-to-profit.

Competition within the industry – through the entry of new MFIs, increased competition for clients, and innovation in financial products – is frequently advocated as the path that will bring down interest rates. Citing the example of BancoSol's lowering of its interest rate to keep up with its direct competitors, Rhyne, among others, echoes this view:

Ultimately, the best means of doing so [reducing interest rates] is to promote competition, which spurs the innovation that brings better products at lower prices ... Worldwide, as microfinance has grown and many more providers have entered the market, a CGAP study found that average interest rates dropped by 2.3 percent per year from 2003 to 2006 ... Ultimately, responsible pricing makes good business sense.

But the CGAP study, itself, does not directly ascribe the lowering of microcredit interest rates to competition. In fact its authors are quite ambiguous on the role of competition, saying that: "One cannot assume that competition will always lower interest rates." The 1.2 to 2.3 percent drop in average interest rate of profitable MFIs is observed in all regions except South Asia possibly because the initial interest rates in all other regions were far higher. The analysis conducted by the authors to explore several alternative explanations for the drop in interest rate shows strongest evidence for efficiency improvements of MFIs, that is, lower operating costs. The lowered cost, in turn, is found by them to be strongly correlated with the number of years the MFIs have been in business. These patterns, the authors conclude, add up to providing more weight to the learning curve thesis than to competition lowering interest rates.

Even with the general drop in interest rates, the data presented in the CGAP study show that the median interest income as percentage of gross loan portfolio is at a similar level of 26.4 percent in South Asia, Middle East and North Africa, Latin America and Caribbean, and Sub-Saharan Africa. It is much lower, approximately at about 20 percent, in Eastern Europe and Central Asia, and it is significantly higher, at above thirty percent, in East Asia and the Pacific. Looking beyond the median, however, there are patterns that suggest that the top seventy-fifth percentile and the top ninety-fifth percentile of the gross loan portfolio in Latin America and the Caribbean earned an interest income of above 30 percent and 70 percent, respectively. In sub-Saharan Africa, these were about 40 percent and nearly 70 percent, respectively; in the Middle East and North Africa, these were about almost 30 percent and above 40 percent; and in East Europe and Central Asia, these were in the low 20s and a little above 40 percent, respectively. In South Asia, the interest incomes of the top seventy-fifth and ninety-fifth percentile of the gross loan portfolio were both in the high 20s in percentage, far lower in an internationally comparative perspective.

The profits from microfinance may have different trajectories depending on whether MFI operations are non-commercialized and controlled by nonprofits, NGOs, and governments or commercialized and privately owned by shareholders. In the former arrangement, profits remaining after covering the cost of operation may be directed to subsidizing other programs or work of these organizations that are meant to benefit population groups of a similar or even more disadvantaged socio-economic profile. In the latter type of arrangement, however, the profits ultimately flow upwards to private investors and shareholders of the MFI.

Advocates of commercializing microcredit argue that profits are rightful rewards for private investors for risking their capital in MFI investments. But with repayment rates on microcredit loans to date being as high as 98 percent on average and the median interest income being approximately 26 percent (percentage of gross loan portfolio), it is worth wondering whether the risk in investing in microfinance companies isn't lower than the risk in conventional investments.

It is worth noting that some commercialized corporate MFIs have started offering their employees stock options, a practice derived from conventional business corporations. For example, *Ujjivan* has instituted an Employee Stock Option Plan for all its employees and directors, purportedly "to help attract and retain talent as well as reduce attrition."[39] In a company newsletter dated March 2007, it is reported that "Sign-On Stock options" of 3,198 shares of Rs 100 each were granted to the twenty-two employees who started the organization. This adds up to a significant sum of Rs 3,19,800 at original value.[40] The newsletter goes on to announce that this is part of the Employee Stock Option Plan program in which all employees are eligible to participate. It further states that every year it will award "Performance Stock Options." This is by no means a typical pattern. But it is an important example of what is happening at the frontier of this industry among organizations that consider themselves "market leaders."

Stock options point to what the future may hold for the commercialized part of the microfinance industry. The same newsletter goes on to mention

---

[39] http://www.ujjivan.com/financial_information.htm.
[40] Not knowing how these shares were allocated among the employees, that is, who got how many, it is not possible to comment on how much of this value accrued to each of the twenty-two employees.

that the Head of Operations of their Technology and Credit division will be attending the Harvard Business School-*Accion* Program on Strategic Leadership for Microfinance to be held in Boston. These emerging trends are a reminder of how the shareholder-value model of the firm and part compensation of CEOs through stock options helped produce a new kind of corporate malfeasance (Dobbin and Zorn 2005). Advocates and skeptics alike will agree that commercialized microcredit seems to be inexorably moving in the direction of professionalization. It also appears to be adopting corporate practices on faith rather than based on any real understanding of the possible social implications of these practices for those most affected by this sector of the economy.

Let me sum up my views. Microcredit, at its best, has a poverty ameliorating effect depending on the success of livelihood enterprises funded by the loans. But rural markets have several economic constraints and these need to be changed to make rural livelihoods more plentiful and profitable. Agriculture and livestock based livelihoods need to be made more profitable, a greater diversity of non-farm livelihoods need to be made available, and, very importantly, more profitable livelihoods for women need to be created. The magnitude of the changes these goals necessitate should not be underestimated.

Certainly, microcredit has potential for improving women's agency. In rural India, at least, the improvement in women's empowerment comes about primarily through microcredit's associational mechanism and participatory dimensions. It comes about not because it promotes women's entrepreneurship or because it enhances women's bargaining position within the household. The group-based model of microcredit has the potential of transforming women's lives by embedding the solidarity created by their mutual support within a hierarchical network of microcredit groups and linking their resulting agency in potent ways to both civil society and to formal institutions of governance. What matters most as a policy question is how to strengthen the associational mechanism and participatory aspects of microcredit for all women who participate in its programs.

Participation in microcredit groups has the potential of being transformational. That participation needs the support of public mobilization, legitimization, and engagement. Currently such support comes primarily from governments, some donor agencies, and NGOs. In this context, it is important to mention that the recently launched National Rural Livelihoods Mission (NRLM) in India, a microcredit plus intervention, is modeled on the peer-group, or SHG, model of microcredit with an associational mechanism in place in theory. The NRLM is a combined venture of the Government of India and the World Bank with each contributing $5.1 billion and $1 billion, respectively. Over a seven-year period, twelve states that, combined, contain 85 percent of poor rural Indian households will eventually come under its operation. The program will directly affect seventy million rural households.

Commercialized microcredit falls short, in my view, in its failure to contribute to this public dimension of re-enforcement for microcredit's associational, participatory solidarity. Although it copies the model of lending to women, it is moving away from, or minimizing, the group-based lending model and failing to value or extend the enormous benefits inherent in microcredit's social, participatory aspects. Commercialized microcredit is increasingly emphasizing non-group-based, solo lending and seems to want to reduce the collective dimension of microcredit lending to a initiation rite by which women are inducted into the rituals and obligations of financial borrowing linked to capital markets.

The commercialized microfinance industry is focused on developing and expanding individual lending. It is determined to create new financial products that supposedly better suit the demands of their individual "clients." What is being sacrificed is the potential of creating peer groups and the power of these groups to use solidarity as a non-coercive force to transform individual preferences and habits of poor and often isolated rural women in positively transformative ways.

In the rush to customize loan products to client needs, when commercialized microcredit companies officially make loans available for social ceremonies and celebrations to poor women, they may in fact be exacerbating the pressure families are under not to skimp on such expenses. The families to whom these loans are being offered are for the most part economically vulnerable. Such customary ceremonial costs are non-productive expenses that can severely hamper women's ability to gain increased agency over their own lives and within their households. Ceremonies and celebrations can be important for sustaining social ties, but they are also classic occasions for exploitative extraction. To make more money available than otherwise would be the case for such practices as dowry demands at the time of marriage and afterwards is unethical and does great social harm. Therefore, MFIs need to exercise caution in their current spree of financial product innovation and consumer need driven customization.

The unavoidable truth is that microcredit embodies a paradox. Microcredit can be a means of contributing to rural communities' economic and social development. But the reality is also that the financialized integration into the global economy that microcredit and particularly commercialized microfinance ushers in subjects rural communities to the coercions and even control of distant outside (corporate) forces from which they were previously protected.

The other unavoidable truth about microfinance is that lenders have far more power than borrowers. Until there is oversight and regulation of the terms of lending, power is heavily stacked in favor of MFIs. Because corporate microfinance companies and commercial banks are less accountable to the public than other forms of micro-lending, there is greater reason for worry concerning them. It is a reality that microcredit is not an inexpensive service. The operating cost of providing small loans at a high rate of frequency close to the homes of poor borrowers is high. The resulting high cost of credit raises the question as to whether "self-sustainability" using commercial business models and accounting practices should be the goal of the microfinance industry.

A proponent of commercialization and "financial self-sustainability", Elizabeth Rhyne of Accion writes, "Like sex, microfinance can be safe if practiced responsibly."[41] But looking at all these emergent trends one must ask: Are the pleasures and risks of microfinance being shared equally?

The moral choice facing the microfinance industry need not be framed in the terms that Rhyne sees it – as between "whether to help (a few of) the poor through subsidies or to provide (many of) them with services on a business basis."[42] The moral and policy choice might better be posed as between whether to serve fewer poor households well with more certainty of helping them move out of poverty and greater surety of improving the lives of women involved in microcredit versus whether to serve many poor households with less certain results and measured according to a financial calculus that occludes the indispensable perspective of the social value of women's agency.

It is only the poverty of imagination that draws moral dilemmas in such narrow terms as "subsidy versus business" with no intervening humanitarian calculus. We must not let the dominance of microcredit as a dream of poverty alleviation through a profitable financial capitalist model rob us of our capacity to imagine alternatives that can help women and men find their ways out of poverty and social subordination. Alternatives need to be imagined that are as radical as microcredit once seemed when first proposed.

[41] "Three Secrets of Safe Microfinance," Huffington Post, The Blog, posted Jan 20, 2011. http://www.huffingtonpost.com/elisabeth-rhyne/three-secrets-of-safe-mic_b_811586.html
[42] Ibid.

Appendix

Why qualitative methods?

Qualitative methods include a vast variety of data gathering tools and techniques, analytical strategies, and interpretive procedures and practices.[1] The fundamental contribution of qualitative methods, some experts have argued, has been their "interpretive, naturalistic approach to the world" (Denzin and Lincoln 2003, p.5), that is, studying things in their real world settings and using empirical materials such as participant and non-participant observations, interviews, and conversations[2] in trying to understand the meanings people attach to phenomena as they experience them and making these subjectivities the primary means of understanding social phenomena. A more recent programmatic document on qualitative methods has come out of a workshop on the *Scientific Foundations of Qualitative Research* convened by the National Science Foundation's (NSF) Sociology program in 2003. This was part of a NSF workshop on *Interdisciplinary Standards for Systematic Qualitative Research* (held in May 2005) led by Michele Lamont.[3] The report prepared by this workshop group outlines some analytical objectives for which the use of qualitative methods is particularly apt. These include: "complex social structures, processes, and interactions; *studies of the mechanisms underlying causal processes*, especially over time; naturally occurring processes and phenomena of social life; *studies that*

---

[1] See Denzin and Lincoln (2003) for a full list of these.
[2] Watkins and Swidler (2009) have proposed the method of using conversational journals.
[3] The participants in this workshop included prominent qualitative sociologists including Wendy Espeland, Wendy Griswold, Susan Silbey, Kathleen Blee, Mario Small, and Alford Young Jr., among others.

focus on questions of 'how' and 'why'; and *the use of in-depth interviews to clarify findings from survey research"* (Lamont and White 2008, p. 17[4]) (italicized emphasis mine). My study was centrally focused on deciphering the underlying causal mechanisms behind improvements of women's agency from microcredit programs and to understand the "how" and "why" behind the mechanisms that come to fruition and those that do not.

The NSF workshop report also highlights the particular advantages of qualitative methods, all of which are relevant for this study and set it apart from the numerous quantitative surveys and statistical regression-based studies of microcredit and its effects on poverty and on women:

Qualitative research enables scholars to gather detailed data about the experience of individuals within social contexts in a way that surveys conventionally cannot. Qualitative approaches allow for the inclusion of subjective experience and cultural sense making that play a vital role in understanding all facets of social life [My study gives equal place to the logic and language of the women whose lives I have tried to understand and to my own analytical assessment of changes in their lives and the underlying mechanisms.] ... Other strengths of qualitative work are the flexibility and recursivity it affords researchers that are made possible by a closer engagement to people and groups being studied. A characteristic of much quantitative research is that it presumes to know in advance what the relevant "variables" are, and the boundaries around these variables. What looks rigorous in advance of research may in fact be less rigorous in its execution. [Rather, in my study, "variables," or factors that seem to be associated with and lead to a consistent pattern in the outcome of interest, emerge out of the analysis of interviews.] Many forms of qualitative research permit the researcher to adapt to learning as they become more knowledgeable about the social context they are studying. If in the process of doing interviews, for example, one learns that things that were expected to be important to respondents were not, one can adjust and look for evidence to help understand why. [A powerful example of this is the way in which the women respondents seemed not to attach premium importance to "domestic decision-making power" contrary to social science expectations and theories regarding its absolute centrality in measuring empowerment.] This recursivity can be methodological (if one line of questioning does not work, try another), theoretical (if predicted patterns do not emerge, or conditions unelaborated in theory seem important, then think about how to develop the theory or look elsewhere), or practical (if you do not get access to one group, you try another. (Lamont and White 2008, p.10) [bracketed inclusions are mine]

---

[4] An online version of this report is available at http://www.nsf.gov/sbe/ses/soc/ISSQR_workshop_rpt.pdf.

In recent decades, qualitative studies have made prominent contributions to understanding the experience and effects of poverty within the U.S. context that has followed deindustrialization in America. These studies have focused on the struggles of the working poor, welfare reforms, patterns of family formation, neighborhood effects, class-based patterns of childhood socialization, and so on. Newman and Massengill (2006) provide a magisterial synopsis of the contributions made to this literature by qualitative studies. In the global context, which has been marked by industrialization in the developing world and global commodity chain production, qualitative studies by sociologists and anthropologists have contributed to the transnational "development and gender" literature. At its centerpiece are the economically vulnerable women – mostly rural women in developing countries who are drawn into the global labor force – supplying feminized labor on the global manufacturing shop floor and the choices and constraints these women experience (Fernandez-Kelly 1983; Wolf 1992; Ching-Kwan Lee 1998; Kabeer 2000; Salzinger 2000, 2003). However, sociologists (in the United States) have not shown the same interest in studying programs and interventions to address poverty and other socioeconomic crises in global, transnational contexts, especially using qualitative methods. A recent exception is Ann Swidler's qualitative studies of the cultural and institutional responses to the AIDS epidemic in sub-Saharan Africa (2009; Tavory and Swidler 2009). The task of examining and evaluating global and transnational development problems and institutional interventions to address them has been largely left to economists (who solely rely on quantitative surveys and statistical analyses) and to anthropologists (who rely on a mix of observations and interviews rather than systematic analysis of interviews as done in my study and who seem to disproportionately concentrate on the negative effects of microcredit and cast microcredit programs in a wholly unfavorable light). My book is an attempt to fill this void by using qualitative methods, specifically a systematic analysis of interviews, to study the most widespread and popular anti-poverty/development intervention in recent history.

From the outset the main goal of my study has been to open the "black box" of mechanism through which microcredit programs influence women's agency. Mechanisms are processes that explain and reveal *how the causal connection actually works*. In this sense, explaining mechanisms include but go beyond establishing the causal connection. So, without doubt, causal thinking and trying to isolate and establish the causal association between microcredit and women's agency was an essential part of the methodological exercise of this study.

To understand the power of qualitative causal analysis, we must first recognize some defining features of causality that are laid out by Miles and Huberman (1994) in their foundational text on qualitative methods. Multiple streams of causes might operate behind the same phenomenon (Abbott 1992) and causes may have simultaneous influence on each other and on the object or outcome of interest (Ragin 1987). This makes it a difficult task to establish causality. Moreover, there is always an underlying dimension of context – it is within a specific local context that a particular configuration of causes has an effect. In the case of this study, it is a context of patriarchy and control. Then there is a dimension of temporality, which in the case of this study was to discover how changes in women's capabilities took effect and expressed themselves over time in relation to their participation in microcredit groups, taking out loans, and other important changes in their family life. For the most part, causality has to be discovered retrospectively, that is, after the fact. Finally, fully understanding causality entails identifying the variables and the processes, that is, the stories, the events in sequence that connect the variables. Considering these features of causality, qualitative causal analysis is particularly powerful. Miles and Huberman write the following:

Qualitative analysis, with its close-up looks, can identify *mechanisms*, going beyond sheer association. It is unrelentingly *local*, and deals well with the *complex* network of events and processes in a situation. It can sort out the *temporal* dimension, showing clearly what preceded what, either through direct observation or *retrospection*. It is well equipped to cycle back and forth between *variables* and *processes* – showing that "stories" are not capricious, but include underlying variables, and that variables are not disembodied, but have connections over time. (Miles and Huberman 1994, p. 147)

In this study, I followed the methodology of drawing out or developing *"causal networks"* for each of the cases as the penultimate analytic exercise at the end of data collection (outlined in Miles and Huberman 1994, pp. 151–63). "A *causal network* is a display of the most important independent and dependent variables in a field study and of the relationship among them. The plot of these relationships is *directional*, rather than solely correlational. It is assumed that some factors exert an influence on others: X brings Y into being or makes Y larger or smaller" (p. 153). In addition to this, finding intervening variables that mediate the influence of the independent variable (the microcredit program: group participation and loan use) on the dependent variable (women's agency) was also an important part of the analytic exercise. In this stage of the analysis, to identify the variables in a systematic way I used the qualitative coding software *Atlas.ti*. These "variables," more appropriately thought of in qualitative studies as local factors, in the words of Miles and Huberman (1994), "are not little lizards hiding under stones turned over by the researcher in the course of investigating the local terrain. Rather, they are a mental map that you gradually elaborate in the course of piecing together discrete bits of data. The abstracted web of meaning is an achievement, not a given ... So much of field research has to do with schema absorption and re-elaboration; you go around recording individuals' mental cause maps, putting them together, and making connections with your own evolving map of the setting" (p. 152). The final goal in this analytic strategy is to move from the locally causal to the translocally causal in order to suggest an explanation that is generalizable within the particular context of the study and makes theoretical sense (p. 237).

Selection of sites and microcredit programs

In India, microcredit programs were first launched during the late 1990s in the southern states of Tamil Nadu (where it started with statewide intervention backed by the state government) and Andhra Pradesh (where it started with private MFIs). In West Bengal, microcredit did not begin in a fully developed way until a few years later in the early 2000s when CARE launched its CASHE project (Credit and Savings for Household Enterprise). CARE is a U.S.-based non-profit relief organization with global reach. It is the world's largest private humanitarian organization with an international focus.

Through the decade of the 1990s, Sisterhood and Self-Reliance,[5] the two NGOs featured in my study, had been trying to promote Grameen-style savings groups and individual savings and lending models. But they had limited success. At that time, there was apprehension and distrust in the minds of villagers regarding NGO-run microcredit programs. Some villagers had lost money in "chit-funds." These funds are locally floated investment plans offered by private companies and are not monitored or regulated by the Reserve Bank of India. Many such programs in the past have proven to be fraudulent, and people (villagers included) who have invested in them have lost their money.

---

[5] These are pseudonyms.

Consequently villagers had a negative impression of financial schemes not backed by the government.

The requirement that women be allowed to participate in these groups was another obstacle against the uptake of microcredit during these early years. A flood disaster in the year 2000 changed these attitudes dramatically and, in conjunction with the launch of CASHE, promoted the sudden growth of microcredit groups in the flood-affected districts of West Bengal. How the flood promoted the mushrooming of microcredit groups is an interesting story. Both Sisterhood and Self-Reliance provided aid, in the forms of food and waterproof sheltering materials, to the members of its early microcredit groups. This act of material provision led to public rumors that the NGOs would give various kinds of material goods, like blankets and lanterns, to all those who joined microcredit groups. The list of goods kept expanding from hearsay. Tempted by the prospect of receiving free household goods in the post-flood devastation, women volunteered in great waves to form and enroll in microcredit groups.

A secondary reason for the change in attitude was the disbursement of loans to the early microcredit groups. When villagers saw these members receiving loans, some of them realized (as one woman put it) that the risk for the organization in loaning them money was far greater than their own risk of losing their savings, since the savings were far smaller in amount than the loans. As more and more microcredit groups got established during that period, the rumor about the disbursement of free goods proved to be just that. This resulted in some disappointment, but the women continued their membership in microcredit groups initially inspired by the prospect of accumulating personal savings. Gradually, as months passed, the rumor was no longer in circulation. Since then, group-formation came to be fuelled by the NGO staff spreading the concept of microcredit and by women hearing about such groups from other sources.

By the time I began this study in 2004, microcredit groups in West Bengal had been in existence for three to four years. My decision to focus this study on microcredit groups in West Bengal was principally guided by methodological concerns. I wanted the benefit of being able to compare my findings with the findings that had emerged from the voluminous research on microcredit programs in Bangladesh. The modern-day regions of West Bengal and Bangladesh were formerly part of the undivided region of Bengal during the British colonial and Mughal rules and during the region's medieval and early modern history.

West Bengal in India and Bangladesh lie directly opposite each other along the international boundary.[6] Given the centuries of shared history up until 1947, the two regions represent commonalities in language and ethnicity and, importantly, in marriage and kinship systems (both are patrilocal and patrilineal).[7] Alongside these commonalities, there is an important difference in their overall socio-religious composition. West Bengal has a majority Bengali Hindu population (72.5% Hindus and 25.2% Muslims compared with an overall Indian ratio of 80.5% Hindus to 13.4% Muslims[8]) and Bangladesh has a majority Bengali Muslim population (89.5% Muslims and 9.6% Hindus[9]).

In the first wave of research on microcredit's impact on women (a body of research that was largely based on studies coming out of Bangladesh), I had noticed a failure to account for the social composition of microcredit groups and to be aware of how socio-religious identity and community may influence or interact with the financial aspects of microcredit intervention. (A few very recent studies have begun to address these issues.) This made me curious about the socio-religious composition of microcredit groups. Brief pilot visits to microcredit groups made me keenly aware of how distinct these groups could be in their composition depending on the neighborhood in which they were located. I wanted to include in my study microcredit groups of varied composition, that is, groups that were composed of Hindu women, Muslim women, and both. Apart from one other state (Assam: 30.9% Muslims; but no microcredit intervention at the time), West Bengal has the second-highest proportion of Muslim population among all the Indian states where Muslims are the numerical minority (there is only a single state where Muslims are the majority and that is Jammu and Kashmir). There was no better place in India than West Bengal in which to systematically study microcredit groups made up of Hindu and Muslim women, both separately and in mixed groups.

Also, the qualitative interview-based method of this study meant that proficiency in the local language was of paramount importance for

---

[6] Independence from the British empire was accompanied by the partition of the country by the departing British regime into India and Pakistan (West and East). The region of Bangladesh was at the time East Pakistan and became the modern nation of Bangladesh after its Liberation War (fought against Pakistan) in 1971.

[7] See Basu and Amin (2000) for more points on the similarities.

[8] Source: 2001 Census of India.

[9] As of 2004 as reported in the CIA World Factbook. https://www.cia.gov/library/publications/the-world-factbook/geos/bg.html

collecting quality data. I am a native speaker of Bengali (*bangla*), the vernacular language of West Bengal, and this was an important advantage that worked in favor of selecting this state as the site for this research.

A few basic statistics will help provide readers necessary background on this state. West Bengal is the fourth most populated state in India. Its total population stands at 91,347,736 according to the 2011 Census, having risen from the 80,221,171 figure reported in the 2001 Census. In the last decade, West Bengal has gone from being the most densely to the second most densely populated state in the country. West Bengal's sex ratio (number of females per thousand males) has improved from 917 in 1991 to 934 in 2001 to 947 in 2011. These statistics lie above the national average, which was 933 in 2001 and 940 in 2011. However, several states have far better sex ratios than West Bengal. The sex ratio reflects the desirability of girl children in society, and it is often used by social scientists as a crude but powerful indicator of the degree of patriarchy, patrilineal or matrilineal heritage, women's subordination, and the status and value of women in society. Below is a map of the sex ratio in all the Indian states and union territories. Note that, compared to West Bengal, the female sex ratio is higher (a positive) in all of the Southern Indian states (Andhra Pradesh, Karnataka, Tamil Nadu, and Kerala) and most of the Northeast Indian states (except for two).[10] If the sex ratio is taken as an indicator of women's value and status in Indian society, then West Bengal is similar in these regards to all the states in the West, the center, and to two of the most populous Northern Indian states (U.P. and Bihar).

West Bengal has remained largely rural and agrarian over the decades, with paddy (rice) and vegetable cultivation being the dominant forms of agriculture in addition to the significant presence of fisheries. Most rural families are peasant families, and agriculture is their primary occupation. Landed families have mid- to small-sized land holdings, which makes large-scale mechanized cultivation impossible.[11] Most farmers practice labor-intensive subsistence agriculture, primarily satisfying their family's consumption needs and selling whatever remains after that. There are very few big landholders in West Bengal of the kind that may be found

---

[10] Out of these states, kinship and inheritance systems in some communities in Kerala and in the Northeastern states were noted for their historically unique matrilineal character.

[11] Therefore, the contribution of agriculture to the state's Gross Domestic Product is relatively low, at 27 percent, compared to a 51 percent contribution from the service sector (with industry providing the remaining 22%).

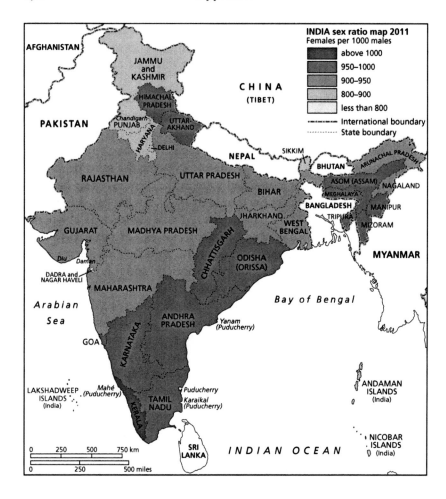

in Northern India. This is due to the Land Reform movement (adopted to counter the feudal means of agricultural production that had continued on from the colonial period) that swept Bengal in the late seventies and eighties, and the successful redistribution of land to landless cultivators by the Left-front led government.

Landless families practice agriculture by leasing-in land from non-cultivating landowners, or they practice sharecropping, that is, the acquisition of land use rights in exchange for one third of the crops. In addition to agriculture, many families engage in agriculture-based businesses (for example, vending agricultural produce and rice-husking) and practice non-agricultural trades in order to earn regular cash income. In the poorest families, men and women hire themselves out as agricultural laborers. This work is both very poorly paid and seasonal. The daily wage for this type of work in this part of the country was Rs 40 for men and Rs 35 for women in 2004.[12] In addition, men and women work in home-based cottage industries in various arts and crafts traditions that are specific to particular regions of the state and include handloom weaving, embroidery, and *bidi*-making. In addition to the socio-religious factors operating in West Bengal, the petty commodity production and subsistence economy of the area made it an ideal site in which to study the impact of microcredit on rural Indian women's agency.

On arriving in Kolkata (formerly Calcutta), the capital city of West Bengal, I contacted people who could tell me more about the major microcredit programs operating in the state and the principal organizations implementing them. The first individual I spoke with, a retired high-ranking bank official, put me in touch with the state-level director of the CARE, CASHE project and mentioned the names of Sisterhood and Self-Reliance as two NGOs running large-scale microcredit operations.

My meeting with the Director of the CASHE project gave me access to the list of NGOs administering microcredit groups under this program. Sisterhood (in Nadia district) was the largest in scale. Self-Reliance (in Uttor Chobbish Pargana district) came second. These two NGOs were in two different districts providing a wide geographic coverage.

I devised a methodological design that would help me identify any unique effects related to organization or context acting separately on outcomes apart from the direct influence of microcredit itself. Both NGOs followed the standard group-based lending model with identical institu-

---

[12] This wage differential is to a large extent gender-based, as it exists even in similar types of agricultural tasks and represents the undervaluation of feminized agricultural tasks. A powerful example establishing this point can be drawn from one of the interviews, in which the respondent (a middle-aged woman and current member of the group *Shantimata*) narrates how this wage differential was justified to her some three decades back by the Punjabi farmer under whose employ she and her husband used to work as migrant farm-laborers: "At that time, both of us would work in the fields; we would sow and harvest paddy and wheat. He would earn five rupees a day, and I would earn four and a half rupees a day. I would ask the Punjabi: 'Why, just because he is a man you pay him five rupees? Why do you pay me four and a half? Do I work any less?' He would say in reply, 'You will return home and make the "roti" (staple bread, used here as an analogy of women's domestic responsibilities). If I pay you the same as him then, once you return home, you will no longer make the "roti." Rather, you'll say (to your husband), "You have earned five rupees and I have earned five rupees as well; you do half the work, and I will do the other half!" That is why I keep you a little low, and I pay you eight annas (fifty paisa, or half a rupee) less (laughs).'" (Kanan Mondol)

tional structures (as per the SHG model) and membership requirements of ten to twenty members. I also had in reserve a third NGO (in Howrah district) that was implementing microcredit under the auspices of the CASHE project. Eventually, after seven months of fieldwork and conducting four hundred interviews, I decided to drop the third NGO-run microcredit program. This decision was due to my sense that I had reached saturation in the patterns I was observing in the interviews. This third potential district was right next to the urban center of Kolkata, the capital. This made it different from the two other districts that were rural and shared an international boundary with Bangladesh.

Once I had decided to focus on the microcredit programs run by Sisterhood and Self-Reliance, I contacted the respective organizations and sought their permission for the study. I described my project in general terms as exploring the influence of microcredit programs on women. Both organizations accepted my request to study them. There was one difference in the procedure they asked me to follow. For Self-Reliance, the smaller and newer of the two organizations, an informal telephone conversation with the program director of the microfinance division was sufficient to gain me entry. The founder-director was traveling abroad at the time, and he was contacted by the program director and sent his approval through him. Sisterhood, the bigger and more reputable of the two organizations required that I write a letter stating that my decision to conduct research on their groups was based on their superior reputation in the field. This difference underscores Sisterhood's careful guardianship of its reputation.

Sisterhood was founded in 1972 by a woman from an educated local family from a village in West Bengal. The organization was staffed by women recruited from different parts of the state after graduating from college or university or employment in other NGOs. All of them resided in the organizations' residential facility. The organization's website at the time described itself as a "voluntary organization of the women, by the women, and for the women."[13] Its mission statement described its goals as the "holistic development of rural community, keeping its focus on poor women suffering from abject poverty, deprivation, gender discrimination and social evils." The organization stated its belief that "poor women can be proactive and are willing to change their lives." Sisterhood's main emphasis has always been on women and income generation. One of its initial efforts was to form women's savings groups. Sisterhood was established six years prior to the launch of the IRDP (Integrated Rural

[13] Extracted from NGO's mission statement.

Development Programme), one of the largest national-scale federal programs sponsored by the Government of India under the Department of Women and Children in Rural Areas (DWCRA). The government partnered with NGOs to implement this program and to perform the ground-level tasks of forming poor rural women into groups, facilitating savings, and providing them vocational training. At the time, Sisterhood partnered with the government to implement the IRDP scheme and received financial contracts from the state.

When microcredit emerged into this scene in the late 1990s, and more fully in the early 2000s, Sisterhood adopted it as the centerpiece of its interventions. Its other interventions included programs on health, education, youth development, community welfare, disaster preparedness, environment, emergency outreach service, and a hotline for at-risk children. By 2005 Sisterhood reported having approximately three thousand microcredit groups, having extended $2.95 million in credit with a 98 percent loan recovery rate. Its work covered approximately five hundred villages in four districts of the state. It had been recognized as the state-level resource and training center for microcredit.

Self-Reliance was formed in 1989, almost two decades later, by a young city-born-and-bred man who had returned to Kolkata after obtaining a post-graduate degree from a U.S. university with the hope of working in India at the grassroots. After some years working at another well-known local NGO, he decided to form his own organization. The organization's mission statement emphasized the fostering of "holistic development of the community in order to make them [villagers] self-reliant" and the involvement of "the indigenous people of the region."[14]

Younger and smaller in scale, Self-Reliance had a more experimental approach to development. It envisioned itself as an innovative organization ready to develop new models of rural development and disseminate them across large geographical areas. Its programs included microcredit, education, health, youth groups, disaster preparedness, and innovations in sustainable agriculture. In keeping with its guiding philosophy, the staff members at Self-Reliance were all local residents from the surrounding villages. The staff was predominantly male. Its microcredit program, by the middle of 2005, included about five hundred groups operating in fifty-eight villages with approximately six thousand members, and it had extended $1.14 million in credit and reported a 93 percent loan recovery rate. Instead of viewing microcredit as its program's centerpiece, the leader

---

[14] Both extracts have been drawn from the NGO's online mission statement.

of Self-Reliance defined it as a peripheral activity, "something Self-Reliance does because it's become a staple activity."[15] CARE was the major fund provider for both microcredit programs.

Sampling

I started my fieldwork with Self-Reliance and followed the same procedures a few months later with Sisterhood. I traveled to the district headquarters of the organization planning to stay in the NGO's residential facilities for the entire period of the data collection. I first met with the program manager for the microcredit division and again explained the purpose of my project. In selecting the sample of groups to study, I had to rely on the help of the respective program managers and organization staffs. The organizations had proprietary rights over the membership and financial data regarding the microcredit groups. Information regarding the groups' social composition was not available in any external database. Only group and member names and their financial information were recorded. Given practical constraints, it became necessary for me to rely on the staffs' experience, and "soft knowledge" (Anand, Manz, and Glick 1998, p. 797) to efficiently identify a sample of microcredit groups that had varied socio-religious composition and were spread across several different villages covering the major regions of microcredit implementation within these two districts. The staffs knew which villages had a Hindu or Muslim concentration and where the microcredit groups would reflect these compositional characteristics. For locating and selecting heterogeneous groups, the program director had to ask the regional program managers who had fine-grained knowledge of groups in their specific regions and who were in regular contact with group supervisors. A final condition for the selection of groups was that they needed to be within commutable distance (by public transportation) of the NGO's district headquarters (also a village) where I was residing for the period of fieldwork. This was a practical consideration and also a consciously adopted strategy that would allow me to gain greater geographic coverage in the dispersion of the groups from which I would interview the members. I should clarify here that this did not mean that the groups were all located near the NGO's headquarters. Many of them were far enough to require an hour or two of travel each way, requiring me to

---

[15] This conclusion is based on my interview with him, in which he emphasized their innovations in alternative education for poor urban children and organic agriculture.

start very early in the morning and start my journey back by 5–6 P.M. in the evening.

I could have decided on a more anthropological approach, selecting one or two villages and studying the microcredit groups only in those villages, interviewing microcredit enrollees and non-enrollees, and spending time on making nonparticipant observations and interacting with a broad spectrum of female and male villagers. Although this approach has the advantage of interpretive depth, it prevents breadth of observation. It also runs the risk of village characteristics becoming consequential to the findings if the villages are not selected with extreme care. Nearly all the existing qualitative studies on microcredit in Bangladesh have been conducted through such an anthropological approach in which observations and interviews have been from a small number of villages and groups. Instead, I decided on a strategy that would allow me to conduct interviews with a relatively large number of microcredit members in groups dispersed widely across multiple neighborhoods and villages.

Another important decision was to suspend caste as an analytical category in the sample selection process. For Hindus, local caste/*jati* identities are classified into three main constitutional categories – "general caste," "other backward caste (OBC)," and "scheduled caste" (SC, also known as "*dalits*," the former "untouchable castes"). The last names of the Hindu interviewees revealed an overwhelming majority of OBC and SC categories. There were negligibly few representatives of "general castes." Muslims in rural West Bengal are largely non-Ashrafs (that is, they are "lower caste" Hindus who converted to Islam). However, for Muslims, to the present day, the socially and economically less advanced castes have only the OBC category constitutionally available to them although scholars of the Muslim community have argued that a substantial number of them are former converts from the "untouchable castes." Any attempt at caste categorization of my sample across religions, therefore, would have been inherently conditioned by constitutional restrictions.

I relied instead on distinguishing between socio-religious identities and group compositions (the Hindu-Muslim distinction). There are pan-Islamic features that are relevant for microcredit and gender norms – like the Qur'anic prohibition against the payment or charging of interest in lending (impacting financial practices and institutions) and the explicit delineation of women's roles and rights in the Sharia. These features pointed to the potential salience of socio-religious distinction for this study. The implications of caste have not been completely ignored, even though they were not rigorously explored. Wherever caste surfaced in the interviews as an important factor in the outcome or process, I have given it due attention.

I sampled on the basis of groups, not on the basis of the individual characteristics of members. By sampling groups rather than individual members, I left myself room for variation in respondents. Even if some of the groups in the sample list were chosen by the organization because they were perceived as being successful, there was still much room for variation among its members in terms of whether and how their agency had been influenced. Most of the groups were approximately three to five years old by the time I conducted this research and each group was allowed to have a maximum of twenty members.

On average, most groups had about twelve to fifteen members. I started with an initial sample of twenty-three groups from Self-Reliance's microcredit program. But sometimes, one or two women from other microcredit groups neighboring the group selected for the study would arrive on the scene of interviewing driven by their curiosity of what was going on and, later, they would want to participate in the interviews. I presume their volunteering to take part in an interview (even though they were not from the notified sample groups) came from their desire to experience the novelty of giving their interview and talking about their lives and experiences. Typically, it was the case that these women were the leaders in neighboring microcredit groups. In these cases, early on, I decided not to reject these women in favor of maintaining a rigid sampling frame, as that would appear inhospitable in this context. So, in all such cases, I also interviewed the women who came forth of their own accord from microcredit groups not in the initial sample list.

At the end of the interviewing period in Self-Reliance there were nine such women who had shown up from seven additional microcredit groups. There was one member each (all leaders or cashiers) from five different groups, and there were two members each (leader and lay member) from two groups. At the stage of analyzing the qualitative data, I made the decision to retain their interviews in the final database since, in my opinion, their interviews were no less important as sources of data. I analyzed the interviews they gave as I did all the others with regard to their agency outcome and prior agency-enhancing circumstances or subsequent microcredit related mechanisms.

The inclusion of these interviews did raise the question of whether this might introduce a bias into the data. It is known that people with extreme opinions (positive or negative) are the ones who most easily volunteer their opinions. Presumably, in this case, the potential bias would be positive since most of these women were position holders in their respective micro-credit groups. Given their relatively insignificant proportion out of the total number of interviews I conducted in Self-Reliance (only 9 (7 leader/cashier) unsolicited volunteer interviewees out of 221), I judged that any potential bias would be trivial.

From Self-Reliance's microfinance program I interviewed 221 women from 30 different microcredit groups that were spread over 16 villages. Of these 30 groups, 18 groups had some Muslim members or were entirely Muslim in composition. The remaining 12 groups were entirely Hindu in composition. Thus of the 221 interviews, I was able to interview 104 Muslim and 117 Hindu microcredit enrollees. Table A.1 gives details on the groups and the number of members from each group that I was able to interview.

When I moved on to the second district to interview members of the microcredit groups run by Sisterhood, I followed the same procedure, but had somewhat different results. With the assistance of the organization staff, an initial sample of twenty-three groups was selected for my study based on my criteria of geographic dispersion and socio-religious composition. After completing the entire round of interviewing, I realized that only two of the sampled groups had any Muslim members (the heterogeneous groups *Shaheli* and *Matri*). Out of these two groups only five Muslim women had showed up for the interview. Neither group was entirely Muslim in its composition. This meant serious under-representation of Muslim microcredit members in the groups sampled from this organization. Once I realized this, I made a second attempt with the organization staff at soliciting a sample of microcredit groups composed of Muslim women. This attempt yielded me access to three groups in two nearby villages where I was told I would find Muslim women enrolled in microcredit groups. On the days of my visits, few Muslim women turned up, and I was able to interview only five additional Muslim women, who belonged to three different microcredit groups (homogeneously Muslim microcredit groups: *Nabashakhi* & *Shuhashini*; and a heterogeneous group: *Baishakhi*).

My being allowed access to one of these groups (*Baishakhi*) displeased the organization leader when I happened to talk about my visit to the group during an informal interaction. The reaction was based on the view that this particular group was ridden with conflicts (a fact) and "on the verge of disintegrating." I was therefore able to interview only ten Muslim women from Sisterhood's microcredit groups. By itself, this would have been a serious problem had I not already interviewed over a hundred Muslim microcredit members from Self-Reliance. The strategy of sampling

TABLE A.1: *Uttar Chobbish Pargana*

Village-regions	Names & Nos. of Microcredit Groups	No. of Members Interviewed	Totals
1. Bhojpara	1. Janakalyan	13	31
	2. Radharani	10	
	3. Probhati	8	
2. Polta	1. Beautiful	13	24
	2. Duti Pata	11	
3. Kamdebkati	1. Shantimata	14	23
	2. Shathi	4	
	3. Ashirbad	2	
	4. Shatadal	1	
	5. Shanti	1	
	6. Barnali	1	
4. Teghoria	1. Shanti	9	14
	2. Agni	5	
5. Shompur	1. Nari Mukti	6	13
	2. Shatarupa	5	
	3. Janakalyan	1	
	4. Nazrul	1	
6. Aturia	1. Banani	13	13
7. Piara	1. Udayan	7	12
	2. Mangaldeep	5	
8. Belgoria	1. Tajmahal	12	12
9. Dakshin Media	1. Ujjal	12	12
10. Magurkhali	1. Iti	12	12
11. Shimulia west	1. Diamond	12	12
12. Jashaikati	1. Adhunik	11	11
13. Kefayetkati	1. Ujjaini	10	10
14. Shimulia north	1. Ananya	9	9
15. Durgapur	1. Shonar Tori	3	5
	2. Agni Bina	2	
16. Sharparajpur	1. Bipasha	5	5
16 villages	30 groups		221 interviews

groups from more than one organization had paid off. Of course, it would have been ideal if I had access to more Muslim microcredit members from Sisterhood. But the final control was in the hands of the organization, and its reluctance to provide access to microcredit groups with a Muslim composition was data of sorts and demanded its own analysis.

There were three cases where the group leaders (all Hindu women) from three additional non-selected microcredit groups came forward to participate

TABLE A.2: *Nadia*

Village-regions	Names & Nos. of Microcredit Groups	No. of Members Interviewed	Totals
1. Duttapulia	1. Unnayan	10	47
	2. Shabitri	9	
	3. Sanjog	8	
	4. Shatadal	8	
	5. Ma Sharada	7	
	6. Rajlakshmi	4	
	7. Kamala	1	
2. Aranghata	1. Deepshikha	10	19
	2. Gram Sangathan	9	
3. Uttar Bhayena	1. Rita	10	19
	2. Shadhana	9	
4. Baliadanga	1. Sharada	10	18
	2. Shanchayita	8	
5. Durgapur	1. Durgapur	9	17
	2. D. Tribeni	8	
6. Bosta, Mathpara	1. Shyama'ma	8	16
	2. Shanti'ma	8	
7. Roopdaha, Ramnagar	1. Matri Gram Sang.	7	16
	2. Sabuj	5	
	3. Suryamukhi	4	
8. Srirampur	1. Pubali	5	12
	2. Nabashakhi	2	
	3. Shaheli	2	
	4. Shuhashini	2	
	5. Shalpagram	1	
9. Hudo	1. Baishakhi	6	11
	2. Bonophool	4	
	3. Nandita	1	
10. Matikumra	1. Debdashi	4	4
10 villages	29 groups		179 interviews

in the interviews. Altogether from Sisterhood's microfinance program I was able to interview 179 women from 29 microcredit groups that were spread over ten villages. Out of these 29 groups, five groups had some or were entirely composed of Muslim members. The remaining 24 groups had entirely Hindu members. Out of the 179 interviews, only 10 were with Muslim enrollees. Table A.2 gives detailed information.

Adding the two samples, total interviews stand at 400 (286 Hindu women; 114 Muslim women) from 59 microcredit groups with 34 groups entirely Hindu, 17 groups entirely Muslim, and 8 groups having Hindus and Muslims in varied proportions.

The hesitation from Sisterhood, the state's leading organization in operating microcredit groups, to provide access to some of its groups can be interpreted in light of the sociological literature of nonprofit organizations. This literature suggests that social approval regarding its work is crucial for NGOs. Several factors are active here: lack of financial autonomy; critical importance of reputation for garnering resources in a crowded, competitive market; difficulty of evaluating outputs; the need to gain legitimacy and the institutional pressures to deliver transparency (Sanyal 2006; DiMaggio and Anheier 1990). Nonprofits, in general, respond to the pressure of gaining social approval through "manipulation" (Oliver 1991, p. 146) and control tactics targeted to gain dominance over external constituencies (Pfeffer and Moore 1980), including controlling researchers' access to discrediting information and negative cases.

Scholars researching development interventions, typically implemented by NGOs, have expressed concern regarding the frequently exclusive focus on successful cases of such interventions. In view of these risks, some of the measures I adopted were targeted to minimize the bias introduced by any particular organization. These included my decision to draw my sample from microcredit programs administered by two NGOs that were somewhat different in their orientations. The samples of interviewees were not pre-selected, and the procedure of the interviews left little control in the hands of the organizations. Both are described in the following section.

Enlisting respondents and interview procedures

After the sample selection had been completed, in Self-Reliance, the program director introduced me to the regional program managers (four managers, all men, responsible for four broad regions) and informed them about the groups I would study. These men individually accompanied me on my first trip to the first village (only one way) in their respective regions (in three cases, as a pillion rider in their motorbikes for part of the way). There, the group supervisor would be waiting for me, and the program manager would leave after I had been introduced to the group supervisor. In Sisterhood, information about my identity and purpose and the list of the groups selected were passed on directly to the group supervisors. I would go to the village directly, unaccompanied (following the routes, modes of transportation, and directions given by the program manager), and I would be met by the group supervisor at the village bus stand or *mor* (intersection with main road). The group supervisor would accompany me to my first meeting with the first group and introduce me to the group leader who would then gather the group members in a location of their choice. The supervisor would then leave and return to their home or work.

Within both organizations out of all the supervisors with whom I crossed paths, only two were male (one, a Hindu man; another, a Muslim man who had taken the job over from his wife who had been the original group supervisor). Most women supervisors would use bicycles in traveling between the groups under their supervision. Between their group-related workload and their domestic responsibilities, these women did not have the time to linger on while I was conducting interviews throughout the day. So they would leave once they had handed me over to the group leader. On the subsequent days, if I was visiting the same group or a nearby group, I would make the entire trip from the NGO's headquarters to the village of the sampled group and back on my own using locally available means of public transportation, which included buses, cycle-vans, over-crowded jeeps, and for one region, a boat crossing a river. There was no supervision of my interviews with the women by any NGO staffs or group supervisors beyond the latter's initial introductory presence (never lasting more than half an hour) on the first day of my visit with any new group.

The selected groups had prior information regarding my visit. Whether or not the group members showed up on the days of my fieldwork to interact with me was voluntary and depended to some extent on the effectiveness of the group leader in disseminating the information about my visit and encouraging group members to be present. Tables A.1 and A.2 provide information on the group turnout for participating in the interviews. There was group-to-group variation, and there were more interviewees from some groups (as many as twelve to fourteen in a few cases) and fewer in others. In groups where there were a sizeable number of members willing to participate, I returned for a second or third day to complete the interviewing.

The number of women to be interviewed from each group was not predetermined. I did not ever turn away anyone who wanted to participate in the interview. I adopted this strategy in order to elicit as many respondents from each group as possible, knowing that having a predetermined number would not work well. Having a predetermined number would require me to randomly select a specific number of members from each group to be interviewed, women who might not all be available or able to participate on the days of my field visit. Choosing only those women who arrived first up to the specified number to be interviewed would appear somewhat unfair when household care-giving and work responsibilities would delay some women unpredictably.

Following the second strategy might have also led to a bias in the data assuming that the first few women to volunteer to be interviewed might give precedence to the ones who already had prior agency or had a strongly positive or negative opinion of microcredit. Interviewing all those women from a group who made themselves available seemed to be the best way to make the qualitative data as inclusive as possible and to avoid obvious biases.

There is still the question of those women who did not show up on the day(s) of my visit and how being able to interview them might have influenced the patterns found in this study. Based on the total number of interviews (four hundred) and the saturation of observations I was able to obtain in each of the pathways that emerged through inductive analysis, I believe any other method of selecting interviewees would not have provided any observations that I was not able to capture in this study. Using a different selection method, however, might have altered the proportion of observations within each pathway.

In all cases, the women decided the location where they wanted their interactions with me to take place and where they would be at ease being interviewed. In most cases the place of meeting was the courtyard surrounding the group leader's home or the home of another member where all the women congregated for the introductions. The main feature of the locations chosen by the groups turned out to be the absence of family members such as husbands or in-laws. Because I only conducted the interviews during the daytime (9 A.M.–5 P.M.), most of the working age men were out of their homes plying their trades or working in their fields. Men often have a main meal in the morning before they leave for work and have their second main meal in the evening when they return home. Some return home briefly for an afternoon meal. Women who needed to be at their homes for serving their families afternoon meals excused themselves for that time and returned later to be interviewed.

There was no external influence on the interviews in the form of the presence of NGO staffs, group supervisors, or male and female family members who were relationally senior to the women and not part of the group. If women who were sisters-in-law were present at the interaction, it meant that they were members of the same microcredit group. I believe I was able to have relatively unrestricted communication with women in both Hindu and Muslim neighborhoods.

The interviews were conducted in Bengali (*Bangla*) and lasted approximately forty-fifty minutes each. With group leaders or other women holding leadership positions in their groups (as co-leaders and cashiers) or in cases in which groups had conducted interventions, the interviews were sometimes longer. With women who were not very articulate, the interviews were shorter. These inarticulate cases were often women deficient in agency who experienced restricted participation in the microcredit group and who did not experience positive changes in their social situation.

All the interviews were tape-recorded, and I transcribed and translated them into English over a six-month period following the conclusion of the fieldwork. The process was very rewarding despite its tedium because it allowed me to develop a deep command over the qualitative data I collected. The in-depth interviews were semistructured around several key themes of women's capabilities and connections, as discussed in Chapter 2. The questions were presented in an open-ended way that allowed women to answer at length and in their own words. Factual questions focused on the background details of the interview subject (education, work, family, and income); household information (type and composition); group characteristics (age, size, and composition); and experience of group enrollment and participation (frequency and nature of participation, community or family reaction, and feeling toward the group).

I went on to collect individual loan histories – the amount of microcredit loans the women and their families had taken out from the group and for what purpose they had used it; who made the loan decisions as to how much to borrow, how to use the loan, and how to repay it; how much they had saved in the group; and borrowing and savings patterns prior to enrollment in microcredit and concurrently outside of microcredit.

Loans were used for a variety of economic activities: leasing agricultural land, ponds, and seasonal fruit-bearing trees; purchasing farming supplies; purchasing dairy cows, goats, and hens; setting up poultry farms; running small-scale enterprises of pisciculture (fish-farming) and honey-production (with bee-boxes); buying paddy for home-based rice husking businesses; setting up or expanding grocery stores; and purchasing *cycle* or *engine-vans* (pedal- or motor-powered vehicles) used in villages for transporting people and goods. Loans were also used to pay for basic amenities for the household such as laying private ground-water taps (tube-well), constructing toilets, and wiring electricity connections; to pay for medical expenses; and to finance marriages and funerals. In Table A.3, I have provided an

TABLE A.3: *Loan history of interviewed members of a group: an example*

No.	Members	No. of Loans	Total Loans (in Rupees)	Loan Amounts and Uses (in Rupees)
1.	Kanika	3	Rs 18,000	Rs 2000: invested in "rakhi" business Rs 4000: invested in "rakhi" business Rs 4000: paid for daughter's wedding expenses Rs 8000: paid for daughter's child delivery costs
2.	Krishna	4	Rs 16,000	Rs 5000: bought supplies for bicycle shop Rs 3000: bought sewing machine Rs 8000: electricity connection for the house, paid off outstanding debts, bought supplies for the bicycle shop
3.	Shikha	4	Rs 16,000	Rs 2000: vegetable vending business Rs 4000: puffed rice and hot gram business Rs 6000: bought a van Rs 4000: bought two cows
4.	Parul	3	Rs 12,500	Rs 2500: set up a snack food business Rs 5000: took five "kathas" of land on lease Rs 5000: registered the land under their own name
5.	Dipali	3	Rs 11,000	Rs 2000: bought a van Rs 3000: set up a snack food ("phuchka") business Rs 6000: expanded the scale of the same business
6.	Uma	3	Rs 11,000	Rs 2000: bought supplies for grocery store Rs 4000: bought supplies for the same store Rs 5000: paid for children's education expenses
7.	Shankari	3	Rs 10,000	Rs 2000: used for cultivation, paid for children's education expenses Rs 5000: for cultivating paddy Rs 3000: for partially financing her surgery
8.	Aparna	3	Rs 9000	Rs 2000: bought palm trees Rs 2000: repaid outstanding debts Rs 5000: bought cyle-van fitted with engine

TABLE A.3: (*cont.*)

No.	Members	No. of Loans	Total Loans (in Rupees)	Loan Amounts and Uses (in Rupees)
9.	Bishakha	3	Rs 7000	Rs 1000: to make fishing nets
				Rs 3000: to make bamboo baskets
				Rs 3000: to make fishing nets
10.	Kamala	3	Rs 6000	Rs 2000: bought date palm trees
				Rs 2000: bought date palm trees
				Rs 2000: took a pond on lease
11.	Usha	3	Rs 4000	Rs 1000: bought a cow
				Rs 1000: sunk a tube-well in her house
				Rs 2000: acquired back land given up for lease
12.	Basanti	1	Rs 2000	Rs 2000: for husband's fruit vending business
13.	Jinnah	2	Rs 2000	Rs 1000: laid a tap in the house
				Rs 1000: bought a calf

example of the loan histories of all the members interviewed from a single group (Banani).

In the interviews, I explored in detail the choices, use, and management decisions behind each of these loans. Questions were used to build rapport with the respondents and to gain critical information before moving on to more sensitive questions pertaining to agency and social capital. For assessing the state of women's social capital, I asked questions regarding the number of social contacts women had, their ability to seek or offer help in times of personal or domestic crisis, and instances of collective action before or after joining the microcredit group. Throughout the interview, I explored alternative factors and causal mechanisms that could explain the social or economic improvements that women claimed to have experienced or the failure to do so. Was success or failure due to microcredit loans, or due to the group's associational mechanism, or due to extraneous factors related to household circumstances? Factors I considered included: widowhood or being deserted by husbands, education and employment, membership in political parties or other associations, prior NGO involvement, transition from an extended to a nuclear household, husband's work-related migration, husband's egalitarian or conservative attitude.

Problems of informant recall in this study were not serious because the groups had been operating on average for three to four years, and the women could clearly remember the social and economic conditions of their lives prior to joining these groups. Among the biggest advantages of the interview as qualitative evidence was the fact that the passage of time and the women's intervening experience of group membership enabled women to compare their previous economic and social condition with their present situations. Through the interview format, they were able to evaluate past experiences in light of present transformations (or their lack) occasioned by their participation in microcredit groups. Women themselves were able to identify the capabilities that they had previously lacked as valued "beings and doings" that they had not been able to achieve in the past. Through the interview format, they were equally able to declare candidly that there had been no change or improvement in their situation or that things had worsened. The retrospective aspect of the data presented here poses no serious methodological flaws that would put the study's findings in doubt.

As to how my identity influenced the interview process, I believe that my shared gender identity and linguistic familiarity greatly helped this study. At the outset, I was concerned about whether my urban and class identities would matter in my interactions with the women and influence the quality of the information that I would be able to elicit from them. A matter of specific concern was whether my interactions with the Muslim women would be hampered in any way because of my being non-Muslim (which they would know from my name).

Being aware of the "intersectionality" of identity, I was prepared to encounter difficulties in achieving openness in communication because of my urban and class identities. Events in the field proved to be moments of proximity rather than distance except in one instance. It was my practice to take a very simple packed lunch prepared by the cook at the NGO residence facility. I had this meal in between waiting for the women to arrive from their own mealtime for their turn at being interviewed. My intention was not to be a burden on the group members. Usually this practice did not attract any attention and was understood as part of my desire to devote as much of my time in the village as possible to interacting with the women. Only once, on the very first day of my fieldwork, I decided to have a meal at a group member's house, the designated location for the day's interviewing. My initial refusal of her offer of lunch had raised the suspicion in her mind that I was unwilling to partake of food at her house because of caste. I became aware of this as she subtly implied this and enquired into it. I hoped that my consuming the food offered by her would lay to rest her suspicions. This was the single incident when the issue of caste identity was obliquely referred to.

There were only two instances in which my social location was explicitly called into question. In the first I was singled out as an outsider, and in the second I was mistaken for an insider. In the first, a male villager stopped me on my way from the village ferry to the interior neighborhood (seeing me for the third day) and asked who I was and what had brought me to the village. In another, more surprising incident, a male villager called out to me from behind and asked if I was going to my uncle's house, obviously mistaking me for somebody else. I took the fact that this person could not tell me apart from behind as a good sign of my having been able to blend into the social context I was studying.

Sometimes women asked about my family, if I was married, and how many siblings I had. On one occasion, on hearing that I had only one sibling, a sister, a group member commented, "Well, your mother's fate is also like mine." The group member saw the absence of a son as being the equalizer of the fate of two women from vastly different life situations.

Nevertheless, the determining reality, I believe, all differences notwithstanding, was that the interview presented a rare opportunity for the women to talk about their lives. Many women, even if they were initially hesitant, opened up once they started and experienced a wide and subtle range of emotions as they recounted the events of their lives and episodes surrounding the group. For some, it was a cathartic experience to be able to talk about their hardships and their struggles. There were times when I was struck by the candor with which some of the women described the physical violence they had suffered at the hands of their husbands.

I gradually came to realize that the notion of privacy that prevailed in these village societies was somewhat different from that in urban societies even within the same country. The residential space in rural households spills out from the one or two brick-walled or earthen rooms into the open ledge and courtyard surrounding the house. Many daily activities are conducted in this space in the view of neighbors and villagers passing by. This feature combined with the dense location of houses in rural neighborhoods means that when it comes to domestic disputes between couples (including physical violence), most of it happens within the view and earshot of their immediate neighbors who live in close proximity. Privacy in such matters therefore does not mean that close neighbors do not know of these incidents; rather, it means that no one intervenes in the internal domestic matters of another household.

I believe that the women's ability to share such intimate information with me is explained by the fact that their domestic happenings were not new information for their immediate neighbors, some of whom were now their fellow group members whom they may have known for three to four years by the time of the interview. In fact, sometimes the presence of other group members hovering near the scene of my interviewing (often these were women waiting to give their interviews) emboldened the woman being interviewed to talk more openly about her travails, the struggles and misfortunes she had faced, how she had suffered, or how she had overcome her hardships. I believe that this was a way the women were able to express themselves forcefully and indirectly seek solace and even praise from each other.

This pattern of fellow group members listening while others were being interviewed emerged very early in the fieldwork. At first I felt consternation and surprise. On my very first day of fieldwork, after the introduction to the group, I requested all the group members to leave the room and return one-by-one later so that I could start interviewing the first person. All the women lived close to each other and this suggestion was in no way inconvenient for them. But, as soon as I had said this, the woman whom I was about to interview reacted with great shock. She asked what I was going to interrogate her about that I couldn't do it in front of the others. And the women laughed at the idea of leaving the room.

I had no other way than to begin interviewing my first interviewee in the presence of her fellow group-members. I noticed that the women did not feel any discomfort in talking about their lives in front of their fellow group members. Gradually, as the novelty of the event wore off for these women or as they were needed back in their households, the women started leaving. Some lingered on even after their own interviews had been completed. Following this incident, in my subsequent visits to the different groups, I refrained from intervening and let the situation be shaped by the women being interviewed. So, in the end, some of the one-on-one interviews were conducted in the presence of an audience of group members and, in some instances, they were conducted with the interviewee alone. I left the decision to the woman being interviewed.

Among the benefits of the presence of multiple group members during the interview was the unanticipated role of group members in facilitating the recall process, as when they would mention incidents pertaining to the interviewee's household and press her to say more about it. The residential proximity of group members meant that, in many groups, there were few group members who were not aware of the happenings in other households. Even if they were not well acquainted with each other, they knew of each other's lives before joining the group. Group members' observations and comments on changes in a fellow group member were often astute and valued by the interviewee.

For the women in groups who were involved in imposing sanctions or collective action, the interview was an opportunity to highlight the deeds of the group that they viewed and highly valued as reflecting their increased capability. Concerning Muslim women in entirely Muslim groups, I am not aware that my difference of religious identity created any barrier in my communications with them or affected their openness during the interview. These women spoke in equally personal measure about their domestic situations and experience with microcredit, displaying emotions very similar to their Hindu counterparts. Some of them spoke quite openly with me about the opposition they faced both from their families and from elders and other community members. I doubt very much that the women's responses to questions would have been significantly different had I hired a Muslim research assistant to interview the Muslim women.

So, in conclusion, in recognizing the importance of reflexivity I have tried to make explicit how my own positionality in terms of gender, ethnicity, and as a city person all played into the dynamics of the interaction with the respondents and the interview process. Ultimately, any interview is an interactive process and the facts and information elicited in the course of an interview are to some extent contingent on the interactional and situational dynamics (it is much the same for surveys administered by enumerators in the course of collecting statistical data). And any situational dynamics that might be present in an interview must be accounted for in analyzing the data from that interview. But this is no reason to diminish the validity of the information obtained from interviews as long as the researcher can reasonably conclude that there was no influence or interference that might make the respondents falsify information or excessively withhold it. Respondents may not share each and every intimate detail of their lives (although in many cases they share a lot, as this study shows abundantly). And scientific skepticism demands that we not take everything a respondent says in an interview at face value, but seek to ask to same question in different ways and at different points in the interview to verify whether the response is consistent and challenge respondents if needed. But to operate with the assumption that respondents never tell the truth and what they say is not to be trusted seems to be an ideological bias, which like all biases overlooks the strength of the object of critique. The interview method, like all methods, has its strengths and weaknesses.[16]

---

[16] For an excellent and authoritative discussion, see Lamont and Swidler (2013).

In this study, I have tried to capitalize on the strengths of the interview method on a topic that has been explored using statistical and ethnographic methods. This book is the first fully interview-based study of microcredit and women's agency and systematically brings to light the causal links between microcredit and women's capabilities and gives analytical prominence to how women experience this intervention.

Bibliography

Abbott, Andrew. 1992. "From Causes to Events: Notes on Narrative Positivism." *Sociological Methods and Research*, 20(4): 428–455.

Ackerly, Brooke A. 1995. "Testing Tools of Development: Credit Programmes, Loan Involvement, and Women's Empowerment." *IDS Bulletin: Getting Institutions Right for Women in Development* 26(3): 56–68.

Agarwal, Bina. 1997 "'Bargaining' and Gender Relations: Within and Beyond the Household." *Feminist Economics* 3(1): 1–51.

Ahmed, Fauzia E. 2008. "Microcredit, Men, and Masculinity." *National Women's Studies Association (NWSA)* 20(2): 122–155.

2008. "Hidden Opportunities: Islam, Masculinity and Poverty Alleviation." *International Feminist Journal of Politics* 10(4): 542–562.

Anderson, Deborah J., Melissa Binder, and Kate Krause. 2003. "The Motherhood Wage Penalty Revisited: Experience, Heterogeneity, Work Effort, and Work Schedule Flexibility." *Industrial and Labor Relations Review* 56(2): 273–294.

Anthony, Denise. 1997. "Micro-Lending Institutions: Using Social Networks to Create Productive Capabilities," *International Journal of Sociology and Social Policy* 17: 156–178.

2005. "Cooperation in Microcredit Borrowing Groups: Identity, Sanctions, and Reciprocity in the Production of Collective Goods." *American Sociological Review* 70(3): 496–515.

Anthony, Denise, and Christine Horne. 2003. "Gender and Cooperation: Explaining Loan Repayment in Microcredit Groups." *Social Psychology Quarterly* 66(3).

Appadurai, Arjun. 2004. "The Capacity to Aspire: Culture and the Terms of Recognition." In *Culture and Public Action*. Vijayendra Rao and Michael Walton (eds.). Stanford, CA: Stanford University Press. Pp. 59–84.

Ardener, Shirley, and Sandra Burman. 1996. *Money Go-Rounds: The Importance of ROSCAs for Women (Cross-Cultural Perspectives on Women)*. Berg Publishers.

Armendariz de Aghion, Beatriz, and Jonathan Morduch. 2005. *The Economics of Microfinance*. Cambridge, MA: MIT Press.

Aubert, Vilhelm. 1956. "The Housemaid: An Occupational Role in Crisis." *Acta Sociologica* 1(3): 149–158.

Avellar, Sarah, and Pamela J. Smock. 2003. "Has the Price of Motherhood Declined over Time? A Cross-Cohort Comparison of the Motherhood Wage Penalty." *Journal of Marriage and Family* 65(3): 597–607.

Axelrod, Robert. 1986. "An Evolutionary Approach to Norms." *American Political Science Review* 80(4): 1095–1111.

Baiocchi, Gianpaolo, Patrick Heller, and Marcelo K. Silva. 2011. *Bootstrapping Democracy: Transforming Local Governance and Civil Society in Brazil.* Stanford, CA: Stanford University Press.

Banerjee, Abhijit, Esther Duflo, Rachel Glennerster, and Cynthia Kinnan. 2010. "The Miracle of Microfinance? Evidence from a Randomized Evaluation." BREAD working paper, No. 278: 1–52.

Banfield, Edward C. 1958. *The Moral Basis of a Backward Society.* New York: Free Press.

Bartholomew, Michael. 2002. "James Lind and Scurvy: A Revaluation." *Journal for Maritime Research* 4(1): 1–14.

Basu, Amrita. 1992. *Two Faces of Protest: Contrasting Modes of Women's Activism in India.* Berkeley: University of California Press.

Basu, Srimati. 1999. *She Comes to Take Her Rights: Indian Women, Property, and Propriety.* Albany: State University of New York Press.

Bateman, Milford, and Ha-Joon Chang. 2008. "The Microfinance Illusion." Mimeo, University of Juraj Dobrila Pula and University of Cambridge.

Becker, Markus C., Thorbjorn Knudsen, and Richard Swedberg (eds.). 2011. *The Entrepreneur: Classic Texts by Joseph A. Schumpeter.* Stanford, CA: Stanford University Press.

Bendix, Rheinhard. 1960. *Max Weber: An Intellectual Portrait.* Garden City, NY: Doubleday.

Berman, Sheri. 1997 a. "Civil Society and Political Institutionalization." *American Behavioral Scientist* 40(5): 562–574.

1997 b. "Civil Society and the Collapse of the Weimar Republic." *World Politics* 49: 401.

Biggart, Nicole W. 2001. "Banking on Each Other: The Situational Logic of Rotating Savings and Credit Associations." *Advances in Qualitative Organization Research* 3: 129–153.

Biju, B. L., and K. G. Abhilash Kumar. 2013. "Class Feminism: The Kudumbashree Agitation in Kerala." *Economic and Political Weekly* XLVIII (9): 22–26.

Blair-Loy, Mary. 2003. *Competing Devotions: Career and Family among Women Executives.* Cambridge, MA: Harvard University Press.

Blair-Loy, Mary, and Jerry A. Jacobs. 2003. "Globalization, Work Hours, and the Care Deficit among Stockbrokers." *Gender and Society* 17(2): 230–249.

Bloomberg Businessweek. 2007. "Compartamos: From Nonprofit to Profit." Dec. 13 edition.

Bourdieu, Pierre. 1977. *Outline of a Theory of Practice.* New York: Cambridge University Press.

1985. The Forms of Capital. In *Handbook of Theory and Research for the Sociology of Education.* J. G. Richardson (ed.). New York: Greenwood.

Bruck, Connie. 2006. "Millions for Millions." *The New Yorker*, Oct. 30.

Budig, Michelle, and Paula England. 2001. "The Wage Penalty of Motherhood." *American Sociological Review* 66(2): 204–225.

Burke, Jason, and Saad Hammadi. 2011. "Muhammad Yunus Loses Appeal against Grameen Bank Dismissal." *The Guardian*, Mar. 8.

Burroughs, Valentine J., Randall W. Maxey, and Richard A. Levy. 2002. "Racial and Ethnic Differences in Response to Medicines: Towards Individualized Pharmaceutical Treatment." *Journal of the National Medical Association* 94(10) (SUPPL): 1–26.

Burt, Ronald S. 1992. *Structural Holes: The Social Structure of Competition.* Cambridge, MA: Harvard University Press.

Butler, Judith. 1999 [1990]. *Gender Trouble: Feminism and the Subversion of Identity.* New York: Routledge.

2004. *Undoing Gender.* New York: Routledge.

Carpenter, Kenneth. 1966 (1988). *The History of Scurvy and Vitamin C.* Cambridge University Press.

Cassar, Alessandra, Lucas Crowley, and Bruce Wydick. 2007. "The Effect of Social Capital on Group Loan Repayment: Evidence from Field Experiments." *The Economic Journal* 117(517): 85–106.

Cassar, Alessandra, and Bruce Wydick. 2010. "Does Social Capital Matter? Evidence from a Five-Country Group Lending Experiment." *Oxford Economic Papers* 62(4): 715–739.

Chaudhuri, Shubham, and Patrick Heller. 2003. "The Plasticity of Participation: Evidence from a Participatory Governance Experiment." New York: Columbia University ISERP Working Paper.

Coleman, James S. 1990. *Foundations of Social Theory.* Cambridge, MA: Harvard University Press.

Constable, Nicole. 2007 (1997). *Maid to Order in Hong Kong: Stories of Migrant Workers.* Ithaca, NY: Cornell University Press.

Cornwall, Andrea. 2004. "Spaces for Transformation? Reflections on Issues of Power and Difference in Participation in Development." In *Participation: From Tyranny to Transformation? Exploring New Approaches to Participation in Development.* Samuel Hickey and Giles Mohan (eds.). London and New York: Zed Books.

Coser, Lewis A. 1973. "The Obsolescence of an Occupational Role." *Social Forces* 52(1): 31–40.

Crepon, Bruno, Florencia Devoto, Esther Duflo, and William Pariente. 2011. "Impact of Microcredit in Rural Areas of Morocco: Evidence from a Randomized Evaliation." Working Paper.

Denzin, Norman K., and Yvonna S. Lincoln (eds.). 2003. *Collecting and Interpreting Qualitative Materials* (2nd ed.). Thousand Oaks, CA: Sage Publications.

Desai, Manali. 2007. *State Formation and Radical Democracy in India.* London and New York: Routledge.

Dixon-Mueller, Ruth. 1978. *Rural Women at Work: Strategies for Development in South Asia.* Baltimore: Johns Hopkins University Press.

Dobbin, Frank, and Dirk Zorn. 2005. "Corporate Malfeasance and the Myth of Shareholder Value." *Political Power and Social Theory* (17): 179–198.

Dyson, Tim, and Mick Moore. 1983. "On Kinship Structure, Female Autonomy, and Demographic Behavior in India." *Population and Development Review* 9: 35–60.

Ehrenreich, Barbara, and Arlie R. Hochschild (eds.). 2003. *Global Woman: Nannies, Maids, and Sex Workers in the New Economy*. New York: Metropolitan Books.

Eliasoph, Nina, and Paul Lichterman. 2003. "Culture in Interaction." *The American Journal of Sociology* 108(4): 735–794.

Emerson, Richard. 1962. "Power Dependence Relations." *American Sociological Review* 27(1): 31–41.

Emirbayer, Mustafa, and Ann Mische. 1998. "What Is Agency?" *American Journal of Sociology* 103(4): 962–1023.

Fernandez-Kelly, Maria P. 1983. *For We Are Sold, I and My People: Women and Industry in Mexico's Frontier*. Albany: State University of New York Press.

Fernando, Jude L. 1997. "Nongovernmental Organizations, Micro-Credit, and Empowerment of Women." *Annals of the American Academy of Political and Social Science* 554(Nov): 150–177.

Fraser, Nancy. 1990. "Rethinking the Public Sphere: A Contribution to the Critique of Actually Existing Democracy." *Social Text* 25/26: 56–80.

Garikipati, Supriya. 2009. "The Impact of Lending to Women on Household Vulnerability and Women's Empowerment: Evidence from India." *World Development* 36(12): 2620–2642.

Giddens, Anthony. 1976. *New Rules of Sociological Method: A Positive Critique of Interpretive Sociologies*. London: Hutchinson.

  1979. *Central Problems in Social Theory: Action, Structure and Contradiction in Social Analysis*. Berkeley and Los Angeles: University of California Press.

  1981. *A Contemporary Critique of Historical Materialism*. Vol. 1: *Power, Property and the State*. London: Macmillan.

  1984. *The Constitution of Society: Outline of the Theory of Structuration*. Berkeley and Los Angeles: University of California Press.

Glauber, Rebecca. 2007. "Marriage and Motherhood Wage Penalty Among African Americans, Hispanics, and White." *Journal of Marriage and Family* 69(4): 951–961.

Goetz, Anne M., and Rina Sengupta. 1996. "Who Takes the Credit? Gender, Power, and Control over Loan Use in Rural Credit Programs in Bangladesh." *World Development* 24(1): 45–64.

Goffman, Erving. 1959. *The Presentation of Self in Everyday Life*. New York: Doubleday.

  1967. *Interaction Ritual: Essays on Face-to-Face Behavior*. Garden City, NY: Anchor.

Government of India. 2001. *Census of India*. Registrar General and Census Commissioner.

Government of India. 2006. *Social, Economic and Educational Status of the Muslim Community in India: A Report*. Prime Minister's High Level Committee, Cabinet Secretariat.

Government of West Bengal. 2004. *West Bengal Human Development Report*. Development and Planning Department.

Gramsci, Antonio. 1971. *Selections from the Prison Notebooks*. New York: International Publishers.

Granovetter, Mark. 1985. "Economic Action and Social Structure: The Problem of Embeddedness." *American Journal of Sociology* 91(3): 481–510.

Hasan, Zoya, and Ritu Menon. 2005. *Educating Muslim Girls: A Comparison of Five Indian Cities*. New Delhi: Women Unlimited.

Hashemi, Syed M., Sidney Ruth Schuler, and Ann P. Riley. 1996. "Rural Credit Programs and Women's Empowerment in Bangladesh." *World Development* 24(4): 635–653.

Hays, Sharon. 1996. *The Cultural Contradictions of Motherhood*. New Haven, CT: Yale University Press.

Hecht, J. Jean. 1956. *The Domestic Servant Class in Eighteenth Century England*. London: Routledge & Kegan Paul.

Hechter, Michael, and Karl-Dieter Opp (eds.). 2001. *Social Norms*. New York: Russell Sage Foundation.

Heckathorn, Douglas. 1993. "Collective Action and Group Heterogeneity: Voluntary Provision versus Selective Incentives." *American Sociological Review* 58(3): 329–350.

Heller, Patrick G. 2009. "Democratic Deepening in India and South Africa." *Journal of Asian and African Studies* 44(1): 97–122.

Heller, Patrick G., K. N. Harilal, and Shubham Chaudhuri. 2007. "Building Local Democracy: Evaluating the Impact of Decentralization in Kerala, India." *World Development* 35(4): 626–648.

Hochschild, Arlie Russell. 2000. "Global Care Chains and Emotional Surplus Value." In *On the Edge: Living with Global Capitalism*. Will Hutton and Anthony Giddens (eds.). London: Jonathan Cape.

Hoff, Karla, Mayuresh Kshetramade, and Ernst Fehr. 2009. "Caste and Punishment: The Legacy of Caste Culture in Norm Enforcement." Institute for the Study of Labor, IZA Discussion Paper No. 4343 (August), Bonn, Germany.

Hondagneu-Sotelo, Pierrette. 2001. *Domestica: Immigrant Workers Cleaning and Caring in the Shadows of Affluence*. Berkeley: University of California Press.

Horne, Christine. 2001. "Sociological Perspectives on the Emergence of Norms." In *Social Norms*. Michael Hechter and Karl-Dieter Opp (eds.). New York: Russell Sage Foundation.

2004. "Collective Benefits, Exchange Interests, and Norm Enforcement." *Social Forces* 82(3): 1037–1062.

John, Mary E. 2005. "Feminism, Poverty, and the Emergent Social Order." In *Social Movements in India: Poverty, Power, and Politics*. Raka Ray and Mary Fainsod Katzenstein (eds.). Lanham, MD: Rowman and Littlefield.

Kabeer, Naila. 1998. *"Money Can't Buy Me Love?" Re-Evaluating Gender, Credit and Empowerment in Rural Bangladesh*. Institute of Development Studies, University of Sussex.

1999. "Resources, Agency, Achievements: Reflections on the Measurements of Women's Empowerment." *Development and Change* 30: 435–64.

2001. "Conflicts over Credit: Re-Evaluating the Empowerment Potential of Loans to Women in Rural Bangladesh." *World Development* 29(1): 63–84.

2000. *The Power to Choose: Bangladeshi Women and Labor Market Decisions in London and Dhaka*. London and New York: Verso.

Karim, Lamia. 2011. *Microfinance and Its Discontents: Women in Debt in Bangladesh*. Minneapolis and London: University of Minnesota Press.

2011. "The Fall of Muhammad Yunus and Its Consequences for the Women of Grameen Bank." University of Minnesota Press Blog, March 31.

Karlan, Dan. 2005. "Using Experimental Economics to Measure Social Capital and Predict Financial Decisions." *American Economic Review* 95: 1688–1699.

Khandker, Shahidur R. 2005. "Microfinance and Poverty: Evidence Using Panel Data from Bangladesh." *World Bank Economic Review* 19(2): 263–286.

Kishwar, Madhu. 1999. *Off the Beaten Track: Rethinking Gender Justice for Indian Women*. New Delhi and New York: Oxford University Press.

Krishna, Anirudh. 1997. "Participatory Watershed Development and Soil Conservation." In *Reasons for Hope: Instructive Experiences in Rural Development*. Anirudh Krishna, Norman Uphoff, and Milton J. Esman (eds.). West Hartford, CT: Kumarian Press.

2000. "Creating and Harnessing Social Capital." In *Social Capital: A Multifaceted Perspective*. Partha Dasgupta and Ismail Serageldin (eds.). Washington, DC: The World Bank.

2002. *Active Social Capital: Tracing the Roots of Development and Democracy*. New York: Columbia University Press.

Krishna, Anirudh, and Abusaleh Shariff. 2011. "The Irrelevance of National Strategies? Rural Poverty Dynamics in States and Regions of India, 1993–2005." *World Development* 39(4): 533–549.

Kristof, Nicholas D., and Sheryl WuDunn. 2009. *Half the Sky: Turning Oppression into Opportunity for Women Worldwide*. New York: Alfred A. Knopf.

Lamont, Michele, and Patricia White (eds.). 2008. *The Evaluation of Systematic Qualitative Research in the Social Sciences*. Washington, DC: National Science Foundation.

Lamont, Michele, and Ann Swidler. 2013. "In Praise of Methodological Pluralism: From a Methods to a Theory Debate." Pp. 1–27 in American Sociological Association Conference. New York City: NY.

Larson, Gerald J. (ed.). 2001. *Religion and Personal Law in Secular India: A Call to Judgment*. Bloomington: Indiana University Press.

Lee, Ching Kwan. 1998. *Gender and the South China Miracle: Two Worlds of Factory Women*. Berkeley: University of California Press.

Lichterman, Paul. 2012. "Religion in Public Action: From Actors to Settings." *Sociological Theory* 30(1): 15–36.

Light, Ivan, and Edna Bonacich. 1988. *Immigrant Entrepreneurs: Koreans in Los Angeles, 1965–1982*. Berkeley and Los Angeles: University of California Press.

Lin, Nan. 2000. "Inequality in Social Capital." *Contemporary Sociology* 29(6): 785–795.

Lin, Nan, Karen Cook, and Ronald S. Burt (eds.). 2001. *Social Capital: Theory and Research*. New York: Aldine de Gruyter.

Lynch, Caitrin. 2007. *Juki Girls, Good Girls: Gender and Cultural Politics in Sri Lanka's Global Garment Industry.* Ithaca, NY: ILR Press/Cornell University Press.

Mahmood, Saba. 2005. *Politics of Piety: The Islamic Revival and the Feminist Subject.* Princeton, NJ: Princeton University Press.

Mandal, N. K., S. Mallik, R. P. Roy, S. B. Mandal, S. Dasgupta, and A. Mandal. 2007. "Impact of Religious Faith and Female Literacy on Fertility in a Rural Community in West Bengal." *Indian Journal of Community Medicine* 32(1): 12–14.

Marwell, Gerald, Pamela E. Oliver, and Ralph Prahl. 1988. "Social Networks and Collective Action: A Theory of Critical Mass. III." *American Journal of Sociology* 94: 502–34.

Marx, Karl. 1987 (1852). *The Eighteenth Brumaire of Louis Bonaparte.* New York: International Publishers.

Mayoux, Linda. 1995. "From Vicious to Virtuous Circles? Gender and Micro-Enterprise Development." UNRISD, U.N., Occasional Paper 3.

Menon, Nidhiya. 2003. "Consumption Smoothing in Microcredit Programs." EconPapers.

Miles, Mathew B., and A. Michael Huberman. 1994. *Qualitative Data Analysis: An Expanded Sourcebook.* Thousand Oaks, CA: Sage Publications.

Molyneux, Maxine. 1985. "Mobilization without Emancipation? Women's Interests, State, and Revolution in Nicaragua." *Feminist Studies* 11 (2): 227–253.

Montgomery, Richard, Debapriya Bhattacharya, and David Hulme. 1996. "Credit for the Poor in Bangladesh." In *Finance Against Poverty.* D. Hulme and P. Mosley (eds.). London: Routledge.

Morduch, Jonathan. 1998. *The Microfinance Schism.* Cambridge, MA: Harvard Institute for International Development.

   1999. "The Microfinance Problem." *Journal of Economic Literature* 37: 1569–1614.

Mukherjee, Arghya K., and Amit Kundu. 2012. "Microcredit and Women's Agency: A Comparative Perspective across Socio-Religious Communities in West Bengal, India." *Gender, Technology and Development* 16(1): 71–94.

Murray, Sarah. 2008. "Overview: Microfinance Unlocks Potential of the Poor." *Financial Times,* June 2 edition.

Newman, Katherine S., and Rebekah Peeples Massengill. 2006. "The Texture of Hardship: Qualitative of Sociology of Poverty, 1995–2005." *Annual Review of Sociology* 32: 423–446.

Olson, Mancur. 1965. *The Logic of Collective Action.* Cambridge, MA: Harvard University Press.

Ong, Aihwa. 1987. *Spirits of Resistance and Capitalist Discipline: Factory Women in Malaysia.* Albany: State University of New York Press.

Ostrom, Elinor. 1994. "Constituting Social Capital and Collective Action." *Journal of Theoretical Politics* 6(4): 527–562.

Ostrom, Elinor, and James Walker (eds.). 2003. *Trust and Reciprocity: Interdisciplinary Lessons from Experimental Research.* New York: Russell Sage Foundation.

Parrenas, Rachel S. 2001. *Servants of Globalization: Women, Migration, and Domestic Work*. Stanford, CA: Stanford University Press.

Pike, Edgar Royston. 1967. *"Golden Times": Human Documents of the Victorian Age*. New York and Washington, DC: Praeger.

Pitt, Mark, and Shahidur Khandker. 1998. "The Impact of Group-Based Credit Programs on Poor Households in Bangladesh: Does the Gender of Participants Matter?" *Journal of Political Economy* 106: 958–996.

Pitt, Mark M., Shahidur R. Khandker, and Jennifer Cartwright. 2006. "Empowering Women with Micro Finance: Evidence from Bangladesh." *Economic Development and Cultural Change* 54(4): 791–831.

Polanyi, Karl. 2001. *The Great Transformation: The Political and Economic Origin of Our Times*. Foreword by Joseph E. Stiglitz. Introduction by Fred Block. Boston: Beacon Press.

Polgreen, Lydia, and Vikas Bajaj. 2010. "India Microcredit Faces Collapse from Defaults." *New York Times*, Nov. 17 edition.

Portes, Alejandro, and Julia Sensenbrenner. 1993. "Embeddedness and Immigration: Notes on the Social Determinants of Economic Action." *American Journal of Sociology* 98: 1320–1350.

Putnam, Robert D., Robert Leonardi, and Rafaella Y. Nanetti. 1993. *Making Democracy Work: Civic Traditions in Modern Italy*. Princeton, NJ: Princeton University Press.

Putnam, Robert D. 2000. *Bowling Alone: The Collapse and Revival of American Community*. New York: Simon and Schuster.

Ragin, Charles C. 1987. *The Comparative Method: Moving Beyond Qualitative and Quantitative Strategies*. Berkeley: University of California Press.

Rahman, Aminur. 1999. "Micro-Credit Initiatives for Equitable and Sustainable Development: Who Pays?" *World Development* 27(1): 67–82.

  2001. *Women and Microcredit in Rural Bangladesh: An Anthropological Study of Grameen Bank Lending*. Boulder, CO: Westview Press.

Raka, Ray, and Seemin Qayum. 2009. *Cultures of Servitude: Modernity, Domesticity, and Class in India*. Stanford, CA: Stanford University Press.

Rao, Vijayendra, and Paromita Sanyal. 2010. "Dignity through Discourse: Poverty and the Culture of Deliberation in Indian Village Democracies." *The Annals of the AAPSS* 629: 146–172.

Ravitch, Diane. 1994. "Somebody's Children: Expanding Educational Opportunities for All America's Children." *Brookings Review* (Fall): 4–9.

Ray, Raka. 1999. *Fields of Protest: Women's Movements in India*. Minneapolis and London: University of Minnesota Press.

Reuf, Martin. 2010. *The Entrepreneurial Group: Social Identities, Relations, and Collective Actions*. Princeton, NJ: Princeton University Press.

Rhyne, Elizabeth. 2010. "Why are Microfinance Interest Rates So High?" Huffington Post, The Blog, posted May 28.

  2011. "Three Secrets of Safe Microfinance." Huffington Post, The Blog, posted Jan 20.

Ridgeway, Cecilia L., and Lynn Smith-Lovin. 1999. "The Gender System and Interaction." *Annual Review of Sociology* 25: 191–216.

Ridgeway, Cecilia L., and Shelley J. Correll. 2004. "Unpacking the Gender System: A Theoretical Perspective on Gender Beliefs and Social Relations." *Gender and Society* 18(4): 510–531.

Riley, Dylan. 2005. "Civic Associations and Authoritarian Regimes in Interwar Europe: Italy and Spain in Comparative Perspective." *American Sociological Review* 70(2): 288–310.

Robinson, Marguerite. 2001. *The Microfinance Revolution, Vol. 1*. Washington, DC: The World Bank.

Roodman, David, and Jonathan Morduch. 2009. "The Impact of Microcredit on the Poor in Bangladesh: Revisiting the Evidence." Center for Global Development, Working Paper No. 174.

Rosenberg, Richard. 2007. "CGAP Reflections on the Compartamos Initial Public Offering: A Case Study on Microfinance Interest Rates and Profits." Focus Note 42. Washington, DC: CGAP.

Rosenberg, Richard, Andrian Gonzalez, and Sushma Narain. 2009. "The New Moneylenders: Are the Poor Being Exploited by High Microcredit Interest Rates?" Occasional Paper 15. Washington, DC: CGAP.

Safilios-Rothschild, Costantina. 1982. "Female Power, Autonomy and Demographic Change in the Third World." In *Women's Role and Population Trends in the Third World*. Richard Anker, Mayra Buvinic, and Nadia H. Youssef (eds.). London: Croom Helm.

Salzinger, Leslie. 2000. "Manufacturing Sexual Subjects: 'Harassment,' Desire and Discipline on a Maquuiladora Shopfloor." *Ethnography* 1: 67–92.

2003. *Genders in Production: Making Workers in Mexico's Global Factories*. Berkeley: University of California Press.

Sanyal, Paromita. 2009. "From Credit to Collective Action: The Role of Microfinance in Promoting Women's Social Capital and Normative Influence." *American Sociological Review* 74(4): 529–550.

Schild, Veronica. 2000. *"Gender Equity" without Social Justice: Women's Rights in a Neoliberal Age*. NACLA Report on the Americas, 25–28.

Schneider, Mark, Paul Teske, Melissa Marschall, Michael Mintrom, and Christine Roch. 1997. "Institutional Arrangements and the Creation of Social Capital: The Effects of Public School Choice." *The American Political Science Review* 91(1): 82–93.

Schuler, Sidney R., Syed M. Hashemi, Ann P. Riley, and Shireen Akhter. 1996. "Credit Programs, Patriarchy, and Men's Violence Against Women in Rural Bangladesh." *Social Science Medicine* 43(12): 1729–1742.

Schuler, Sidney R., Syed M. Hashemi, and Shamsul Huda Badal. 1998. "Men's Violence Against Women in Rural Bangladesh: Undermined or Exacerbated by Micro-Finance Programmes?" *Development in Practice* 8(2): 148–156.

Sen, Amartya K. 1993. "Capability and Well-Being." In *The Quality of Life*. Martha Nussbaum and Amartya Sen (eds.). Oxford: Clarendon Press.

1999. *Development as Freedom*. New York: Knopf.

Sewell, William H., Jr. 1992. "A Theory of Structure: Duality, Agency, and Transformation." *American Journal of Sociology* 98(1): 1–29.

Shramajibee, Mahila Samity. 2003. "'Shalishi' in West Bengal: A Community-Based Response to Domestic Violence." *Economic and Political Weekly* 38 (17): 1665–1673.

Shyamsukha, Rahul. 2011. "India: Post Microfinance Crisis results." *MIX Microfinance World*, November.

Simmel, Georg. 1982 (1978). *The Philosophy of Money*. Translated by Tom Bottomore and David Frisby. Boston, London, and Melbourne: Routledge & Kegan Paul.

Small, Mario L. 2009. *Unanticipated Gains: Origins of Network Inequality in Everyday Life*. Oxford and New York: Oxford University Press.

Srinivas, Mysore N. 1978. *Religion and Society Among the Coorgs of South India*. London: J.K. Publishers.

State Institute of Panchayat and Rural Development (SIPRD). 2000. *Study of Self-Help Groups and Micro Finance in West Bengal*. Draft Report. Kalyani, Nadia: West Bengal.

Stone, Pamela. 2007. *Opting Out? Why Women Really Quit Careers and Head Home*. Berkeley: University of California Press.

Stuart, Guy. 2007. "Institutional Change and Embeddedness: Caste and Gender in Financial Cooperatives in Rural India." *International Public Management Journal* 10(4): 415–438.

Sun, Yat-Sen. 1927. *San Min Chu I: The Three Principles of the People*. Translated by Frank W. Price. Edited by L. T. Chen. Shanghai, China: China Committee, Institute of Pacific Relations.

Swedberg, Richard. 2000. *Entrepreneurship: The Social Science View*. Oxford and New York: Oxford University Press.

Swidler, Ann. 2009. "Responding to AIDS in Sub-Saharan Africa." In *Successful Societies: Institutions, Cultural Repertoires and Population Health*. Peter Hall and Michèle Lamont (eds.). Cambridge University Press.

Tavory, Iddo, and Ann Swidler. 2009. "Condom Semiotics: Meaning and Condom Use in Rural Malawi." *American Sociological Review* 74(2): 171–189.

Thapa, Ganesh B. 1993. *Banking with the Poor: Self-Help Groups, NGOs and Banks as Financial Intermediaries*. Saarbrücken and Fort Lauderdale, FL: Verlag Breitenbach.

The Economist. 2008. "Face Value: Google's Guru of Giving." Jan. 17 edition.

The Washington Post. 1986. "Third World Bank That Lends a Hand." Nov. 2 edition.

The Washington Post. 2006. "Micro-Credit Pioneer Wins Peace Prize; Economist, Bank Brought New Opportunity to Poor." Oct. 14 edition.

Tilly, Charles. 1998. *Durable Inequality*. Berkeley: University of California Press.

Tocqueville, Alexis. 1988. *Democracy in America*. New York: Perennial.

Trollope, Frances. 2009 (1832). *Domestic Manners of the Americans*. Cambridge, New York, and Melbourne: Cambridge University Press.

Varshney, Ashutosh. 2001. "Ethnic Conflict and Civil Society: India and Beyond." *World Politics* 53(3).

Watkins, Susan Cotts, and Ann Swidler. 2009. "Hearsay Ethnography: Conversational Journals as a Method for Studying Culture in Action." *Poetics* 37(2): 162–184.

Weber, Max. 1892. *Die Verhaltnisse der Landarbeiter im ostelbischen Deutschland* (Vol. LV of *Schriften des Vereins fur Sozialpolitik*). Berlin: Duncker and Humblot.

Whyte, Martin K. 1978. *The Status of Women in Preindustrial Societies*. Princeton, NJ: Princeton University Press.

Wijayaratna, C. M., and Norman Uphoff. 1997. "Farmer Organization in Gal Oya: Improving Irrigation Management in Sri Lanka." In *Reasons for Hope: Instructive Experiences in Rural Development*. Anirudh Krishna, Norman Uphoff, and Milton J. Esman (eds.). West Hartford, CT: Kumarian Press.

Wisnes, Hanna. 1868. *For Tjenestepiger*. Christiania.

Wolf, Diane L. 1992. *Factory Daughters: Gender, Household Dynamics, and Rural Industrialization in Java*. Berkeley: University of California Press.

Wolf, Margery. 1972. *Women and the Family in Rural Taiwan*. Stanford, CA: Stanford University Press.

Woolcock, Michael. 1998. "Social Capital and Economic Development: Towards a Theoretical Synthesis and Policy Framework." *Theory and Society* 27(2): 151–208.

    1999. "Learning from Failures in Microfinance: What Unsuccessful Cases Tell Us About How Group-Based Programs Work." *American Journal of Economics and Sociology* 58 (1): 17–42.

    2001. "Microenterprise and Social Capital: A Framework for Theory, Research, and Policy." *Journal of Socio-Economics* 30: 193–198.

Wright, Erik Olin. 2000. "Working-Class Power, Capitalist-Class Interests, and Class Compromise." *American Journal of Sociology* 105(4): 957–1002.

Yancey Martin, Patricia. 2003. "'Said and Done' versus 'Saying and Doing': Gendering Practices, Practicing Gender at Work." *Gender and Society* 17(3): 342–366.

Zelizer, Viviana. 2006. "Circuits in Economic Life." *European Economic Sociology Newsletter* 1. (Nov.): 30–35.

Index

CPSIA information can be obtained at www.ICGtesting.com
Printed in the USA
LVOW06*1921010315

428799LV00007B/61/P